Interactive Reader and Study Guide

HOLT

WORLD HISTORY

Human Legacy

HOLT, RINEHART AND WINSTON
A Harcourt Education Company
Orlando • Austin • New York • San Diego • London

Printed in the United States of America

ISBN- 978-0-03-093783-5
ISBN 0-03-093783-3

8 9 10 11 1689 14 13 12 11
4500298681

Contents

Unit 5: New Ideas, New Empires

Unit 6: Changes in European Society

Unit 7: Industrialization and Nationalism

Unit 8: The World at War

Contents

How to Use this Book

The *Interactive Reader and Study Guide* was developed to help you get the most from your world history course. Using this book will help you master the content of the course while developing your reading and vocabulary skills. Reviewing the next few pages before getting started will make you aware of the many useful features in this book.

Chapter Summary pages help you connect with the big picture. Studying them will keep you focused on the information you will need to be successful on your exams.

The Chapter Summary graphic organizers help you to summarize each chapter. They are a valuable study tool to help you prepare for important tests.

Answering each question will help you to understand the graphic organizer and ensure that you fully comprehend the content from the chapter.

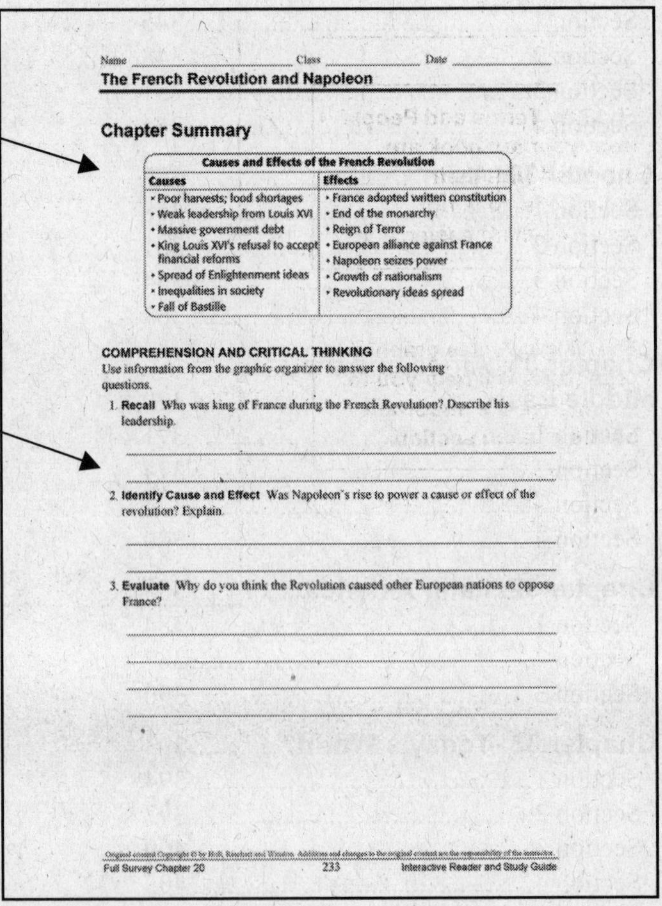

Name ____________ Class ____________ Date ____________

The French Revolution and Napoleon

Chapter Summary

Causes and Effects of the French Revolution	
Causes	**Effects**
• Poor harvests; food shortages • Weak leadership from Louis XVI • Massive government debt • King Louis XVI's refusal to accept financial reforms • Spread of Enlightenment ideas • Inequalities in society • Fall of Bastille	• France adopted written constitution • End of the monarchy • Reign of Terror • European alliance against France • Napoleon seizes power • Growth of nationalism • Revolutionary ideas spread

COMPREHENSION AND CRITICAL THINKING

Use information from the graphic organizer to answer the following questions.

1. **Recall** Who was king of France during the French Revolution? Describe his leadership.

2. **Identify Cause and Effect** Was Napoleon's rise to power a cause or effect of the revolution? Explain.

3. **Evaluate** Why do you think the Revolution caused other European nations to oppose France?

Original content Copyright © by Holt, Rinehart and Winston. Additions and changes to the original content are the responsibility of the instructor.

Full Survey Chapter 20 233 Interactive Reader and Study Guide

Section Summary pages allow you to interact easily with the content and key terms from each section.

Clearly labeled page headers make navigating the book very simple.

The Main Idea statement from your textbook focuses your attention as you read the summaries.

The Key Terms and People from your textbook are provided with their definitions, making studying them easier.

The Taking Notes graphic organizers will help you to summarize the important points of each section.

Name ______________ Class ______________ Date ______________

The French Revolution and Napoleon

Section 1

MAIN IDEA
Problems in French society led to a revolution, the formation of a new government, and the end of the monarchy.

Key Terms and People

Old Order France's social and political structure that places the king at the top and three estates below him

King Louis XVI ruler during early years of the French Revolution

Marie-Antoinette Austrian wife of King Louis XVI, serving as queen during his reign

First Estate small, privileged class made up of Roman Catholic clergy in France

Second Estate the class in France that was made up of the nobility

Third Estate the class of 97% of France, made up of the bourgeoisie, artisans, merchants, and peasants

bourgeoisie city-dwelling merchants, factory owners, and professionals

sansculottes "without knee breeches"; a nickname for workers of the Third Estate

Declaration of the Rights of Man and of the Citizen document written by the National Assembly advocating equality, freedom of speech, and freedom of religion

radicals people favoring extreme change

Taking Notes

As you read the summary, use the graphic organizer below to record events that occurred before and after the revolution.

Events Before the Revolution

↓

Events After the Revolution

Original content Copyright © by Holt, Rinehart and Winston. Additions and changes to the original content are the responsibility of the instructor.

Full Survey Chapter 20 234 Interactive Reader and Study Guide

Notes throughout the margins help you to interact with the content and understand the information you are reading.

Simple summaries explain each section in a way that is easy to understand.

Headings under each section summary relate to each heading in the textbook, making it easy for you to find the material you need.

The Key Terms and People from your textbook have been boldfaced, allowing you to find and study them quickly.

Be sure to read all notes and answer all of the questions in the margins. They have been written specifically to help you keep track of important information. Your answers to these questions will help you study for your tests.

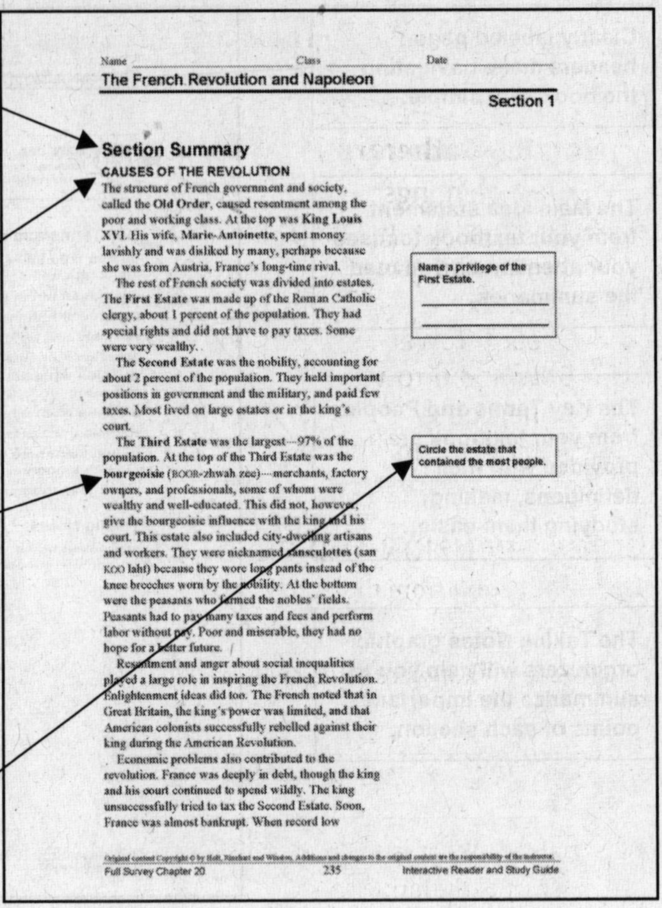

Name ____________ Class ____________ Date ____________

The French Revolution and Napoleon

Section 1

Section Summary

CAUSES OF THE REVOLUTION

The structure of French government and society, called the **Old Order**, caused resentment among the poor and working class. At the top was **King Louis XVI**. His wife, **Marie-Antoinette**, spent money lavishly and was disliked by many, perhaps because she was from Austria, France's long-time rival.

The rest of French society was divided into estates. The **First Estate** was made up of the Roman Catholic clergy, about 1 percent of the population. They had special rights and did not have to pay taxes. Some were very wealthy.

The **Second Estate** was the nobility, accounting for about 2 percent of the population. They held important positions in government and the military, and paid few taxes. Most lived on large estates or in the king's court.

The **Third Estate** was the largest—97% of the population. At the top of the Third Estate was the **bourgeoisie** (BOOR-zhwah zee)—merchants, factory owners, and professionals, some of whom were wealthy and well-educated. This did not, however, give the bourgeoisie influence with the king and his court. This estate also included city-dwelling artisans and workers. They were nicknamed **sansculottes** (san KOO laht) because they wore long pants instead of the knee breeches worn by the nobility. At the bottom were the peasants who farmed the nobles' fields. Peasants had to pay many taxes and fees and perform labor without pay. Poor and miserable, they had no hope for a better future.

Resentment and anger about social inequalities played a large role in inspiring the French Revolution. Enlightenment ideas did too. The French noted that in Great Britain, the king's power was limited, and that American colonists successfully rebelled against their king during the American Revolution.

Economic problems also contributed to the revolution. France was deeply in debt, though the king and his court continued to spend wildly. The king unsuccessfully tried to tax the Second Estate. Soon, France was almost bankrupt. When record low

Name a privilege of the First Estate.

Circle the estate that contained the most people.

Original content Copyright © by Holt, Rinehart and Winston. Additions and changes to the original content are the responsibility of the instructor.

Full Survey Chapter 20 235 Interactive Reader and Study Guide

Chapter Summary

Tools and Art of Early People

Hunter-Gatherers
- Cave paintings
- Carvings
- Sharpened stones
- Hand ax
- Spear thrower
- Bow and arrow
- Bone hooks
- Fishing spears

Early Farmers
- Hoes
- Plows
- Pestles
- Grindstones
- Pottery
- Baskets
- Megaliths

First City Dwellers
- Metalwork
- Written records
- Statues
- Temples

COMPREHENSION AND CRITICAL THINKING

Use information from the graphic organizer to answer the following questions.

1. **Recall** What were tools such as sharpened stones and spear throwers used for?

____

____

2. **Analyze** What is the major difference between the tools of hunter-gatherers and those of early farmers?

____

____

3. **Develop** How did the creations of an artist in an early city differ from an artist who lived as a hunter-gatherer?

____

____

4. **Evaluate** Would you have preferred to live as a hunter-gatherer or an early farmer? Why?

____

____

Name ______________________ Class ______________ Date ______________

Section 1

MAIN IDEA
Scientific evidence suggests that modern humans spread from Africa to other lands and gradually developed ways to adapt to their environment.

Key Terms and People

artifacts any objects that people made or used

culture a society's knowledge, art, beliefs, customs, and values

hominids early humanlike creatures that many experts believe are ancestors of humans

Mary Leakey anthropologist who found bones in East Africa that were more than 1.5 million years old

Donald Johanson anthropologist who found a partial Australopithecine skeleton that was more than 3 million years old

Louis Leakey anthropologist who found hominid remains that he called Homo habilis

Paleolithic Era the first part of the Stone Age which lasted until about 10,000 years ago

nomads people who move from place to place following migrating animal herds

hunter-gatherers people who hunt animals and gather wild plants, seeds, fruits, and nuts to survive

animism belief that all things in nature have spirits

Taking Notes

As you read, record information about studying the past, human origins, early migration, and the Stone Age in a graphic organizer like the one below.

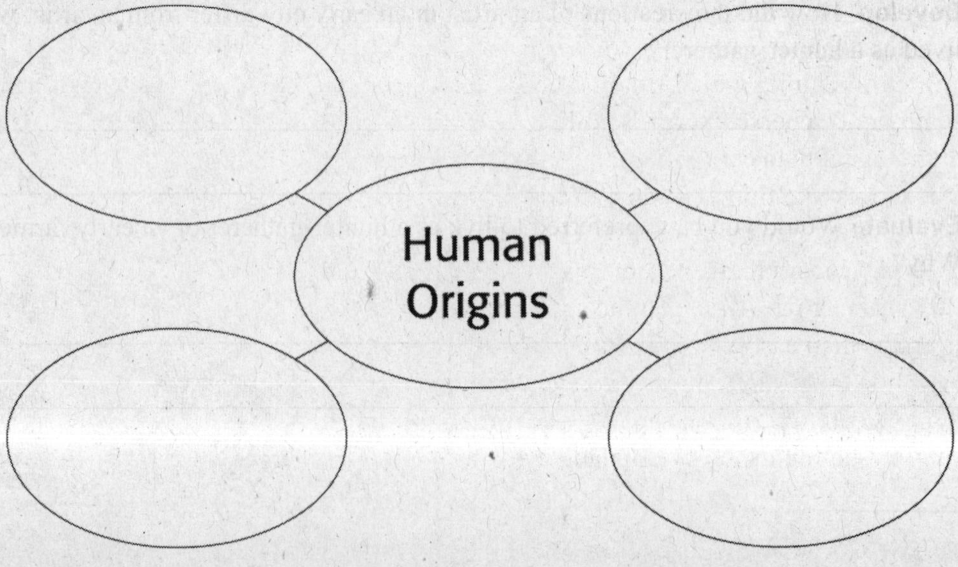

Section Summary

STUDYING THE DISTANT PAST

To study prehistory, the time before written records, scientists use a wide variety of clues. They look to **artifacts** such as tools, art, tombs, and weapons left behind by ancient people. These scientists include anthropologists, who study human **culture**, or a society's knowledge, art, beliefs, customs, and values. Anthropologists called archaeologists dig into settlements to find objects used by early people. Workers then use tools to unearth objects people have left behind. By analyzing the remains archaeologists find, they can draw conclusions about long-ago people's lives and culture.

HUMAN ORIGINS

Based on bones and footprints that have been found, many experts believe that **hominids** are early ancestors of humans. Anthropologists made several significant discoveries in East Africa. In 1959, **Mary Leakey** found hominid bones that were more than 1.5 million years old. **Donald Johanson** uncovered an Australopithecine skeleton in Ethiopia that he named Lucy. Lucy lived over 3 million years ago and walked upright. Recently, a French team in Central Africa found 6-7 million-year-old remains with features from both an Australopithecine and a chimpanzee. **Louis Leakey** found hominid remains he called Homo habilis, which he believed was more closely related to modern humans than Lucy.

Name two famous anthropologists and their discoveries.

____

____

A type of hominids called Homo erectus, or "upright man," appeared 2 to 1.5 million years ago. More intelligent than earlier hominids, they used more advanced tools like flint hand axes. Scientists also think that Homo erectus was the first hominid to control fire. Modern humans, Homo sapiens, appeared 200,000 years ago in Africa. Homo sapiens have larger brains than earlier hominids, developed more sophisticated tools and shelters, and eventually learned to create fire. Homo sapiens were probably also the first hominids to develop language.

The Beginnings of Civilization

SPREADING AROUND THE WORLD

Early human ancestors began to migrate around the world, from Africa to Asia and beyond. About 1.6 million years ago, long periods of freezing temperatures caused ice sheets to cover the land and lower ocean levels. These times were called ice ages. They created bridges of land between continents, which hominids could cross. In time, hominids died out and early humans began to migrate. By at least 9000 BC, humans lived on all continents except Antarctica.

How did human ancestors cross from one continent to another?

____

____

Two early groups of Homo sapiens that developed as people moved around the world were Neanderthals and Cro-Magnons. Neanderthals lived about 35,000 to 150,000 years ago. Cro-Magnons appeared about 45,000 years ago. They were physically identical to modern humans. They left behind fine tools, figurines, and cave art.

LIFE IN THE STONE AGE

Early humans lived during the Stone Age, which is divided into three sections based on the kinds of tools used at the time. The first part of the Stone Age is called the **Paleolithic Era**, (PAY-lee-uh-li-thik) a time in which people used tools made of stone. People lived as **nomads**, moving from place to place following migrating animal herds.

As the Stone Age continued, new technology helped early humans survive and improve life. People made tools from chipped stones, wood, and bone. They invented spears for easier hunting. Other technological developments included the bow and arrow, fishing hooks, canoes, needles for sewing clothes from animal skins, and shelters called pit-houses. Scholars call these people **hunter-gatherers** because they hunted animals and gathered the fruit, seeds, and nuts of wild plants for food. People also made art as well as musical instruments. Elaborate images of people and animals were painted on rocks and in caves. They may have been created to honor the spirits of the people and animals, a belief called **animism**. Figures were also carved out of many different materials such as animal teeth and bone.

Circle six examples of Stone Age technology.

What did hunter-gatherers eat?

____

____

Describe the artwork of hunter-gatherers.

____

____

Name ______________________ Class ______________ Date ______________

The Beginnings of Civilization

Section 2

MAIN IDEA

The development of agriculture was one of the most important turning points in human history and significantly changed the way in which many people lived.

Key Terms and People

Neolithic Era time period known as the New Stone Age which followed Paleolithic Era

Neolithic Revolution the shift from hunting and gathering to farming

domestication the process of changing plants and animals for better human use

pastoralists people who ranged over wide areas and kept herds of livestock

megaliths huge stone monuments that Neolithic Europeans built for burial or spiritual purposes

Bronze Age time period following the Stone Age, characterized by the use of bronze

Taking Notes

As you read, record details about the causes and effects of the development and spread of agriculture on a graphic organizer like the one below.

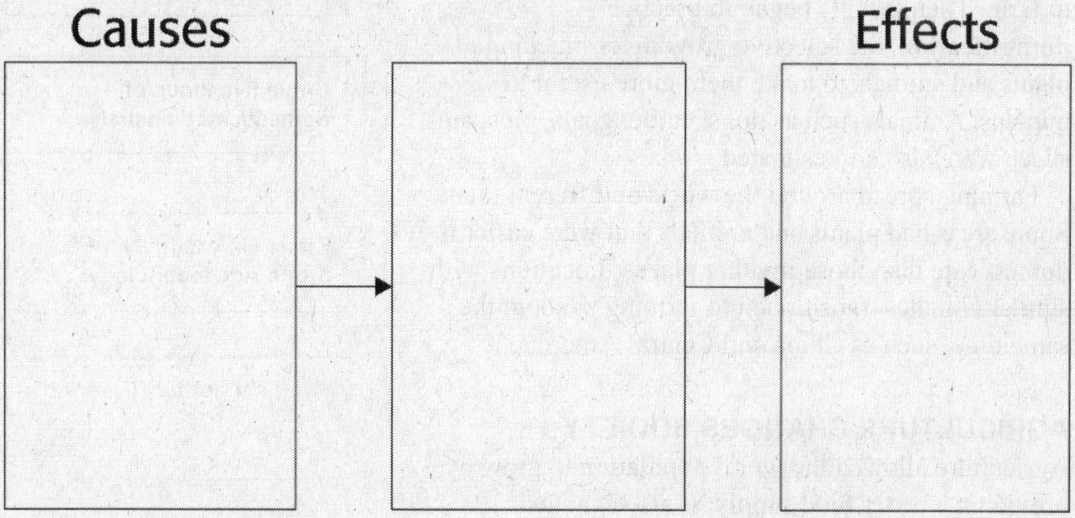

Section Summary

THE NEW STONE AGE

After the Paleolithic Era came the **Neolithic Era**, or New Stone Age. People learned to make tools and weapons with sharper edges, which led to the development of chisels, drills, and saws.

DEVELOPMENT OF AGRICULTURE

The lives of early people changed dramatically about 10,000 years ago. People began to grow crops. By growing their food instead of just hunting animals and gathering food, early people greatly improved their chances of survival and forever changed history. The shift to farming is called the **Neolithic Revolution**.

What happened during the Neolithic Revolution?

____

____

Farming started around the time the last ice age ended. Wild grains such as barley and wheat appeared due to the warmer weather. People began to gather the wild grains for food. This new food source caused the population to grow and need even more food. In time, people experimented with planting seeds and learned to farm. Then, people began to practice **domestication**, the selective growing or breeding of plants and animals to make them more useful to humans. Animals such as dogs, cattle, goats, pigs, and sheep were also domesticated.

What impact did the end of the ice age have on early people?

____

____

Circle five kinds of domesticated animals.

Farming spread around the world at different rates. Some areas had plants and animals that were easier to domesticate than those in other places. Locations with similar climates transitioned to farming at about the same time, such as China and Central America.

AGRICULTURE CHANGES SOCIETY

Agriculture allowed the world population to grow by providing a better food supply. It also changed people's ways of life. Some people became **pastoralists**, ranging over wide areas and keeping herds of livestock to use for food and other materials. Others began staying in the same place and settling into permanent villages. By about 7000 BC some settlements grew into towns. Now, instead of hunting and gathering food, many people worked in the fields and tended livestock. Since more food was available, some people could spend more time doing activities

What changed around 7000 BC?

____

____

other than food production. For example, some people became skilled at making crafts or tools. As people produced extra food and products, trade increased. Settlements traded with each other to obtain materials and products that they lacked. Societies became more complex and prosperous, and differences in social status began to emerge. Some people gained more wealth and influence than others. Others rose to positions of authority such as overseeing the planting and harvesting or running building projects. Because men performed the heavier work in farming, they often held positions of authority. As a result, men began to gain dominance and status over women in many agricultural societies.

Why did trade increase as food increased?

____

____

Societies began to build structures such as **megaliths** for religious purposes. Megaliths are huge stone monuments that some Neolithic people in Europe built for burial or spiritual purposes.

Agricultural societies also had some negative effects. Warfare increased as societies fought over land and resources. Crop failures made life difficult for people dependant on farming. Disease increased and spread rapidly among groups of people.

Circle three negative effects of agricultural societies.

Technology continued to develop. Animals pulled plows to produce larger fields of crops. Pestles and grindstones were used to prepare grains. Pottery was used for cooking and storing food. Wool from goats and sheep was weaved into cloth.

When people began to use metal the Stone Age gave way to the **Bronze Age**. Bronze is a mixture of copper and tin that produces objects that are stronger and harder than copper alone.

Çatal Hüyük (cha-tal hoo-yuk) in present-day Turkey is an example of a Neolithic village. Some 5,000 to 6,000 people lived there around 6000 BC. The village covered more than 30 acres, making it the largest Neolithic site that archaeologists have found.

Our knowledge of Neolithic societies continues to increase due to recent discoveries. In 1991 in the Italian Alps a 5,300 year-old frozen hunter nicknamed Ötzi the Iceman was found by hikers. The cold had preserved his clothing and belongings, adding to scholars' information about this time period.

Who is Ötzi the Iceman and what have scholars learned from him?

____

____

____

Name ______________________ Class ______________ Date ______________

MAIN IDEA
From farming villages arose cities, and with them, the first civilizations, marking the beginnings of recorded history.

Key Terms and People

surplus excess of food

division of labor job specialization that lets people concentrate on one type of work

traditional economy an economy based on long-standing practices

civilizations complex cultures with several important characteristics including cities, government, religion, and arts

artisans skilled crafts workers

cultural diffusion the spreading of cultural traits from one society to another

Taking Notes

As you read, use the graphic organizer below to record details about the first cities and civilizations, including why civilizations change.

Cities	Civilizations

Section Summary

FROM VILLAGES TO CITIES

Over time, farmers worked to increase the food production of their farms. Their most important advance was the irrigation system, a network of canals or ditches linking crop fields to streams or to water storage basins. Irrigation enabled people to farm more land in drier conditions, producing more food. Some farmers began to produce a **surplus**, or excess, of food. Surplus food allowed villages to support larger populations.

Circle the result of irrigation.

Now that fewer people were needed to produce food, some people could devote all of their time to specialized jobs like making tools or weapons. Others became weavers, potters, or religious leaders. **Division of labor** refers to the economic arrangement that allows workers to specialize in a particular job or task. Division of labor is different than the system of traditional economies that early farming villages had used. In a **traditional economy**, custom, tradition, or ritual is the basis of economic decisions.

Having surplus food allowed villages to grow into cities because not everyone had to farm. Cities differ from early villages in four ways. First, they are larger and more populated. Second, city populations usually included many unrelated people who came from a wide area. Third, most early cities had a defined center containing palaces, temples, government buildings, marketplaces, and defined boundaries, often marked by defensive walls. Fourth, early cities served as centers of trade for merchants and farmers from the surrounding villages. The first known city was Uruk, located between the Tigris and Euphrates rivers in what is now Iraq.

Name two ways of the four in which early cities differed from villages.

____

____

____

THE FIRST CIVILIZATIONS

Civilizations, or complex cultures, grew out of early cities. The first civilizations grew up along river valleys that had enough fertile land to produce food to support a growing population. Civilizations use record keeping and have social classes, specialization of labor, government, religion, and arts. Major cities in early river valley civilizations include Ur and Uruk

Name two main characteristics of early civilizations.

____

____

near the Tigris and Euphrates rivers in Mesopotamia, Memphis on the Nile River in Egypt, Mohenjo-Daro on the Indus River in India, and Anyang near the Huang He in China.

Circle the names of four early civilizations.

Governments in the first civilizations created laws and systems of justice, gathered taxes, and organized defense. Religious institutions included priests who performed rituals, such as sacrificing animals, to try to gain the gods' favor. Priests often became powerful and closely connected with governments.

As cities grew, the division of labor increased, and many new jobs developed. Skilled craft workers, or **artisans**, created useful everyday objects such as baskets and pottery.

Over time, clear social classes emerged. Rulers and priests had the highest positions, followed by merchants, artisans, farmers and unskilled workers. Slaves often formed the bottom of the social order.

Systems of writing developed about 5,000 years ago in order to keep records such as tax records. Calendars developed to help farmers keep track of the changing seasons. Most public buildings in large cities featured elaborate statues of gods and rulers. Art and architecture reflected the wealth and power of the city and its leaders.

Why did systems of writing develop?

____

____

CHANGE IN CIVILIZATIONS

Civilizations constantly changed once they were established. Something as simple as the weather could help a city grow…or destroy it with drought. People still had to deal with disease and warfare. Early civilizations met challenges with new technologies and knowledge from other societies. Trade, migration, and invasion led to **cultural diffusion**. For example, artisans adopted styles from other civilizations and traders learned multiple languages.

What factors led to changes in early civilizations?

____

____

Civilizations went to war to control rich farmland, important sea ports, or regions with valuable resources. Through conquest, civilizations expanded their control over land and people. Conflicts also arose between civilizations and nomadic groups, who sometimes launched raids on villages and cities. Further conflicts also arose as nomads and farmers competed over land.

Name ______________________ Class ______________ Date ______________

The Ancient Near East

Chapter Summary

The Ancient Near East

In Mesopotamia, the first known civilization arose, along with culture and innovations that influenced civilizations for thousands of years.	Indo-European invaders brought new technologies and adapted old ones that had been developed by the civilizations they encountered in the Fertile Crescent.	The ancient Hebrews and their religion, Judaism, have been a major influence on Western Civilization.	Persians formed one of the largest best-governed empires in the ancient world and made great cultural achievements.

COMPREHENSION AND CRITICAL THINKING

Use information from the graphic organizer to answer the following questions.

1. **Recall** Where was Mesopotamia located and why did civilization appear there?

____

____

2. **Make Inferences** Why did the Indo-European invaders adapt some of the technologies developed by the civilizations they encountered in the Fertile Crescent?

____

____

3. **Develop** How did the ancient Hebrews and their religion, Judaism, influence Western civilization?

____

____

4. **Elaborate** What made the Persian Empire able to grow so large and have many cultural achievements?

____

____

Name ______________________ Class ______________ Date ______________

MAIN IDEA

The first known civilization arose in Mesopotamia, and its culture and innovations influenced later civilizations in the region for thousands of years.

Key Terms and People

Fertile Crescent region between the Mediterranean Sea and the Persian Gulf

Mesopotamia Fertile Crescent area between the Tigris and Euphrates rivers

ziggurat pyramid-shaped temple dedicated to a Sumerian city's chief god

city-state a political unit with its own government made of a city and its lands

polytheism the worship of many gods

dynasty a series of rulers from one family

cuneiform Sumerian writing

Sargon Akkadian ruler who was the first to create a permanent army

Hammurabi King of Babylon famous for his code of laws

Taking Notes

As you read, use the diagram below to record details about Sumerian society.

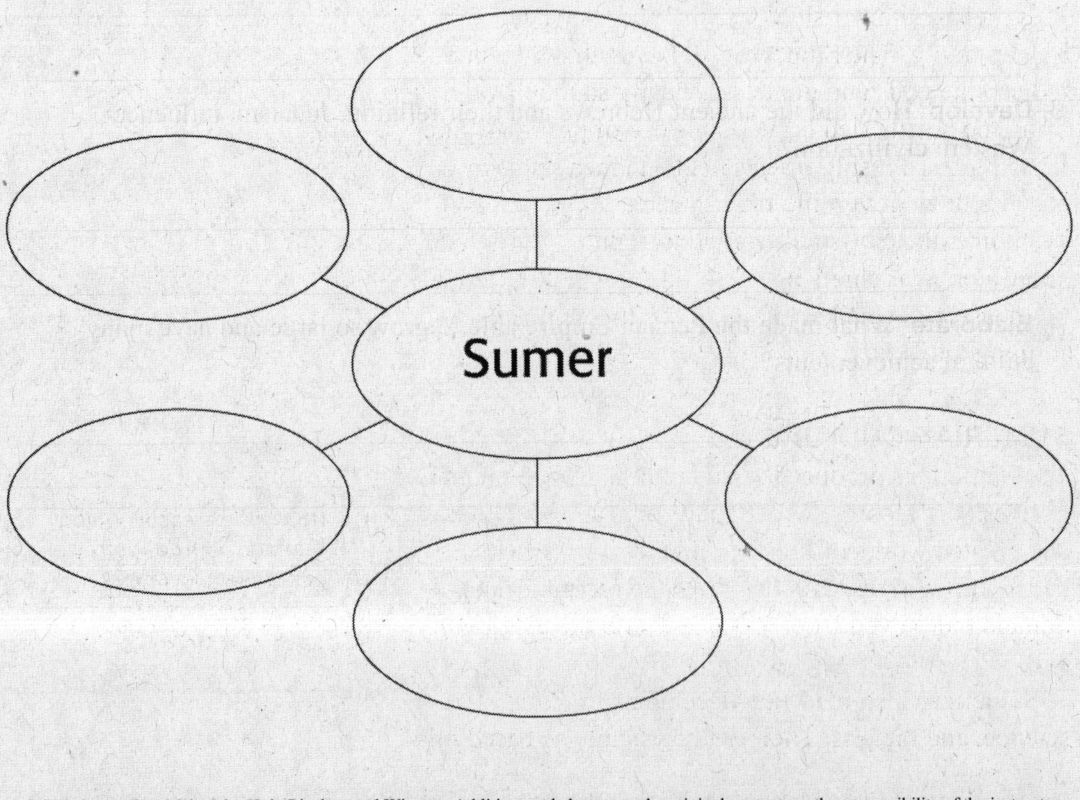

Section Summary

GEOGRAPHY PROMOTES CIVILIZATION

The **Fertile Crescent** is found between the Mediterranean Sea and the Persian Gulf in Southwest Asia. Within the Fertile Crescent, an area called **Mesopotamia** developed. It was home to the world's first civilization.

As early as 5500 BC people farmed grains in Mesopotamia's silt, rich soil left behind when the Tigris and Euphrates rivers flooded every spring. In time, people learned to control the rivers' flooding and store rainwater to use during the hot, dry summers. As a result, food was plentiful. Villages grew larger and governments formed. Slowly, a civilization emerged.

What problem did farmers face due to nearby rivers?

____

SUMER

Sumerians (soo-MER-ee-unz) developed the first civilization. Their first large cities began to appear by 4000 BC. Each Sumerian city had structures made of mud bricks and a large pyramid-shaped temple called a **ziggurat** to honor its chief god.

Over time, each Sumerian city and its lands formed a **city-state**, a political unit with its own government. **Polytheism**, the worship of many gods, shaped Sumerian life. The Sumerians believed that they had to keep the gods and goddesses happy so they would bring the people rich harvests instead of problems like flooding. As a result, priests held a higher status in society, often governing the city-states.

Circle the religious belief of the Sumerians. What does the word mean?

____

In time, the city-states started to fight more for land and water. War chiefs began to rule as kings. Often, a king passed his leadership on to family members, forming a **dynasty**.

SUMERIAN CULTURE

The Sumerians produced great cultural achievements. Scribes kept records, wrote about laws and grammar, and created works of literature in a writing system called **cuneiform**. With the ability to record events, humankind moved from prehistory into the historical age.

Underline areas in which Sumerians produced cultural achievement.

Sumerians also made advancements in math, science, and the arts. Their math system was based on the number 60. Because of this, even today we divide an hour into 60 minutes and a circle into 360 degrees. The Sumerians also invented the wheel and the plow, and learned to use bronze to make stronger tools and weapons. They even built sewer systems and performed medical surgeries. In addition to architecture and sculpture, Sumerian artists created engraved stone cylinders that when rolled over wet clay created a seal to serve as a signature or to show ownership. They traded with other groups to obtain materials. It was through trade that a social hierarchy, or ranking, developed. At the top were the kings, priests, and their principal agents. Then came large landowners and wealthy merchants, followed by the majority of Sumerians who worked as craftspeople, farmers, and laborers. At the bottom of the ranking system were the slaves, many of whom had been captured during battles. Men held political power and made laws while women took care of the home and children. Some upper-class women received educations and served as priestesses in the temples.

How did social hierarchy develop in Sumer?

____

____

EMPIRES IN MESOPOTAMIA

Frequent warfare weakened Sumer's city-states. **Sargon**, ruler of the Akkadians, was the first to use a permanent army. This army helped him to create the world's first empire, a land that includes different kingdoms and people under one rule. The Akkadian Empire stretched from the Mediterranean Sea to the Persian Gulf.

After Sargon's empire fell, one hundred years of disorder followed. As several tribes battled for Mesopotamia, one tribe, the Amorites, settled in Babylon. **Hammurabi**, their leader, was a brilliant warrior. He brought all of Mesopotamia into his Babylonian Empire. During his rule, he wrote Hammurabi's Code. The code contains 282 laws dealing with a variety of crimes. Now people knew what kind of behavior was considered criminal. Upon his death, Babylonian power declined. Within two centuries the empire had ended.

Underline why Sumer's city-states weakened. Who were two rulers who came to power as a result?

____

____

MAIN IDEA

Indo-European invaders introduced new technologies to the Fertile Crescent while adapting earlier technologies developed by the civilizations they encountered there.

Key Terms and People

Indo-Europeans tribes that spoke related languages and invaded Mesopotamia

steppes arid grasslands

Nebuchadnezzar II Chaldean king who rebuilt Babylon

Taking Notes

Use a chart like the one below to describe the peoples who conquered the Fertile Crescent. Add extra boxes as needed.

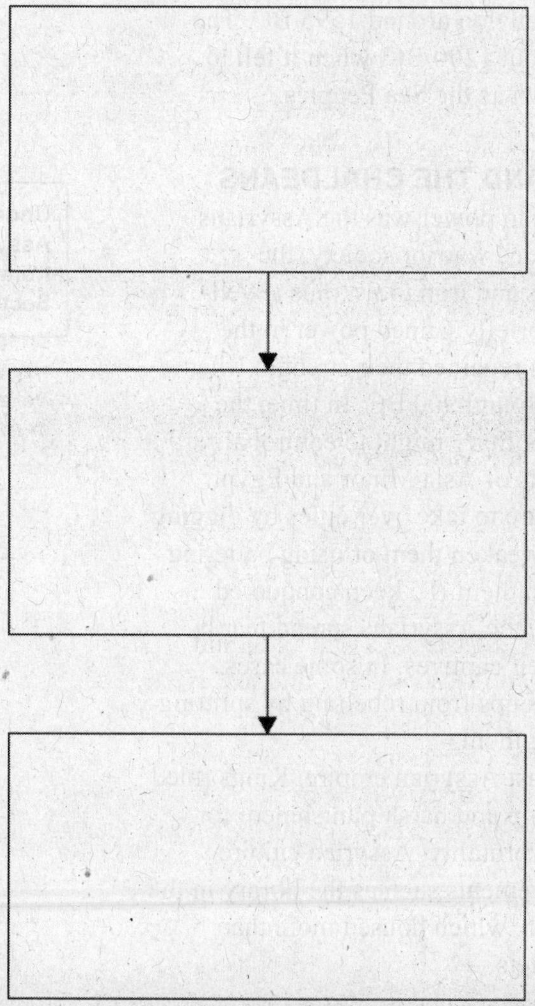

Section Summary

THE HITTITES

After the fall of the Babylonian Empire, **Indo-European** tribes invaded Mesopotamia. Speaking related languages, the tribes likely traveled from the **steppes**, or arid grasslands, north of the Black Sea.

> Circle the words that show what the Indo-European tribes had in common.

One of these tribes was the Hittites. Around 2000 BC, they conquered the surrounding people to build a strong empire in Asia Minor, which is now Turkey. They used iron, not bronze, to make better weapons, becoming the first people in the region to master iron making techniques. They also improved the horse-drawn war chariot, making it lighter, quicker, and able to hold an extra man. Their culture was a blend of their own and those around them. For example, they used Sumerian cuneiform to write their own language. The Hittites sacked Babylon around 1595 BC. The empire lasted until about 1200 BC, when it fell to powerful raiders known as the Sea Peoples.

THE ASSYRIANS AND THE CHALDEANS

The next group to rise to power was the Assyrians (uh-SEER-i-unz). A fierce warrior society, the Assyrians had chariots and iron tools, plus a well-armed cavalry. They briefly gained power in the 1300s BC, lost it, then regained their strength when they built an empire around 900 BC. In time, the Assyrians used their military might to control all of Mesopotamia and parts of Asia Minor and Egypt. They used siege warfare to take over cities by digging beneath city walls to weaken them or using battering rams to pound through them. To keep conquered people from rebelling, the Assyrians spread fear by killing or maiming their captives. In some cases, however, they kept groups from rebelling by splitting them up and resettling them.

> Underline how the Assyrians were different from groups described in Section 1.

Roads linked the vast Assyrian empire. Kings ruled through local leadership and harsh punishment for rebels. In spite of this brutality, Assyrian culture produced great achievements such as the library in the capital city of Nineveh, which housed more than 20,000 cuneiform tablets.

As the Assyrians' power declined, the Chaldeans formed an empire with the old city of Babylon as its capital. King **Nebuchadnezzar II** built a grand palace there. It is said to have housed the Hanging Gardens, one of the seven wonders of the ancient world. According to legend, he built this magnificent structure for his wife, who missed the mountains and forests of her birthplace. Nebuchadnezzar also built numerous palaces and temples, including an immense multistoried ziggurat, in Babylon, and the Euphrates River flowed through the center.

Why did Nebuchadnezzar build the Hanging Gardens of Babylon, according to legend?

____

____

The Chaldeans built temples to Sumerian gods, developed a lunar calendar, and made advancements in astronomy. When the Persians conquered Babylon in 539, the Chaldean empire ended, less than 100 years after rising to power.

THE PHOENICIANS

While great empires rose and fell, smaller states emerged in Phoenicia (fi-NI-shuh) in western Asia at the western end of the Fertile Crescent along the Mediterranean Sea in present-day Lebanon. Wealthy city-states such as Sidon and Tyre became centers for trade.

Phoenicians could not easily farm the rugged hills and mountains of their homeland, so they turned to trade for their livelihood. Many became expert sailors who traveled to faraway ports. Along the way, they founded colonies such as Carthage (KAHR-thij), which became a powerful city on the Mediterranean coast of northern Africa.

Underline ways in which many Phoenicians earned a living. Write why this was a good career for someone who lived in Phoenicia.

____

____

While exporting valuable goods brought the city-states wealth, the Phoenicians' greatest achievement was their alphabet. As traders traveled from port to port, more people began to use the alphabet. The Greeks modified the Phoenician alphabet for their own alphabet, which is the ancestor of the one we use to write English today.

The Ancient Near East

Section 3

MAIN IDEA
Jews and their religion, Judaism, have been a major influence on Western civilization.

Key Terms and People

Judaism the religion of the Hebrews

Torah most sacred text of Judaism

Abraham father of the Hebrew and Jewish people

covenant a solemn agreement

patriarch ancestral "fathers"

Moses Israelite leader who led his people out of Egypt

Exodus the journey of the Israelites out of Egypt, led by Moses

Diaspora the dispersal of the Jews outside of Judah

monotheism the belief in one God

Taking Notes

As you read about the ancient Hebrews, complete a chart like the one below.

Key Events	Key Teachings

Section Summary

THE EARLY HEBREWS

The Hebrews (HEE-brooz), ancestors of the people called Jews, appeared in Southwest Asia between 2000 and 1500 BC. **Judaism** (JOO-dee-i-zuhm) is the religion of the Hebrews. Accounts of their early history form the **Torah**, the most sacred text of Judaism. The Torah and other writings became the Hebrew Bible, which also appears as the Old Testament within the Christian Bible.

The Torah tells about a man named **Abraham**. According to the Torah, God made a **covenant**, or promise, to lead Abraham and the rest of the Hebrews to a new land where his people would form a mighty nation. Later Hebrews considered Abraham their **patriarch**, or ancestral "father" because in Canaan (KAY-nuhn), his grandson Jacob had 12 sons. Each of them established a tribe. Later, all Hebrews could trace their roots to one of these tribes.

Still later, some Hebrews moved to Egypt, where the pharaoh made them slaves. According to the Torah, God told a Hebrew leader named **Moses** to demand the Hebrews' freedom. Around 1200 BC, after a series of plagues struck Egypt, the pharaoh finally agreed. The journey of the Hebrews out of Egypt led by Moses is called the **Exodus**. Jews today still celebrate the Exodus during the Passover holiday in the spring.

After the Exodus, the Hebrews wandered through the desert for 40 years. According to the Torah, God gave Moses two stone tablets that contained the Ten Commandments. Over time, the commandments greatly influenced the laws and values of Western civilization. When the people reached Canaan, which later became known as Israel, the Hebrews renamed themselves the Israelites.

Circle the name of the people who appeared in Southwest Asia sometime between 2000 and 1500 BC.

Where did the Hebrews move?

____

Why was Moses an important Hebrew leader?

____

____

THE KINGDOM OF ISRAEL

At first the Twelve Tribes did not have a central government. They lived in communities scattered in Canaan, where they farmed and raised livestock. Each community had judges to enforce laws and settle problems between people. This system worked until the Philistines invaded in the mid-1000s BC. To get rid of the Philistines, the Israelites made Saul their first king. He had some military success but never won full support from the people. The next king, David, did have the tribes' backing. He was able to unite the kingdom, which grew strong as he conquered new territory. He also made Jerusalem the capital of his kingdom. David's son Solomon later built a great temple there when he became king.

After Solomon's death around 931 BC, Israel could not agree on who would be the next king. So it became two kingdoms: Israel and Judah (JOO-duh). Within a few centuries, both had fallen. In 722 BC, Israel was conquered by the Assyrians, who scattered the people of Israel throughout their empire. Judah, the other Hebrew kingdom, fell to the Chaldeans, who destroyed Solomon's Temple and enslaved the Jews in Babylon. These events marked the start of the **Diaspora**, the scattering of the Jews outside Judah. After fifty years of enslavement, the Persian Empire conquered the Chaldeans and let the Jews return to Jerusalem. They were allowed to rebuild Solomon's Temple, renaming it the Second Temple. Many Jews, however, moved other places in Persia instead of returning to Jerusalem.

Circle the names of the three Hebrew kings. Which one made Jerusalem the capital of his kingdom?

____

THE TEACHINGS OF JUDAISM

Ancient Hebrew society was based on religion, just as it was later for Jews. The most important belief in Judaism is that only one God exists. This belief is called **monotheism**. Because most other ancient peoples worshipped many gods, the Jews' monotheism set them apart. Other central beliefs are obedience to the law, justice, and righteousness. The most important laws of Judaism are the Ten Commandments, but a whole system of laws guides many areas of Jewish life such as how to pray, when to worship, and what to eat. This system of laws is called Mosaic Law. These beliefs are recorded in sacred texts such as the Torah and the Talmud (TAHL-moohd). The Torah is the most sacred of these texts. The Talmud contains explanations and interpretations of the other sacred texts.

Underline important beliefs in Judaism. Where would someone look to find out what the beliefs mean?

____

Name ______________________ Class ______________ Date ______________

MAIN IDEA

The Persians formed one of the largest and best-governed empires in the ancient world and made great cultural achievements.

Key Terms and People

Cyrus the Great Persian king who, by 530 BC, ruled the largest empire in the world

Darius I ruler who followed Cyrus, restoring order to Persia

satraps governors who ruled a region in the emperor's name

Xerxes Persian emperor who was the son of Darius I

Zoroaster man whose religious teachings became the basis of Zoroastrianism

dualism the belief that the world is controlled by two opposing forces, good and evil

Taking Notes

As you read, add information to this chart to keep track of the politics and religion of the Persian Empire.

The Persian Empire	
Politics	Religion

Section Summary

GROWTH AND ORGANIZATION

The Medes were another Indo-European tribe that came to power. They settled in Media, on the plateaus of what is now Iran. Among the neighboring groups the Medes conquered were the Persians. In 559 BC, **Cyrus the Great** led a Persian revolt that united Persia and Medes under his rule. Cyrus then conquered the wealthy kingdom of Lydia, several Greek cities in Ionia, and Babylon. Cyrus also freed the Jews from slavery and allowed them to return to Jerusalem and rebuild their temple there.

Underline the person who led the Persian revolt. What places did he conquer?

____

____

At the time of Cyrus's death in 530 BC, he ruled the largest empire in the world. His son Cambyses became emperor, but unlike his father, he was described as a tyrant and a madman. After Cambyses's death, **Darius I** became leader of Persia. He strengthened the empire by creating a permanent army of paid, trained soldiers. Some soldiers were even more skilled and they served as bodyguards for the emperor. Darius gained new lands in the east, although he was unable to conquer Greece.

How did Darius change the Persian Empire?

____

____

____

To help rule his vast empire, Darius had **satraps** govern different regions. Even though they were in charge, the satraps still had to obey Darius's orders. Darius also built roads and minted the first Persian coins. Trade made Persia very rich, and most historians consider Darius's reign the high point of Persian culture. His son **Xerxes** (ZUHRK-seez) was the last strong leader of Persian. Later emperors faced rebellion and a decline of trade until around 330 BC, when the Greek king Alexander the Great conquered Persia.

ZOROASTRIANISM

During the reigns of Cyrus and Darius, a religion called Zoroastrianism took hold in Persia. Based on the teachings of **Zoroaster**, it was one of the first religions to teach **dualism**, the belief that the world is controlled by two opposing forces, good and evil, or Ahura Mazda and Ahriman.

Underline the teachings of Zoroaster. What did he think people should do?

____

____

The Avesta, Zoroastrianism's sacred text, told people to live good lives in the service of Ahura

Mazda so that they could go to heaven. Zoroastrianism almost disappeared when the Persian Empire fell to the Greeks, but gradually, Zoroaster's teachings spread again in Persia and other parts of the world.

Why did Zoroastrianism almost disappear?

____

____

PERSIAN ACHIEVEMENTS

The Persian Empire stretched across most of Asia. Because it was huge, it contained dozens of peoples with their own customs and traditions. Emperors like Cyrus and Darius encouraged their cultures to blend because this built Persian unity. The people lived at peace with each other, so instead of fighting, they were able to work together to improve the empire.

Underline the names of Persian emperors who encouraged cultures to blend. How did this help the empire?

____

____

To ensure that leaders in the capital stayed aware of what was happening throughout the empire, a network of high quality roads was build. Messengers traveled the Royal Road, more than1,500 miles long, that was the world's first long highway. Urgent messages were carried by a series of messengers who worked like runners in a relay race.

The Persians were also widely admired for their art, especially delicate drinking vessels made of gold and set with precious gems. These were used in the royal court. Animals were common Persian decorations, appearing on the walls, gates, and columns of the empire's cities.

Architectural achievements are another part of Persia's culture. Persepolis was a city designed by Darius I to be a monument to Persia's glory. At its center was a huge, highly decorated hall. There was nothing else like it in the ancient Near East.

Chapter Summary

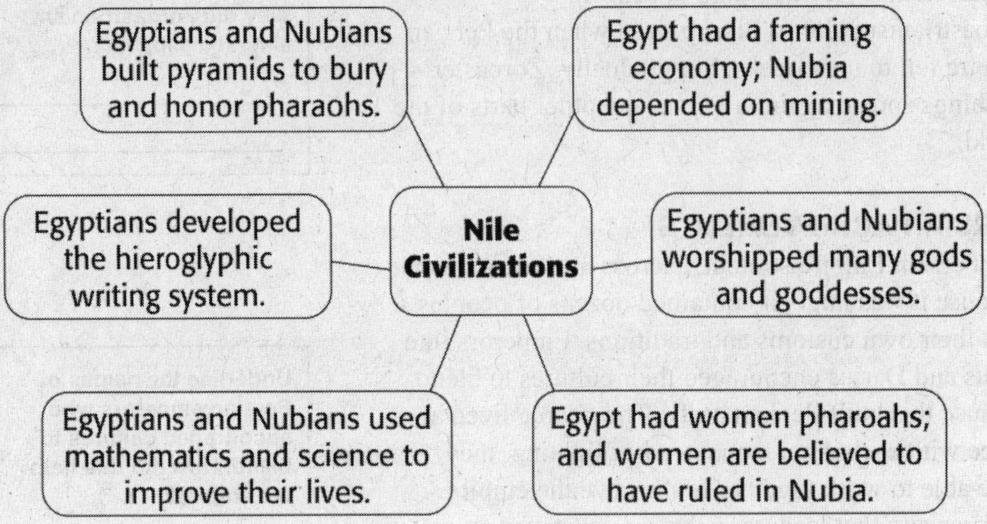

COMPREHENSION AND CRITICAL THINKING

Use information from the graphic organizer to answer the following questions.

1. **Recall** What writing system did the Egyptians use?

____

____

2. **Compare and Contrast** How were the cultures of Egypt and Nubia similar and different?

____

____

3. **Make Inferences** How might Egyptian civilization have been different if it had not lasted so long?

____

____

4. **Evaluate** Which aspect of Nile culture do you think has had the most powerful impact on the modern world? Why?

____

____

Name ______________________ Class ______________ Date ______________

Section 1

MAIN IDEA

Egypt was one of the most stable and long-lasting civilizations of the ancient world.

Key Terms and People

delta an area at the mouth of a river, often triangle-shaped, made up of silt deposits

cataracts rocky stretches of water marked by rapid currents and waterfalls

Menes ruler who may have united Upper and Lower Egypt to found Egypt's first dynasty

pharaoh an Egyptian king whom ancient Egyptians believed was a god in human form

theocracy a state ruled by religious figures

bureaucracy a highly-structured organization managed by officials

Hatshepsut one of the few women to rule Egypt as a pharaoh

Ramses the Great Pharoah of the New Kingdom who agreed to a truce with Hittite invaders

Taking Notes

As you read the summary, take notes about Egyptian history. Use a graphic organizer like the one below to record key events from each period.

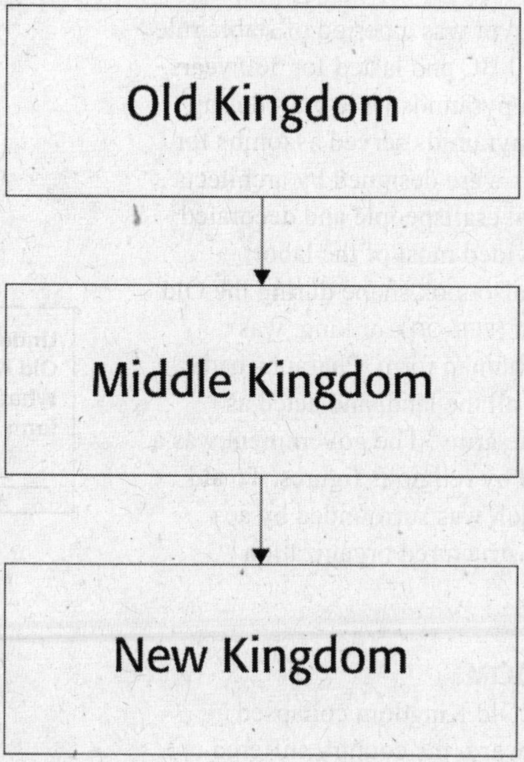

Section Summary

GEOGRAPHY AND EARLY EGYPT

The Nile River is the longest river in the world, and the most important physical feature in Egypt. Without its waters, no one could live there.

Egyptian civilization depended on the Nile for two main reasons. People farmed the fertile soil called silt that was left behind when the river flooded. The best soil was found in the **delta**, the area at the mouth of the river that is made up of silt deposits. The Nile also protected the Egyptians from invasion. Its **cataracts**, or rocky stretches marked by rapid currents and waterfalls, kept invaders' boats out.

Why did Egyptian civilization depend on the Nile River?

____

____

The early Egyptians formed two kingdoms. Lower Egypt, in the north, occupied most of the Nile Delta, where the climate was mild. Upper Egypt lay along the river's southern upper stretches. The two kingdoms were first unified around 3100 BC. According to legend, this happened when **Menes** (MEE-neez) a ruler from Upper Egypt, conquered the north. Menes founded the first of Egypt's 31 dynasties.

THE OLD KINGDOM

The Old Kingdom in Egypt was a period of stable rule that began in about 2650 BC and lasted for 500 years.

Most of the Egyptian pyramids were built during the Old Kingdom. The pyramids served as tombs for Egypt's rulers. Pyramids were designed by architects and built by professional craftspeople and decorated by artists. Peasants provided most of the labor.

Egypt's government also took shape during the Old Kingdom. The **pharaoh** (FER-OH), or king, was believed to be a god in human form. Pharaohs had absolute power, owned all the land, and acted as judges and leaders of the army. The government was a **theocracy**, a state ruled by religious figures. To aid him in ruling, the pharaoh was surrounded by a **bureaucracy**, a highly-structured organization managed by officials.

Underline the powers of Old Kingdom pharaohs. What is the term for this form of government?

____

THE MIDDLE KINGDOM

The government of the Old Kingdom collapsed around 2100 BC. Afterward, the country suffered from economic problems, invasions, and civil wars. In about 2055 BC, a new dynasty rose to power and the Middle Kingdom began.

How did the Old Kingdom's collapse affect Egypt?

____

____

The leaders of the Middle Kingdom encouraged trade and made the routes safer, built fortresses along the Nile, and enlarged the kingdom. Around 1650 BC, the Middle Kingdom ended when the Egyptian army was defeated by the better-armed Hyksos (HIK-sos) from Syria.

THE NEW KINGDOM

The Hyksos ruled Egypt for almost 100 years before the Egyptians rose up and drove them out. The army that defeated the Hyksos was led by nobles from Thebes. They became the new rulers of Egypt, and with this, the New Kingdom began.

Underline the event that marked the beginning of the New Kingdom.

During the New Kingdom, Egyptians realized that a permanent army and more land would help keep the kingdom safe. They attacked and took over Nubia, the Sinai Peninsula, and parts of Phoenicia and Syria.

The pharaohs of the New Kingdom made important changes in Egyptian society. **Hatshepsut**, one of the few women to rule Egypt, took power in around 1500 BC when her husband, the pharaoh, died.

Around 1353 BC, the pharaoh Amenhotep IV, also known as Akhenaten, forbid the Egyptian people from worshipping many gods. He forced them to worship only the sun god Aten, and built a new capital, Akhenaten. The very next pharaoh, Tutankhamen, or Tut, restored Egypt's worship of traditional gods and brought the capital back to Thebes.

Circle the names of four New Kingdom pharaohs. Which pharaoh changed Egypt's form of religion?

____

Egypt enjoyed peace until around 1250 BC, when the Hittites from Mesopotamia invaded. Pharaoh Ramses II, also called **Ramses the Great**, eventually agreed to a truce. Ramses' long reign of 60-plus years brought many political and artistic achievements, making him the most admired and famous pharaoh. His reign marked the last period of Egypt's greatness.

After Ramses, Egypt lost control of its empire and broke into small states. It was controlled by many foreign rulers. In the 330s BC, the Greek armies of Alexander the Great conquered Egypt and brought an end to its history as an independent kingdom.

What event brought an end to Egypt's independence?

____

____

Name ______________________ Class ____________ Date ____________

Nile Civilizations

Section 2

MAIN IDEA
The ancient Egyptians are famous for their religion, their burial practices, and their advances in art, writing, and science.

Key Terms

obelisks tall, thin pillars with pyramid-shaped tops found on many Egyptian temples

mummification the making of mummies to prevent the breakdown of a dead body

hieroglyphics main Egyptian writing system, which used picture symbols

papyrus reedy plant whose pulp Egyptians dried to make writing surfaces

Rosetta Stone stone with passages in different languages that unlocked the mystery of Egyptian writing

Taking Notes

As you read the summary, take notes about ancient Egyptian culture. Use a graphic organizer like the one below to record information.

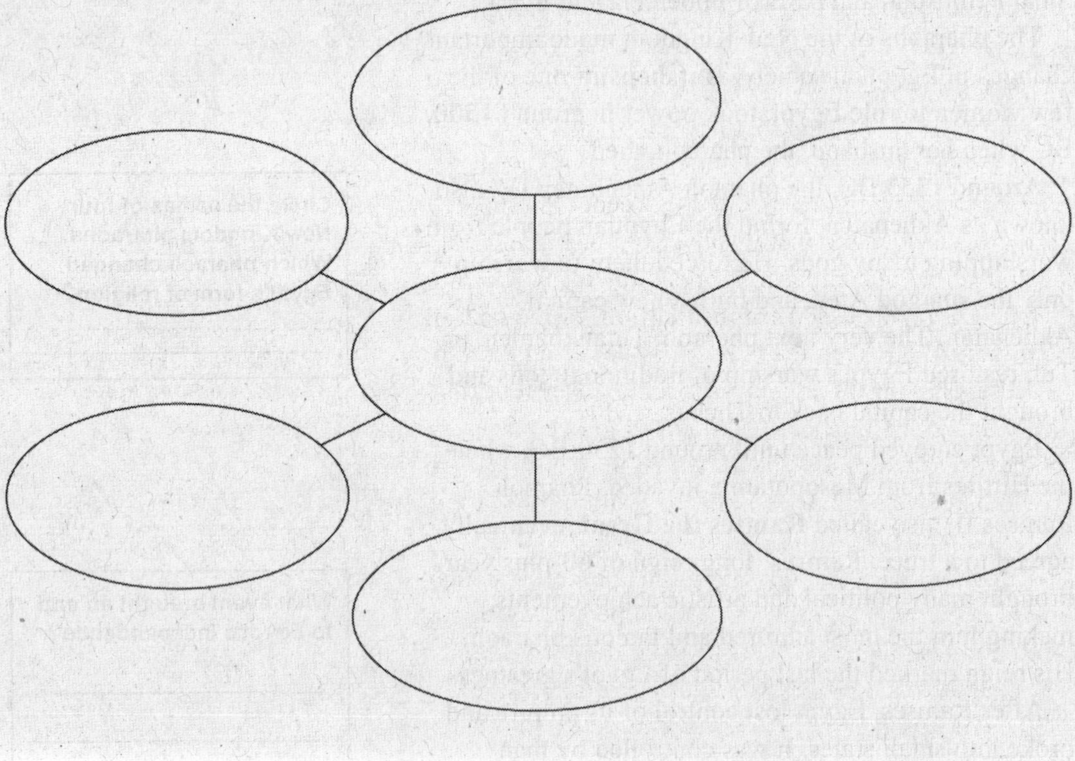

Section Summary

EGYPTIAN RELIGION

The Egyptians worshipped many gods. They believed that gods controlled natural events, such as the Nile flooding.

Some of the Egyptians' gods and goddesses were thought to have power over a small area or household but some were worshipped by all. One of these was the god of the sun, first called Re (RAY), then when he was linked to the sky god, Amon or Amon-Re. Anubis, the protector of the dead, was also widely worshipped, as were the trio of Osiris, Isis, and Horus. Other important gods were Hathor and Thoth.

The Egyptians built temples to honor their gods and also to provide homes for them. Many temples featured **obelisks**, tall, thin pillars with pyramid-shaped tops. In the temples, priests performed rituals so that the gods would bring peace, prosperity and eternal life for their pharaoh. Common people had no part in these rituals.

Underline the two purposes of Egyptian temples. Who performed religious rituals?

____

MUMMIFICATION AND BURIAL

The Egyptians believed that when a person died, a life force called the ka lived on in the land of the dead. The Egyptians believed that the ka needed food and drink to survive, and that its physical body could not be allowed to decompose, or break down.

The Egyptians used **mummification**, or the making of mummies, to keep the body from decaying. In this process, all internal organs were removed except for the heart. Then, the body was packed to keep its shape, dried with salts, and wrapped in strips of linen. The outside was painted to look as it did in life so the ka could recognize its body.

Egyptians were buried with all the possessions they might need in the afterlife. Common people were buried with little other than food and drink for their ka. Pharaohs and nobles were buried with treasures, statues of servants (believed to come to life to serve the ka), and even chariots and boats. The walls of the tombs were often painted with stories about the mummy's life or the gods.

Why do you think pharaohs were buried with so many objects?

____

____

DAILY LIFE

Egyptian society was highly stratified, or layered. At the top were the pharaoh and the royal family. Other top Egyptians were government officials, priests and priestesses, scribes, military leaders, landowners, and doctors. The next level of society included artisans, craft workers, and merchants who made and sold goods such as jewelry and clothing. About 90 percent of Egyptian society was made up of peasant farmers. They also helped build large public works such as pyramids, worked in mines, and served in the army. Egyptians also had a small number of slaves, mostly convicted criminals or prisoners of war. Sometimes, people could gain social status through education and better jobs, such as working as scribes.

Who made up the upper class in Egyptian society?

____

____

Home life and quality of housing varied but most people lived as family units with the father heading the household. Egyptian women's most important roles were as wife and mother, but they had more rights than women in most ancient civilizations. Nearly all children were educated. People enjoyed caring for their appearance, sports, and board games.

ART, WRITING, AND SCIENCE

Egyptian art is easily recognizable. Paintings are detailed and colorful. They often show people with torsos shown straight on, but with heads, arms, and legs shown from the side. Important figures are often larger than other people. Egyptian sculptures of gods or pharaohs are large, symbolizing the subjects' power.

The Egyptians' main writing system was **hieroglyphics**, which used picture symbols to represent objects, sounds, and ideas. **Papyrus**, a reedy Nile plant, was used to make paperlike sheets to write on. The **Rosetta Stone** helped historians decipher the Egyptian languages because some of the stone's writing was in Greek.

Why was the discovery of the Rosetta Stone important?

____

____

The Egyptians used math and science as tools to improve their lives. The Egyptians also made great advances in medicine. Through mummification, they understood human anatomy. Doctors used this knowledge to treat patients at their homes and in healing centers.

MAIN IDEA

One of ancient Africa's most advanced civilizations, Kush developed along the Nile south of Egypt in a region called Nubia.

Key Terms and People

Piankhi ruler who led the Kushites north into Egypt and ruled his kingdom as a pharaoh

smelt to extract, as in heating ore to remove iron

Taking Notes

As you read the summary, take notes about Kushite civilization. Use a graphic organizer like the one below to record information about Kushite lands, kingdoms, and culture.

Lands
Kingdoms
Culture

Section Summary

THE REGION OF NUBIA

Nubia was located south of Egypt along the Nile. Two rivers, the Blue Nile and the White Nile, flow together to form the Nile. The point where these two rivers meet served as Nubia's southern boundary. Nubia extended north as far as Egypt's southern border.

Like the Egyptians, the Nubians depended upon the Nile, but not for farming purposes. Nubia's landscape was too rocky to farm, but it was rich in minerals. Its mines produced gold, granite, and precious stones that could be exported and sold. Its location made Nubia a place where goods bound for central Africa, Egypt, and the Red Sea passed.

Underline Nubia's main exports. Why was farming difficult in Nubia?

____

____

The Nubian people were skilled at pottery, trade, and archery. During the time of the Egyptian Old Kingdom, the Nubians formed their own kingdom, which grew wealthy from trade. Before long, Nubia and Egypt became rivals, competing for control of the same land and resources. During Egypt's Middle Kingdom, Egypt conquered Nubia and the Nubians adopted some elements of Egyptian culture, such as religion and architecture.

THE GROWTH OF KUSH

While northern Nubia was controlled by Egypt during the Middle Kingdom, a powerful Nubian state called Kush began to develop in the south. After the Middle Kingdom collapsed in around 1700 BC, Kush expanded its rule, taking over all of Nubia.

When did Kush take over all of Nubia?

____

____

The rulers of Kush made an alliance with the Hyksos, the invaders who had gained control of Egypt, ending the Middle Kingdom. When the Hyksos were in power, the Kushite kingdom became very wealthy. After Egyptian nobles drove out the Hyksos in about 1550 BC, Egypt conquered Kush and added its land to their empire. Egyptian rulers, including Ramses the Great, built temples throughout Kush.

After the reign of Ramses the Great, Egyptian power over Kush declined. By about 1100 BC, Kush was free from Egypt. In around 750 BC, a new Kushite kingdom grew up. Its ruler, **Piankhi**, decided to expand the kingdom to the north, into Egypt. In the end, Piankhi (PYANG-kee) conquered all of Egypt and declared himself pharaoh. The Kushites ruled Egypt until the mid-600s BC, when they were driven out by the Assyrians.

The Kushite pharaohs saw themselves as guardians of Egyptian culture. They adopted Egyptian customs in art and architecture, built pyramids like those used in the Old Kingdom, and used the hieroglyphic writing system. The Kushites kept some of their own customs as well, such as clothing. Their pharaoh's crown symbolized the union of Egypt and Kush.

Underline the Egyptian customs adopted by the Kushites. What Kushite custom did they keep?

____

LATER KUSH

The period immediately following the Kushite expulsion from Egypt is a mystery to historians. Knowledge of Kushite history resumes in the mid-200s BC, when the Kushites moved their capital city from Napata to Meroë (MER-oh-wee). Kushite culture changed greatly at that point.

Meroë was located within a triangle formed by three rivers, near a forest. The new capital was abundant in copper, gold, precious stones, and iron. Iron quickly became Kush's most valuable resource, and it was shipped all over Africa. Money from the sale of iron funded new buildings and the expansion of the kingdom.

Circle the natural resources found in Meroë. Which resource was most valuable?

____

With the move to Meroë, Kush's rulers abandoned many elements of Egyptian culture. They created their own alphabet and writing system, but historians have not deciphered it yet. Based on carvings, women appear to have enjoyed a fairly high status in Kush. Many pyramids were built for women. Though this suggests that female rulers were common, historians have not been able to learn about their lives.

Meroë prospered until trade declined in the 200s AD, when it faced increased competition for iron and other goods. Its trade routes were disrupted by raids from hostile peoples. The Kushites also did not have enough wood for their forges in order to **smelt**, or extract, iron from ore. These factors led to Meroë's decline. In about AD 350, the kingdom of Aksum, located in present-day northern Ethiopia, invaded and destroyed Meroë.

Name ______________________ Class ______________ Date ______________

Chapter Summary

Development of India

Indus River Valley → agriculture, caste system → Hinduism, Jainism, Buddhism

Development of China

Chang Jiang and Huang He river valleys → agriculture, ancestor worship → Confucianism, Daoism

COMPREHENSION AND CRITICAL THINKING

Use information from the graphic organizer to answer the following questions.

1. **Recall** Where did the first civilizations develop in India and China? Why?

____

____

____

2. **Contrast** How was society different in ancient India and in ancient China?

____

____

____

3. **Evaluate** How is Hinduism similar to and different from Confucianism?

____

____

____

4. **Elaborate** How are Buddhism and Daoism alike and different?

____

____

____

Section 1

MAIN IDEA
Early civilization arose in the Indus River Valley, flourished, and then mysteriously died out. Later India's Vedic civilization developed a culture based on old and new beliefs.

Key Terms

subcontinent a large landmass that is part of a continent

monsoons seasonal winds that bring heavy rains and warm air or cool, dry air

citadel fortress

Vedas sacred writings about Aryan history and society

rajas regional leaders in Vedic society who protected a group of villages

varnas social classes that divided Vedic society into four groups

castes divisions of *varnas* that determined what jobs one could hold and whom a person could marry

Taking Notes

As you read the summary, take notes about India's earliest civilizations. Use a graphic organizer like this one.

Indus Valley	Vedic Period

Section Summary

INDIA'S GEOGRAPHY

One of the ancient world's great river valley civilizations originated along the Indus River. This river flows across the northwest edge of the Indian **subcontinent**, a large landmass that is part of a continent, Asia. The Indian subcontinent is divided into three geographic zones. In the far north, the Himalaya and Hindu Kush mountains separate India from the rest of Asia. The Northern Plains cover the middle of the subcontinent, where society first developed in India. This area is covered by rich soil deposited by floods from the Indus, Ganges, and Brahmaputra rivers. The southern part of the Indian subcontinent is the high, flat, and dry Deccan Plateau.

Flooding in the Northern Plains is caused by heavy rains. These rains are brought by seasonal winds called **monsoons**. Monsoon winds during the summer bring warm air from the Indian Ocean, along with most of the annual rainfall. In the winter, northeast monsoons blow cool, dry air from Central Asia.

India's first civilizations depended on the monsoons to bring water. Monsoon rains flooded rivers, leaving behind fertile soil. However, monsoons could also destroy crops and homes. If rains came too late or were not heavy enough, crops would not grow. If that happened, famine became a threat.

How did monsoons affect life in the Indus valley?

____

____

____

INDUS VALLEY CIVILIZATION

People have lived in the northern parts of the Indian subcontinent for thousands of years. The first people to live there were hunter-gatherers. Later, people settled in farming communities. In the Indus river valley, farming communities grew into India's first civilization. Historians believe this civilization started around 2500 BC, when people there developed a system of writing.

Ruins of this civilization were discovered in the 1920s. Archaeologists found remains of two large cities, Harappa and Mohenjo Daro. The civilization is sometimes called the Harappan civilization, after the first ruins found. Ruins of more large cities and hundreds of smaller towns have also been found.

What development occurred as the Indus civilization came about?

____

____

Indus settlements were planned and laid out carefully, suggesting that a strong central authority was in power. Streets ran in a grid pattern and people shared wells and a drainage system. In the largest cities, a walled, elevated **citadel**, or fortress, protected government buildings. Homes, workshops, and shrines were built outside the citadel's walls.

The economy of the Indus civilization focused on agriculture and trade. Most people farmed and herded livestock. Others made pottery, metalwork, and jewelry. Trade took place with nearby communities and distant peoples. Scholars know little else about Indus society because no one has been able to read Indus writing. Some believe the Indus civilization was a single society, not a group of independent ones.

Underline the crafts created and traded by the Indus Valley civilization.

The Indus Valley civilization thrived from about 2500 BC to 2000 BC. Repeated flooding, the disappearance of a river that ran through the valley, invasion, and disease may have been factors in the decline of the civilization.

THE VEDIC PERIOD

After 2000 BC, a group known as the Aryans ruled nearly all of India. The word Aryan comes from a Sanskrit word meaning "noble." Much of what is known about Aryan history and society comes from sacred writings called the **Vedas** (VAY-duhs). The Aryan period is sometimes called the Vedic period.

According to the Vedas, early Vedic people settled in villages much smaller than the cities of the Indus Valley. Later, groups of villages banded together. Regional leaders known as **rajas** (RAH-juhz) protected groups of villages in exchange for food or money.

Vedic society was divided into four social classes called ***varnas***. Each *varna* played a particular role in society. Later, the varnas were divided into hundreds of smaller groups called **castes**. A person's caste determined what job they could hold and whom they could marry.

How did castes affect life during the Vedic period?

____

____

People in Vedic society prayed to many aspects of a single eternal spirit. The *Vedas* describe fire sacrifices and the chanting of sacred hymns. Over time, the religious rituals became more complicated and the priests became powerful.

Ancient India and China

MAIN IDEA

The religion of Hinduism developed and evolved over a long time in India, giving rise to a variety of beliefs and practices and to other religions, including Jainism.

Key Terms and People

Hinduism one of the world's oldest religions, practiced by most people in India today

reincarnation Hindu belief that the *atman* (soul) will be released from the body after death and later reborn in another; also called *samsara*

karma the sum effect of a person's deeds and actions during life

moksha escape from the cycle of rebirth, considered by Hindus to be the ultimate goal of human existence

dharma set of spiritual duties and obligations for Hindus

yoga a series of physical and mental exercises that aid meditation

Jainism religion founded by Hindus who broke away because they believed *moksha* could be achieved through giving up worldly goods and controlling one's actions

ahimsa nonviolence; idea that is central to Jain teaching

Taking Notes

As you read the summary, use a graphic organizer like the one below to take notes about Hinduism and Jainism.

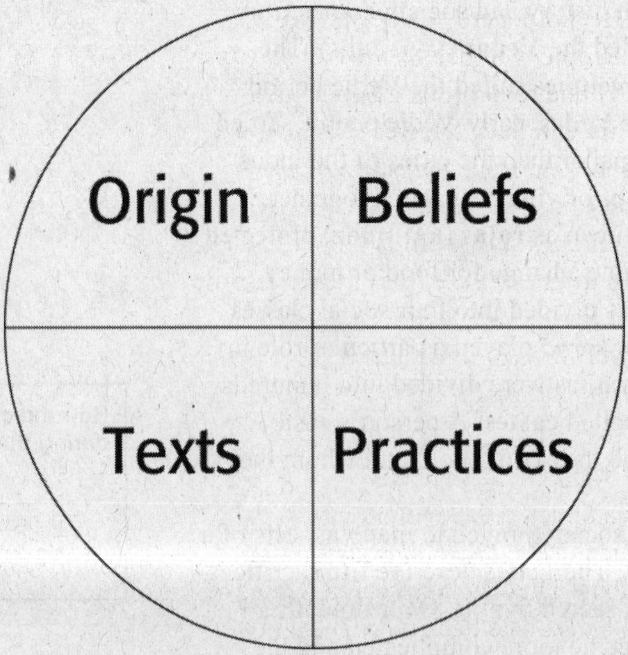

Section Summary

BASIC TEACHINGS OF HINDUISM

Most people in India today practice **Hinduism**. One of the oldest religions in the world, Hinduism has no single founder. Instead, it evolved over thousands of years and was influenced by many cultures.

One of the most basic teachings of Hinduism is the belief in Brahman, the eternal spirit that created and preserves the world. Hindus believe that because Brahman makes up all of creation, the human mind is not capable of understanding it.

Underline the description of Brahman. Why can't people understand Brahman?

____

____

Hindus also believe that each person has an *atman*, or soul, that is part of Brahman. The *atman* shapes personality and cannot be destroyed, even by death. Most Hindus believe that various aspects of Brahman called *devas* (DAY-vuhs) help maintain order in nature. The widely recognized *devas* are Ganesha the lord of wisdom, Lakshmi the grantor of wealth, Brahma the Creator, Vishnu the Preserver, and Siva the Destroyer.

Hindus believe that the universe and everyone in it are part of a continual pattern of birth, death, and rebirth. They believe that after death the *atman* is released from the body and reborn in another. This process is called **reincarnation**, or *samsara*. A person's **karma** determines the nature of the new life. Karma is the sum effect of a person's deeds and actions during life. People who behaved well have good karma. They will be reborn into a better station. Those with bad karma will have a lower station.

Underline the phrase that describes what Hindus believe happens to the *atman* after death.

The ultimate goal of Hindus is ***moksha***, escape from the cycle of rebirth. When a person achieves *moksha*, the *atman* reunites fully with Brahman. Hindus look forward to this release from the cares and difficulties of life on Earth. They believe they can achieve *moksha* by fulfilling their **dharma**, or spiritual duties and obligations.

SACRED TEXTS AND PRACTICES

Sacred writings have directed the evolution of Hinduism over the centuries. The *Vedas* are among the earliest Hindu texts. They include sacred hymns of praise. Some of the *Vedas* date back more than 3,000 years. They are considered the core of Hinduism even today. The *Upanishads* are sacred texts that built upon the *Vedas*. They deal with the nature of the world and the meaning of life.

Hindus believe the *Vedas* and the *Upanishads* were not written, but were revealed. Other sacred texts that shared themes with the Vedas are believed to have been composed by people. Two important texts are epic poems, the *Ramayana* (rah-MAH-yuh-nuh) and the *Mahabharata* (muh-HAH-BAH-ruh-tuh). The *Ramayana* tells of the relationship between Rama (Vishnu in human form) and his wife, Sita. Because of their devotion to each other and obedience to their dharma, Rama and Sita are considered a model for Hindu couples. The *Mahabarata* teaches about dharma and proper behavior through a story about two warring families.

Circle the names of the people in the *Ramayana* who are considered a model for Hindu couples. What makes them the ideal couple?

____

____

The *Bhagavad Gita* is found within the *Mahabarata*. It is a dialogue between the warrior Arjuna and Krishna, again Vishnu in human form, regarding Hindu belief and philosophy. It is considered the most sacred of all Hindu texts.

Circle the names of Hindu texts named in this summary. How do the epic poems differ from the *Vedas*?

____

____

Hindu worship takes place in temples, shines, and in homes. Hindus at home might offer food or gifts to a *deva*. They also say special prayers or meditate. To help them meditate, some Hindus practice a series of physical and mental exercises called **yoga**. Yoga teaches people to focus their bodies and minds.

Many Hindus make a pilgrimage to a holy place at least once during their lives. Hindus believe the water of the Ganges River, thought to flow from the feet of Vishnu and over the head of Siva, is sacred. Many believe that bathing in the Ganges will purify them.

JAINISM

Around 500 BC, a group of Hindus broke away from the religion and founded **Jainism** (JYN-iz-uhm). The Jains believed that rituals were unnecessary. Instead, people could achieve *moksha* by giving up their possessions and controlling their actions. One of Jainism's central ideas is ***ahimsa***, or nonviolence. Jains avoid harming any living creature, even insects. They promise to be truthful, to avoid the emotions of anger, greed, and prejudice, and to avoid stealing. The most devout Jains become monks or nuns.

Why did Jains break away from Hinduism?

____

____

MAIN IDEA

Buddhism, which teaches people that they can escape the suffering of the world through the Buddha's teachings, developed in India and spread to other parts of Asia and the world.

Key Terms and People

Buddhism religion whose followers seek enlightenment and an end to human suffering

Buddha founder of Buddhism; translated as Enlightened One

Four Noble Truths beliefs described by Buddha that explain the connections between life, desire, and suffering

Eightfold Path the way to find the Middle Way: right view, attitude, speech, action, livelihood, effort, mindfulness, and concentration

nirvana a state of peaceful existence free from suffering

Middle Way a life lived in moderation, avoiding extremes of comfort and discomfort in the search for enlightenment

Taking Notes

As you read the summary, use a graphic organizer like the one below to take notes on the history of Buddhism.

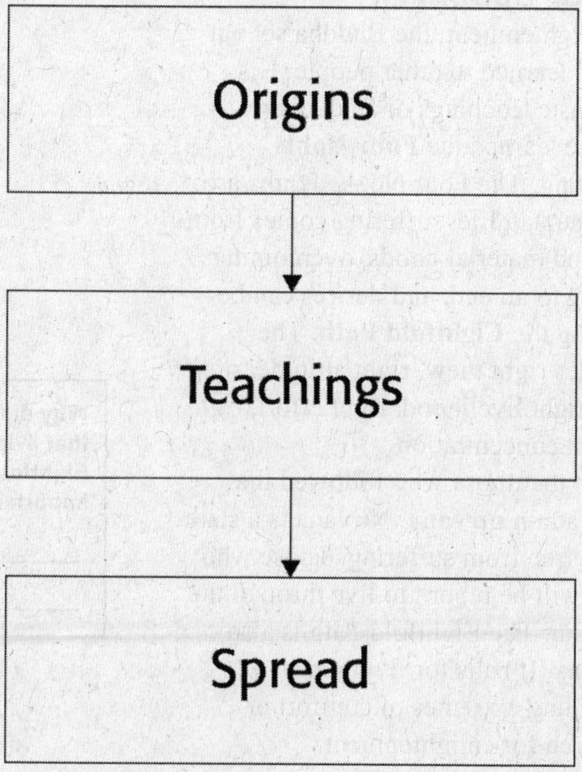

Section Summary

THE LIFE OF BUDDHA

Buddhism, another of the world's major religions, originated in ancient India. It was founded by a single person, called the **Buddha**. Buddhist writings tell of a prince named Siddhartha Gautama who was born in the 500s BC. His life was so sheltered that he did not know suffering existed until he was almost 30. When he did learn of sickness and death, he left his palace to try to find a way to end human suffering.

For six years, Gautama sought enlightenment, or spiritual understanding. He lived alone in the forest, then with gurus who taught him meditation, and finally with monks who denied themselves basic necessities. Gautama decided that neither the gurus nor the monks could teach him the way to enlightenment. He decided to sit under a tree until he found the way to end human suffering. After meditating for a long time, he was transformed: he had found enlightenment. He then became known as the Buddha, which means "Enlightened One."

Where and when did Buddhism start?

____

____

THE TEACHINGS OF BUDDHISM

After he achieved enlightenment, the Buddha set out to spread what he had learned to other people. His lessons became the basic teachings of Buddhism. Buddha is said to have learned the **Four Noble Truths** while meditating. The Four Noble Truths are: suffering is a part of human life, suffering comes from desires for pleasure and material goods, overcoming desire brings suffering to an end, and desires can be overcome by following the **Eightfold Path**. The Eightfold Path includes right view, right attitude, right speech, right action, right livelihood, right effort, right mindfulness, and right concentration.

The Buddha taught that those who followed the Eightfold Path could attain **nirvana**. Nirvana is a state of peaceful existence free from suffering. Those who do not reach nirvana will be reborn to live through the cycle of suffering again. The Eightfold Path is also called the **Middle Way**. It calls for living in moderation, and avoiding extremes of comfort or discomfort in the search for enlightenment.

Why did Buddha believe that living according to the Eightfold Path was important?

____

____

After the Buddha died, three main Buddhist traditions formed—Theravada, Mahayana, and Tibetan Buddhism. Theravada is based on the oldest known Buddhist writings. Theravada teaches that the best way to attain nirvana is to become a monk or a nun and spend all of one's time in meditation. Mahayana teaches that people can help each other find enlightenment. Bodhisattvas, people who have found enlightenment but have not yet passed on to nirvana, are said to remain on Earth to help others find their way to nirvana. The third Buddhist tradition, Tibetan Buddhism, shares many teachings with Mahayana. However, Tibetan Buddhists also believe that they can use special techniques to harness spiritual energy and achieve nirvana in a single lifetime.

Underline the names of the three main Buddhist traditions.

THE SPREAD OF BUDDHISM

Unlike Hinduism, which largely remained an Indian religion, Buddhism spread to other parts of the world. Today, more than 350 million people are Buddhists, most of them in Asia. Relatively few people in India are Buddhists today.

After his death, the Buddha's followers spread his teachings. These teachings were not written down until the first century BC. Buddhism reached its peak in India in the 200s BC during the reign of the emperor Ashoka. Ashoka helped spread Buddhism into all parts of India. He encouraged missionaries to carry the Buddha's message to lands outside of India.

Trade also helped to spread Buddhism beyond India into Central Asia and China. In China, Buddhism slowly spread and blended with native Chinese philosophies. From there, Buddhism went to Korea and Japan, making it the leading religion in all of East and Southeast Asia.

By what two means did Buddhism spread throughout India and into the East and Southeast Asia?

____

As Buddhism encountered other religious traditions outside of India it continued to change and develop. Because of this blending, various smaller traditions developed within Theravada and Mahayana. For example, a branch of Mahayana known as Zen emphasizes self-discipline and meditation. Buddhism today is a very diverse religion with a wide range of adherents and practices.

Name ______________________ Class ______________ Date ______________

MAIN IDEA

China's river valley civilizations built the foundations of a long-shared Chinese culture. The achievements of the Shang and Zhou dynasties can be felt to this day.

Key Terms

loess a fine dusty soil carried into China by desert winds

court gathering of wealthy nobles

oracle bones inscribed bits of animal bones or turtle shell that were used to seek advice from dead ancestors

Mandate of Heaven principle stating that the gods would support a just ruler, but they would not allow anyone corrupt to hold power

dynastic cycle the rise and fall of dynasties

Confucianism philosophy that stresses treating others humanely, practicing traditional rituals, and honoring one's ancestors

Daoism philosophy that teaches that harmony is found by finding one's place in nature

Taking Notes

As you read the summary, use a graphic organizer like the one below to take notes on the development and achievements of China's earliest dynasties.

Shang dynasty	Zhou dynasty

Section Summary

CHINA'S GEOGRAPHY

The first Chinese civilizations grew in river valleys created by the Chang Jiang river, also known as the Yangzi, and the Huang He, or Yellow River. Annual floods left behind rich soil in both valleys. The Huang He valley also benefited from **loess** (LES), a fine dusty soil carried into China by desert winds.

Mountains, hills, and desert protected early Chinese civilizations from invaders. Historians believe Chinese civilization began in the Huang He valley, where people started growing crops about 9,000 years ago. According to legend, this civilization was ruled by the Xia (SHYAH) dynasty.

Underline the names of the two river valleys where the first Chinese civilizations developed. What geographic features helped the development of civilizations in China?

____

____

THE SHANG DYNASTY

Because no evidence of the Xia dynasty has been found, most historians date Chinese civilization to the beginning of the Shang dynasty around 1766 BC. Shang kings ruled from their capital of Anyang where they were surrounded by a **court**, or gathering of wealthy nobles. Shang rulers appointed governors to keep order in distant parts of the kingdom. The king's army fought invaders and prevented rebellions.

Most people in Shang China were farmers. Sometimes, they had to serve in the army or build tombs, palaces, or walls. The wealthy had time for leisure, such as hunting for sport. Much of what historians know about the Shang comes from studying royal tombs. Most of these tombs contained valuable items made of bronze and jade, as well as sacrificed prisoners of war. From this evidence, historians have concluded that the Shang believed in an afterlife in which a ruler would still need his riches and servants.

Shang religion centered on ancestor worship. The Shang offered gifts to keep their ancestors happy in the afterlife. **Oracle bones** made of inscribed bits of animal bone or turtle shell were used to seek advice from dead ancestors. The earliest Chinese writings are questions written on oracle bones. Picture symbols were used to represent objects or ideas.

How were oracle bones related to ancestor worship in Shang China?

____

____

The Shang became skilled at making items out of bronze and they learned to build huge structures, such as tombs. In addition, Shang astronomers created a precise calendar based on the cycles of the moon.

THE ZHOU DYNASTY

The Shang ruled until about 1100 BC, when an army of the Zhou invaded. The Zhou convinced the Chinese people to accept them as rulers by saying that they ruled by the **Mandate of Heaven**. This principle stated that the gods would support a just ruler, but not a corrupt ruler. Later, rulers explained the **dynastic cycle**, or the rise and fall of dynasties, as a result of the Mandate of Heaven.

The Zhou learned to make objects from iron, which could be cast more cheaply than bronze, and produced stronger weapons. New farming techniques created a surplus of food. Cities grew, canals and roads were built, and transportation improved. The Zhou introduced coins and pioneered the use of chopsticks.

What technological developments were made during the Zhou dynasty? How did each benefit society?

____

____

____

Conflict in the later years of Zhou rule weakened the kingdom. Rebellions waged from 403 BC to 221 BC, called the Warring States Period. Eventually, the Qin dynasty arose, ending both the Warring States Period and the Zhou dynasty.

NEW PHILOSOPHIES

Among the many new philosophies developed during the late Zhou period were **Confucianism** and **Daoism** (DOW-iz-uhm). Confucianism is based on the teachings of Kongfuzi, also known as Confucius. It stresses treating others humanely and with respect, practicing traditional rituals, and honoring one's ancestors. His teachings on how to improve society were collected in a book called the *Analects* and had a lasting impact on China. Confucius taught that a ruler should be advised by qualified people, so China's emperors selected their advisors based on merit.

What does Confucianism have in common with the religion practiced during the Shang dynasty?

____

____

Daoists believe in the dao, or the way, a limitless force that connects all things in nature. Daoism teaches that finding one's place in nature leads to harmony. Daoists embrace the Chinese concept of yin and yang, the balancing aspects of nature. Among the first people to write about Daoist teachings was Laozi (LOW-dzuh), who wrote the *Dao De Jing*.

Name ______________________ Class ______________ Date ______________

Classical Greece

Chapter Summary

The first two cultures of ancient Greece were the Minoan and the Mycenaean. After the downfall of Mycenaean civilization, a dark age descended. Around 800 BC, a new Greek society emerged, one centered on the polis, or city-state. Each polis developed its own government, but all Greeks worshipped the same gods.

Athens's government gradually developed the world's first democracy. As this was going on, Greece was forced to fight against two invasions by Persia. Later, the Peloponnesian war pitched Athens and their allies against a group of cities led by Sparta.

The golden age of Greek philosophy was led by Socrates, Plato, and Aristotle. Written poetry, drama, and history also developed at this time. The Greeks developed distinct styles of art and architecture, and made many advances in science and math.

Macedonian king Philip II invaded Greece, and his son Alexander the Great went on to also conquer lands ruled by Persia and beyond. The new empire he created mixed several cultures into a Hellenistic society. The exchange of ideas led to new advances in philosophy, art, literature, and science.

COMPREHENSION AND CRITICAL THINKING

Use information from the graphic organizer to answer the following questions.

1. **Identify** What types of writing developed in Greece during the golden age of philosophy?

____

____

2. **Cause and Effect** How did Hellenistic society develop?

____

____

3. **Evaluate** Why do you think each polis developed its own government?

____

____

Name ______________________ Class ______________ Date ______________

MAIN IDEA

The earliest cultures in Greece, the Minoans and the Mycenaeans, were trading societies, but both disappeared and were replaced by Greek city-states.

Key Terms

polis city-state, the basic political unit in Greece

acropolis a walled, high area around which a polis was typically built

agora marketplace, usually found below a polis's acropolis

helots state slaves of Sparta who farmed so that the Spartans could train for war

hoplites Spartan foot soldiers

hubris great pride that often led heroes to tragic ends

Taking Notes

As you read the summary, use a graphic organizer like the one below to take notes on the first Greeks, city-states, and mythology.

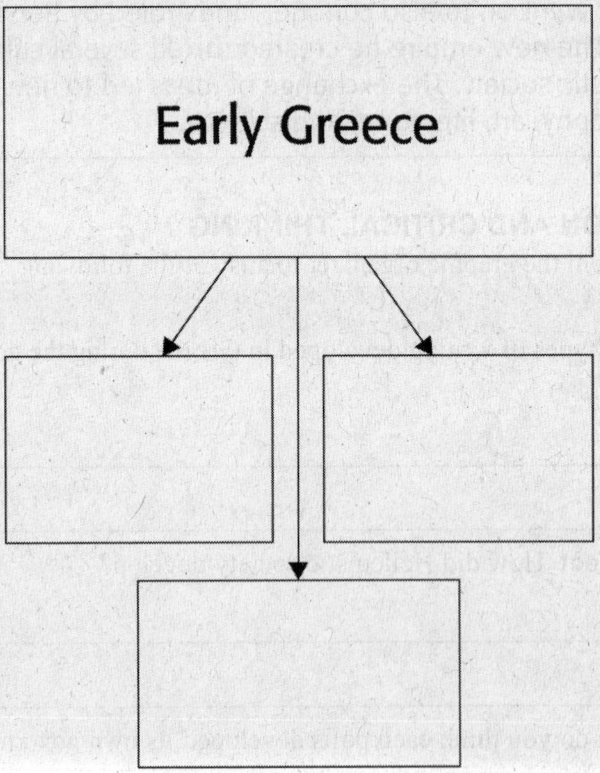

Section Summary

MINOANS AND MYCENAEANS

Much of early Greek history is still unknown. We do know that two cultures developed in early Greece. Minoan civilization developed on the island of Crete around 2100 BC and lasted at least 700 years. Minoans settled on many Aegean islands and traded among these colonies and Crete. We know about Minoans from excavations at Knossos on Crete, particularly from the artwork; Minoans had writing, but historians have not been able to translate it. Minoan life was tied deeply to the sea. Women had important roles in society, and warfare did not seem to be a part of life. We know their civilization fell apart quickly. The eruption of the volcano on Thera, near Crete, may have weakened society. The Mycenaeans from the Greek mainland conquered the Minoans.

Name three known aspects about Minoan civilization.

____

____

____

The Mycenaeans (my-sun-NEE-uhz) built city-states that often fought one another. Because they spoke an early form of Greek, they are considered the first Greek civilization. They traded with the Minoans, then expanded their own trade after conquering Crete. Mycenaean civilization was dominated by war, competition, and powerful kings who built palaces and monuments. One legend tied to the Mycenaeans is about the Trojan War, in which Greeks, led by Mycenae, fought against the city of Troy. It is unclear whether the Trojan War really happened. But it is known that war, along with drought, famine, the collapse of trade, and invasion from outside, helped to end Mycenaean civilization. Their cities were mostly in ruins by 1100 BC, and a dark age followed. As people struggled to feed and protect themselves, the use of writing was lost for several centuries. Greek civilization almost disappeared.

How were the Minoans and Mycenaeans similar? How were they different?

____

____

____

____

____

____

GREEK CITY-STATES

By the 800s BC, a new type of society emerged in Greece, centered around the **polis**, or city-state. The polis was the basic political unit and center of daily life and culture. People were very loyal to their polis. The typical polis was built around a high area called an **acropolis**, which held temples to the gods and space for ceremonies. Below the acropolis was the **agora** or marketplace, surrounded by shops, houses, more temples, and a gymnasium. Around the polis was a wall for defense, and outside the wall were fields for crops. Each polis developed its own political system. For example, Corinth was an oligarchy, Athens a democracy, and Thebes an aristocracy.

Why do you think each polis followed the layout described here?

____

____

____

Sparta was a mighty city-state, but unlike the others. It conquered nearby towns and made the people **helots** or state slaves. Helots were given to Spartans to do their manual labor so that the citizens could spend all their time training for war. This was believed to be the only way to keep order because the helots outnumbered the Spartans and might rebel at any time. So Spartans demanded that their citizens be tough from birth. Babies who were not healthy were left in the wild to die. Boys entered a school for combat at age 7. At 20, they became **hoplites** or foot soldiers, and served in the army for 10 years. Women were also expected to be physically fit and helped to run the city when men were away at war. Sparta was led by two military commander kings but eventually, an elected council of elders made many decisions.

Do you think the Spartans' focus on readiness for war was worthwhile? Why or why not?

____

____

____

____

GODS AND HEROES

Ancient Greeks believed in hundreds of gods and goddesses. Each ruled over one part of nature or life. The Greeks believed the gods would protect them in exchange for sacrifices. About 12 of the gods were especially important and were thought to live on Mount Olympus, the highest mountain in Greece. The gods were powerful, but they were not perfect. They often got jealous or made mistakes.

Most Greeks worshipped the same gods, but each polis also claimed one god or goddess as its protector. In addition, all Greeks considered some locations sacred, such as Delphi, where priestesses were thought to receive visions of the future, and Olympus, where games were held every four years. Athletes from different city-states competed in honor of the gods. Greeks also had myths about heroes that could inspire people to live virtuously but without **hubris**, great pride that often led heroes to tragic ends.

How did living in a particular city-state affect people's worship of gods and goddesses?

____

____

____

Name ______________________ Class ______________ Date ______________

Classical Greece

Section 2

MAIN IDEA

The Classical Age of ancient Greece was marked by great achievements, including the development of democracy, and by ferocious wars.

Key Terms and People

democracy government run by the people

Solon Athenian lawmaker who revised laws and created an elected council to help govern, the first step toward democracy

tyrant a leader who seizes power by force and claims to rule for the good of the people

Cleisthenes Athenian reformer, often called "the father of democracy"

direct democracy system of government in which all people vote directly on an issue

archon elected official who acted as the head of both the assembly and the Council of 500

phalanx a tight rectangle formation in which soldiers held long spears out ahead of their shields

Pericles military and political leader of Athens who is credited with most of the rebuilding of city after the Persian Wars

Taking Notes

As you read the summary, use a graphic organizer like the one below to take notes about the achievements and wars of Greece's classical age.

Achievements	Wars

Section Summary

ATHENIAN DEMOCRACY

The government of Athens was the world's first **democracy**, run by the people. But Athens had not always been democratic. First it was ruled by kings, then aristocrats. Most Athenians were poor and had little power. This led to conflict between rich and poor. Harsh laws made the dispute between rich and poor worse, so in the 590s BC, a lawmaker named **Solon** got rid of the harshest laws, introduced trial by jury, and created a council of 400 elected men to help govern. Men from any social class could be elected. This was the first real step toward democracy. But tensions in Athens flared again, so Peisistratus (PY-sis-truht-uhs), a **tyrant**, seized power by force. After he died, **Cleisthenes** (KLYS-theuh-neez) took over. He increased the council to 500 and gave men from every class the same rights.

How did Solon change law and government in Athens?

____

____

____

____

However, only free male Athenians over age 20 who owned property and had military training were allowed to vote. In the 300s BC, that was about 10 percent of the population. Those who could were expected to vote in all elections, to serve if elected, and to serve on juries and in the military if needed. At its height, Athenian democracy consisted of three parts. The assembly included all people eligible to vote, a system called **direct democracy**. The Council of 500 wrote the laws that would be voted on by the assembly. The third part was the courts. Members of the courts came from the assembly. One elected official was the **archon** (ahr-kahn), who acted as the head of both the assembly and the Council of 500.

Name three different groups that helped govern Athens at the height of democracy.

____

____

____

THE PERSIAN WARS

In the 500s BC, Persia had conquered Greek cities in Ionia, in what is now Turkey. When the Ionians rebelled, they asked their fellow Greeks for help. The Persians quickly put down the revolt, then attacked the Greek mainland, especially Athens, in revenge. In 490 BC, thousands of Persians landed near a town called Marathon. The Athenians surprised the Persians and defeated them. The Athenians fought in a **phalanx**

(FAY-lanks), a tight rectangle formation in which soldiers held long spears out ahead of their shields.

The Persians planned revenge. In 480 BC, a huge army entered Greece. The city-states worked together. The Persians burned Athens, but the entire Greek fleet was in the nearby Bay of Salamis. The Greeks destroyed Persian supply ships that tried to reach the mainland, stranding the Persia army. In 479, Sparta led the Greek army to victory in the Persian Wars.

The Persians invaded Greece twice looking for revenge. What made them seek revenge each time?

____

____

____

____

THE GOLDEN AGE OF ATHENS

Eventually, Athens became the leading city-state in Greece. It led the Delian League, an alliance of several city-states for defense. Those who resented Athens' power and rebelled were attacked. The league was basically an Athenian empire.

Athens had been burned and had to be rebuilt after the Persian Wars. Several temples including the Parthenon, roads, and walls were built, and the port was expanded. Much of the rebuilding was due to **Pericles** (PER-uh-kleez), a military and political leader in the 460s BC. Although he had a lot of power, he supported democracy. He also supported the arts, wanting Athens to be the most glorious city in Greece. During this Golden Age, trade brought wealth to Athens, and merchants brought new food and customs, making the city very cosmopolitan. There were also festivals, religious games, and great dramas.

Underline the elements that contributed to Athens's Golden Age.

THE PELOPONNESIAN WAR

Sparta wanted to end the Delian League's dominance, so they formed the Peloponnesian League with allies. Athens and Sparta declared war on each other in 431 BC. At first, Sparta dominated on land, Athens at sea. After a few years, they agreed to a truce. This lasted six years, then Athens attacked one of Sparta's allies. This time, Sparta destroyed the Athenian fleet. Athens had to surrender. The war nearly destroyed Athens, and also damaged Sparta. Sparta tried to dominate Greece, but it was worn down. In 371 BC Thebes defeated Sparta but could not maintain control either. In the 350s BC, Macedonia, a Greek-speaking kingdom to the north, took control of all of Greece.

Why do you think that Sparta could not maintain control over Greece?

____

____

____

Name ______________________ Class ______________ Date ______________

Classical Greece

Section 3

> **MAIN IDEA**
> The ancient Greeks made great achievements in philosophy, literature, art, and architecture that influenced the development of later cultures and ideas.

Key Terms and People

Socrates first of the great Athenian philosophers, believed that working through a series of questions led people to discover the basic nature of life

Plato great philosopher and student of Socrates, wrote about government and other topics, founded the Academy

Aristotle Athenian philosopher who studied at the Academy, used philosophy to pursue every kind of knowledge

reason clear and ordered thinking

logic the process of making inferences

Homer legendary poet from the 800s BC who composed the Iliad and the Odyssey

lyric poetry poetry which was sung with the accompaniment of an instrument called a lyre

Herodotus first major historian; lived during the wars with Persia and wrote about them

Thucydides historian who wrote about the Peloponnesian War

Taking Notes

As you read the summary, keep a list of key people and developments in Greek philosophy, literature, art, and architecture in a graphic organizer like the one below.

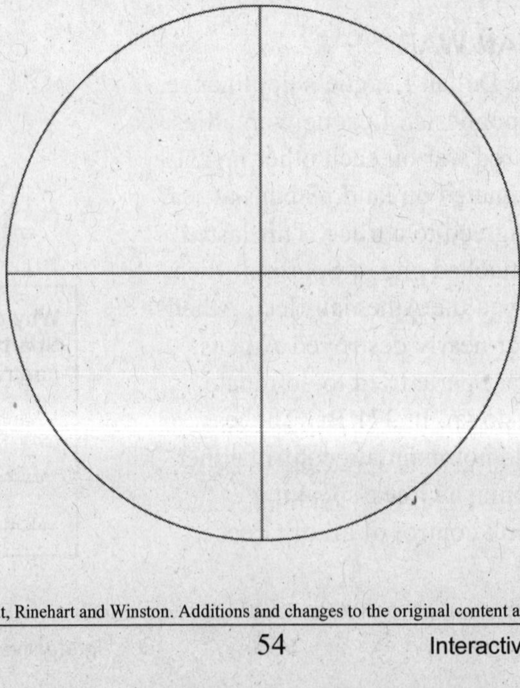

Section Summary

GREEK PHILOSOPHY

The people of ancient Greece were great believers in philosophy. The golden age of Greek philosophy was the 400s–300s BC, when the three greatest Greek philosophers lived: Socrates, Plato, and Aristotle.

What we know about **Socrates** (SAHK-ruh-teez) comes from his students. He was interested in concepts like truth, justice, and virtue. He asked questions like, "What is truth?" When someone answered, he challenged the answer with more questions. This is known as the Socratic method.

What is the Socratic method?

____

____

____

Plato (PLAYT-oh) was Socrates' student and a great philosopher also. He wrote on topics like truth and government. He believed governments should be led by philosophers. To spread philosophical ideas, he founded the Academy. It became the most important philosophy school in Greece.

Why do you think Plato believed that political leaders should be philosophers? Do you agree? Why or why not?

____

____

____

____

____

____

Aristotle (ar-uh-STAH-tuhl) became another great philosopher. He was more concerned with the nature of the world than with human nature, which had been Socrates' and Plato's focus. He emphasized the importance of **reason**, or clear and ordered thinking, and **logic**. This is the process of making inferences, using what we already know to learn something new.

GREEK LITERATURE

The ancient Greeks' development of poetry, drama, and history still influence European culture. Around 800 BC, heroic stories began to take form. The legendary blind poet **Homer**, who may or may not have been a real person, told a mixture of history and legend about the Trojan War in two epics, the *Iliad* and the *Odyssey.* The *Iliad* describes the long conflict. The *Odyssey* describes the efforts of Odysseus to get home after the war. In both stories, the gods argue and take sides, and there are human heroes and villains. These stories influenced Greek culture for centuries.

Why do you think Homer's epics influenced Greek culture for centuries?

____

____

____

____

The earliest examples of Greek poetry are epics like the *Iliad* and *Odyssey*. Literature started when these oral stories were written down. At about the same time, the poet Hesiod (HEEZ-ee-od) wrote poems about everyday Greek life, and also about the gods. By the

600s BC, Greeks such as Sappho and Pindar were composing **lyric poetry**, which was sung with the accompaniment of an instrument called a lyre.

At first, drama was much like poetry: a chorus of singers told a story. Over time the stories became more complicated. At the festival of Dionysus, playwrights competed for prizes. Aeschylus (EES-ky-luss) created drama based on myths. Sophocles specialized in tragedy, the destruction of noble characters by their fatal flaws. Euripides also wrote tragedies, many of them about women. Comedy also developed, usually in the form of satire. The greatest Athenian comic writer was Aristophanes.

Around the same time that drama was being developed, Athenians were also writing history. The first major historian was **Herodotus**, who lived during the wars with Persia and wrote about them. He used prose, and tried to describe major events as they actually happened. **Thucydides** (thoo-SID-id-eez) lived during the Peloponnesian War and used primary sources like speeches to write about it in detail. Both historians tried to understand why events happened as they did. Xenophon picked up when Thucydides left off, but concentrated more on describing famous men.

How are the histories written by Herodotus similar to the *Iliad*? How are they different?

____

____

____

____

____

GREEK ARCHITECTURE AND ART

The Greeks appreciated the natural world, and tried to understand it using math and science. They wanted art and architecture to represent the world as they saw it, and to create balance, proportion, and harmony. Painting and sculpture portrayed real human beings as ideals. Architecture used clean, simple geometry arranged for balance.

What features did the ancient Greeks use in their art and architecture?

____

____

____

The Greeks developed methods for exploring scientific subjects that last to this day, such as the use of reason and logic. Pythagoras, who believed that the universe was held together by mathematics, helped discover the rules of geometry in the 500s BC. In the 300s BC, Euclid wrote books on geometry and math that formed the basis for later European studies. In the late 400s, Hippocrates (hip-OCK-rah-teez) studied human illnesses, trying to cure them. Today, doctors swear a "Hippocratic oath" naming their ethical duties and the methods they will use.

MAIN IDEA
Alexander the Great formed a huge empire, spread Greek culture into Egypt and many parts of Asia, and paved the way for a new civilization to develop in those areas.

Key Terms and People

Alexander the Great Macedonian leader who ruled Greece and conquered Persia

Hellenistic Greeklike; describes a culture that was no longer purely Greek, but included elements from Persia, Egypt, Central Asia, and other regions

Euclid Egyptian who formulated many of the geometry ideas we still learn today

Eratosthenes Egyptian scientist who calculated the size of the world, arriving at a figure remarkably close to the actual circumference of the globe

Archimedes one of the ancient world's greatest inventors, used mathematics and physics to create devices that would make life easier

Taking Notes

As you read the summary, use a graphic organizer like the one below to take notes on Alexander's empire and the Hellenistic world.

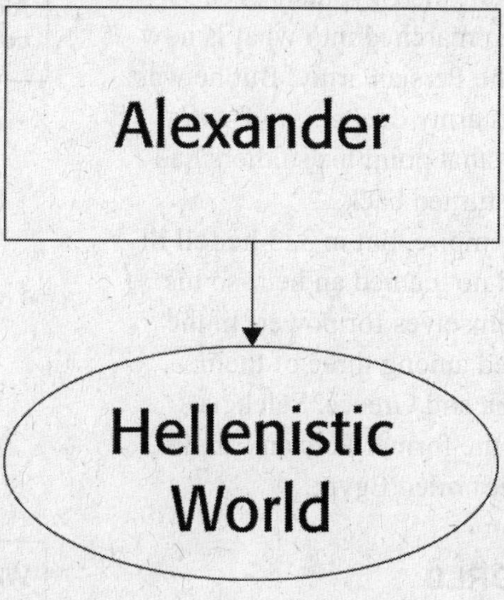

Section Summary

ALEXANDER THE GREAT

In 359 BC, King Philip II took power in Macedonia, the country just north of Greece. He reorganized the army. Then he set out to conquer Greece. Most city-states did not realize the danger, so he faced little opposition. The Macedonians quickly crushed the armies that stood against them, and conquered every major Greek city-state except Sparta. King Philip was assassinated in 336 BC, so his 20 year old son took over. We now know him as **Alexander the Great**.

Alexander had been trained to rule from birth, so he was ready to lead. As soon as he took over, there were rebellions in Greece. He used harsh measures to reestablish his rule: when Thebes rebelled, he crushed its army and burned the city. After getting Greece under control, he went into Asia to fight the large but disorganized Persian army. Alexander's army was smaller but well-trained and loyal. He won several major victories in Asia Minor, then went into Phoenicia and Egypt, which were also ruled by Persia. He was greeted as a liberator; the Egyptians even made him pharaoh. He then marched into what is now Iraq, where he destroyed the Persian army. But he was not yet satisfied. He led his army deeper into Central Asia, to the Indus river. At that point his soldiers had had enough, so Alexander turned back.

Alexander built a huge empire, but in 323 he fell ill and died at age 33. He had not named an heir, so his generals fought among themselves for power. In the end, the empire was divided among three of them: Antigonus ruled Macedonia and Greece, Seleucis (suh-LOO-kuhs) took over the former Persian Empire, and Ptolemy (TAHL-uh-mee) ruled Egypt.

Why was Philip II able to conquer Greece so easily?

____

____

____

Underline the places that Alexander the Great conquered.

THE HELLENISTIC WORLD

By creating a huge new empire, Alexander brought about a new culture, blending elements from Greece, Persia, Egypt, Central Asia and other regions. Historians call this culture **Hellenistic**, or Greeklike.

Alexander worked to bring people and ideas together. He appointed officials from various cultures to help rule. He also built dozens of new cities (most

Why do you think Alexander made such a strong effort to blend the cultures in his empire?

____

____

____

named Alexandria) throughout the empire and encouraged Greeks to move to them. The most famous of these was in Egypt at the mouth of the Nile. It became Egypt's capital and at one time had the busiest harbor in the world. Palaces and monuments were built, such as the Pharos lighthouse and the great library. It became a center for culture and learning.

Many other cities throughout the empire also became trading centers. Traders went to East Africa, Arabia, India, and even China. Traders helped spread not only goods but ideas like the teachings of Judaism.

How did life change in cities in the Hellenistic world?

____

____

____

The shift to a Hellenistic world brought drastic changes to people's lives. Perhaps most importantly, the city-state was no longer the main political unit. Traditional forms of government such as democracy were replaced with monarchy. Women's lives also changed: for the first time, they were given the rights to be educated and to own property.

HELLENISTIC ACHIEVEMENTS

The blending of cultures in the Hellenistic world led to an exchange of ideas, which then led to advances in philosophy, literature, and science.

Interest in philosophy spread, and new schools of philosophy developed. One was the Cynics. They rejected pleasure, wealth, and social responsibility, believing people should live according to nature. The Epicureans, on the other hand, thought people should seek out pleasure and try to avoid pain. Stoics emphasized reason, self-discipline, emotional control and personal morality.

What was the focus of each of the three new schools of philosophy?

____

____

____

Artists in this period learned to convey emotion and movement in their works. Women became much more common subjects of art. This was also true in literature, where love stories became popular for the first time. There were also important advances in science, especially in Egypt. **Euclid** formulated many ideas about geometry, while **Eratosthenes** calculated the circumference of the globe. Others studied the movement of the stars and the workings of the human body. **Archimedes**, one of the greatest inventors of the ancient world, used math and physics to design machines such as pulleys to lift heavy loads and a mechanical screw for drawing water out of a well.

Name _______________ Class _______________ Date _______________

Chapter Summary

The Rise and Fall of the Roman Empire

Early Success	Cultural Legacy	End of Empire
• Favorable location in the center of Mediterranean region • access to trade • routes • strong military expanded throughout Mediterranean	• system of law • Latin language • education • many systems of government • scientific knowledge • new techniques in engineering and architecture • Christianity	• lacked strong rulers after Pax Romana • weakened by civil war and inflation • invaded by tribes from the frontiers • western empire defeated by tribes in 400s

COMPREHENSION AND CRITICAL THINKING

Use information from the graphic organizer to answer the following questions.

1. **Recall** What two factors made Italy an ideal location for an empire to grow?

____

____

2. **Cause and Effect** How was the Roman Empire affected by the tribes at its boundaries?

____

____

3. **Evaluate** What do you think was the Roman Empire's most important contribution to later societies?

____

____

4. **Design** Outline a plan that the Roman Empire could have used to prevent its fall in the west. Explain why your plan would have succeeded.

____

____

Name ______________________ Class ______________ Date ______________

Rome and Early Christianity

Section 1

MAIN IDEA
From a small town on the banks of an Italian river, Rome grew to control the entire Mediterranean region.

Key Terms and People

republic a type of government in which elected officials govern the state

patricians elected officials from aristocratic families in the Roman Republic

plebeians nonaristocrats in the Roman Republic

veto rejection of harmful or unjust laws

Forum central square in Rome

constitution Roman political structure that created new offices and government institutions

Senate a body of legislators who acted as advisors, controlled public finances, and handled foreign relations in the Roman Republic

consuls elected magistrates that replaced the king as chief executives of the state

dictator a ruler who has nearly unlimited power

Taking Notes

As you read the summary, take notes on Rome's origin, government, and expansion. Use a graphic organizer like the one below to record key points.

Origin
Government
Expansion

Section Summary

ROMAN CIVILIZATION DEVELOPS

From a tiny village, Rome grew into the largest city of the ancient world. Italy was a logical place for an empire to develop. Its mountains provided protection from invaders and the coastline offer a rapid means of transportation via sea travel. Rich soil and a pleasant climate made it possible for many people to live there.

Underline the reasons Italy was an ideal location for an empire to develop.

According to legend, Romulus and Remus, twin brothers who were raised by a she-wolf, founded the city of Rome in 753 BC. The people who built Rome were members of an Indo-European tribe known as the Latins. Rome prospered under the Latins, partly because of its access to trade routes on land and sea.

Around 600 BC, Rome came under the control of the Etruscans of northern Italy. The Etruscans shaped Rome's government and architecture. They also introduced an alphabet and a number system, as well as gladiator games and chariot races.

ROME BECOMES A REPUBLIC

Around 509 BC the Roman aristocracy overthrew the Etruscan monarchs to establish a **republic** in which elected officials governed the state. At first, aristocratic families called **patricians** controlled every aspect of society. Then, the **plebeians** (pli-BEE-uhns), or common people, challenged patricians for power.

The plebeians eventually gained more rights. They were given the right to elect officials known as **tribunes** to protect them from unjust treatment by patrician officials. Tribunes eventually gained the right to **veto**, or ban, unjust laws. Around 450 BC, the plebeians forced the patricians to write down all laws. The laws were displayed on 12 large bronze tablets in the Roman **Forum**, or central square.

How did plebeians protect their rights?

____

____

The patricians and plebeians together created a **constitution**, or political structure. The government had three parts. The **Senate**, a body of legislators who acted as advisors, controlled public finances and foreign relations. Various assemblies allowed all citizens to vote on laws and elect officials. Officials known as magistrates put the laws into practice.

Circle the three parts of the new Roman government.

Two magistrates, called **consuls**, became the chief executives of the state and commanded the military. Lesser magistrates handled other administrative duties. All Roman city leaders worked in the Forum, the public square, home to important buildings and temples. The Forum was an important meeting place for the public to shop, gossip, and hear speeches.

Romans considered farming and land ownership the noblest careers, as shown in the story of Cincinnatus. The Romans asked General Cincinnatus to save them from attack. They made him a **dictator**, giving him nearly unlimited power. Cincinnatus stopped plowing his fields only long enough to defeat his enemies. He wanted only to return to his farm.

Why do you think the Romans admired Cincinnatus?

____

____

THE REPUBLIC EXPANDS

As Rome's government changed, its population grew. More land was needed. Rome acquired land by attacking nearby lands with a large, organized, and well-trained military. By about 265 BC, the Romans had defeated the Etruscans and the Greek cities in southern Italy. When Rome's army moved on Sicily, it came into conflict with the powerful trading city of Carthage. The military conflicts that followed are known as the Punic Wars.

The first Punic War began in 264 BC. Rome defeated Carthage and demanded money and control of Sicily. This victory got Romans more interested in expansion. They later seized Sardinia and Corsica.

What two generals battled in the second Punic War?

____

____

Relations between Rome and Carthage became worse. In 218 BC, during the Second Punic War, the great Carthaginian general Hannibal invaded Italy, defeating many Roman armies. In the end, the Roman general Publius Cornelius Scipio (SIP-ee-oh) sailed to Africa and attacked Carthage itself. Scipio's defeat of Hannibal ended the Second Punic War in 202 BC.

In 149 BC Rome decided to destroy Carthage once and for all, declaring a Third Punic War. After Carthage fell, the Romans enslaved the population and destroyed the city. Rome went on to conquer Macedonia and Persia, who had both allied with Carthage. They also annexed Greece and were greatly influenced by Greek art, architecture, and religion.

How did the Punic Wars end?

____

____

Name ________________ Class ____________ Date ____________

Rome and Early Christianity

Section 2

MAIN IDEA

Governmental and social problems led to the end of the Roman Republic and the creation of a new form of government.

Key Terms and People

Gracchi Two brothers, Tiberius Gracchus and Gaius, who tried to redistribute land to small farmers

Gaius Marius a talented general who, as consul, allowed anyone to join the army

Lucius Cornelius Sulla a general who became consul in 88 BC and later dictator

Julius Caesar helped end the Republic and became dictator of Rome in 44 BC

triumvirate the rule of three men

Augustus a title of honor given to Octavia in 27 BC, meaning "the revered one"

Pax Romana the Roman Peace, which lasted from 27 BC to AD 180

Taking Notes

As you read the summary, make a list of major events in Rome's change from a republic to an empire. Use a graphic organizer like the one below to record key points.

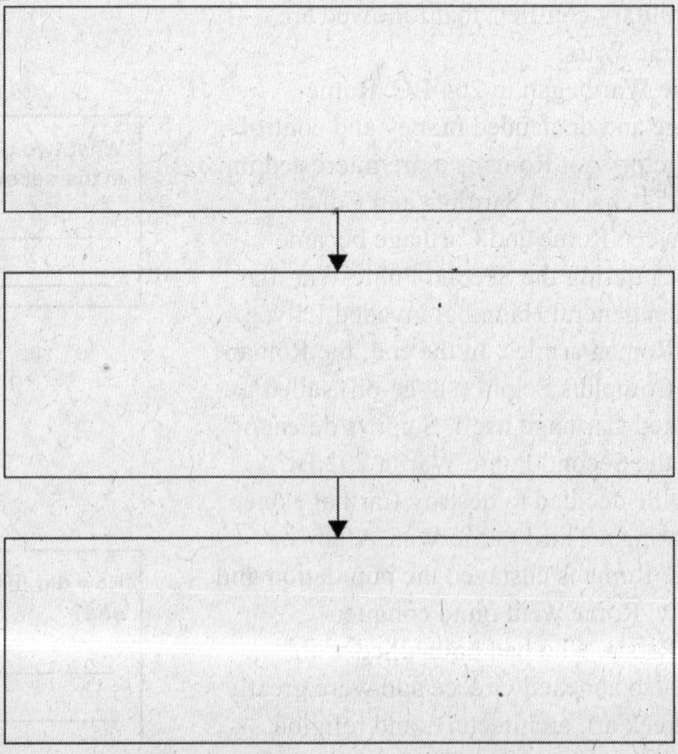

Section Summary

PROBLEMS IN THE LATE REPUBLIC

By the mid-100s BC, Rome had no rival anywhere in the Mediterranean world. However, the task of running a vast empire and the tension growing between social classes began to cause problems for the Romans. In 133 BC Tiberius Gracchus and his brother Gauis, known as the **Gracchi**, were murdered at the Senate's urging after planning to distribute public land to unemployed ex-soldiers.

In 107 BC the social unrest reached a new level. When General **Gaius Marius** became consul, he changed the rule about soldiers having to own property to join the army. Poor people with hopes of gaining plunder through war joined the army. The army then became a private force devoted to Marius, not Rome itself. In 90 BC, Rome's allies wanted to obtain Roman citizenship, but the Senate refused. This led to the Social War. In the end the rebels were defeated, but the Senate granted them citizenship.

In 88 BC General **Lucius Cornelius Sulla** became consul. Marius and his supporters did not want Sulla to command the military, as earlier consuls had. A civil war began. Sulla won and became dictator, executing all those who had opposed him. He paved the way for major changes in Rome's government.

Why were the Gracchi murdered?

____

____

Underline the names of two Roman generals that became consuls.

ROME BECOMES AN EMPIRE

Within a generation of Sulla's death, the old Republic was practically gone. In 60 BC Julius Caesar, Gnaeus Pompey, and Licinius Crassus dominated the Roman state. Their rule became known as the First **Triumvirate**, or rule of three men. After Crassus's death, Caesar defeated Pompey and took total control of Rome. In 44 BC he became dictator for life.

Caesar was murdered by a group of senators in a failed attempt to save the Republic. However, in 43 BC, the Second Triumvirate took power. Its members were Caesar's adopted son, Octavian, the officer Marc Antony, and the high priest Lepidus. Lepidus was pushed aside so that Antony and Octavian could each rule half of the empire. In time, civil war broke out between Antony and Octavian.

Underline the definition of triumvirate. List the three rulers of the Second Triumvirate.

____

____

Octavian defeated Antony and his ally, Queen Cleopatra of Egypt, in 31 BC. When he took control of the empire, a new period in Roman history began.

Octavian created a new political order known as the Principate. In 27 BC the Senate gave Octavian a title of honor: **Augustus**, or "the revered one," the name by which he is still known today. Augustus remained the head of the state for more than 40 years. He took special care of Rome, initiated a vast building program, and presided over moral and religious reforms. Great writers such as the poet Virgil flourished in the Augustan Age.

Which Roman leader was given the title Augustus?

____

Augustus died in AD 41, and for the next 54 years relatives of Julius Caesar, called the Julio-Claudian Emperors, ruled Rome. The abilities of these emperors varied widely. After AD 68, a series of emperors known as the Flavians took control of Rome and reestablished order. After the Flavians came a dynasty of five leaders known as the Good Emperors. Most of them were from the provinces, rather than from Rome. During their rule, the empire reached its largest size and built fortifications against invaders.

THE PAX ROMANA

The period from the beginning of Augustus's reign in 27 BC until the death of Marcus Aurelius in AD 180 is often called the **Pax Romana**—the Roman Peace. Stable government, law, widespread trade, and an extensive network of roads helped the Romans build their empire and maintain peace.

What aspects of the Pax Romana helped the Romans build the empire and maintain peace?

____

____

____

The Roman government was the strongest force in holding the empire together. The Roman Empire was divided into provinces with governors appointed from Rome. Through this provincial organization, the empire helped all Mediterranean cities become more alike, complete with local senates and magistrates.

The stable system of Roman law also unified the empire. With few exceptions, the same laws applied to everyone in the empire. The empire also provided many opportunities for trade because of two factors: its many Mediterranean settlements and its extensive road network. However, most roads were used for military purposes, while the majority of goods were shipped by sea.

MAIN IDEA

The Romans developed a complex society and pioneered cultural advances that, even today, affect life all over the world.

Key Terms and People

villa a Roman country home that had conveniences such as running water and baths

circus racetrack used for chariot racing

paterfamilias the family father, the oldest living male in a family

augurs priests who specialized in interpreting signs from the gods in natural phenomena

Galen physician whose medical writings established him as the greatest medical authority for centuries

Ptolemy astronomer who said that the earth was the center of the universe

aqueducts manmade channels used to bring water to cities

Latin the language of Rome and root of French, Italian, Spanish, Romanian, and Portuguese languages

civil law system of law based on written codes

Taking Notes

As you read the summary, take notes on Roman life, entertainment, society, religion, and culture. Use a word web like the one below to record key points.

Section Summary

LIFE IN IMPERIAL ROME

The Pax Romana provided prosperity to many people, but citizens did not share equally in this wealth. Rich citizens usually had both a city home and a country home, or **villa**, that included conveniences such as running water and baths.

Wealthy Romans also controlled politics. Because public officials were not paid, only the wealthy could afford to hold office. Wealthy Romans met frequently with public officials and political groups with common interests. Ties of marriage, friendship, and family alliances were as important to them as class interests. They also worked to improve the public speaking skills they used in popular assemblies.

How was Roman politics controlled by the wealthy?

____

____

Nearly one million poor Romans, on the other hand, lived in dangerous, crowded conditions. Fire posed a constant threat. In part to prevent the poor from rebelling, free food and public entertainment became a major feature of city life in Rome.

Romans of all classes enjoyed many forms of entertainment. Comedies and satires were staged at theaters. Chariot racing at the **circus** was popular, too. Romans also favored bloody spectacles such as gladiator fights in the amphitheaters. Public baths were another popular place for entertainment. The Romans were well aware of the importance of bathing and hygiene for health, but the baths also offered an opportunity to socialize and relax.

Circle forms of popular entertainment for Romans.

Roman families were headed by a **paterfamilias**, or family father. He was the oldest living male and had extensive powers over other family members. Romans often adopted a teenage boy or young man to ensure that family names carried on. Roman women had few freedoms, although many lower class women worked outside the home.

What was the role of the paterfamilias in Roman families?

____

____

Most Romans of the upper classes were at least partly literate. Children were educated either at home or, if they were wealthy enough, by tutors or in schools.

Religion was central to Roman life. When the Romans conquered Greece, they adopted Greek mythology. They also worshipped gods from the

Egyptians, the Mesopotamians, and other peoples. In short, they would pray to any god they believed might ensure prosperity. Each family also worshipped local household gods called penates. The Romans believed that the gods sent signs and warnings to human beings in the form of natural phenomena, like the flight of birds. These signs were read by highly respected priests known as **augurs**.

ROME'S CULTURAL LEGACY

Although the Western Roman Empire fell in 476, much of what was Rome endured, influencing life for centuries. The Romans influenced later people through their knowledge of science and engineering. The physician **Galen** wrote several volumes that summarized the medical knowledge of his day. He was regarded as the greatest medical authority for centuries. Similarly, **Ptolemy** created a single theory of astronomy, that the earth was the center of the universe. Roman engineers applied scientific knowledge to create amazing roads, bridges, buildings, and **aqueducts** – manmade channels used to bring water to cities. Romans also developed concrete, which made it possible to build large public structures, many of which still stand today.

What building material was invented by Roman engineers?

____

The Roman legacy in architecture is strong. Their use of the round arch and the vault allowed them to construct much larger buildings than earlier societies. The ruins of Roman buildings inspired generations of architects including Michelangelo and Thomas Jefferson.

Also part of Rome's legacy are the Romance languages, which developed from **Latin**, the language of Rome. The French, Italian, Spanish, Romanian and Portuguese languages all have roots in Latin. Many words in English also come from Latin, such as et cetera, veto, and curriculum.

Circle the languages that have roots in Latin. Write one English word that comes from Latin.

____

Roman law left its imprint on the world, too. The Romans used a system of law based on written codes called **civil law**. This system was adopted by many countries in Europe after the empire fell. Roman influence can still be seen in the legal systems of many of the world's countries.

Name ______________ Class ______________ Date ______________

MAIN IDEA

A new religion called Christianity developed within the Roman Empire and gradually spread throughout the Roman world.

Key Terms and People

Christianity a religion based on the teachings of Jesus of Nazareth

Messiah a spiritual leader who, according to prophecy, would restore the ancient Kingdom of David

Jesus of Nazareth a spiritual leader who taught people to seek forgiveness for their sins

disciples followers

Apostles twelve disciples chosen by Jesus

martyrs people who suffer death for the sake of their faith, inspiring others to believe

Paul Jewish apostle who helped spread Christianity in the eastern Mediterranean region, formerly called Saul

Eucharist a religious ceremony that commemorated Jesus's last supper

bishop a priestly official who oversaw church affairs in a particular city, had authority over other priests in the region

pope bishop of Rome

Taking Notes

As you read the summary, take notes about key events and ideas in the early history of Christianity. Use a graphic organizer like the one below to list key points.

Events	Ideas

Section Summary

CHRISTIANITY AND JUDAISM

Over time, the teachings of Jesus of Nazareth developed into a new religion called **Christianity**. Many of those teachings were rooted in the beliefs and customs of Judaism. Unlike many conquered peoples living in the Roman Empire, the people living in the kingdom of Judea strived to keep their monotheistic religion as it was. They did not want it mixed with Rome's polytheistic state religion. Most Roman emperors allowed the Jews religious freedom. Judaism, however, had many different branches. One group, the Zealots, wanted to overthrow Roman rule. Others preferred to wait for the coming of a spiritual leader known as the **Messiah**, who they believed would restore the ancient Kingdom of David. When the Zealots rebelled in AD 66–70, the Romans killed thousands of Jews and destroyed Jerusalem, including most of the Second Temple, leaving only the western wall.

How did the people of Judea differ from other peoples in the empire?

____

____

JESUS OF NAZARETH

From the chaos in Judea, a spiritual leader named **Jesus of Nazareth** emerged. Our knowledge of Jesus comes almost entirely from the Gospels, or the first four books of the New Testament. The New Testament together with the books of the Hebrew Bible make up the Christian Bible.

Underline the spiritual texts that make up the Bible.

According to the Gospels, Jesus was born in Bethlehem, near Jerusalem, and grew up in the town of Nazareth. In time, Jesus began to preach. He gathered a group of **disciples**, or followers. According to the Bible, Jesus performed miracles of healing and defended the poor and the oppressed.

Jesus instructed people to repent for their sins, seek God's forgiveness, and love God and all people. Jesus's teachings and the crowds he drew alarmed authorities. He was arrested and put to death.

What messages did Jesus spread to his followers?

____

____

According to the New Testament, after being executed, Jesus rose from the dead, then spent another 40 days teaching his disciples before ascending into heaven. His followers believed that Jesus was the Messiah and the Son of God. They began calling him Jesus Christ, after Christos, the Greek word for Messiah.

THE SPREAD OF CHRISTIANITY

After Jesus's death, 12 of the disciples he had chosen specifically—known as the **Apostles**—began to spread Jesus' message. They taught that all people could receive salvation, or the forgiveness of sins and the promise of everlasting life. The disciples were persecuted and some were killed. Those killed were seen as **martyrs**, people who suffer death for their faith's sake, and thus inspire others to believe.

Had it not been for the work of a man named **Paul**, Christianity might have remained a branch of Judaism. Paul convinced the disciples that Jesus had given him a special mission to convert non-Jews, or Gentiles. Paul changed some rules for non-Jews and wrote epistles that would later be placed in the New Testament. Many new followers joined the church.

How did Paul help spread Christianity?

____

____

Christianity spread quickly through the Roman world. Its message of love and life after death appealed to many. The emperor Constantine joined the religion and made Christianity legal within the empire, which helped the religion flourish in the 300s.

THE EARLY CHRISTIAN CHURCH

The earliest Christian congregations were spiritual organizations that were like close-knit families. As Christianity grew, however, its organization became more complex. Part of the church's early success came from the development of special ceremonies and rituals. One such ceremony was the **Eucharist**, which commemorated Jesus's last supper with his disciples. In this ceremony, Christians ate bread and drank wine in memory of Jesus's death.

Over time, those who organized and performed church ceremonies became known as priests. Soon a single priestly official, called a **bishop**, emerged to oversee church affairs in most cities. Bishops had authority over the other priests in an area. Many bishops believed that the **pope**, or bishop of Rome, had authority as the head of the entire church.

Circle the titles of officials within the early Christian church.

Name _______________________ Class _______________ Date _______________

MAIN IDEA

Events and conditions inside as well as outside the Roman Empire weakened it and led to its collapse in the west in the 400s.

Key Terms and People

inflation a dramatic rise in prices

Diocletian a capable Roman emperor who assumed the throne in 248 and created an absolute monarchy to strengthen the empire

Attila the leader of the Huns

Taking Notes

As you read the summary, keep track of the problems that faced the Roman Empire on a graphic organizer like the one below.

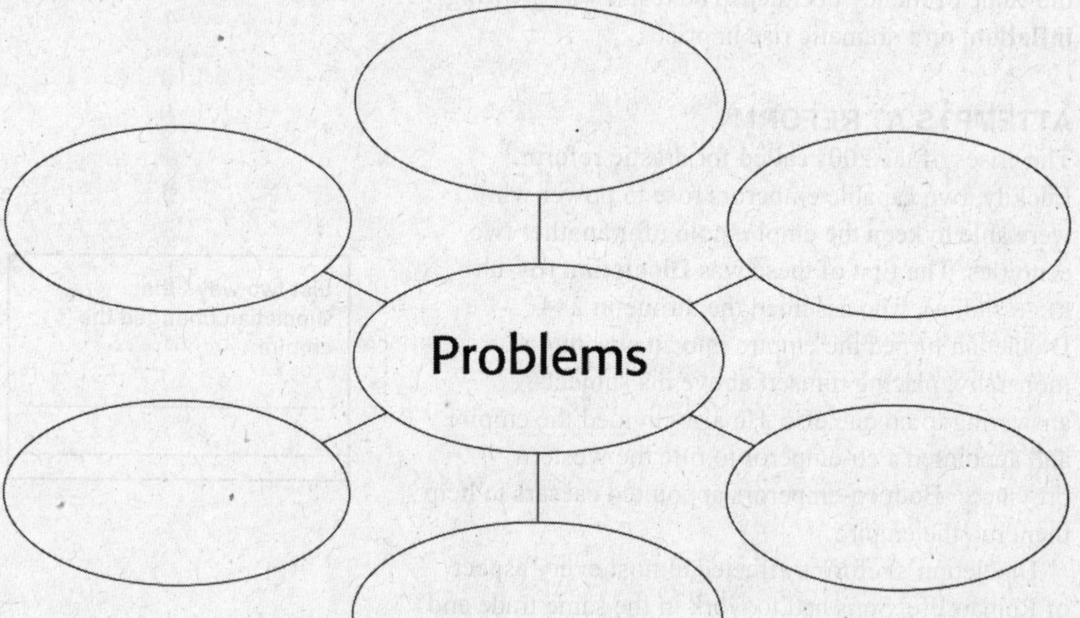

Section Summary

THE EMPIRE WEAKENS

The inability of the Roman army to stop the Huns was just one sign of the empire's weakness after the Pax Romana ended. When the last of the Good Emperors died, Rome was left without a strong leader. The empire endured a series of civil wars and more invasions by the tribal peoples along its borders. The expense of increasing the military to deal with these issues caused an economic crisis. Between 235 and 284, twenty emperors reigned. All but one died violently. The military legions became the center of power, deposing unpopular emperors and elevating their own leaders to the throne.

The civil wars and invasions affected many aspects of Roman life. Travel became unsafe, taxes rose, and the value of money declined. The result was growing **inflation**, or a dramatic rise in prices.

Underline the causes of inflation in Rome after the Pax Romana.

ATTEMPTS AT REFORM

The crises of the 200s called for drastic reform. Luckily, two capable emperors rose to power who were able to keep the empire going for another two centuries. The first of these was **Diocletian** (dy-uh-KLEE-shuhn), who assumed the throne in 284. Diocletian turned the empire into an absolute monarchy, placing himself above his subjects, answering to no one else. He also divided the empire and appointed a co-emperor to rule the western provinces. Both co-emperors appointed caesars to help them run the empire.

Diocletian's reforms affected almost every aspect of Roman life. Sons had to work in the same trade and have the same social position as their fathers. Peasants were connected to the land they farmed for life. The imperial economy also came under state direction. Diocletian did manage to save the empire from collapse.

Diocletian and his co-emperor retired in 305. Both emperors' caesars became the new co-emperors, but they soon quarrelled. A civil war broke out, lasting until 312 when Constantine, a son of the original caesar, took control.

List two ways that Diocletian changed the empire.

____

____

Constantine continued Diocletian's policies of rigid state control over society. He also made two decisions that affected the future of the empire. First, he converted to Christianity. Second, he built a new capital, Constantinople, or "the city of Constantine." Constantinople was built in the eastern half of the empire, which was richer and better defended than the west.

INVASION AND FALL

Despite the reforms of Diocletian and Constantine, the empire's serious problems continued and were worsened by invading forces along the empire's borders. In the late 300s, a new nomadic Central Asian people, the Huns, stormed out of the east and began defeating many Germanic tribes. The Huns were fierce and lived by looting and plundering. They struck terror in the people they attacked. Many of their victims fled south.

The Huns formed a vast empire in Eurasia. Around 370 they attacked the Ostrogoths, who lived north of the Black Sea. This motivated the Visigoths to avoid the Huns by moving into Roman lands. In 410 the Visigoth king Alaric captured and sacked Rome.

Why did the Visigoths go to Rome?

____

____

Pushed by the Huns, other tribes also soon attacked the Roman Empire. The Vandals, infamous for destroying everything in their path, invaded Rome in the 450s. The word vandal comes from this destructive tribe.

In the mid-400s **Attila** (at-UHL-uh), the leader of the Huns, led an attack on Gaul. The Roman army allied with the Visigoths and together they defeated the Huns in a great battle in 451. After Gaul, Attila set his sights on Rome but after speaking with Pope Leo I, Attila and his troops left Italy instead.

Despite the Huns' retreat, the Western Empire lay in a shambles. Germanic tribes ruled most of the western provinces, including Italy. In 476, the Ostrogothic commander Odoacer (oh-doh-AY-surh) defeated Romulus Augustus, the last emperor in the west. With this, the Western Roman Empire ended. The Eastern Roman Empire, however, remained.

Circle the name of the leader who ended the Western Roman Empire.

Chapter Summary

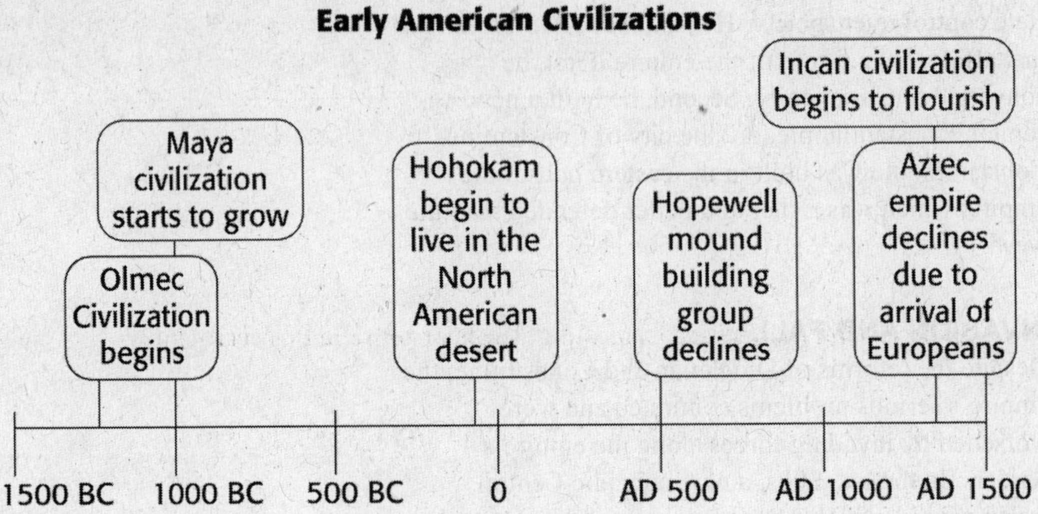

COMPREHENSION AND CRITICAL THINKING

Use information from the graphic organizer to answer the following questions.

1. **Recall** When did the Inca civilization begin to grow rapidly in South America?

____

____

2. **Sequence** Describe two civilizations that lived at the same time in the Americas.

____

____

3. **Evaluate** What impact did the arrival of Europeans have on civilizations that already lived in the Americas?

____

____

4. **Elaborate** What are some reasons civilizations grew and eventually declined? Explain your answer.

____

____

MAIN IDEA
As people settled in North America, they adapted to different types of geography by developing different styles of housing and ways of getting food.

Key Terms and People

adobe a mixture of clay and straw used to build dwellings

pueblo Anasazi dwellings that had many rooms and were several stories high

kivas underground rooms used as meeting places or for religious ceremonies

maize a type of corn farmed by the Iroquois

Iroquois League a joint government formed by the six Iroquois nations

Taking Notes

As you read the summary, record details about how the early cultures of North America adapted to their environment. Place your notes in a graphic organizer like the one below.

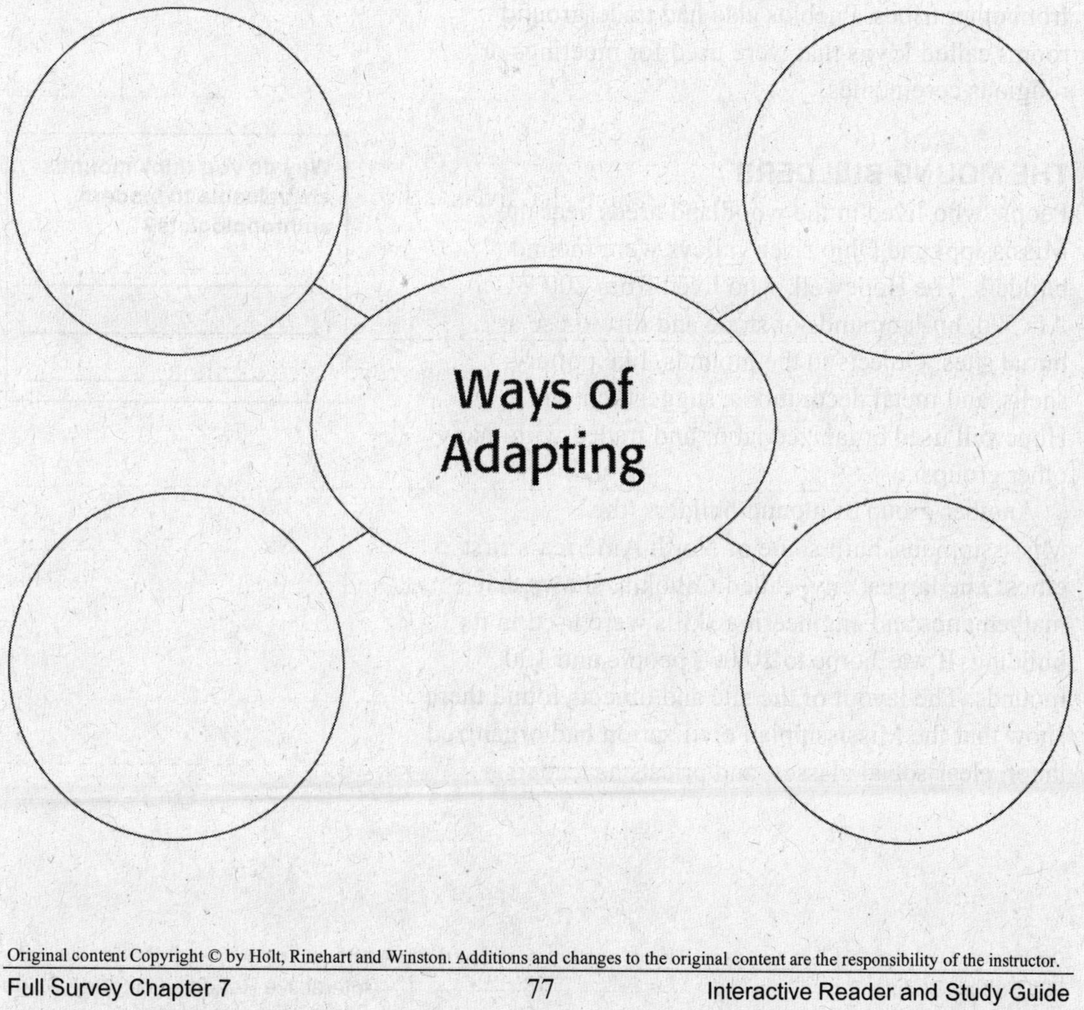

Section Summary

CULTURES OF THE DESERT WEST

Early people in North America adapted to a wide variety of environments. Those in the Desert West of what is now the southwestern United States and northern Mexico lived where it is very dry. One group, the Hohokam, lived from 100 BC to AD 1500. They built a system of canals with dams made of woven mats to water their crops. The crops were planted in nearby mounds made of earth. The Hohokam also brought irrigation and water storage to their villages. Their homes were pithouses, built-in holes in the ground. They used a mixture of clay and straw called **adobe** as a building material.

Another group, the Anasazi, lived in pithouses and also developed a new kind of home called the **pueblo**. Similar to today's apartment buildings, pueblos were several stories tall and had many rooms. Some pueblos were built in the sides of cliffs, for protection from other tribes. Pueblos also had underground rooms called **kivas** that were used for meetings or religious ceremonies.

Describe two types of dwellings built by early people in North America.

____

____

____

THE MOUND BUILDERS

People who lived in the woodland areas near the Mississippi and Ohio river valleys were mound builders. The Hopewell, who lived from 200 BC to AD 500, built mounds of stone and dirt to use as burial sites. Objects in the mounds, like pottery, shells, and metal decorations, suggest that the Hopewell used organized labor and traded with many other groups.

Another group of mound builders, the Mississippians, built some of North America's first cities. The largest city, called Cahokia, shows that mathematics and engineering skills were used in its building. It was home to 20,000 people and 100 mounds. The layout of the site and objects found there show that the Mississippian civilization had organized labor, clear social classes, and priests as leaders.

Why do you think mounds are valuable to modern anthropologists?

____

____

____

OTHER CULTURES OF NORTH AMERICA

The people living in North America found creative ways to deal with a variety of environments. For example, the Inuit people lived in the cold Arctic regions where farming was impossible. Instead, the Inuit hunted seals and caribou, and fished, using kayaks or holes in the ice. They used skins and furs for warm clothing and ice blocks for the igloos in which they lived.

The Iroquois lived in the forests of eastern North America. They lived in longhouses made of elm bark and trapped animals for food. The Iroquois farmed several different crops, including squash, beans, and **maize**, another word for corn. The Iroquois were made of five different nations, or tribes: the Cayaga, Mohawk, Oneida, Onondaga, and the Seneca. Later, the Tuscarora people joined them. In time, the different nations formed a common government body called the **Iroquois League**.

Plains Indians also had different groups, but because they did not all speak the same language, they developed a common sign language to communicate. They lived in the Great Plains region in the middle of the continent. At first they lived near rivers and streams. This was the area where the land was most fertile for farming. When Europeans brought horses to North America, the Plains Indians used them to follow buffalo, greatly changing the way the tribes lived. Buffalo became very important to the Plains Indians, who found ways to use different parts of the animal for meat, clothing, tents, and tools.

What did Inuit people eat?

____

____

Which culture in North America likely had the greatest variety of food?

____

____

How did life change for Plains Indians when horses arrived?

____

____

MAIN IDEA

Civilizations in Mesoamerica were some of the earliest and most advanced in the Americas.

Key Terms and People

elite high-ranking members of society

slash-and-burn agriculture a method of farming in which vegetation is burned to clear land for planting

glyphs Mayan writing symbols that represented objects and sounds

codex a type of bark paper book used for keeping written records

alliances groups of people or nations who agree to cooperate to meet common goals

tribute a type of tax collected from conquered people

Taking Notes

As you read the summary, take notes about the characteristics of Maya and Aztec societies. Fill in a chart like the one below with the details you find.

Maya	Aztec

Section Summary

THE FIRST CIVILIZATIONS

Mesoamerica includes what is now southern Mexico and northern Central America. Excellent farming conditions led to civilizations that had large cities, complex social structures, and cultural achievements. The Olmec lived along the Gulf coast in southern Mexico between 1200 BC and AD 300. They built large towns with monuments and pyramids. The Olmec **elite**, or high-ranking members, controlled a large trade network along the Pacific coast. They invented a calendar and used writing. The Zapotec people lived from 1500 BC to AD 750 and built Monte Albán, the first true city in the region. It had a large plaza with elaborate buildings, such as temples, and a population as high as 25,000. The Toltec civilization lasted from AD 900 to 1200. Its main city, Tula, was a trade center near obsidian mines. Toltec art and architecture show that they were warriors.

Circle the names of the first three civilizations in Mesoamerica.

Write two facts about the city of Monte Albán.

____

____

THE MAYA

The Maya civilization, which developed around 1000 BC, was much larger than the others in Mesoamerica. At its height, it had more than forty cities. The Maya began as farmers who used **slash-and-burn agriculture** to clear dense rainforest. They also flattened hillsides for farming. Small villages began trading with one another, and the population grew. Most Maya cities were built between AD 250 and 900. Each worked as a city-state with its own government and links to others for trade and war.

Religion played an important role in Maya culture. The Maya worshipped many gods and offered them sacrifices of blood and, sometimes, humans. Priests were part of the upper class, along with professional warriors. Below them were merchants and craftspeople. Most people were in the lower class, working as farmers or slaves.

The Maya civilization made advancements in architecture, as seen in their pyramids and palaces, and in astronomy, writing, and math. They charted movements of the sun, moon, and planets to create an accurate 365-day farming calendar. The Maya also

When were most Maya cities built?

____

____

Describe the role religion played in Maya culture.

____

____

used a 260-day religious calendar. They had a writing system that used **glyphs**, or symbols that stood for objects or sounds. Records were carved on stone monuments or kept in a bark paper book called a **codex**. The Maya civilization began to decline around AD 900, probably due to drought, warfare, and poor leadership. Some Maya people moved to cities that stayed strong for centuries.

What are glyphs? What do they have to do with a codex?

____

____

____

THE AZTECS

The Aztec people began as farmers in northern Mexico where they were likely controlled by the Toltecs. They migrated south in the 1100s. In 1325 they founded Tenochtitlán, a city on an island in Lake Texcoco. The Aztecs eventually formed key **alliances** with two nearby city-states. This empire ruled more than 400 cities and 5 million people in Mesoamerica. The Aztecs made conquered people pay **tribute**, or taxes, and built roads to make trade more efficient. Through tribute and trade, the empire grew wealthy.

Name two reasons the Aztecs were very wealthy.

____

____

Tenochtitlán was one of the largest cities in the world at the time, with a population of around 200,000. It had a walled center with a huge pyramid inside. The city was on an island without adequate farmland. Instead, city dwellers got their food from rafts or "floating gardens" in the lake that linked to canals leading to a big market at Tlatelolco, where goods such as cotton and rubber were sold.

Aztec society, like that of other civilizations, had a strict class system. At the top was the king. Priests came next. They tried to keep the gods happy by conducting many bloody sacrifices. Next in the social order came warriors, merchants, and artisans. The lower class consisted of farmers and slaves. Farmers could become warriors or government officials, but slaves could only hope their children were born free. Slaves were often sacrificed to the gods. The Aztecs calculated the movement of some planets and created a solar calendar like the Maya. Their system of writing recorded taxes, business deals, poetry, riddles, and historical accounts. Advanced artisans created beautiful works in metal and stone. The Aztec empire came to an end in the 1500s with the arrival of the Europeans.

List at least five roles of people in Aztec society in order from those in the highest classes to those in the lowest.

____

____

____

Name ______________________ Class ______________ Date ______________

MAIN IDEA

Several early cultures in South America adapted to extreme environmental conditions. One of them, the Inca, built one of the biggest and most powerful empires in the Americas.

Key Terms and People

Pachacuti Inca leader who started to expand the empire in the 1400s

quipu a set of colored and knotted cords used by the Incas for record-keeping

census data about a population

Taking Notes

As you read the summary, record notes on early South American cultures and the Inca empire. Place the details in a graphic organizer like the one below.

Early Cultures	Inca

Section Summary

EARLY CULTURES IN SOUTH AMERICA

Despite the geographical extremes of western South America, many groups created civilizations here. The Chavín (chah-VEEN) lived from 800 to 400 BC and built a religious and trading center called Chavín de Huantar in the Andes Mountains. They grew each of their crops at the altitude of the mountain that was best for it. Irrigation carried water to the corn planted in the warm valleys. The Chavín raised llamas and alpacas high in the mountains where nothing would grow well.

When did the Chavín and Moche live?

____

____

____

The Moche lived from 400 BC to AD 600 in the coastal desert regions of South America. They built canals to water crops planted in the desert and fished in villages. Metalwork and pottery with military images show that the Moche used war to expand their empire and had warrior-priests as leaders.

How did the Moche and Nazca deal with their desert climate?

____

____

____

Finally, the Nazca people lived from 200 BC to 600 AD. They are best known for Nazca Lines, huge designs of animals and geometric shapes in the desert floor. It is believed that the designs gave information about where water was found, because like the Moche, the Nazca were a desert culture that farmed. Their use of canals, natural springs, and an annual flood raised enough food to support a large population.

THE INCA EMPIRE

The Inca civilization flourished many centuries after the Chavín, Moche, and Nazca. Once a small tribe, the Inca reached the height of their power in the early 1500s when 12 million people were part of the empire. Expansion started in the 1400s when the Inca leader **Pachacuti** began to bring territory under Incan control through political alliances and military force. The central government was strong, with most power in the hands of one emperor. However, loyal leaders were sent out to rule each of the conquered areas.

What did Pachacuti do during his reign?

____

____

____

The government controlled the economy and collected labor taxes called the mita from the people. The government ordered each family to do a certain kind of work and was in charge of supplying goods to all people and storing the excess for emergencies. A set of knotted cords called a **quipu** helped Incas keep track of goods because there was no written language. The Incas used quipus to record a variety of information, such as **census** data that told about the population. A complex network of roads helped link cities.

The Inca government also grouped families in communities called ayllu (EYE-yoo) to work on projects together. Ten ayllus had one chief who reported to higher levels of government. There were class divisions in Inca society. Members of the lower class were limited in what they could own. They had to serve the upper class. The upper class lived in the capital city of Cuzco, where they had fine stone houses and wore nice clothes. They were not forced to pay the labor tax like the lower class. They were generally either priests or government officials. People worshipped a variety of local gods as well as the sun god, who was considered to be the most important. The Incas believed their kings were related to the sun god. Priests performed ceremonies in which llamas, food, or cloth was sacrificed. Unlike the Aztec, Incas rarely sacrificed humans to the gods but they did mummify important people sometimes.

Which god was most important to the Inca?

____

The Inca civilization made many important achievements because of its organized government. The empire's builders used large stone blocks that fit perfectly together without mortar to hold them, creating impressive temples, forts, and roads. Many structures built this way still stand today. Inca artists were skilled at weaving wool and cotton, and working with metal. They created everything from delicate jewelry to a large decorative field of corn made from gold and silver for a temple's courtyard. Weavers created everyday clothing as well as special fabrics for royalty and religious ceremony. The pattern of the fabric showed the owner's status in society.

Circle two things created by Inca builders and artisans.

The Inca empire remained strong for about 100 years. It had been declining by the time the Spanish arrived in 1532, ending the empire for good.

Name ______________________ Class ______________ Date ______________

Empires of China and India

Chapter Summary

	CHINESE EMPIRES	INDIAN EMPIRES
Dynasties	Qin and Han	Mauryan and Gupta
Roles of women	Family ruled by father or husband; few rights; expected to bear sons, daughters less valued than sons because daughters join husband's families	ruled by parents or husband; few rights; protected from abuse by husbands; expected to be mothers and wives, widows had even lower status
Social system	clear class system: king, royal family, nobles, peasants, artisans, merchants, slaves	caste system with clear roles and rules for each caste
Religious Life	Qin: rejected Confucianism Han: Confucianism and Buddhism	Mauryan: Buddhism; Gupta: Hinduism
Trade	Silk and other valuable goods; use of Silk Road during Han Dynasty	trade with China and central Asia; in Gupta Dynasty, increased trade with Southeast Asia and Roman Empire, sea routes

COMPREHENSION AND CRITICAL THINKING

Use information from the graphic organizer to answer the following questions.

1. **Recall** What were the names of important ancient empires in China and India?

____

2. **Compare and Contrast** How did life for women in the Chinese empires compare to women's lives in the Indian empires?

____

____

3. **Make Judgments** Do you think life in Han China would be better for a wealthy merchant of low status or for a peasant farmer with higher status?

____

____

MAIN IDEA

The Qin and Han dynasties created strong centralized governments that unified China and shaped Chinese civilization for thousands of years to follow.

Key Terms and People

Shi Huangdi "first emperor," title the Qin ruler gave himself when he unified China

Legalism a political philosophy that taught that a powerful and efficient state was the key to control and order

Liu Bang founder of the Han dynasty who defeated Qin forces in 206 BC

Wudi greatest Han ruler, brought the dynasty to new heights from 141 to 187 BC

civil service a system in which passing an exam is required to obtain government jobs

Xiongnu nomads who lived in the steppe, or grasslands, north of China and posed the biggest military threat to the Han dynasty under Emperor Wudi

Taking Notes

As you read the summary, take notes in the graphic organizer like the one below. Record the key people, events, and policies of each dynasty.

Qin	Han

Section Summary

THE QIN DYNASTY

After the decline of the Zhou dynasty in the 300s BC, local warlords battled for control of China. This was known as the Warring States period. It ended in 221 BC when the state of Qin (CHIN) on China's western frontier defeated the other states and unified China.

The first ruler of the new Chinese empire took the title **Shi Huangdi** (SHEE hwahng-dee), which means "first emperor." He boasted that the Qin dynasty would last a very long time. He made some changes to ensure that his predictions would come true. First, he instituted a system of **Legalism**. This political philosophy taught that a powerful and efficient state was the key to control and order. Shi Huangdi led by force, not virtuous example, as previous emperors had. He believed people were bad by nature, and so punishment for even minor crimes was severe. He also made the government stronger by taking land from powerful nobles and making them move to the capital, where he could watch them. He seized and destroyed the people's weapons and split China into 36 districts. These were controlled by officials who were loyal to the emperor, not the noble families.

The Qin dynasty's rule unified China. Shi Huangdi standardized China's laws, writing, coins, weights and measures, and even the width of axles on carts traveling its roads. He made improvements in building, crop irrigation, transportation, and trade. Peasants had to pay heavy taxes to fund these projects and often were forced to work on them.

Underline the ways in which the Qin dynasty united China.

Shi Huangdi protected the new empire from invaders, especially the fierce nomads who came from the north to raid the frontier. The Qin army pushed out these tribes along with others to the south. Then Shi Huangdi had peasants work hard, for years, to connect defensive walls already in place in the north. They formed one Great Wall, which was later rebuilt and extended to form the structure still found there today.

In the end, Shi Huangdi's harsh policies were the Qin dynasty's downfall. After Shi Huangdi died in 210 BC, his dynasty quickly fell apart. In 206 BC a rebel leader named **Liu Bang** (lee-OO-bang) defeated the Qin forces and founded the Han dynasty.

THE HAN DYNASTY

The Han dynasty is one of the greatest in Chinese history, ruling China for more than 400 years. Liu Bang gained the support of the people by softening many of Qin's harsh Legalist policies and lowering taxes. He gave large blocks of land to his supporters. The government became more stable with the addition of a large bureaucracy, or ranked body of officials.

What strategies did Liu Bang use to gain support for his rule?

____

____

____

After Liu Bang's death in 195 BC, his young son became king but his mother, Empress Lü, ruled in his place until he was older. She worked to keep her family's power until her death, when a group of officials and princes seized the throne and had the whole Lü family killed. Such power struggles were a common part of many later Chinese dynasties.

How did Empress Lü gain control of China?

____

____

The greatest of the Han rulers was **Wudi** (WOO-dee), who ruled from 141 to 187 BC. He promoted economic growth by building new roads and canals to make trade easier. To raise money, Wudi controlled the nation's salt, iron, and alcohol trades. To limit threats to his rule, he took power and land from large landowners, and placed limits on merchants so they could not become too wealthy.

Wudi ran the government based on Confucian values such as loyalty to the emperor. He established a **civil service** system which made people pass a test in order to get government jobs. This system was used until 1912.

Which of the Han dynasty rulers established the civil service system in China? How long was the system used?

____

____

Because of his military successes, Wudi was called the Martial Emperor. He defeated the **Xiongnu** (shee-UNG-noo), nomadic raiders who lived in the grasslands north of China. Wudi expanded the Chinese empire to the northeast, south, and west, and opened up important trading routes with other civilizations.

Battles for power, weak rulers, instability, and high taxes that caused debt and poverty for many peasants eventually weakened the Han dynasty. In 184 a Daoist sect called the Yellow Turbans rebelled. The central government lost power to local warlords and nomads destroyed the cities. The 350 years that followed are called the Period of Division.

MAIN IDEA
The Han dynasty was a time of social change, the growth of trade, and great achievements in the arts and sciences.

Key Terms and People

filial piety obedience and devotion to parents and grandparents

Ban Zhao female Confucian scholar and writer who had high status and bold views

Zhang Qian Han official whose reports on Central Asia led to increased trade to the west

Silk Roads a network of trade routes that stretched from China to the Mediterranean Sea

Sima Qian writer whose history of early Chinese dynasties became the model for all Chinese historical writing

acupuncture the practice of inserting fine needles through the skin at specific points to cure disease or relieve pain

Taking Notes

As you read the summary, take notes in the graphic organizer like the one below. Record notes for each topic under Han China.

Section Summary

HAN SOCIETY

During the Han dynasty, Confucianism shaped society. Strong families were believed to strengthen China as a whole. Under Confucianism, fathers had complete control over other family members. Children were expected to show **filial piety**, or obedience and devotion to parents and grandparents. A son was considered valuable because he would carry on the family line. A daughter had fewer privileges. She was considered less important because when she married, she left her own family to join her husband's. Women were expected to obey their husband and mother-in-law. One of the few women who attained a position of status was the writer **Ban Zhao**. Though she directed women to be humble and obedient, she said husbands should respect their wives and women should be educated—bold views at the time.

Underline the reason why family was important in Confucian China.

Han society was highly structured and divided into classes. The emperor was at the top of society and ruled with the mandate of heaven. Below him were classes of nobles and government leaders, peasant farmers, artisans, merchants, and at the bottom, slaves. The military was not a separate class, but those who joined it could raise their status.

Which class was more respected in Han society, merchants or farmers?

____

Peasant farmers had a higher status than merchants, but were usually much poorer. In Han China, the wealthy lived in luxurious houses, and many had large estates and hired people to do their work. Most Chinese, however, lived in mud huts. They had no choice but to work hard to feed their families, raise extra crops to sell, and pitch in on building projects like the Great Wall. High taxes and poor harvests forced many peasants into debt. Chinese farmers split their land equally between their sons. Over time, the land became too small to support the families, forcing the son to sell his land and go work for someone else.

TRADE AND BUDDHISM

Artisans in Han China produced many valuable items such as iron armor and swords, pottery, objects of jade and bronze, and lacquerware—carved wooden items covered with layers of hard varnish. The most prized product, however, was silk. The method of making silk fabric from the cocoons of silkworms was a carefully guarded secret for centuries. The strong, lightweight fabric was highly sought in other parts of the world, and silk became a major Chinese industry.

Underline the valuable products made in China during the Han dynasty, and circle the most valuable product.

One Chinese official, **Zhang Qian**, returned from Central Asia with news about both the area's wealth and horses the Han believed were blessed. As a result, Emperor Wudi conquered more land there and increased trade. Merchants traveled on the **Silk Roads**. This network of trade routes stretched 4,000 miles from China to the Mediterranean Sea. Merchants often traveled in large camel caravans through the difficult terrain that was home to bandits seeking to rob them.

What were the Silk Roads?

____

____

Buddhism, a religion from India, came to China through contact with traders. For many Chinese, Buddhism's belief in rebirth and the end of suffering brought comfort at a time when the Han dynasty grew less stable and more violent. Buddhism's growth in China is an example of diffusion, the spread of ideas from one culture to another.

HAN ACHIEVEMENTS

During the Han period, the arts flourished. Among the paintings, figurines, and carvings, Buddhist artwork stands out. Architectural models show palaces and towers that were built but did not survive. In literature, new styles of poetry were developed. Han writers also produced important works of history. The writer **Sima Qian** (jee-EN) wrote a history of China's dynasties that became a model for all Chinese historical writing.

Han inventors made advancements in science and technology. They created paper from fibers such as hemp. They also invented the iron plow and the wheelbarrow, along with the seismograph to measure earthquakes, water clocks to monitor time, the compass for navigation, the water mill for grinding grain, and the rudder to improve steering on boats. The Han also made advances in **acupuncture**, the practice of inserting fine needles through the skin at specific points to cure disease or relieve pain.

Circle the products and machines invented during the Han dynasty.

MAIN IDEA

The Mauryas and Guptas created powerful empires that united much of India, while trading kingdoms thrived in southern India.

Key Terms and People

Chandragupta Maurya first leader to unite India, founder of the Mauryan Empire

Kautilya advisor to Chandragupta Maury and advocate of strict government control

Ashoka grandson of Chandragupta and one of India's greatest rulers

Chandra Gupta II leader whose expansion of the Gupta Empire brought prosperity and cultural achievement

Taking Notes

As you read the summary, take notes in the graphic organizer like the one below. List key facts about each empire or region.

Mauryan
Regional Kingdoms
Gupta

Section Summary

THE MAURYAN EMPIRE

By the 300s BC, India was controlled by small, independent kingdoms. Around 321 BC, a military leader named **Chandragupta Maurya** (kuhn-druh-GOOP-tuh MOUR-yuh) seized a northeast Indian kingdom. This launched the Mauryan Empire, India's first empire. With an army of some 600,000 men aided by chariots and war elephants, Chandragupta conquered more kingdoms. By 303 BC, the Mauryan Empire controlled northern India and much of what is now Afghanistan.

To secure his power and crush resistance, Chandragupta established a strong, centralized government. He followed the advice of **Kautilya**, a Brahman, or member of the priest caste. Kautilya is most likely the author of a government handbook that called for strict rule, the use of spies, and even assassination to maintain power and control. Chandragupta set up districts run by a bureaucracy of loyal supporters and a secret spy society to root out threats to the state. The government also controlled the economy. It taxed the farmers and made them pay rent for the government land they used.

Underline words that tell how Chandragupta maintained control over his empire.

Although his reign brought prosperity, little crime, and a capital with fantastic palaces, temples, and parks, Chandragupta gave up his throne in 301 BC to become a monk. His son and grandson followed him as emperors. Chandragupta's grandson, **Ashoka**, became one of India's greatest rulers after he took the throne in 270 BC. Ashoka continued to expand the Indian empire to the south. However, after a particularly brutal military campaign, Ashoka converted to Buddhism. He adopted a policy of nonviolence, turning his efforts from military conquest to improving the lives of his subjects. He dug wells, made travel better, and urged people to practice Buddhism.

Which religion did Ashoka promote during his reign?

____

After Ashoka died in 232 BC, his sons battled for power as invaders threatened the empire. Control weakened as distant provinces slipped away. The last Mauryan emperor was killed in 184 BC by one of his own generals, ending an empire that lasted 140 years.

REGIONAL KINGDOMS

Once again, India split into smaller kingdoms. Invaders from central Asia poured into northern India and set up new dynasties. Greeks invaders also appeared. People called Kushans conquered much of northern India around 100 BC, holding onto control until about AD 250.

South of India's Deccan Plateau other kingdoms developed. The Andhra kingdom expanded across south and central India, and controlled central India wfrom the 100s BC to about AD 300. In the far south, small kingdoms made up what was called the Tamil kingdoms. They carried on an active sea trade with Southeast Asia and other regions. The result was a wealthy, sophisticated culture known for its poets.

Who controlled India after the Mauryan Empire ended?

____

____

THE GUPTA EMPIRE

It was not until the AD 320s that India was again united as a single empire. That empire was ruled by the Gupta (GOOP-tuh) dynasty. Its founder was Chandra Gupta I. His armies invaded and conquered neighboring lands, eventually bringing much of northern India under his control.

Chandra Gupta I's heirs further expanded the empire to the east, west, and south. The Gupta Empire reached its height under Chandra Gupta I's grandson, **Chandra Gupta II**. He further expanded the empire and strengthened its economy. His reign was a period of prosperity and cultural achievement in India.

Circle the names of the Gupta dynasty's founder and of its greatest leader.

During this period, a Chinese Buddhist monk named Faxian (FAH-shee-en) described the people of the empire as rich and prosperous. He also wrote that punishments were fair and that the government did not use capital punishment.

Under the Guptas, Hinduism became the main religion in India. The Gupta rulers supported the building of Hindu temples and promoted a revival of Hindu writings.

Gupta rule remained strong until the late 400s when nomads invaded from Central Asia. By the mid-500s, the Gupta dynasty ended and India again divided into small kingdoms.

How did the rule of the Gupta dynasty differ from the rule of the Mauryan dynasty?

____

____

____

MAIN IDEA
The strength, prosperity, and stability of the Gupta Empire helped lead to a golden age in Indian society, culture, and trade.

Key Terms and People

Kalidasa poet and playwright who was the greatest writer of the Gupta period

Hindu-Arabic numerals today's numbering system; numerals created by Indian scholars, then taken to Europe by Arabs

Aryabhata astronomer who argued that the Earth rotates on its axis and revolves around the sun, and calculated the circumference of the Earth, among other discoveries

Taking Notes

As you read the summary, take notes in the graphic organizer like the one below. Record notes for each topic.

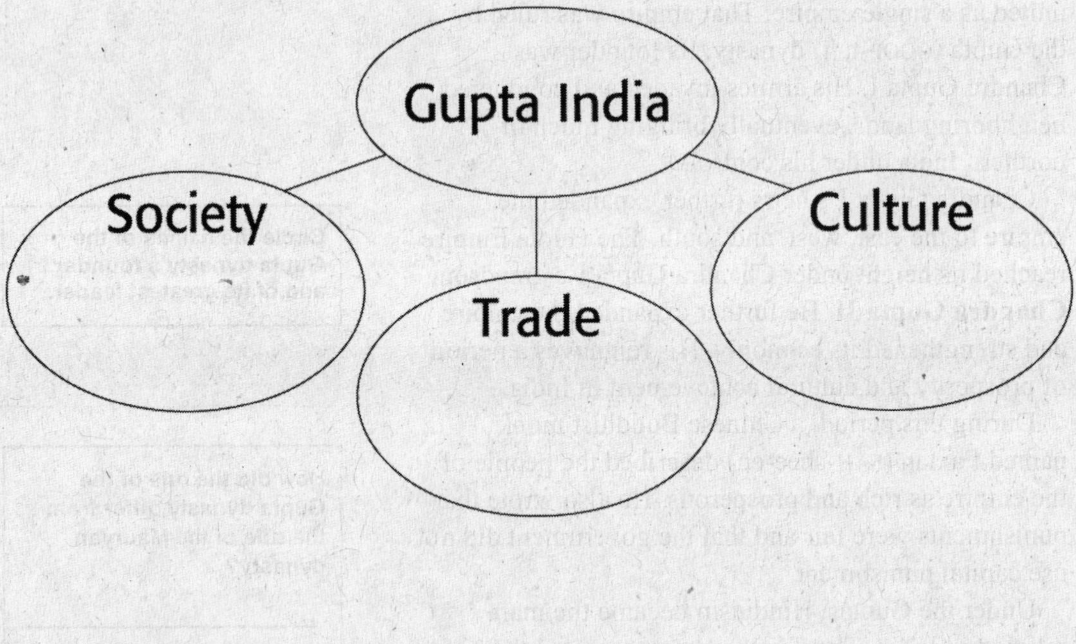

Section Summary

LIFE IN GUPTA INDIA

During the Gupta period, India developed strong trade relationships with markets from China to the Mediterranean Sea. Indian merchants traded goods across the Silk Roads that linked markets in China and central Asia. Navigators discovered that they could use the monsoon, a wind system, to sail directly across the Arabian Sea.

How did Indian goods reach China and central Asia?

____

India's Gupta period prosperity produced a thriving society. It was admired for its wealth and beauty. Its cities had shopping districts and young residents who were encouraged to develop an appreciation for the arts. Wealthy residents sought luxury and pleasure. As the use of money became commonplace, a new class of bankers and moneylenders emerged. Most people, however, led simple lives in small farming villages.

Strict rules regarding caste and gender shaped society in the Gupta period. People's castes determined what jobs they could hold and how they should interact with others. During the Gupta period, the number of castes grew, and many castes developed their own rules and customs. Hindu legal codes also defined proper behavior for people of various stations.

In general, men had more rights and authority than women did. For instance, most families were patriarchal, or headed by the father or eldest male. Marriages were arranged, and young women were taught that their role was to marry and have children. Once married, women were to obey their husbands. At the same time, men were expected to treat women with respect, and Hindu laws gave abused wives the right to leave their husbands.

What was a woman's primary role in Gupta Indian society?

____

A GUPTA GOLDEN AGE

Many great poems and plays were written during the Gupta era. Most were written in Sanskrit, the language of the ancient Aryans. The greatest writer of the age was **Kalidasa** (kahl-ee-DAHS-uh), a poet and playwright. His most famous play, Sakuntala, uses lyric poetry to tell the story of a king who falls in love with a maiden named Sakuntala.

Another popular work of the period was the *Panchatantra* (PUHN-chuh-TAHN-truh), or "Five Books." This collection of stories taught people lessons such as how to think before acting.

Gupta rulers also funded the building of temples and monasteries. Hindu temples often had huge towers covered with carvings. Some of the most spectacular architecture from the period is cave monasteries. Carved out of the stone of a cliff and a hillside, they are filled with wall paintings and sculptures. Many show details from Buddha's life.

The ancient Indians were pioneers of working with iron. Indian iron was valued for its hardness and purity. Gupta society also made advancements in areas such as science and mathematics. Indians were the first people to use a symbol for zero, which is an essential part of modern math. The numerals we use today are called **Hindu-Arabic numerals** because Indian scholars created them. Afterward, Arabs brought the number system to Europe.

What are the numerals we use today called? Why?

____

____

____

Doctors made medicines from plants and minerals, and protected people against disease by using vaccines. They could also perform surgery, repair broken bones, and treat wounds.

The astronomer **Aryabhata** correctly argued that the Earth rotates on its axis and revolves around the sun. Indian astronomers also identified seven of the planets in our solar system and accurately predicted eclipses of the sun and the moon.

Circle three accomplishments of Indian astronomers.

Chapter Summary

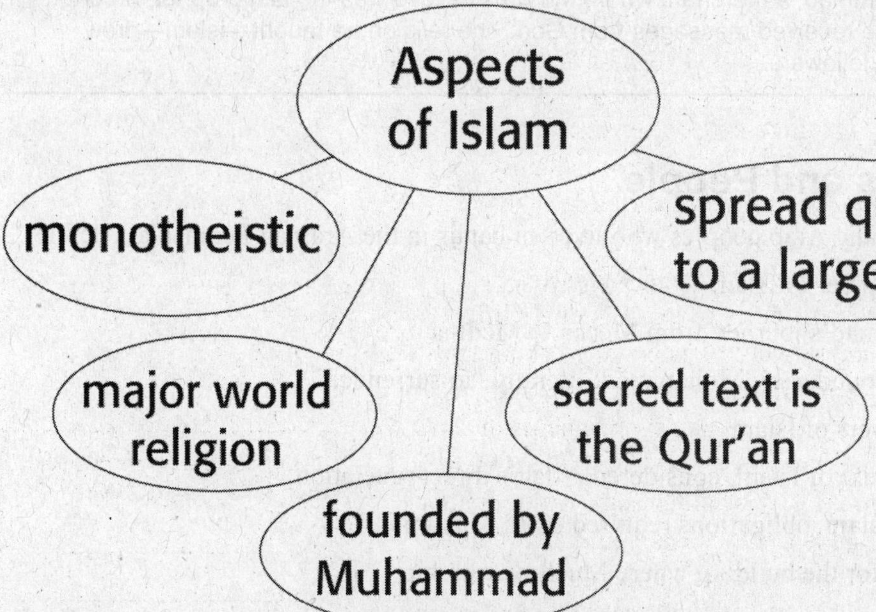

COMPREHENSION AND CRITICAL THINKING

Use information from the graphic organizer to answer the following questions.

1. **Recall** What is the sacred text of Islam?

   ____

2. **Identify Cause and Effect** How was trade related to the spread of Islam?

   ____

   ____

3. **Evaluate** Which of the above characteristics does Islam share with Judaism and Christianity?

   ____

   ____

MAIN IDEA
Muhammad, a merchant whom Muslims believe was the last prophet, reported that he received messages from God. The religion he taught—Islam—drew many followers.

Key Terms and People

bedouins nomadic Arab peoples who lived in bands in the Arabian Peninsula's desert

Muhammad founder of Islam

hegira Muhammad's journey from Mecca to Medina

Islam religion founded by Muhammad; literally "to surrender"

Muslims followers of Islam

Qur'an sacred text of Islam, considered Allah's direct revelation

Five Pillars of Islam obligations required of all Muslims

mosque name for the building where Muslims worship

jihad word that can be translated as "struggle for the faith" or "holy war" and can also mean the struggle to defend the Muslim community or convert people to Islam

Taking Notes

As you read the summary, use a graphic organizer like the one below to take notes on the origins of Islam. Add circles as needed.

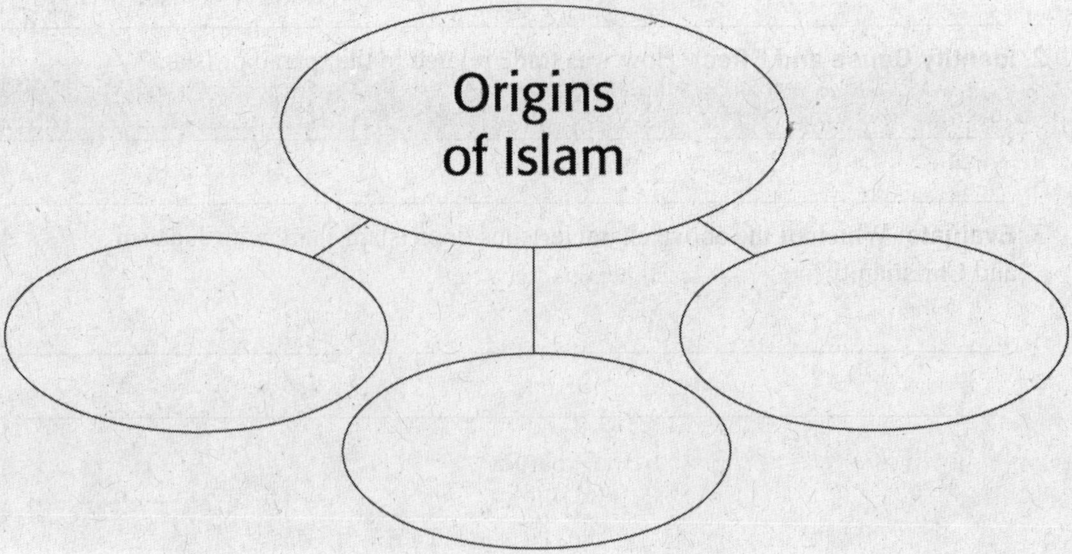

Section Summary

THE ARABIAN PENINSULA

Some 1,500 years ago, the Arabian Peninsula's vast desert interior had very few people living within it. Small bands of **bedouins**, or nomadic Arab peoples, moved their herds between oases. Farming was limited but trading was plentiful. Goods and ideas were exchanged in the trading towns that had popped up. Mecca (MEH-kuh) was the most important of these. Near the Red Sea, it was a trade center that also had a religious purpose. In the heart of the city was a large, ancient cube-shaped structure called the Kaaba (KAH-bah). This sacred site attracted pilgrims who came to see its idols and a stone said to be a relic from heaven. In Mecca, many gods and goddesses were worshipped. Allah was considered the supreme god.

MUHAMMAD THE MESSENGER

Muhammad was born in Mecca around 570. He was raised by his uncle, a powerful clan leader. Muhammad grew up to be a well-respected merchant. Always a religious man, Muhammad sometimes went to a cave to pray and reflect on spiritual matters. On one of these visits in about 610, Muhammad had an experience that changed his life. Later, he explained that an angel commanded him to speak messages from Allah, or God. Those words eventually became the first scripture Muhammad brought to his followers.

About how old was Muhammad when he was first visited by an angel?

____

Muhammad's wife, Khadijah, helped him understand what had happened. After more visits from the angel, Muhammad concluded that Allah had chosen him to be a prophet. In time, he also became a political leader.

Muhammad reported many messages from the angel. One was that Allah was the one true and all-powerful God. Other messages were about how people should live if they wanted to reach paradise after death. When he started preaching in public, Muhammad attracted many followers. However, some powerful people in Mecca were angry that he criticized their traditional beliefs.

Why were some people upset by Muhammad's teachings?

____

____

After the death of his uncle in 619, Muhammad and his followers were no longer safe in Mecca. He moved from Mecca to the city of Yathrib. Later, Yathrib was called Medina, or "the Prophet's city." Muhammad's journey is called the **hegira** (hi-JY-ruh).

Muhammad's community of believers grew over the next decade. The faith was called **Islam**, which means "achieving peace through submission to God." The followers, who were known as **Muslims**, fought many battles against the people of Mecca. The Meccans were defeated, and by 630, Muhammad controlled Mecca. His influence in the western part of the Arabian Peninsula was greater than anyone else's.

BASIC IDEAS OF ISLAM

Since Muhammad could not read or write, he recited the messages from Allah. Eventually, his followers wrote them down. The writings were collected in a book called the **Qur'an** (kuh-RAN), the sacred text of Islam. Muslims believe that the original Arabic version of the Qur'an is the direct revelation of Allah.

The Qur'an outlines the five basic acts of worship that are central to Islam and that Muhammad fulfilled. These acts are called the **Five Pillars of Islam**. The first is the profession of faith. The second is to pray five times every day. The third obligation is to give charity to the poor. Muslims are also required to go without food and drink from dawn to dusk during the month of Ramadan. Finally, those Muslims who are able to must complete a hajj, or journey to Mecca to pray in the city's vast **mosque** and perform a variety of other rituals. Another requirement for devout Muslims is **jihad**, which can be translated as "struggle for the faith." Jihad can also mean the struggle to defend the Muslim community. It has also been translated as "holy war."

What is the name for the basic acts that are central to Islam?

____

The Qur'an provides guidelines for moral behavior, but so do other texts. One of these, the Sunna, includes hundreds of lessons from Muhammad's daily life and teachings. Muslims also developed a legal system known as Sharia (shuh-REE-uh). The Qur'an teaches that Allah is the same God found in the Jewish and Christian traditions. Likewise, Muslims believe that the sacred texts of those faiths also come from Allah, though the Qur'an carries the greatest authority as God's final message to humanity.

What is the Sharia?

____

____

____

Name ______________________ Class ______________ Date ______________

MAIN IDEA

After Muhammad's death, Islam spread beyond the Arabian Peninsula, shaping a major empire within 100 years. While the empire eventually broke into smaller parts, Islam continued to spread.

Key Terms and People

Abu Bakr successor to Muhammad as leader of Islam

caliphs title given to leaders of Islam after Muhammad, means "successors"

caliphate area ruled by a caliph

Umayyad a powerful clan from Mecca whose struggle to regain control led to civil war

Sunnis Muslims who accepted the Umayyad caliph

Shia supporters of Muhammad's cousin Ali, who refused to accept the Umayyad caliph

Sufis a group within Islam that seeks a mystical, personal connection with God

Abbasid family that ruled Islam after the Umayyads lost control

Harun al-Rashid most prominent Abbasid caliph, helped Muslim culture reach greatness

Taking Notes

As you read the summary, use a graphic organizer like the one below to take notes on the spread of Islam. Add boxes as needed.

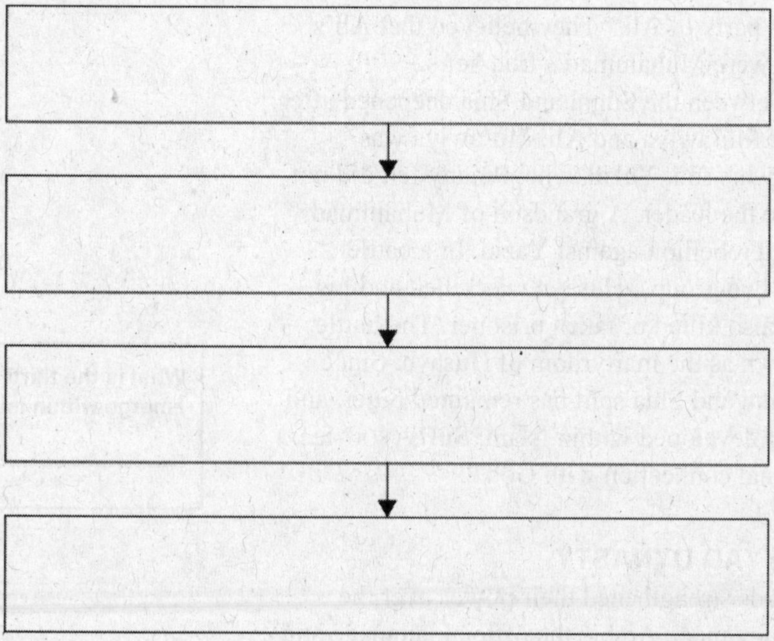

Section Summary

ISLAM AFTER MUHAMMAD'S DEATH

After Muhammad's death in 632, **Abu Bakr** was chosen to replace him as leader. He and later leaders of Islam were called **caliphs**, which means "successors." Abu Bakr built up a strong army to reunify Arabia then gained more territory. By 661, the area ruled by a caliph, known as a **caliphate**, stretched from northern Africa to Persia.

However, there were conflicts among Muslim leaders. The tension dated back to when Abu Bakr was chosen as caliph; some leaders had supported Muhammad's cousin Ali instead. In 644, Ali was defeated again for caliph by Uthman, who was supported by the powerful **Umayyad** (oom-Y-yuhd) clan of Mecca. Rebels killed Uthman, and Ali finally became caliph. Civil war broke out between Ali's forces and the Umayyads. It ended with the Umayyads taking control after Ali was killed.

Underline the sentence that explains when and how the conflict within Muslim leadership began.

Most Muslims reluctantly accepted the Umayyad caliph, Mu'awiya. They were called **Sunnis** (SOOH-neez), which meant "followers of the Sunna," or "way of the Prophet." Ali's supporters, however, refused to go along with the Umayyads. They became known as the **Shia**, or "party of Ali." They believed that Ali's descendants were Muhammad's true heirs.

Conflict between the Sunni and Shia deepened after the deaths of Mu'awiya and Ali. Mu'awiya was succeeded by his son, Yazid, whom many felt did not deserve to be the leader. A grandson of Muhammad, Husayn, led a rebellion against Yazid. In a battle between the two groups, Husayn was killed and his forces were also killed or taken prisoner. The battle became known as the martyrdom of Husayn. Since then, the Sunni and Shia split has remained bitter, and a third group developed within Islam. **Sufis** (SOO-feez) seek a personal connection with God.

What is the third group to emerge within Islam?

____

THE UMAYYAD DYNASTY

The Umayyads strengthened their power over the caliphate. They made Arabic the official language and made the money system uniform throughout the empire. They also began the Dome of the Rock in

Jerusalem, considered the first great work of Islamic architecture.

Muslim armies conquered territory all the way to the borders of China and the Indus River Valley in the east. In the west, they conquered North Africa and most of Spain. The military conquests spread the Muslim faith. Jews and Christians were allowed to practice their religion but paid heavy taxes and endured some restrictions on their daily lives.

The Shia continued to oppose Umayyad rule. Wars were fought over who would be the next caliph. The creation of a powerful, privileged leading class also led to further opposition. Eventually, the Umayyad dynasty was weakened by rebellion. Led by a direct descendent of Muhammad's uncle, a family known as the **Abbasids** united many of the Umayyads' enemies. The Abbasids took power in the late 740s.

Why did the Shia continue to oppose the Umayyads?

____

____

____

THE ABBASID DYNASTY

The Abbasids relocated the caliphate's capital to Baghdad in what is now Iraq. The Abbasids cut themselves off from the people and relied on Persian government officials. They also changed the nature of Islam by inviting all people to join it. As Muslim traders traveled, they took Islam as far as West Africa and Southeast Asia. Caliph **Harun al-Rashid** (hah-ROON ahl-rah-SHEED) helped bring Muslim culture to great heights during his reign from 786 to 809.

THE END OF UNITY

Abbasid political power began to weaken, and by the 900s a number of small, independent states broke away. The caliph became a powerless figurehead.

In the 1000s, Christian armies pushed Muslims out of Spain and went to war against Muslims in and around Jerusalem in quests called the Crusades. They wanted to make the Holy Land region Christian.

Other threats to the Abbasids came from Egypt. Later, a group of Turks that supported the Abbasids created their own empire, further shrinking the Muslim empire. The Mongols, who had already conquered China and Central Asia, killed the Abbasid caliph, finishing the caliphate.

Circle the name of the group that finally ended the rule of the caliphate. What territories had this group already conquered?

____

Name ______________________ Class ______________ Date ______________

Muslim Civilization

Section 3

MAIN IDEA

For the first Muslims, Islam was more than a religion. It was a guide to a political, social, and cultural life. The early Muslims responded with spectacular achievement in many fields.

Key Terms and People

Ibn Rushd Muslim scholar who writings on the relationship between reason and faith influenced Muslim, Christian, and Jewish thinking into the 1400s

astrolabe instrument for finding the positions and movements of stars and planets

Ibn Sina Persian doctor who was a famous medical scholar, also contributed to the fields of logic, music, and psychology

Ibn Khaldun Muslim scholar who wrote a history of the world in the 1300s

calligraphy beautifully styled writing that is a distinctive feature of Islamic art

minarets tall towers found on mosques from which the faithful were called to prayer

Rumi poet, Sufi mystic, and founder of an order known as the Whirling Dervishes

Omar Khayyam author of a collection of four-line poems called *The Rubaiyat*

Taking Notes

As you read the summary, take notes on aspects of Muslim civilization in the graphic organizer below.

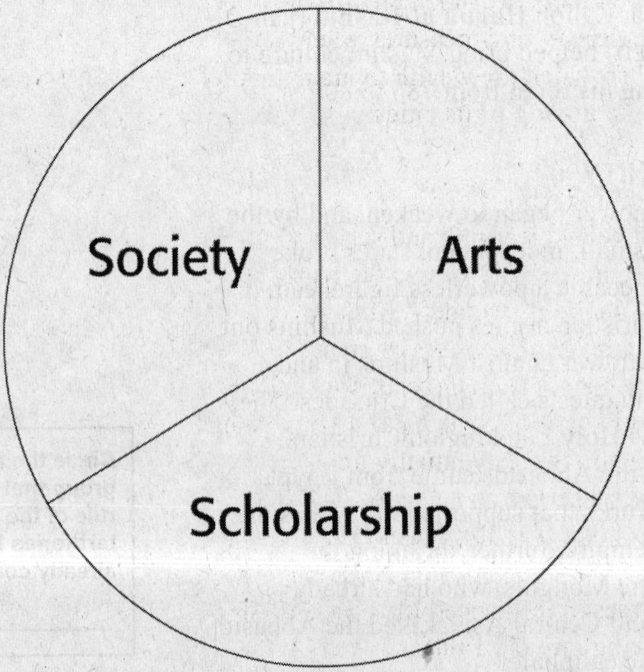

Name ______________________ Class ______________ Date ______________

Muslim Civilization

Section 3

Section Summary

MUSLIM SOCIETY

Even after the Abbasid empire broke up, Muslim civilization remained distinct. One reason is that Islam affected practically all aspects of daily life. Islamic texts provided guidance on how Muslims should deal with many issues, including each person's role within the family, the main unit of society. The man was the head of the family. He could marry several wives, but was supposed to treat his wives equally.

What is the main unit of Muslim society?

____

Women played important roles in the early Muslim community. According to the Qur'an, women are equal to men before Allah. According to Islam, women could inherit property and seek divorce. However, women lost status during the Abbasid dynasty. It became common for women to cover their hair and wear a veil during Abbasid rule.

Muslims were allowed to own slaves, but had to treat their slaves fairly. Freeing slaves was praised as a religious act, but slavery remained a part of daily life and of the economy. Muslim merchants traded slaves over a wide area.

Trade was important to the Muslim community, partly because of ancient trade routes that crossed the Arabian peninsula. Traders expanded the use of coins, and used the same weights and measures wherever they traded. Trade provided the wealth to maintain the empire and led to the growth of its cities.

MUSLIM SCHOLARSHIP

The Muslim world valued learning and scholarship. Islam requires its followers to examine the world and seek evidence of Allah in its wonders. Muslim scholars translated into Arabic works of great scientists and philosophers from Greece. Those texts inspired further study by Muslim scholars. The Arabic versions of many works were eventually translated into Latin and used by European scholars.

How are learning and scholarship linked to the Muslim faith?

____

____

____

One important scholar was **Ibn Rushd** (IB-uhn-ROOSHT), who wrote commentaries on Aristotle. His work on faith and reason influenced Muslim, Jewish, and Christian thinking into the 1400s.

The study of astronomy was important because Muslims needed to predict the phases of the moon. Islamic religious festivals and rites are determined by the lunar calendar. Muslim scholars used texts from Persia and India, but the most important influence was Ptolemy's work, the *Almagest*, which helped them understand the movements of the planets and stars.

Muslim scholars helped perfect the design of the **astrolabe**, an instrument that helps find the positions and movements of stars and planets. Sailors used astrolabes to determine their position at sea, and to calculate time of day.

In what areas did Muslim scholars make advances?

____

____

Muslim doctors had to pass rigorous tests before they could practice medicine. They developed many skills, including ways to conduct eye surgery. **Ibn Sina** (IB-uhn SEE-nah) was probably the most famous medical scholar of his time. He also contributed to the fields of logic, music, and psychology.

Geographers created travel guides to help pilgrims find their way to Mecca. One geographer measured the earth's circumference with considerable accuracy. In the 1300s, **Ibn Khaldun** (IB-uhn kal-DOON) wrote a history of the world that is still influential.

ARTS AND LITERATURE

Muslim artists worked in a range of materials. One feature is common: none of the religious works contains human or animal figures. Muslims believe that portraying people or animals could tempt people to worship those images. Worship of anyone but Allah is a terrible sin. Instead, Islamic art features geometric patterns, floral designs, and **calligraphy**, a beautifully styled writing. Architecture developed distinctive features throughout the Muslim world. Mosques have domes and **minarets**, tall towers from which the faithful are called to prayer.

Underline the words that describe a common feature of Islamic art. Why did artists develop this style of art?

____

____

The most significant literary work of Islam is the Qur'an. In nonreligious literature, *Arabian Nights* is still popular. The poet Jalal ad-Din **Rumi** wrote Persian-language poems in the 1200s. These poems are still popular today. Another writer whose work is still known today is **Omar Khayyam**. His collection of four-line poems is called *The Rubaiyat*.

Name ______________________ Class ______________ Date ______________

African Kingdoms

Chapter Summary

The Growth of Trade in Early Africa

- Early Africans moved from hunting and gathering to farming and raising livestock.
- Extended families worked with larger groups: clans and age-sets.
- Iron tools enabled Africans to clear more land for farming.

→

- Aksum's location by the Red Sea made it an ideal site for trade.
- Coastal kingdoms traded across Indian Ocean with Persia, Arabia, India, and Southeast Asia.
- Mixing of cultures through trade led to new Swahili communities.

→

- Northern Berber traders introduced Islam to other kingdoms.
- Kingdoms of Ghana, Mali, and Songhai became wealthy from increased trade.
- African kingdoms experienced a golden age of culture.

COMPREHENSION AND CRITICAL THINKING

Use information from the graphic organizer to answer the following questions.

1. **Recall** How did early African farmers benefit from the use of iron tools?

____

____

2. **Analyze** How did trade among African kingdoms affect African culture?

____

____

3. **Elaborate** How did geography and climate affect the development of development of empires in Africa? Give examples.

____

____

4. **Evaluate** What do you think was the most important result of trade in Africa?

____

____

MAIN IDEA

Africa's earliest people adapted to a wide range of geographic conditions to establish societies based on family ties, religion, iron technology, and trade.

Key Terms and People

Sahel a region of Africa that divides the Sahara desert from wetter areas

savanna an area of open grassland, such as those in southern Africa

griots storytellers who passed on oral tradition, helping to keep history alive for each new generation and were highly respected in their communities

Nok one of the earliest known African peoples to practice ironworking

Bantu a group of related languages spoken by early African peoples

Taking Notes

As you read the summary, take notes in a graphic organizer like the one below. Record details about the geography, early societies, and the Iron Age of Africa.

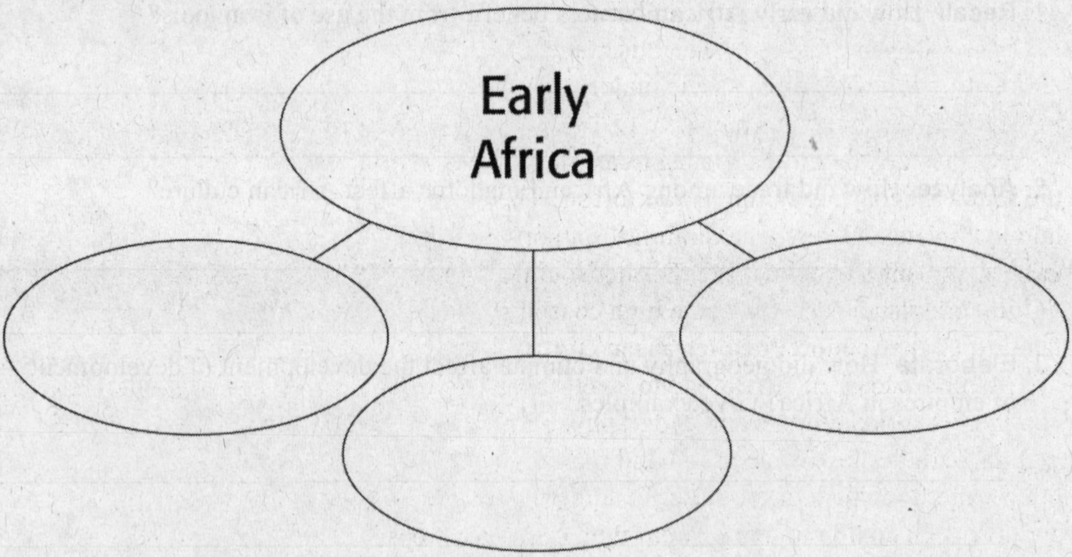

Section Summary

THE GEOGRAPHY OF AFRICA

Africa is more than three times the size of the United States, and is home to a wide variety of climates and vegetation. Each region has its own terrain and resources that have led to distinct cultures and ways of life. Africa also has a varied landscape. In the central and southern interior are plateaus, or high plains. Elsewhere in the interior are low, wide plains. Around the rim of Africa are several mountain ranges. Near the coastline, the land drops off to coastal plains of farmland, desert, swamp, and sandy beaches.

Circle the terrain of the central and southern interior of Africa. Where are the mountain ranges located?

____

Africa's climate is also quite varied. The world's largest desert, the Sahara, fills much of northern Africa, stretching over 3,000 miles from the Atlantic Ocean to the Red Sea. Rain is rare and temperatures can climb very high. Just south of the Sahara is the **Sahel** (sah-hel), a strip of land that divides the desert from wetter areas. Mighty rivers flow across the plains, which have enough vegetation to support grazing animals. Farther south is a band of tropical **savanna**, or open grassland, which is home to a variety of wild herd animals. The majority of Africa's people live on the savannas.

Near the equator and on Madagascar, an island off the southeast coast, are tropical rainforests. The hot, humid climate and year-round rainfall supports a large variety of plant and animal life. Farther south, a region of hilly grasslands, deserts, and a high coastal strip of land experience a more Mediterranean climate.

The early people in Africa had to adapt to the continent's varied climate and geography. Farming was difficult because of poor soil and rainfall that was often either too much or too little. In addition, people and livestock could not live in areas with certain insects that spread deadly diseases.

List two challenges faced by early African farmers.

____

____

EARLY AFRICAN SOCIETIES

Anthropologists think the first humans lived in East Africa and were hunter-gatherers. About 7,000 years ago, some people began to grow crops such as sorghum, cotton, and yams. Other early Africans practiced pastoralism, the raising of herd animals.

African Kingdoms

Section 1

About 8,000 years ago, people farmed and raised animals in the Sahara. When the climate changed and the Sahara became drier, they moved to other areas.

Many African societies developed village-based cultures. A typical West African family included the mother, father, children, and close relatives, all living in one household. Families with common ancestors formed clans. In some areas, people formed age-sets. These were groups of people born within the same two or three years, who had a duty to help each other.

In a village, everyone had specific duties. The men hunted and farmed. Women cared for children, farmed, collected firewood, ground grain, and carried water. Children had their own tasks. The elders, or old people, taught traditions to younger generations.

What were the duties of early African women?

____

____

Many early Africans shared similar religious beliefs such as honoring the spirits of their ancestors. In return, they hoped the spirits would protect them. West Africans also practiced animism—the belief that bodies of water, animals, trees, and other natural objects have spirits.

Oral tradition, not systems of writing, helped many early African societies maintain their identity and remember the past. Storytellers called **griots** (GREE-ohz) helped keep history alive by remembering and sharing stories, poems, songs, and proverbs. Music, dance, and elaborate masks were part of many rituals.

AFRICA'S IRON AGE

After the 500s BC, the spread of iron technology changed farming practices in sub-Sahara Africa. The **Nok**, who lived in what is now Nigeria in West Africa, grew powerful because they had better tools for hunting, farming, and warfare. Iron blades enabled people to clear new land, creating more places to live and farm. Africa's population grew.

List uses of early iron tools.

____

____

A number of groups in Africa spoke related languages called **Bantu**. In the first centuries AD, Bantu-speaking people began to migrate to the east and south, bringing their knowledge of ironworking with them. By the AD 900s Bantu-speaking peoples had established a social system in which women farmed and men cared for cattle, their most important resource.

Name ______________________ Class ______________ Date ______________

MAIN IDEA

The growth of trade led to the development of wealthy kingdoms and city-states in East Africa.

Key Terms and People

Ezana king of Aksum who ruled at the time of Aksum's defeat of the rival trading kingdom of Kush in 350

Ge'ez the written and spoken language of Aksum

Lalibela Zagwe king who built 11 Christian churches out of solid rock in the 1200s

Swahili language that blended a Bantu language and Arab words, also the name of the blended African-Arab culture that developed on East Africa's coast

Taking Notes

As you read the summary, take notes in a graphic organizer like the one below. Record key facts about Aksum and early Ethiopia, the coastal city-states, and Great Zimbabwe.

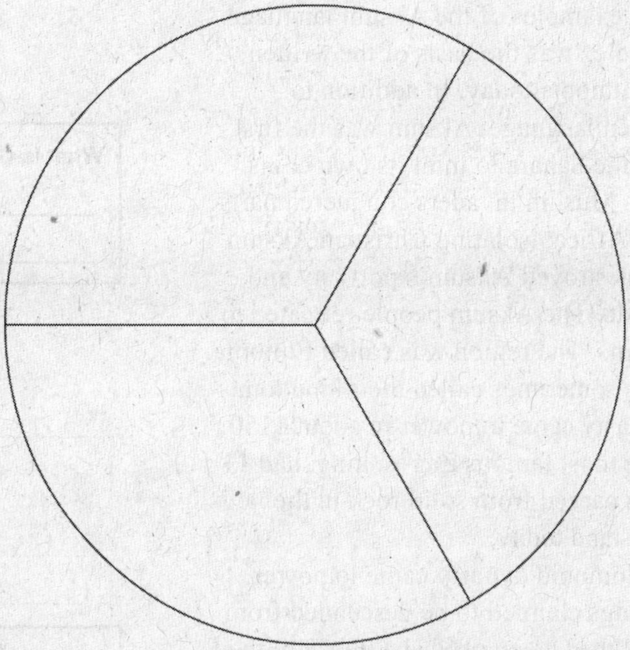

Section Summary

AKSUM AND ETHIOPIA

The kingdom of Aksum (AHK-soom) developed in eastern Africa, in what is now Ethiopia and Eritrea. Aksum's location by the Red Sea made it ideal for agriculture and trade. By AD 100, Aksum was a wealthy and powerful trading kingdom. Traders from the interior brought frankincense, gold dust, ivory, and enslaved Africans to the markets. They traded these items for luxury goods such as cloth and spices.

King **Ezana** came to power in about 320. Under Ezana's rule, Aksum defeated the rival trading kingdom of Kush. Aksum took control of trade and became the dominant power in East Africa.

How did the kingdom of Aksum become so powerful?

____

____

Merchants brought new ideas and goods to Aksum, giving the kingdom a diverse culture. One of these ideas was Christianity, which became the official religion of Aksum when Ezana converted.

Details of important events such as this were inscribed on stone monuments called stelae (STEE-lee). The stelae contain examples of the Aksum language, **Ge'ez** (GEE-ez). Ge'ez was the basis of the written language used in Ethiopia today. In addition to developing a written language, Aksum was the first kingdom south of the Sahara to mint its own coins.

What is Ge'ez?

____

____

During the 600s Muslim invaders conquered parts of East and North Africa, isolating Christian Aksum. In time, Muslims destroyed Aksum's port city and took control of trade. The Aksum people retreated to the inland mountains. The region was called Ethiopia, a name the Aksum sometimes called their kingdom.

The Zagwe dynasty came to power in about 1150. King **Lalibela**, the most famous Zagwe king, had 11 Christian churches carved from solid rock in the 1200s. Many still stand today.

In 1270, the Solomonid dynasty came to power. These Christian kings claimed to be descended from King Solomon and the Queen of Sheba. Early in their 700-year rule, Solomonid kings waged religious wars to try to force Jews to leave Ethiopia. The Solomonid kings also fought attacks from the Muslim kingdom of Adal to the east. They were able to remain independent, and ruled Ethiopia until 1974.

How did the Solomonid dynasty get its name?

____

____

COASTAL CITY-STATES

The East African coast attracted overseas traders who crossed the Indian Ocean on monsoon winds. A trade network linked East Africa with Persia, Arabia, India, and Southeast Asia. By 1100 several towns, such as Mogadishu, Mombasa, Kilwa, and Sofala, had grown into wealthy city-states. In their markets, merchants sold luxury goods from China and India and obtained African materials such as coconut oil, copper, leopard skins, shells, ivory, and gold. In addition, enslaved Africans captured in the interior were exported to slave markets in Arabia, Persia, and India. After Europeans arrived in Africa, enslaved Africans were exported to the Americas. Kilwa was the southernmost city reachable on the monsoon winds. It became the most powerful coastal city-state because it controlled the export of all goods from the south.

Trade led to a blending of African, Arab, and Asian cultures. Muslim Arabs and Persians settled in the coastal city-states. Indonesians settled on the island of Madagascar. A new language called **Swahili** (swah-HEE-lee) developed from a blend of the local Bantu language and Arabic. The term also refers to the blended African-Arab culture that developed along East Africa's coast. As many African rulers adopted Islam, mosques appeared in many cities and towns.

What helped Africa's East coast become an important trading region?

____

____

GREAT ZIMBABWE

In Africa's interior, the Shona people built their kingdom of Great Zimbabwe by the 1300s. The kingdom was located in southeastern Africa along an important trade route. Great Zimbabwe served as a middleman between gold miners and ivory hunters in southern Africa and traders on the coast. All that remains of Great Zimbabwe today are stone ruins. A circular wall about 35 feet high surrounds a structure called the Great Enclosure. It was built with stones so perfectly fitted that no mortar was used.

Sometime in the 1400s, the people abandoned Great Zimbabwe for unknown reasons. Power shifted to the Mutapa Empire. By 1500 the Mutapa Empire controlled much of present-day Zimbabwe and grew wealthy by controlling trade.

What role did Great Zimbabwe serve on the trade route between the interior and the coast?

____

____

Name ______________________ Class ______________ Date ______________

MAIN IDEA
The expansion of trade across the Sahara led to the development of great empires and other states in West Africa.

Key Terms and People

Sundiata Mali king who led the expansion of the empire to the Atlantic Ocean

Mansa Musa famous ruler who led the Mali empire at its height

Sunni Ali strong military leader of the Songhai Empire, who took control of the former Mali empire

Askia Muhammad Songhai leader who ruled during the golden age of Songhai culture

Taking Notes

As you read the summary, use a graphic organizer like the one below to take notes on early West Africa.

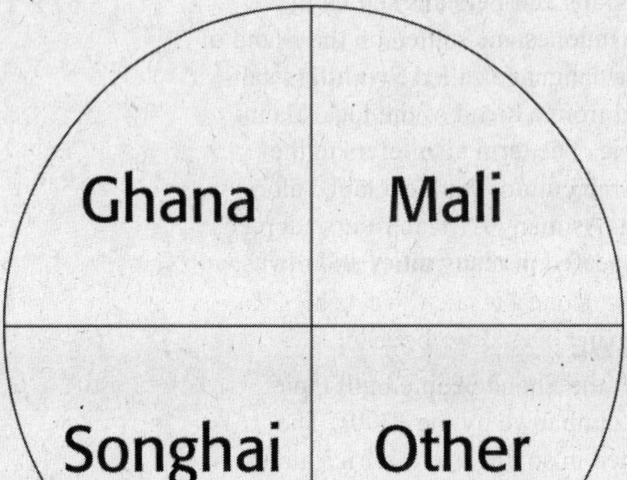

Section Summary

EMPIRE OF GHANA

By about 800 AD, the rulers of Ghana created a huge, powerful empire. Ghana's development was delayed because it did not have an easy access route to the sea. In addition, the Sahara Desert blocked travel between Ghana and other parts of Africa. In the first centuries AD, North African traders such as the Berbers learned to cross the desert in large caravans. They used camels to carry supplies over long distances. Because Ghana's capital, Koumbi-Saleh, was located between the gold mines and the desert trade routes, Ghana soon controlled nearly all of the area's gold and salt trade.

List three ways that North African traders influenced the people of Ghana.

____

____

____

Taxing goods such as salt brought the kingdom great wealth. Gold was not taxed the same way, but kings kept gold prices high by keeping supply low. They issued a law that said only kings could own large gold nuggets. They also kept the mines' locations secret. Ghana's kings enjoyed a lavish lifestyle. They built up huge armies to conquer other peoples and to capture people who could be sold as slaves to Muslim traders.

Ghana began to decline around AD 1000. It tried to expand into lands controlled by the Almoravids, a Muslim Berber kingdom. In 1076, the Almoravids temporarily captured Koumbi-Saleh, weakening the kings of Ghana. As local leaders rebelled, a new trading state rose in Ghana's place.

MALI EMPIRE

In the 1230s, a new empire, Mali, rose to power where Ghana had been, then expanded to the Atlantic ocean. A king named **Sundiata** (soon-JAHT-ah) led Mali's conquest of neighboring people. He ruled for 25 years. Mali reached its height in the 1300s, when it was led by **Mansa Musa**. During Mansa Musa's reign, Mali's territory expanded. The kingdom grew wealthy controlling the gold and salt trade.

Circle the names of two rulers of Mali in this section. Which ruler led Mali during its height?

____

Like many of Mali's leaders after Sundiata, Musa was a Muslim. His pilgrimage to Mecca in 1324 made him well known for his wealth and generosity. When he returned home, Musa brought with him artists and architects who designed beautiful mosques, some of which still stand today. He also built schools and libraries. Many of these were built in Timbuktu, which became West Africa's center for education, religion, and culture. After Musa, the empire declined. Several groups broke away and set up independent kingdoms. After the Tuareg of North Africa captured Timbuktu in 1433, Mali slowly slipped into decline.

How did Musa's pilgrimage to Mecca affect his empire?

____

____

EMPIRE OF SONGHAI

The small trading kingdom of Songhai was located in eastern Mali and its leaders had paid tribute to Ghana and Mali. Songhai grew wealthy by trading along the Niger River. Muslim traders introduced Islam to Songhai, where it became a major cultural influence. By the 1460s, the rising empire took control of the former empire of Mali, thanks mostly to military leader **Sunni Ali**. His first act as leader was to take back Timbuktu from the Tuareg. He then led campaigns to expand the kingdom.

The reign of **Askia Muhammad** is considered the golden age of Songhai culture. Songhai's first Muslim ruler, Askia Muhammad made a pilgrimage to Mecca. On the way he gained the support of the Muslim rulers. As a result, trans-Saharan trade resumed. Askia Muhammad extended Songhai borders into the desert and reformed the government. Eventually, he was overthrown by his son. In 1591, the Songhai empire was conquered by Morocco.

Whose reign is considered the golden age of Songhai culture?

____

OTHER WEST AFRICAN STATES

To the east of Songhai lived a people called the Hausa. They built a society of independent city-states. The Hausa were known as skilled weavers and dyers and their products were in much demand. To the south of Songhai the Yoruba established several strong kingdoms. They were admired for their realistic sculptures in terra-cotta, bronze, brass, and copper.

Just southwest of them was the powerful kingdom of Benin. In the 1400s an ambitious leader, Ewuare, expanded Benin from the Niger River into what is now central Nigeria. The people of Benin began to trade with Portuguese traders. Art from Benin became popular in Europe.

Underline the name of the kingdom that expanded under the leadership of Ewuare.

Name ______________________ Class ______________ Date ______________

Cultures of East Asia

Chapter Summary

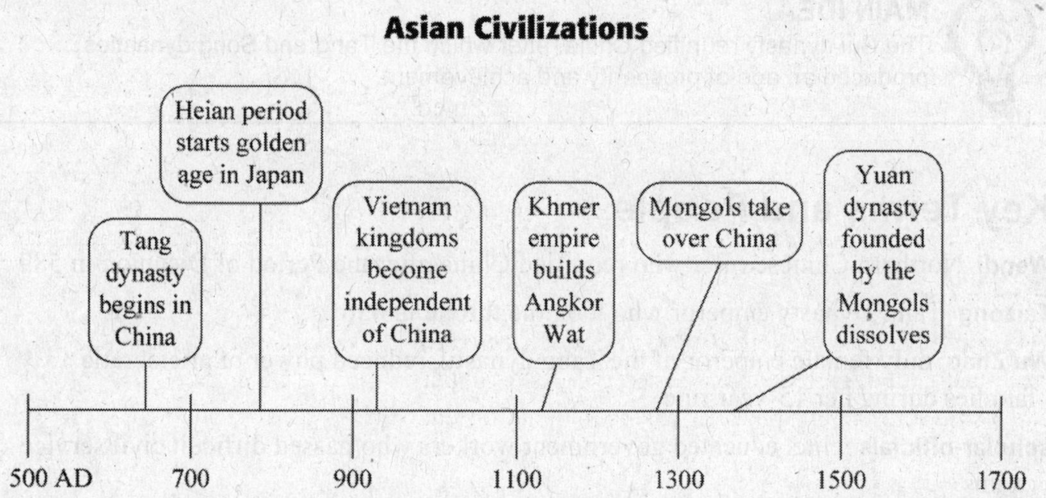

COMPREHENSION AND CRITICAL THINKING

Use information from the graphic organizer to answer the following questions.

1. **Identify** Which group of people took over China in the 1200s?

   ____

2. **Sequence** Which happened first: Mongols taking over China or kingdoms in Vietnam becoming independent of China?

   ____

   ____

3. **Draw conclusions** Angkor Wat still exists today. What can you conclude about the Khmer people?

   ____

   ____

4. **Elaborate** How might a group have protected itself from an invading neighbor during the period covered by the timeline?

   ____

   ____

   ____

MAIN IDEA
The Sui dynasty reunified China, after which the Tang and Song dynasties produced an age of prosperity and achievement.

Key Terms and People

Wendi Northern Chinese ruler who reunified China after the Period of Disunion in 589

Taizong Tang Dynasty emperor who took the throne in 626

Wu Zhao only female emperor of the Tang dynasty, reduced power of aristocratic families during her 15-year rule

scholar-officials elite, educated government workers who passed difficult civil service exams

porcelain a type of ceramic from China that was in demand by foreign traders

pagoda multi-storied Chinese temples

woodblock printing text carved into wooden blocks and covered with ink; pages are then created when the blocks are pressed against paper

movable type faster form of printing than woodblock printing, uses etched metal blocks that could be rearranged and reused

gentry powerful class of scholar-officials and leading landowners

Taking Notes

As you read the summary, use a graphic organizer like the one below to list key facts for each of the four main parts of the section.

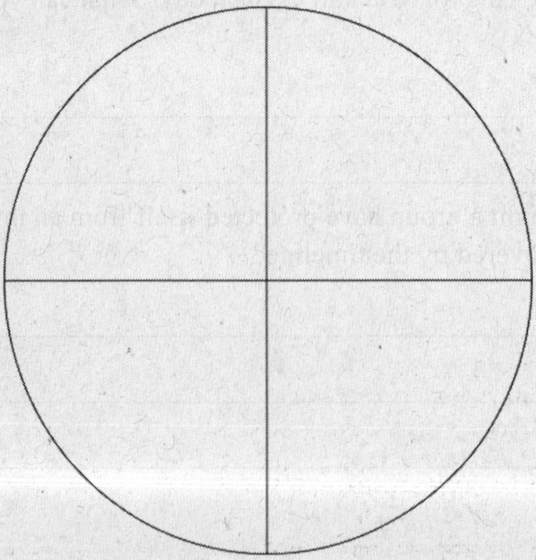

Section Summary

SUI AND TANG DYNASTIES

After the Han Dynasty fell in AD 220, military leaders split China into rival kingdoms. This began the Period of Disunion, when nomads invaded northern China and formed their own kingdoms.

How long did the Period of Disunion last?

____

The Period of Disunion ended in AD 589 when a northern ruler named **Wendi** reunified China. He established the Sui (SWAY) dynasty. The Sui dynasty produced a more centralized government by creating a new legal code, reforming the bureaucracy, and providing all adult males with farming land. Its greatest accomplishment was the completion of a 1,000-mile waterway known as the Grand Canal. Many peasants died from forced work on the canal's construction. In 618, the assassination of the emperor Yangdi ended the dynasty.

Circle the achievements of the Sui dynasty.

Next, a Sui general seized power, founding the Tang Dynasty. The Tang created a flexible law code, established two new capitals, and expanded the civil service examination system, which required government workers to pass written exams to get jobs. **Taizong** (TY-tzoong) was one of China's most admired emperors. He is well-known for his military success. He also sought talented ministers to help him govern and set up schools to prepare people to take civil service exams.

Wu Zhau declared herself emperor upon the death of her emperor husband in 690. She was the only female to hold this title. Her reign lasted fifteen years. The height of the Tang Dynasty came soon afterward during the rule of Xuanzong (SHOO-AN-toong), from 712 to 756.

During the Period of Disunion, many Chinese had turned to Buddhism. By the time of the Tang dynasty, Buddhism was well established in China. In fact, the Tang emperors made Buddhism China's state religion. The period from about 400 to 845 is known as the Age of Buddhism because of its importance. By the the mid-800s, however, the religion had lost official favor. An emperor unhappy with the religion's power had officials burn Buddhist texts and destroy temples.

Why was the period from 400 to 845 known as the Age of Buddhism?

____

____

Name ____________________ Class ____________ Date ____________

Cultures of East Asia

Section 1

THE SONG DYNASTY

The Song dynasty followed after the end of Tang rule in 907. They established a strong central government made of civilians who had to pass a difficult test to get their jobs. The elite, educated workers who did pass the exams were called **scholar-officials**. A new form of Confucianism called Neo-Confucianism gained favor. Song rulers protected their lands by paying tribute to the Jurchen, nomads who created the Jin empire. The Song dynasty lasted for 150 more years.

How did the Song emperors protect their lands?

____

____

CULTURAL ACHIEVEMENTS

The Tang period produced some of China's greatest cultural achievements. Two of the most famous Tang poets are Du Fu and Li Bo. Du Fu wrote about war and Confucianism. Li Bo wrote about friendship, the joys of life, nature, and solitude. Artist Wu Daozi painted lifelike murals that celebrated Buddhism and nature. Artisans created exquisite pottery and beautiful **porcelain**, a type of ceramic often known as china. In architecture, Indian Buddhist temples influenced design of the Chinese **pagoda**, or multi-story temple.

One major Chinese invention was gunpowder, which was used in fireworks, explosives, firearms, and cannons. Other innovations included the magnetic compass, paper money, mechanical clocks, and **woodblock printing**, or text carved into wooden blocks and covered with ink. Pages are then created when they are pressed against paper. A faster form of printing was **movable type**, etched metal blocks that could be rearranged and reused.

Underline the topics of two famous Tang poets. Circle the topics of the artist Wu Daozi. How are these topics related?

____

____

____

PROSPERITY AND SOCIETY

During the Tang and Song periods, new irrigation techniques and new a type of rice made agriculture more productive. More food led to population growth. China's cities became the largest in the world, and trade expanded, bringing prosperity and new money and banking systems. Scholar-officials and leading landowners formed a new, powerful class of people called the **gentry**. Women's status, however, declined as the practice of binding a woman's feet tightly with cloth—resulting in small, deformed feet—increased.

What two factors led to an increased population? Why?

____

____

____

Name ____________________ Class ______________ Date ______________

Cultures of East Asia

Section 2

MAIN IDEA
The Mongols built a vast empire across much of Asia, founded the Yuan dynasty in China, and opened China and the region to greater foreign contacts and trade.

Key Terms and People

khan chief of a Mongol clan

Genghis Khan the "Universal Ruler" of the united Mongol tribes

Pax Mongolia Mongol peace, a time of security in Asia which made travel and trade easier

Kublai Khan grandson of Genghis Khan, became ruler of the Mongols in 1260

Marco Polo Venetian who carried out missions in the Mongol empire and India at Kublai Khan's request

Taking Notes

As you read the summary, use a graphic organizer like the one below to record in order the key events during the Mongol Empire. Add boxes as needed.

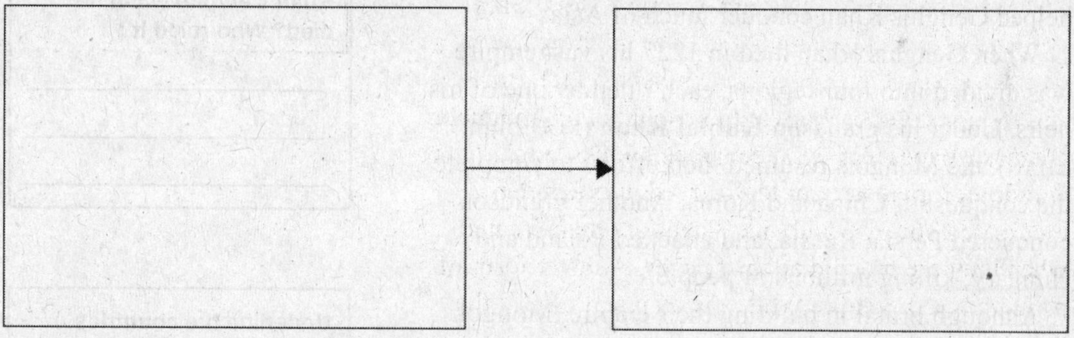

Section Summary

THE MONGOLS

Many nomadic tribes made their home in the steppe region of Central Asia, where they hunted, herded, and traded with China. One group, the Mongols, left this region in the 1200s to create the largest land empire in history. The Mongols were skilled horsemen and herders of sheep and goats. They often raided other tribes for goods and people. Each Mongol tribe was independent and had its own chief, or **khan**, who had demonstrated military and leadership skills.

In the early 1200s, a khan named Temujin united the tribes and was declared **Genghis Khan** (JENG-guhs KAHN), or "Universal Ruler." The fierce Mongol warriors used horses equipped with iron stirrups so that they could accurately shoot arrows while riding. Mongol armies spread terror by burning towns that resisted them and killing the inhabitants. They also sent agents out to describe the Mongol's brutality and huge numbers. These tactics, combined with a well-organized army and a reliable messenger system, helped Genghis Khan conquer much of Asia.

When Genghis Khan died in 1227 his vast empire was divided into four regions, each ruled by one of his heirs. Under his grandson **Kublai Khan** (KOO-bluh KHAN), the Mongols resumed their efforts to complete the conquest of China and Korea. Another grandson conquered Persia, Russia, and attacked Poland and Hungary, killing millions of people.

Although brutal in building their empire, Mongol leaders ruled it peacefully. This period is called the **Pax Mongolia**, meaning the "Mongol Peace." It lasted from the mid-1200s to the mid-1300s and allowed goods, people, and ideas to travel across Asia.

Why were the Mongols effective conquerors?

____

____

____

What happened to Genghis Khan's empire when he died? Who ruled it?

____

____

____

Underline the countries conquered by the Mongols. Circle how many people were killed by them.

THE YUAN DYNASTY

Kublai Khan became the Great Khan of the Mongol Empire in 1260. He completed the conquest of China in 1279, founding of the Yuan dynasty. He moved the Mongol capital to China. The Mongols lived apart from the Chinese. They created different laws and taxes for the Chinese than for themselves. To gain loyalty from the Chinese people, Yuan rulers adapted some Chinese practices. High taxes and profits from trade brought wealth to Mongol rulers and foreign merchants. The government also sponsored irrigation programs, lowered taxes in the war-torn south, and promoted the circulation of paper money.

An Italian trader from Venice, **Marco Polo**, stayed in China and worked for Kublai Khan. Polo went on several missions throughout the China. A book that described his travels brought him fame, and increased European interest in China.

END OF THE YUAN DYNASTY

The Yuan dynasty began to weaken during the last part of Kublai Khan's reign. One cause was a number of military defeats. In an effort to expand his empire, Kublai Khan sent several invading forces into Southeast Asia. All of the invasions failed, and the Mongol army suffered huge losses.

Kublai Khan ordered an invasion of Japan in 1268 because the Japanese refused to surrender to him. Although the Mongols won a brief land battle, a storm destroyed their fleet, killing 13,000. Later, Kublai Khan sent an even larger battle fleet against Japan. For more than 50 days the Japanese held off the Mongol invasion. Then another storm killed 100,000 Mongol troops attempting to invade Japan. The Mongols made no more attempts on Japan.

When Kublai Khan died in 1294, power struggles weakened the empire. A series of disastrous floods and rising taxes increased discontent. In the 1300s many Chinese factions rebelled against the Yuan dynasty and in 1368 a rebel army defeated the Mongols. The Mongols fled to Manchuria, ending foreign rule in China.

What happened when the Mongols tried to invade Japan?

____

____

____

Name ______________________ Class ______________ Date ______________

Cultures of East Asia

Section 3

MAIN IDEA
Geography and cultural borrowing from China shaped the early civilizations of Japan and Korea.

Key Terms and People

archipelago large island chain

Shinto "the way of the gods," a religion based on belief in supernatural beings called kami

Prince Shokotu ruler of Japan between 593 to 622, member of the powerful Soga family

Lady Murasaki Shikibu wrote *The Tale of Genji*, considered the world's first full-length novel

Koryo dynasty Korean dynasty that who ruled from 918 to 1392

Taking Notes

As you read the summary, use a graphic organizer like the one below to take notes about early Japan and Korea.

Japan	Korea

Section Summary

RISE OF JAPANESE CIVILIZATION

The nation of Japan consists of some 3,000 islands. The islands form an **archipelago** (ahr-kuh-PE-luh-goh), or large island chain, along East Asia's mainland. Steep mountains covered with forests leave only a small amount of farmland but this land is fertile and receives much rain. The sea provides food and serves as a barrier against invasion. However, huge waves called tsunamis, storms known as typhoons, and frequent earthquakes pose threats to Japan's safety.

Name three ways the sea affects Japan.

____

____

____

Early Japanese people were hunters and gatherers who arrived from the Asian mainland during prehistoric times. Over time, they developed a religion called **Shinto**, which is based on belief in nature spirits called kami (KAH-mee), whom they believed were their ancestors. Shinto does not have a sacred text or formal structure like many religions. Instead, followers build shrines to kami in natural settings and perform ceremonies to ask for their blessings.

Japanese society was organized into clans based on extended family ties. By the 500s, the Yamato clan became the most powerful. They claimed the sun goddess as their ancestor. All of Japan's emperors are descended from the Yamato. Eventually, other clans gained power and controlled the emperor. Often, the emperor became a figurehead with no real power.

How was Japanese society organized?

____

____

FOREIGN INFLUENCES ON JAPAN

Japan's culture was influenced by nearby Korea and China. Korean traders and travelers introduced Japan to Chinese writing. Buddhism also came to Japan through Korea. One of the people who most helped spread Buddhism in Japan was **Prince Shotoku** (sho-toh-koo). He served as regent for his aunt from 593 until 622. A regent is a person who rules for someone who is unable to rule alone. Shotoku's devout practices helped Buddhism spread. He also sent young scholars to China. Over the next 200 years, many of these missions brought home Chinese fashions, food, tea, artwork, music, dance, gardening and ideas about law.

How did Prince Shotoku influence religion in Japan?

____

____

THE HEIAN PERIOD

In 794 Japan's emperor moved the capital to Heian (HAY-ahn), now called Kyoto (kee-OH-toh). This period, called the Heian period, lasted until 1185.

The nobles at Heian lived in beautiful palaces and enjoyed easy, privileged lives. Lovely gardens, art and poetry were popular. Rules of etiquette governed all aspects of court behavior and dress.

Monogatari, or fictional prose, was especially popular. Noblewomen were discouraged from learning Chinese, so many of them wrote and read in Japanese. By this time, the Japanese had developed a way to write their spoken language by combining Chinese characters with phonetic characters.

How did the Japanese develop a written language?

____

____

____

Heian women produced some of the best works of early Japanese literature. The greatest writer was perhaps **Lady Murasaki Shikibu** (moohr-ah-sahkee shee-kee-boo). Around 1000, she wrote *The Tale of Genji*, considered the world's first full-length novel.

During most of the Heian period, the Fujiwara family controlled Japan until rich landowners with private armies began to challenge them.

KOREA

Korea's location has made it able to share its culture with Japan and China's but it has also made Korea vulnerable to invasion. Korea is a mountainous peninsula with limited land available for farming. The first Koreans came from northeast Asia. Chinese influences in Korea included Confucianism, agricultural methods, writing, political institutions, and, later, Buddhism.

Name two ways Korea's geography has affected the lives of its people.

____

____

____

After China's Han dynasty declined, a kingdom called Silla allied with China to conquer Korea. The Silla then turned on the Chinese and drove them from Korea. They decided, however, to pay tribute to China to ensure harmony and goodwill. When the Silla kingdom weakened, rebels founded the **Koryo dynasty**, which lasted from 935 until 1392. During this time, Korean artisans created a pottery style called celadon and metal movable type.

In the 1200s, the Mongols invaded. They stayed until 1392 when a Korean general founded a new dynasty, which ruled until 1910.

Name ______________________ Class ______________ Date ______________

Cultures of East Asia

Section 4

MAIN IDEA
Geography and the cultures of India and China influenced the early civilizations of Southeast Asia.

Key Terms and People

Anawrata the first great king of Pagan whose conquests spread Theravada Buddhism throughout the region

Angkor Wat famous temple complex built in the 1100s

Trung Trac a leader in Vietnam who raised an army with her sister Trung Nhi in AD 39 to defeat the Chinese and temporarily expel them

Trung Nhi a leader in Vietnam who raised an army with her sister Trung Trac in AD 39 to defeat the Chinese and temporarily expel them

Taking Notes

As you read the summary, use a graphic organizer like the one below to record key facts about Southeast Asia's (1) geography, (2) cultural influences, and (3) ancient kingdoms.

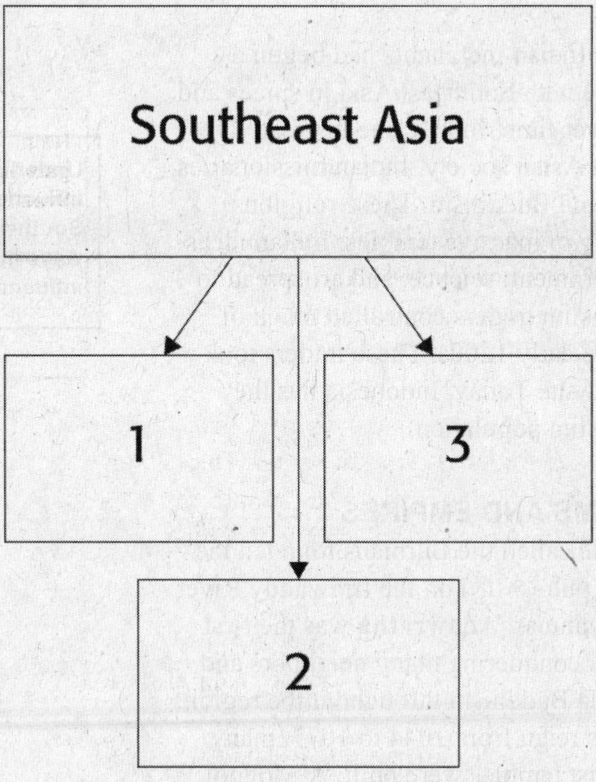

Section Summary

INFLUENCES ON SOUTHEAST ASIA

Southeast Asia lies mostly between India and China. Geography, weather, and trade have played roles in its growth. The region has two sections, mainland (Cambodia, Laos, Myanmar, Thailand, Vietnam, and part of Malaysia) and islands, made up of the rest of Malaysia, Brunei, East Timor, Indonesia, the Philippines, Singapore, Sumatra, Borneo, and Java. Deltas in mainland Southeast Asia have been areas of settlement for a long time because they are good for farming.

Waterways surrounding the island nations served as important trade routes between India and China. The most important trade routes were the Malacca Strait and the Sunda Strait.

Concentrated bursts of rain called monsoons affected trade because ships relied on their winds to travel. As ships sat in ports for months to wait for the next monsoon, cities grew up around them to supply them. These cities became important economic centers.

How did weather influence life in Southeast Asia?

____

____

____

By the AD 100s, Indian merchants had begun a prosperous sea trade with Southeast Asia in spices and aromatic woods. Over time, India came to greatly influence Southeast Asian society. Indian missionaries brought Hinduism and Buddhism. These religions inspired the building of massive temples. Indian ideas about writing, government, science, and art spread to Southeast Asia. Muslim traders controlled much of northern India in the early 1200s. These traders took Islam to Southeast Asia. Today, Indonesia has the world's largest Muslim population.

Underline the ways Indians influenced religion in Southeast Asia. Circle the ways in which Indian ideas influenced the region.

EARLY KINGDOMS AND EMPIRES

In the 800s, a people called the Burmans founded the kingdom of Pagan (puh-GAHN) on the Irrawaddy River in what is today Myanmar. **Anawratha** was the first great king in Pagan, conquering many neighbors and spreading Theravada Buddhism throughout the region. During and after his reign from 1044 to 1077, many magnificent Buddhist temples were built. A Mongol invasion in 1287 caused Pagan to lose its power.

Section 4

The Khmer (kuh-MER) Empire rose in what is now Cambodia. By the early 800s, the Khmer people had begun to conquer the kingdoms around them. They grew into a great empire that reached its height between about 850 and 1250, during which it controlled much of the Southeast Asian mainland.

The Khmer city of Angkor included the famous **Angkor Wat** temple complex with its 200 foot tower. The Khmer kingdom produced large quantities of rice, aided by an irrigation system that covered millions of acres of land. The empire prospered for some 400 years before expensive building projects and outside invaders contributed to its decline.

Approximately how long did the Khmer Empire last?

____

On Java, the kingdom of Sailendra flourished from about 750 to 850. The people of this kingdom relied on agriculture and trade for their livelihood. The kingdom adopted Mahayana Buddhism. The most famous Sailendra achievement is the Buddhist monument at Borobudur.

The Srivijaya (sree-wi-JAW-yuh) Empire controlled important overseas trade routes through the Malacca and Sunda straits. Its capital, located at Palembang on the island of Sumatra, was a center of Buddhist learning. The people also practiced Hinduism. Rulers worked to ensure that trade passed through their empire. The Srivijaya empire was weakened by an Indian attack in 1025. Other nearby kingdoms reduced their control of trade. In time, a Muslim kingdom on the Malay Peninsula came to dominate trade in the region.

Why do you think the Srivijaya rulers encouraged trade to pass through their empire?

____

____

____

Vietnam was conquered in 111 BC by the Han Chinese and was influenced by China, on and off, for the next 1,000 years. The Chinese have influenced Vietnamese language, clothing, hairstyles, government, art, architecture, and religion.

However, the Vietnamese also rebelled at times. In AD 39, sisters **Trung Trac** and **Trung Nhi** raised an army and defeated the Chinese. When the Chinese returned, however, the sisters threw themselves into a river. They remain heroes today.

Why were Trung Trac and Trung Li heroes of the Vietnamese people?

____

____

____

After the collapse of the Tang dynasty, an independent kingdom formed in the northern part of Vietnam called Dai Viet. Prince Tran Quoc Toan defeated the Mongols when they invaded in 1285.

Chapter Summary

Spread of Christianity

Byzantine Empire	Russia	Western Europe
Christianity tied the large empire together.	Christianity spreads due to trade with Byzantines.	Christianity gives hope to people living in harsh medieval times.
City of Constantinople built by Christian emperor Constantine.	Cyril and Methodius, two Greek missionaries, help the religion to spread.	Saints Ambrose, Jerome, Augustine, and Gregory help shape the church.
Eastern Orthodox Church splits from Western Roman Church.	Vladimir I makes Orthodox Christianity the state religion in 988.	Missionaries spread the Christian message.

COMPREHENSION AND CRITICAL THINKING

Use information from the graphic organizer to answer the following questions.

1. **Explain** How did Christianity begin to spread in Russia?

____

____

2. **Interpret** How do you think it benefited kings and emperors to have all their people practicing the same religion?

____

____

3. **Identify Cause and Effect** What caused the pope to have more power as time passed?

____

____

4. **Elaborate** How might converting to Christianity during the Middle Ages help people, beyond giving them the promise of a happy afterlife?

____

____

Name ______________________ Class ______________ Date ______________

MAIN IDEA

The Byzantine Empire, once the eastern half of the Roman Empire, was held together for centuries by strong leaders, profitable trade, and the influence of Christianity.

Key Terms and People

Byzantine Empire the Eastern Roman Empire, the capital of which was Constantinople

Justinian I ruler of the Byzantine Empire from 527 to 565 who dreamed of restoring the original Roman Empire

Theodora wife of Emperor Justinian, who co-ruled the Byzantine Empire with him

Belisarius Emperor Justinian's top general, recaptured Northern Africa and lands in Italy

mosaic pictures created with tiny colored tiles fitted together and cemented in place

icon paintings or sculptures of sacred figures

clergy church officials

Orthodox Church church in the east, after the schism in 1054

Taking Notes

As you read the summary, use a graphic organizer like the one below to take notes on the Byzantine Empire's emperors, culture, and decline.

Emperors
Religion
Decline

Section Summary

EMPERORS RULE IN CONSTANTINOPLE

Roman Emperor Constantine I founded the city of Constantinople in 395. Until 1453, it served as the capital of the Eastern Roman Empire, which later became known as the **Byzantine Empire**. The location of Constantinople allowed it to control trade between Asia and Europe. The city itself was well-fortified by heavy walls on one side and the sea.

The emperor **Justinian I** came to power in 527. With his wife and co-ruler **Theodora** he tried to restore the original Roman Empire. He sent his top general **Belisarius** to recapture northern Africa, which had been taken by the Vandals. Belisarius also restored lands in Italy. Constantinople itself was greatly damaged in 532 when two political groups started a violent uprising called the Nika Revolt. Afterward, the rulers rebuilt with city with grand new monuments. During this time, the spectacular Hagia Sophia (HAH-juh so-FEE-uh) was built. A spectacular blend of domes and arches, the church still stands.

When Justinian came to power he codified, or systematically arranged, existing laws and legal opinions. It included all the existing constitutions from the time of Emperor Hadrian. Later, the code was revised and updated to include laws created by Justinian himself. Together the revised law code is called Justinian's Code.

Under the reign of Heraclius the Persians, who had been a constant threat on the empire's eastern border, were defeated. In the west, he allowed Croats and Serbs to settle. Their borderland acted as buffers against new invaders. The people were converted to Christianity, which brought Byzantine influence into the region, an influence that would last for centuries.

Why is the city of Constantinople significant?

____

____

Circle two reasons Constantinople had such a strategic location.

What was Justinian's Code?

____

____

BYZANTINE CULTURE

Two institutions were central to Byzantine culture: the emperor and Christianity. The emperor was a priest-king, who was considered the deputy of Jesus Christ on Earth and his co-ruler. Although the people of Constantinople referred to themselves as Romans, Greek cultural influences grew stronger. Emperor

Heraclius brought an official end to Roman traditions in the eastern empire by making Greek the official language, replacing Latin. He also replaced the old Roman imperial titles with Greek terms.

Most Byzantine art, architecture, and literature had strong religious themes. An important example of this is **mosaics**, pictures created with tiny colored tiles fitted together and cemented in place. Mosaics decorated the interiors of many Byzantine buildings. Byzantine churches had round domes over square foundations, a style that influenced architects across Europe and Asia.

In the 700s the use of art in churches deeply divided society. A sect called the iconoclasts objected to the use of **icons**, paintings or sculptures of sacred figures. They claimed the practice was too close to the non-Christian worship of idols. Emperor Leo III banned icons. Because few people could read, many of the **clergy**, or church officials, had used sacred images to teach people about Christianity.

Why were icons important to members of the clergy?

____

____

A strong reaction against iconoclasm soon set in and continued until a council in 843 settled the issue by accepting icons. This dispute widened a growing divide between the eastern and western churches. In 1054 the differences became so large that a final schism, or split, occurred between the churches. The eastern church became the **Orthodox Church**; the western church remained the Roman Catholic Church.

What effect did the dispute over iconoclasm have on the eastern and western Christian churches?

____

____

THE EMPIRE DECLINES

In the 600s the Byzantine provinces of Egypt and Syria fell to Muslim conquerors. Leo III managed to stop advancing Muslim forces twice, in 719 and 740. A Macedonian dynasty ruled the empire from 867 to 1056. They improved the condition of the peasantry and established a law school. Parts of Syria were recovered from the Arabs and the Bulgarian kingdom to the north was annexed. However, internal conflict with the military and incompetent emperors caused the dynasty to lose power and territories. By 1391, the empire had been reduced to Constantinople and a few outlying districts. Constantinople fell to the Ottoman Turks after a fierce battle in 1453. The Ottomans renamed the city Istanbul.

How long was it between the founding of Constantinople and its fall to the Ottoman Turks?

____

Name ______________________ Class ______________ Date ______________

Kingdoms and Christianity

Section 2

MAIN IDEA

Starting as a blend of Slavs and northern Europeans, the Russians organized as a state, became Christian, and fought invaders.

Key Terms and People

Rus northern Europeans—perhaps Vikings—who came to help the Slavs in the 800s

Yaroslav the Wise Rus king who made many cultural and administrative improvements to the Kievan state

Cyril and Methodius Two Greek brothers who as Slavonic-speaking monks, helped convert the Slavs in Moravia to Christianity

Cyrillic alphabet written alphabet developed by Cyril and Methodius for the Slavonic language which was based on characters of the Greek alphabet

Vladimir I Grand Duke who made Christianity the state religion of Kievan Russia

Alexander Nevsky Prince of Novgorod who encouraged the Russians not to rebel against the Mongols, and defeated Swedish and German invaders

Taking Notes

As you read the summary, use a graphic organizer like this one to take notes on important people and events in the development of Russia.

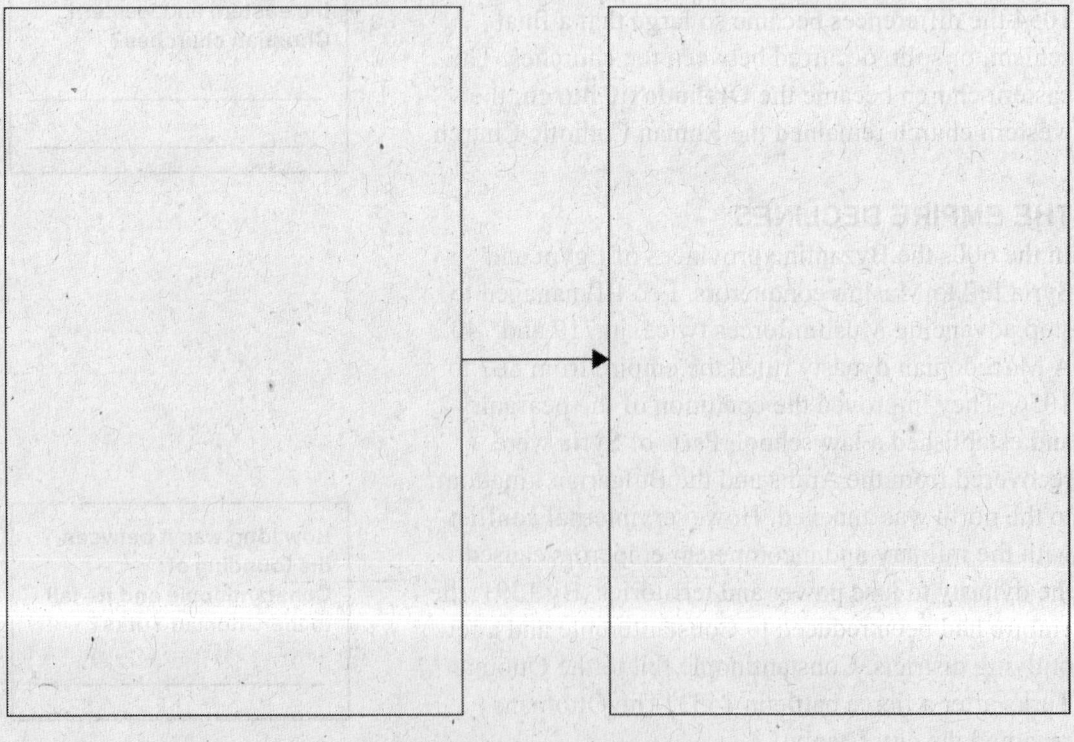

Section Summary

THE RUS AND KIEV

The Russian Primary Chronicle, written in the 1100s, records the early history of the Slavs. It states that during the mid-800s the Slavs along the Dneiper (nee-puhr) River were fighting among themselves. They asked for help from northern Europeans called the **Rus**. One of them, Rurik, brought order to the trading center Novgorod. In 882, Rurik's successor, Oleg, took control of the town of Kiev and united the entire region, which came to be known as Kiev. In order to expand the kingdom's boundaries, Oleg successfully attacked Constantinople in 907. He then demanded an advantageous trading agreement with the Byzantines.

The Rus then defeated a people known as the Khazars and freed several Slavic tribes who had been under the Khazars' control. The region became a state called Kievan Rus. One of its greatest kings was **Yaroslav the Wise**. He employed scribes to translate religious books from Greek into the Slavic language, codified Russian law, and built many new structures to beautify Kiev. Yaroslav also regained lost territory and expanded Kievan territory into the Baltic region. He maintained a good relationship with western Europe, but his forces were crushed when they tried to attack Constantinople.

What did Yaroslav accomplish during his reign as king?

____
____
____
____

CHRISTIANITY IN RUSSIA

In 863, two Greek brothers, monks named **Cyril and Methodius**, went to Moravia (now in the Czech Republic) to convert the Slavs to Christianity. They used the Slavonic language instead of Greek when celebrating Mass. They also developed a written alphabet for the Slavonic language so they could pass on religious texts of Byzantine Christianity. This alphabet was called the **Cyrillic alphabet**. It helped Orthodox Christianity spread through Serbia, Bulgaria, and Russia.

In 988 the Grand Duke **Vladimir I** made Christianity the state religion of Kievan Russia. He built libraries, schools, and churches. Following the schism of 1054, the head of the Orthodox Church in

For what purpose was the Cyrillic alphabet developed?

____
____
____

Kiev set up a semi-independent church in Russia, which became the Russian Orthodox Church.

How did the Russian Orthodox Church begin?

____

____

____

RUSSIA UNDER ATTACK

Kievan Rus was at the height of its power in the mid-1000s, but by the end of the 1100s, it had declined. It then fell under attack by invaders. Internal disputes became common after Yaroslav's death. In 1169 Prince Andrew Bogolyubsky captured Kiev and became the new grand prince. Andrew refused to move his seat of power to Kiev, staying in his home city of Vladimir while his relatives worked from Kiev. This weakened the region's power by dividing it.

In 1223, the Mongols, led by Genghis Khan, entered Rus lands, defeating them and their allies. Upon Genghis Khan's death, the Mongol empire's western edge came under the control of his grandson, Batu Khan. Kiev fell to the Mongols in 1240, and Batu established a Mongol state in southern Russia, ending the era of Kievan Rus dominance. Alexander, Prince of Novgorod, encouraged the Russians not to rebel against the Mongols, keeping them from their usual degree of destruction of conquered land.

Underline the name(s) of those invaders who succeeded in conquering Russia. Circle the name(s) of those invaders who failed in conquering Russia

In 1240 a band of Swedes invaded Russian territory, hoping to take control of the lucrative trade route between Russia and the Byzantine Empire. Prince Alexander launched a surprise attack against them, defeating them and saving Russia from a full-scale invasion. The prince became known as **Alexander Nevsky** for his accomplishment.

Later, an order of German knights tried to force Russians to abandon the Eastern Orthodox Church and convert to Roman Catholicism. Alexander's army met the invaders on an ice-covered strait, and lured them onto the thinning ice. The ice cracked, and men and horses fell through into the freezing water. The massacre on the ice, as the battle came to be called, remains one of the most famous in Russian history.

The Tatars, a Turkic-speaking Central Asian people, succeeded the Mongols, and ruled Russia until 1480. Within Russia, Moscovy, east of Kiev, became the capital of a nation that gradually expanded to occupy much of Asia.

Which city became capital of Russia after Kiev?

____

Name ________________________ Class ________________ Date ________________

Kingdoms and Christianity

Section 3

> **MAIN IDEA**
> The spread of Christianity, largely through the work of missionaries and monks, helped unify western Europe after the collapse of the Roman Empire.

Key Terms and People

Alfred the Great king of Wessex who united the Anglo-Saxon kingdoms,pushed the Danes back to the north, and became ruler of all England

Clovis king of the Franks, was baptized into Christianity with 3,000 followers in 496

medieval times of the Middle Ages, marked by doubt, suffering, and hardship for many

Christendom Christian society that included most of western Europe

Gregory the Great pope whose reforms won respect for the papacy and made the pope one of the most influential figures in Europe

monasticism voluntary separation from society to dedicate one's life to God

Augustine of Hippo influential Christian theologian whose writings helped shape Christian doctrine for centuries

Benedictine Rule guidelines for monks, written in the early 500s by Benedict of Nursia

abbot monastery leader

Taking Notes

As you read the summary, use a graphic organizer like the one below to note the influences of Christianity on the lives of people in western Europe.

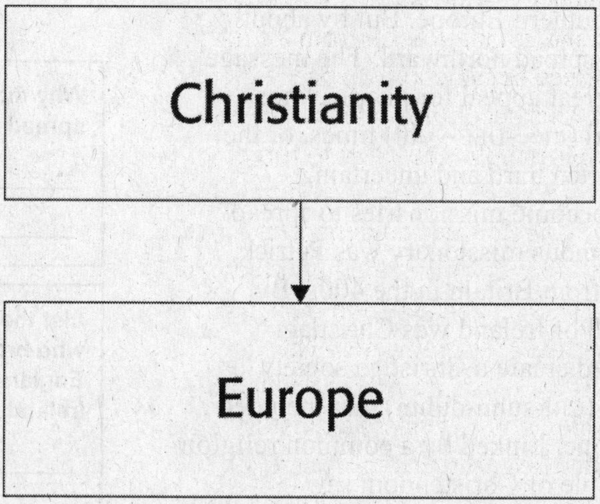

Kingdoms and Christianity

Section Summary

NEW KINGDOMS IN EUROPE

While the Eastern Roman empire flourished and became the Byzantine Empire, Western Europe was fragmented into numerous kingdoms including the Angles and Saxons in England.

In the late 500s, a group of monks led by Augustine of Canterbury brought Christianity to the kingdom of Kent. From there, Christianity slowly spread throughout England. The independent Anglo-Saxon kingdoms united under **Alfred the Great**, king of Wessex, to repel Danish invaders. Later, Alfred became the ruler of all England. He reorganized the army, issued his own code of laws, and reformed his court's financial system. His greatest achievement, however, was establishing a system of schools that educated adults as well as children.

A Germanic kingdom called the Franks was established in modern France in the late 400s. The Franks were led by **Clovis**. In 496, Clovis and 3,000 Franks were baptized into Christianity in a large public ceremony. The Franks eventually became one of the major powers of western Europe.

Why did Alfred the Great accomplish?

____

____

____

CHRISTIAN EUROPEAN SOCIETY

When Rome fell in the late 400s, Christianity was mostly confined to southern Europe. But by about 600, the religion had spread northward. The message of Christianity held great appeal for people whose lives during **medieval** (mee-DEE-vuhl) times, or the Middle Ages, were often hard and uncertain.

Many Europeans become missionaries to spread their religion. One famous missionary was Patrick, who went to Ireland from Britain in the 400s. By around 460, nearly all of Ireland was Christian.

Missionaries helped create a Christian society called **Christendom** (CRI-suhn-duhm) that included most of western Europe. Linked by a common religion and customs, the people of Christendom saw themselves as a community of believers.

Early in the Middle Ages, the pope had little authority. Many saw him as just another bishop. This lack of authority ended with **Gregory the Great**, who

Why did Christianity spread in the Middle Ages?

____

____

List the names of those who brought Christianity to England, the Franks, and Ireland.

____

____

____

undertook reforms that strengthened the papacy and church law. He encouraged both missionary work and **monasticism**, or voluntary separation from society to dedicate one's life to God. He also encouraged people to care for the poor and less fortunate. Gregory's reforms made the pope one of the most influential and respected figures in Europe.

As Christianity spread through the diverse population of Europe, the Mediterranean, and northern Africa, debates arose over questions such as the humanity or divinity of Jesus. Influential theologians like **Augustine of Hippo** wrote explanations that set forth the church's official positions. His writings, based on the Greek philosophy of Plato, helped shape Christian doctrine for centuries. Augustine's greatest writing, the *City of God*, encouraged people to pay less attention to the material world than to God's plan for the world.

Which philosopher did Augustine of Hippo base his writings on? What was Augustine's greatest writing?

____

____

MONKS AND MONASTERIES

The first Christian monks had lived in Egypt in the 200s. They usually lived alone or in small groups. During the Middle Ages, though, a new form of monasticism developed. In it, groups of monks lived in monasteries and abided by a strict code of rules.

Benedictine Monasticism was common in Europe. It was based on a rule written by a monk named Benedict in the early 500s. This collection of guidelines for monks is called the **Benedictine Rule**. It outlined a schedule for a monk's day, including prayer services and periods of work such as farm labor, copying manuscripts from the monastery library, or running schools. An **abbot** led each monastery. Monks helped preserve the knowledge of Greece and Rome by copying ancient manuscripts. Over time, many monasteries grew wealthy, and their monks acted as advisers to European rulers.

Underline the two forms of monasticism in Europe. Circle passages that explain how both types of monks spent their days.

A second branch of monasticism called Celtic (KEL-tik) monasticism developed in Ireland. There, monks often fasted and spent days alone in thought. Many Celtic monasteries were built on small islands far offshore to more fully separate the monks from the rest of society. Lindisfarne, on a small island near the English coast, is one of the most famous.

Chapter Summary

Life in the Middle Ages was governed by the feudal and manorial systems. In the feudal system, knights fought for their lords in exchange for land. The manorial system was an economic arrangement between land-owners and the people who lived on and farmed their land.	Charlemagne briefly tied much of Western Europe together into a single empire, and made social changes. ↓ Invasions by Vikings, Magyars, and Muslims led to widespread damage and turmoil throughout Europe. ↓ The power of kings grew and the nature of monarchy changed across Europe in the Early Middle Ages.	Reform and changes swept through the Christian Church, one of the most influential institutions in Europe. Popes and monastaries made reforms, and the power of popes increased. Popes often clashed with kings over these changes.

COMPREHENSION AND CRITICAL THINKING

Use information from the graphic organizer to answer the following questions.

1. **Identify** Which three groups of invaders caused widespread turmoil in Europe in the early Middle Ages?

____

____

2. **Draw Conclusions** Why do you think the increasing power of popes caused conflicts with kings?

____

____

3. **Evaluate** Do you think the feudal and manorial systems were logical and reasonable ways to organize society in the Middle Ages? Can you think of a better system?

____

____

MAIN IDEA

Through conquest and social change, Charlemagne tied much of western Europe together in a single empire.

Key Terms and People

Charlemagne King of France, also crowned Emperor of the Roman People in 800

Papal States a region in central Italy ruled by the Pope

counts officials chosen by Charlemagne to rule parts of his empire in his name

Taking Notes

As you read the summary, use a chart like this one to record the steps Charlemagne took in building his empire and forming social change.

Empire	Society

Section Summary

BUILDING AN EMPIRE

For two hundred years, the kings of the Franks worked to expand their power and influence over western and central Europe. The most powerful of these kings came from the Carolingian (ka-ruh-LIN-juhnz) family. One of the first of the Carolingians, Charles Martel, served as a political adviser and a war leader for the Frankish king. He led the Frankish army in many battles, including defeating the Muslims from Spain. Charles's son Pippin III became the first king of the Carolingian dynasty by forcing the old king of the Franks to step down and taking the throne for himself. When Pippin died in 768, he passed the kingdom on to his son, who was also named Charles. We remember this king Charles as **Charlemagne** (SHAR-luh-mayn), which means "Charles the Great." Many historians believe he was one of the strongest leaders in the history of Europe.

What parts of Europe did the Franks rule?

____

Charlemagne led armies into battle each year, conquering new lands and incorporating them into his kingdom. This is how the kingdom grew and became more powerful. In 774, the pope asked for Charlemagne's help. The Lombards had attacked the **Papal States**, a region in central Italy ruled by the pope. Charlemagne's army went to Italy and conquered the Lombards. This pleased the pope. In the year 799 he needed Charlemagne's help again. Angry supporters of the previous pope attacked Leo and ran him out of Rome. Charlemagne invaded Italy and returned the pope to power.

Underline descriptions of two events that made the pope grateful to Charlemagne.

The pope rewarded Charlemagne by naming him Emperor of the Roman People on December 25, 800. Charlemagne became the first person to hold that title in over 300 years. By giving him the title, the pope showed that he believed Charlemagne had restored the glory of the Roman Empire in Europe. This honor also let other European leaders know that the church completely supported Charlemagne's actions as king.

What did the pope's naming Charlemagne Emperor of the Roman People tell about the church's view of him?

____

____

____

Charlemagne wanted to make his government more effective. Though no Frankish king before him had established a permanent capital, Charlemagne wanted a place that would reflect his power. He established a capital city in Aachen (AH-kuhn), in what is now Germany. A very religious man, he built a large cathedral there in addition to his palace.

To assist him in ruling his huge empire, Charlemagne appointed **counts**. These officials ruled different regions of the empire in his name. Charlemagne also sent inspectors to make sure the counts were ruling well and remained loyal to their emperor. The inspectors rewarded or punished the counts based on what they found.

Underline the description of a count's job. Who made sure the counts did their jobs well?

____

A NEW SOCIETY

Charlemagne introduced many changes to Frankish society, some of which influenced life for centuries. For example, in Charlemagne's time most people could not read or write. But Charlemagne cared about education so he built many schools, which were run by educated priests and monks. Students learned about religion, music, grammar, and other subjects. Charlemagne also invited European scholars to Aachen to teach; Charlemagne himself was one of their students. The scholars also studied and copied ancient texts, which were then sent to monasteries throughout Europe, where monks made more copies. This helped to preserve many important texts from the ancient world that might otherwise have been lost forever during the Middle Ages.

Charlemagne wanted to preserve Christianity and bring it to new lands. During some military efforts, he ordered the people he conquered to become Christians. He then sent monks and missionaries there to help make Christianity a permanent part of the people's lives.

Another important change Charlemagne made was to the legal system. Before his rule, each tribe within the empire had its own set of laws. Charlemagne organized the many different law codes into one set of rules for everyone in the empire to follow. Many of his laws enforced the teachings of Christianity.

Western Europe's greatness under Charlemagne's rule did not last long after his death in 814. Both internal conflict and outside invaders quickly began to tear the empire apart.

Name three reasons that Charlemagne may have been called "the Great."

1. ______________________

____

____

2. ______________________

____

____

3. ______________________

____

____

MAIN IDEA
Invasions and migrations changed the political and cultural landscapes of western Europe during the early Middle Ages.

Key Terms and People

navigation planning a course of travel, such as the Vikings crossing the sea

sagas long Icelandic stories about great heroes and events

Leif Eriksson Viking who led settlers to the eastern shores of what is now Canada

Taking Notes

As you read the summary, use a graphic organizer like this one to list and describe the peoples that invaded Europe.

People	Description

Section Summary

THE VIKINGS

Charlemagne brought peace to western Europe. But that peace was soon destroyed by invaders who attacked Europe from several different directions. Warriors called the Vikings were perhaps the most feared of these new invaders.

The Vikings came from northern Europe, from the large peninsula of Scandinavia. This region now includes the countries of Norway, Denmark, and Sweden. Vikings are also known as Norsemen or Northmen. The Vikings were farmers and fishers when they were at home. But their land was not very fertile. As the population grew, food shortages happened more often. As a result, the Vikings turned to raiding other lands for supplies.

What was the main reason Vikings began raiding in Europe?

____

____

Their strong ships and special skills at **navigation**, or planning the course across the sea, allowed the Vikings to raid all over Europe. They started in England and northern France, but eventually traveled as far as Kiev and Constantinople. They attacked settlements both along coasts and inland—including Paris and Aachen—by traveling on rivers. The Vikings were greatly feared because they seemed to appear out of nowhere; local people did not have time to prepare to fight them. Those who tried to defend themselves were killed or captured and sold into slavery in a faraway land. The Vikings targeted monasteries because they had treasures made of gold and jewels. Not being Christians, the Vikings only saw the monetary value in these items.

Name two reasons that Vikings were especially feared by Europeans.

____

____

____

Circle places that Vikings invaded. Underline places that Vikings settled.

Some Vikings were looking for faraway lands so they could settle permanently there. Vikings settled in Iceland in the late 700s and lived there for many centuries. According to ancient **sagas**, long Icelandic stories about great heroes and events, they also settled in Greenland in the late 900s. About 100 years later, a Viking leader named **Leif Eriksson** even led some settlers to the eastern shores of what is now Canada.

Viking warriors built a settlement in northern France. A chief named Rollo had raided France many times, leading the French king to offer to make a deal with him. The king offered land in exchange for the

Vikings' promising not to raid France. Rollo agreed, and the northern settlement became known as Normandy, or the land of the Northmen.

THE MAGYARS

The Magyars were another group of invaders who brought fear to the people of Europe. They originally came from central Asia, and were nomads until they settled in what is now Hungary. From there they invaded many parts of Europe including France, Germany, northern Italy, and the Byzantine Empire. The Magyars were fierce warriors and skilled horsemen who planned their raids carefully.

The Magyars raided small settlements, looted them, and then fled. They avoided the larger towns, which had strong defenses. They could easily escape any army sent to stop them. But eventually the Magyars stopped being nomads and settled in a permanent home. After that happened, they could not run away from their opponents. Germany's King Otto the Great ended their raids by destroying the Magyar army in the mid-900s.

Name two ways that the Magyars differed from the Vikings.

1. ______________________

2. ______________________

THE MUSLIMS

Around the same time that Vikings and Magyars invaded northern Europe, Muslims from Spain and north Africa attacked southern Europe. The Muslims had tried to invade in 732 but were stopped by Charles Martel, Charlemagne's grandfather. In the 800s, they made quick raids in southern France and Italy. Among the towns raided was Rome, spiritual center of Christianity and home to the pope. They destroyed many ancient churches there.

Muslim pirates also attacked European ships that sailed on the Mediterranean. They took the goods on board and sold the ships' crews into slavery. More importantly, they cut off Italy from trade with its eastern allies. The popes had little choice but to turn to the Franks for protection. As a result, the balance of power in western Europe shifted.

Why do you think the Muslims used fast raids and pirate attacks instead of a large invasion force?

____

MAIN IDEA

In Europe, during the Middle Ages, the feudal and manorial systems governed life and required people to perform certain duties and obligations.

Key Terms and People

knights highly skilled soldiers who fought on horseback

fief land given to a knight in exchange for his services

vassal a person who accepts a fief from a lord

feudal system the political and social system of exchanging land for service

fealty a knight's loyalty to the lord who gives him land

manorial system an economic system built around large estates called manors

serfs people who were legally tied to the manor on which they worked

Taking Notes

Copy this chart onto a separate piece of paper. Then take notes on each of the roles in medieval society listed in the graphic organizer below. Describe each role, then write one or more of the responsibilities of someone in that role.

Feudal Lord	
Vassal	
Manor Lord	
Peasant	
Serf	

Section Summary

THE FEUDAL SYSTEM

As you have read, invaders caused serious problems for European society. With their sudden attacks in small groups, raiders were able to do serious damage in one area of a kingdom and then disappear before the king's army could get there to oppose them. As a result, a new system of defense came into use.

Local noblemen or lords built castles to protect themselves and their families. They also used trained and heavily armed soldiers on horseback called **knights**. These men were given land by the lord in exchange for their service. This land was called a **fief** (FEEF). The knight who agreed to this service is called a **vassal** of the lord. Exchanging land for service is known as the **feudal system** or feudalism. Of course, feudalism only worked if both sides agreed to certain obligations and duties. A knight swore **fealty**, or loyalty to his lord, promising to fight when asked, and give money to the lord to help pay for his release if captured and on special occasions. In addition to the fief, the lord promised responsible demands, protection if the knight were captured, and help in settling disputes between knights.

The feudal system was very complex. It was possible to be both a lord and a vassal at the same time. A vassal with a large amount of land might further divide it and enlist knights to serve him. In addition, a knight could accept land and provide service to more than one lord. If a knight's lords had a dispute, he would have to choose which lord to fight for in battles between them. And of course, all lords and vassals were expected to be loyal to the king, but some powerful lords did not take that duty seriously. The king, who was the central figure in feudalism, slowly lost authority. Finally, the duties of a vassal varied at different times and in different places, making it difficult to keep track of one's duties.

What is a knight?

____

____

Underline the duties that a knight had towards his lord. Circle the duties that the lord had towards the knight.

Name three reasons why the feudal system could be very complex.

1. ______________________

____

____

2. ______________________

____

____

3. ______________________

____

____

THE MANORIAL SYSTEM

The feudal system governed medieval Europe politically and gave it its social structure. The **manorial system** was its economic system at the time.

Manors were large estates usually owned by lords or knights. People would farm the land for them in exchange for protection and a portion of the crops. Some of the workers were peasants. They were free but did not own the land they farmed. They worked in exchange for a place to live. Others workers were **serfs**. They were not slaves, but they were legally tied to that piece of land and could not leave without the lord's permission. The children of serfs were serfs also.

On a manor, most of the land was used for planting crops and feeding animals. At any given time, one in three fields was left unplanted. This allowed the soil to improve, resulting in a better harvest when it was planted again. The second field was planted in spring for a fall harvesting, and the third field was planted in winter for a spring harvesting. This system is called the three-field crop rotation system. Peasants and serfs all worked this land together. The rest of the land was divided into lots for each family working on the manor. Lords tried to make their manors self-sufficient, or able to produce everything the people on the manor needed. This is why most manors had a mill to grind grain, a blacksmith, and a church.

How are peasants and serfs alike? How are they different?

____

____

DAILY LIFE IN THE MIDDLE AGES

Life in the castle was more pleasant than in a village, but neither was comfortable. Castles were built for safety during attack. They were dark, cold in winter, and stuffy in summer. The lord and his family lived primarily in the main room, called a hall. With soldiers and servants present, privacy was scarce, although in later years separate bedrooms were built.

In the village, families lived in one-room houses usually made of wood. Families slept on a dirt floor on a bed made of straw. Their animals slept there, too. A fire was built right on the floor. While the fire helped with cooking and warmth, it also filled the house with smoke. Sparks reaching the straw roof could send the house up in flames.

All members of the family worked. Men and boys worked the fields, while women and girls cooked, sewed, and took care of their family's vegetables and animals. At harvest time, the whole family worked in the fields all day.

If you lived on a medieval manor, would you rather be a knight or a peasant? Explain your reasoning.

____

____

____

MAIN IDEA

The power of kings grew and the nature of monarchy changed across Europe in the early Middle Ages.

Key Terms and People

Alfred the Great first king of the united England and who drove out the Vikings

William the Conqueror Duke of Normandy, conquered England in 1066

Domesday Book the record of William's survey of England's people and their property

Eleanor of Aquitaine powerful French duchess; divorced the king of France to marry Henry II of England and ruled all of England and about half of France with him

Magna Carta document that restricted the king of England's power, considered to be the first step toward democracy in England

Parliament governing body that was the result of the king's council in the 1260s and which still makes England's laws today

Hugh Capet first ruler from the Capetian dynasty that ruled and expanded France

Otto the Great Saxon duke who became emperor of the Holy Roman Emperor in the early 900s

Reconquista Christian leaders' effort to retake the Iberian peninsula from the Moors

Taking Notes

Copy this chart on a separate piece of paper. As you read the summary, take notes on the growth of monarchies in Europe. In the second box, show how they changed over time.

England	
France	
Holy Roman Empire	
Spain	
Portugal	

Section Summary

THE ENGLISH MONARCHY

England developed a strong monarchy, first under the rule of Anglo-Saxons, and then the Normans. Anglo-Saxons were descendants of the tribes who invaded England in the 400s. For most of their rule, the land was divided into eight small kingdoms. In the 800s, Viking invaders ruled most of these kingdoms until an Anglo-Saxon king called **Alfred the Great** drove them out. As he freed each kingdom from the Vikings, he took over its rule himself. In so doing, he became the first king of the united country.

Explain how Alfred the Great came to unite the kingdoms of England.

____
____
____
____

For the next 200 years, Alfred's descendants ruled England. But in 1066 the king died without an heir. Harold, a nobleman from England, claimed the throne. But a relative of the king, William, Duke of Normandy in France, thought he should be king. William defeated Harold and his supporters at the Battle of Hastings. William, now known as **William the Conqueror**, claimed all of England as his own property. He gave much of it to his Norman soldiers. This meant that the new nobility of England were born in France, spoke French, and had French customs. The lower classes kept their Anglo-Saxon language and habits. For centuries, this cultural divide remained.

List how England changed under William the Conqueror.

____
____
____

William wanted to know exactly who and what he had conquered, so he ordered a survey to be taken. The results were recorded in a document known as the **Domesday Book**. It was used to create a new system of taxing the people of England. Because William was Duke of Normandy, he and his descendants held property both in England and in France. Through inheritance and marriage, such as King Henry's to powerful duchess **Eleanor of Aquitaine**, England came to hold even more land in France. This meant that the kings of England were also vassals to the French king. England's kings, however, largely ignored their duties as vassals.

English nobles rebelled in 1215, after King John lost almost all of England's lands in France, then tried to make the nobles pay a new tax. Instead they made him accept the **Magna Carta**, a document that stated the nobles' rights and limited the king's power to do things like raise taxes, arrest people, and take their property. This was a first step towards a democratic system of government in England.

In the 1260s, another rebellion broke out over nobles' rights. To end it, the king agreed to meet with nobles, churchmen, and members of the middle class to discuss important issues. This council became known as **Parliament**, the body that still governs England today. While it had the power to make new taxes and advise the king on laws, Parliament still had less power than the king at this time.

Name two ways that the English monarchy's power was limited in the 1200s.

____

____

OTHER EUROPEAN MONARCHIES

Rulers of other European countries had different experiences than the English kings. French kings in the early Middle Ages only ruled a small area around Paris. Powerful nobles, including the kings of England, held much of what we now think of as France. But in the mid-900s, **Hugh Capet** (kuh-PAY) became king. He and his descendants, the Capetians, increased the power of the French monarchy. By 1300 they ruled much of modern France.

After Charlemagne's rule, his empire had split into France and Germany. Germany was further divided into several smaller states ruled by dukes. But in the early 900s, one duke convinced the others, and the pope, to grant him the title of Emperor of the Romans. This man was **Otto the Great**. From then on, this area was known as the Holy Roman Empire, but the individual states remained independently ruled by dukes. Each Emperor after Otto was chosen by electors and crowned by the pope.

How was the Holy Roman Empire different from other European kingdoms? Tell at least two ways.

____

____

On the Iberian Peninsula, where Spain and Portugal are today, Muslims, known as Moors, had held most of the land since the 700s. For centuries, Christian rulers in the north tried to drive the Moors out. This effort is known as the **Reconquista** or reconquest. Led by the kingdom of Castile, Portugal and Aragon eventually joined in. The Portuguese declared themselves an independent kingdom in the early 1100s. By the mid-1200s, the Moors only held the tiny kingdom of Grenada in the far south. In the 1400s, they were driven completely off the peninsula, and Aragon and Castile united to become Spain.

What was the Reconquista? Circle the answer in the text.

MAIN IDEA
Reform and changes swept through the Christian church, one of the most influential institutions in medieval Europe.

Key Terms and People

piety a person's level of devotion to religion

Pope Gregory VII pope who excommunicated Henry IV, showing that a pope could stand up to the emperor

pontificate term of office of a particular pope

Henry IV Holy Roman Emperor who clashed with Pope Gregory VII in 1075

Taking Notes

As you read the summary, take notes on a graphic organizer like the one below. Note the major changes that took place in the medieval church.

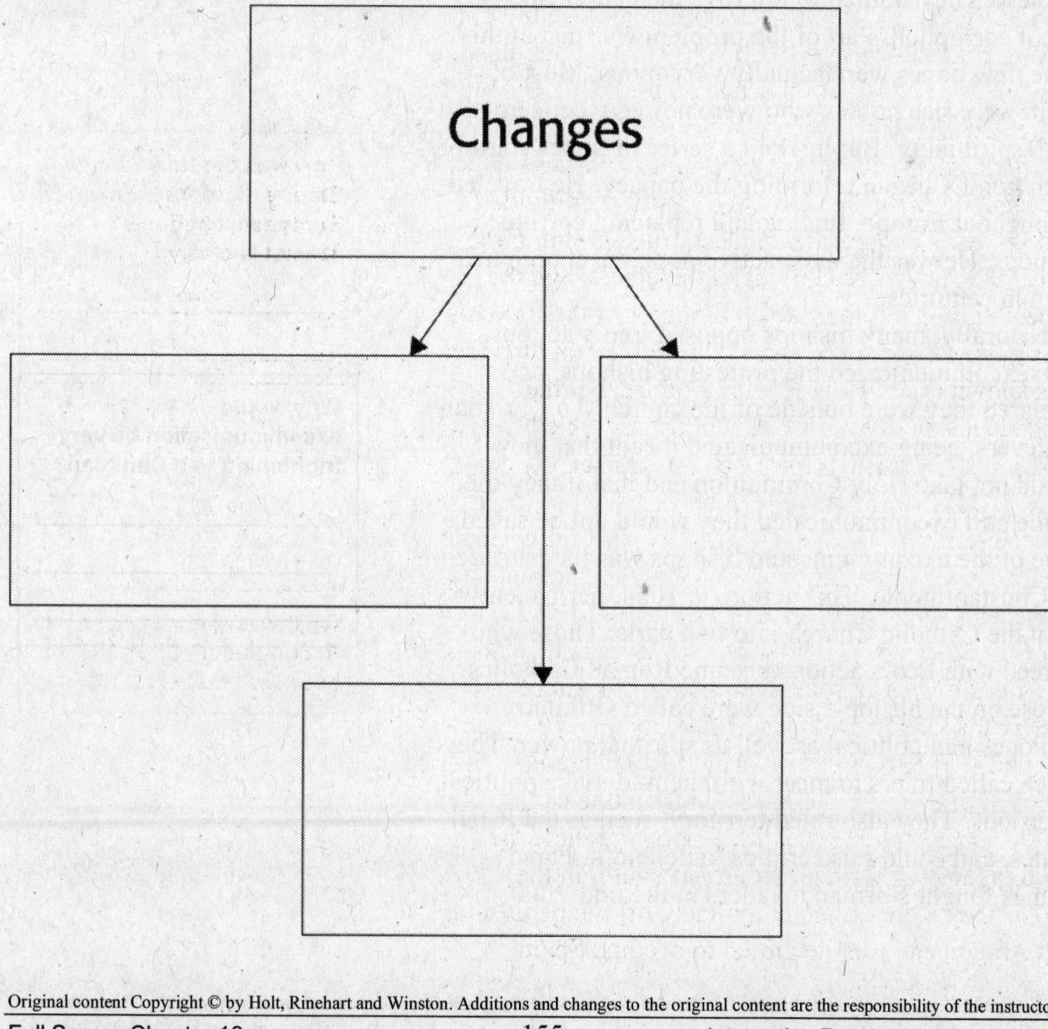

Section Summary

RELIGION IN THE MIDDLE AGES

The pope is the head of the Roman Catholic Church. During the Middle Ages, popes also came to be important political leaders. This happened because almost everyone in Europe at this time was Christian, and religion was central in most people's lives. The church was a common bond for almost everyone throughout Europe. Around the year 1000, the influence of the church increased even more as **piety**, or people's level of devotion to their religion, rose throughout Europe. Many more people became more active members of their churches or joined religious orders in places such as monasteries.

Underline two results of the increase in piety around the year 1000.

GROWTH OF PAPAL POWER

Both regular people and the clergy felt this new surge in piety. They wanted to improve the church and get rid of corruption. Part of the problem was that at this time, few popes were actually very pious. Most of them were rich nobles who were not very concerned with spirituality. But in 1049 a series of popes starting with Leo IX began reforming the papacy. He traveled throughout Europe, finding and replacing corrupt bishops. He was the most active pope the church had seen in centuries.

Naturally, many bishops opposed Leo's actions. Leo excommunicated the protesting bishops, or declared they were outside of the church. To Christian believers, being excommunicated meant that they could not take Holy Communion and that if they died while still excommunicated they would not be saved. One of the excommunicated bishops was the patriarch of Constantinople. This action, in 1054, permanently split the Catholic Church into two parts. Those who agreed with Leo's actions became Roman Catholics. Those on the bishop's side were called Orthodox.

Why would excommunication be very frightening to a Christian?

____

____

____

Popes had political as well as spiritual power. They often called rulers to meet with them to make political decisions. They also ruled territory, such as the Papal States, and could raise armies to defend it. Papal armies fought Norman invaders in the mid-1000s.

Section 5

Popes and other political leaders were often in conflict. One problem area was the appointment of clergy. For years, kings and nobles played an active role in choosing the bishops who served in their lands. The Holy Roman Emperor had even named several popes. But popes in the late 1000s thought only clergy should make decisions about religious positions. During **Pope Gregory VII's** papal term in office, also called his **pontificate**, he clashed with the Holy Roman Emperor **Henry IV** over this issue. Henry chose a bishop for the city of Milan, and Gregory did not approve, so he removed the bishop. Henry told Gregory he had no authority over him or any other ruler. In response, Gregory excommunicated Henry, and called on the leaders within the Holy Roman Empire to replace Henry with another emperor. This frightened Henry into begging for the pope's forgiveness. Gregory eventually gave in, lifting the excommunication. But the issue of who had the right to appoint bishops was not really resolved. A compromise was agreed upon by later popes and rulers: the pope would appoint the bishop, but the bishop still had to answer to his king.

Whose appointment led to conflict between Henry IV and Pope Gregory VII?

____

Underline the compromise that was reached between popes and rulers over the appointment of bishops.

CHANGES IN MONASTICISM

Monks also wanted to reform their religious orders in the Middle Ages. As you have read, monks lived by the Benedictine Rule, a strict code. But by about 900, many monasteries were not observing the Rule very strictly. They often owned large parcels of land, which meant they became involved in the feudal system and, as a result, in politics. This went against the ideal of quiet contemplation. In the early 900s, some unhappy monks set up a new monastery at Cluny, France. They lived strictly by the Benedictine Rule. Their example inspired many other monks all over Europe to reform.

For some, not even the Benedictine Rule was strict enough. They founded new orders such as the Cistercian (sis-TUHR-shuhn) Order. These monasteries were built in wilderness areas and were unheated and undecorated. The monks divided their time between prayer and manual labor. Other monasteries were even more strict, forbidding speaking or even interacting with fellow monks.

How was the Benedictine monastery at Cluny similar to new monastic orders like the Cistercians? How were they different?

____
____
____
____

Chapter Summary

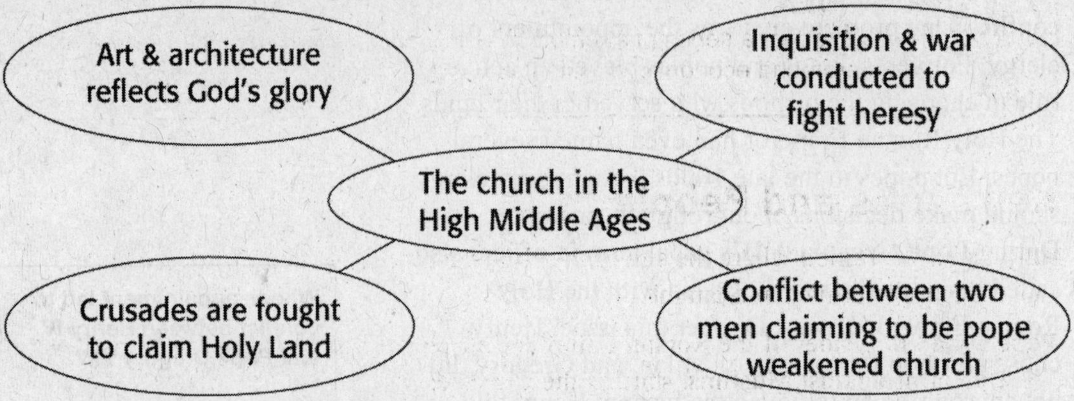

COMPREHENSION AND CRITICAL THINKING

Use information from the graphic organizer to answer the following questions.

1. **Explain** Describe the church's role in art and architecture advancement during the Middle Ages.

____

____

2. **Recall** Why did European Christians fight the Crusades?

____

____

3. **Draw conclusions** What role did the church play in everyday life during the Middle Ages?

____

____

4. **Elaborate** Why did the church continue to have problems even after the conflict between the two competing popes had been resolved?

____

____

Name ______________________ Class ______________ Date ______________

The High Middle Ages

Section 1

MAIN IDEA

The Crusades, a series of attempts to gain Christian control of the Holy Land, had a profound economic, political, and social impact on the societies involved.

Key Terms and People

Holy Land the region where the site of the Holy Temple of the Jews was located and where Jesus had lived and taught

Pope Urban II Leader of the Roman Catholic Church who asked European Christians to take up arms against Muslims, starting the Crusades

Crusades a series of religious wars launched by European Christians in the Middle Ages

Saladin Muslim sultan who overthrew the Seljuk Turks and drove the Christians out of Jerusalem, leading to the Third Crusade

Richard the Lion-Hearted King of England who led forces against the army of Saladin during the Third Crusade

Taking Notes

As you read the summary, use a graphic organizer like the one below to take notes on the causes, the fighting, and the results of the Crusades.

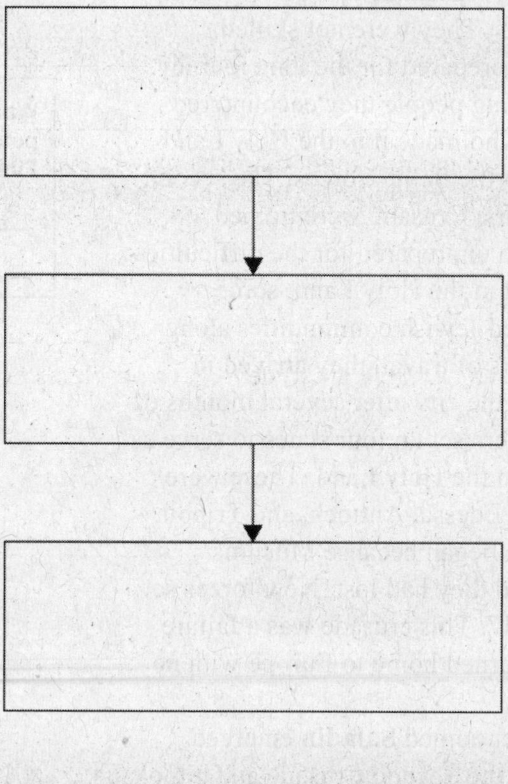

Section Summary

LAUNCHING THE CRUSADES

The **Holy Land** contains the city of Jerusalem, where Jesus lived and taught. It includes several sites sacred to three major religions: Islam, Judaism, and Christianity. During the Middle Ages, Seljuk Turks controlled the Holy Land, along with Persia and southwest Asia. Rumors that Muslims were persecuting Christian visitors spread through Europe. The Seljuk Turks attacked the Byzantine Empire, destroying a large part of its army in 1071. Fearing the Turks would soon conquer Constantinople, the Byzantine emperor turned to **Pope Urban II**. At a meeting in Clermont, France, Pope Urban asked European Christians to fight on behalf of the Byzantine Christians. To claim or protect the Holy Land, they launched several **Crusades**, or religious wars.

What did Pope Urban II do to help the Byzantine Empire?

____

____

What was the goal of the Crusades?

____

____

FIGHTING THE CRUSADES

In all, there would be nine crusades between 1096 and 1291. The First Crusade was made up of two groups. One group was peasants. They were not skilled fighters, nor were they prepared for the long journey. Many were killed fighting people they encountered along the way. Those who made it to the Holy Land were easily defeated by the Seljuk forces. The second group fighting in the First Crusade were trained knights. They were also unprepared for the difficulties of travel. Eager to fight in the Holy Land, some knights brutally attacked Jewish communities along the way. After two years of travel, they arrived in Jerusalem and claimed the city after several months of battle. Christian crusaders set up four states to serve as Christian strongholds in the Holy Land. These were centered on Jerusalem, Edessa, Antioch, and Tripoli.

What happened to the peasant fighters during the First Crusade?

____

____

The Second Crusade began because Muslims started retaking the land they had lost. New forces set out from Europe in 1147. This crusade was a failure for Christians, who returned home to Europe with no new land claims.

A new Muslim leader named **Saladin** emerged about thirty years after the Second Crusade and retook

Jerusalem from the Christians. This caused the Third Crusade. The kings of France and Germany set out on this crusade, but only King **Richard the Lion-Hearted** of England stayed with his forces to fight Saladin. Richard and Saladin had great respect for each other, even as they fought fiercely for control of the Holy Land. Despite some early victories, Richard was not able to take Jerusalem and returned to England defeated. He was captured and held for ransom along the way.

Circle the names of two opponents in the Third Crusade.

A Fourth Crusade began in 1201 in yet another Christian attempt to claim Jerusalem. The Crusaders lacked the funds to pay for passage to the Holy Land. Instead, they agreed to attack a Christian port city called Zara for the Venetians in exchange for passage. Zara had been taken over by the Hungarian king, who was Christian. This attack resulted in the outraged pope excommunicating all the Crusaders, who then attacked Constantinople instead of the Holy Land.

At the end of all the Crusades, who controlled the Holy Land?

____

Five more Crusades were launched in the following years. None was successful. Jerusalem remained in Muslim hands when the Christians were driven completely out of the Holy Land by 1291.

EFFECTS OF THE CRUSADES

The Crusades had long-lasting effects on the economy, society, and politics in Europe and the Holy Land. First, trade increased as people in Europe learned about products from Asia, such as the spices and textiles that had been brought home by Crusaders.

Second, the Crusades brought changes to the political structure of Europe. Because many nobles and knights died during the Crusades, some kings took their land to increase their own power. Also, fighting between European nations decreased because their soldiers were fighting elsewhere.

Name three effects of the Crusades.

____

____

____

Finally, relations between people of different religions suffered as a result of the Crusades. Many Europeans became intolerant, thinking of all non-Christians as enemies. In return, Muslims and Jews viewed Christians as invaders. These attitudes caused strained relations between the groups for centuries.

MAIN IDEA

Towns and cities grew during the high Middle Ages as the amount of trade increased between Europe and other continents.

Key Terms and People

Hanseatic League a group of cities and towns in northern Germany that worked together to promote and protect trade

credit the promise of later payment for goods bought

guilds trade organizations in which all members set standards and prices for their products

apprentice someone who spent several years with a skilled crafter to learn basic skills of the craft

journeyman a person who has learned the basics of a career as an apprentice but is still learning from masters and has not yet opened his own shop

Taking Notes

As you read, use a graphic organizer like the one below to take notes on the growth of trade, cities, and towns.

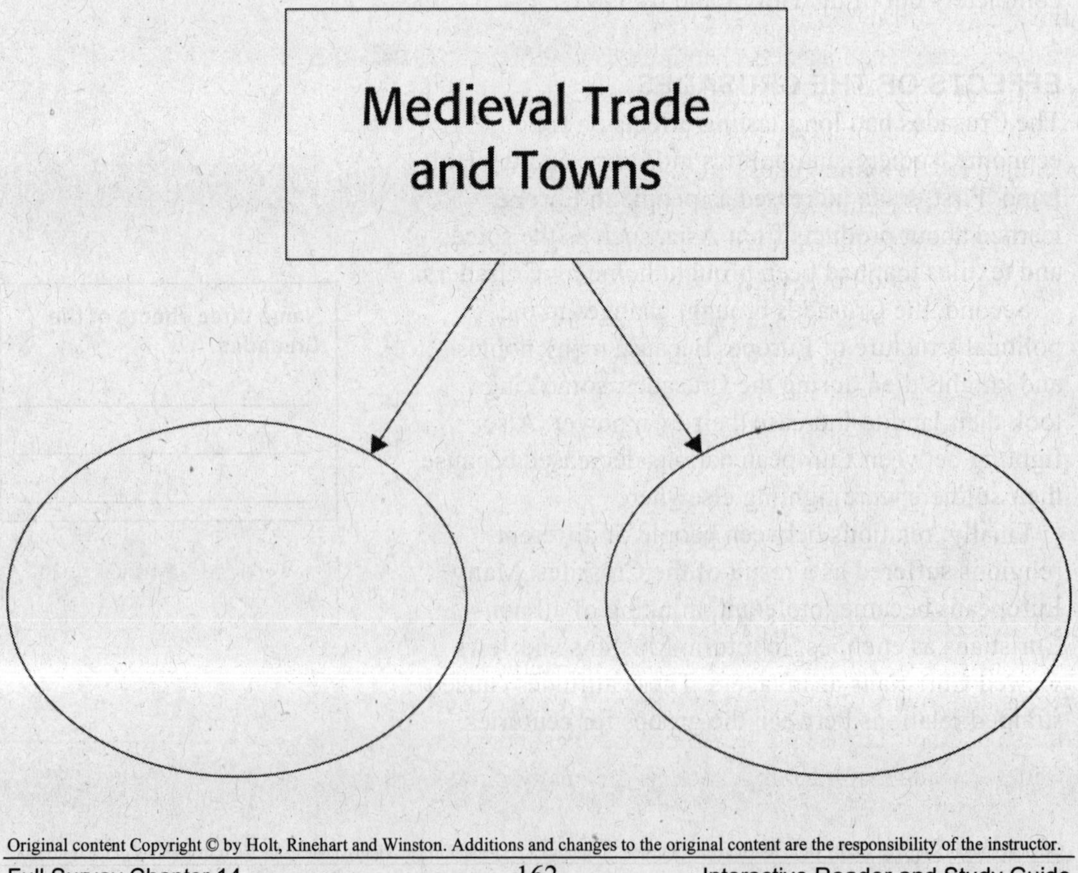

Section Summary

GROWTH OF TRADE

Trade grew after the Crusades ended. Most of it was controlled by merchants in Italy and northern Europe. Italians were good at sailing, able to travel great distances and gather rare and expensive goods such as silk and spices from the Byzantine Empire, Muslim territory, and China. The most significant trading city at this time was Venice. Venetians had the biggest fleet of ships in the Mediterranean Sea. In time, the Italians cities of Genoa, Florence, Pisa, and Milan became major trading cities. Before long, Italy controlled most trade in southern Europe.

What was one reason Italians controlled trade?

____

____

In northern Europe, trade was controlled by the **Hanseatic League**. This was a groups of cities and towns in northern Germany that worked together to promote and protect trade. The league controlled most trade between Europe, Russia, and the Baltic region.

How did trade fairs differ from local markets?

____

____

____

Merchants had to find a way to get their goods to customers. Trade fairs provided one opportunity. Trade fairs were very large and held once per year. Crowds poured into the fairs, which were usually held near a town or monastery. A great variety of goods were offered, such as spices, animals, and fabrics. Some merchants traveled all the time to take part in each fair. Local markets were smaller and held weekly so that people could get essential goods close to home.

As a result of increased trade, many European cities began minting their own coins. People used these to pay workers and buy goods. People used coins to pay taxes to their lords. Some merchants even allowed customers to buy goods on **credit**. Credit is the promise of later payment. Coins and credit led to the first banks in Europe. People could deposit money for safekeeping or request loans in banks. Most money lenders were Jews because of religious laws that kept Christians from charging interest on loans.

Circle two things people could do at Europe's first banks.

GROWTH OF TOWNS AND CITIES

The growth of trade and the use of money helped the cities and towns of Europe grow. People wanted to move off their farms and seek their fortunes through trade. Advances in farming, such as the heavy plow, water mill, and windmill made it possible to produce more food with fewer people working on the farms. As a result, more people could move to cities.

Merchants obtained special charters from kings in order to run their own towns and avoid paying taxes to feudal lords. These merchant-led towns grew very quickly. One example is Paris, which had 100,000 people in the year 1300.

How many people lived in Paris in 1300?

____

Craftspeople in cities created trade organizations called **guilds** to protect their own interests and restrict competition. Guild members worked together to set standards and prices and to train children in the craft. Most guilds were only opened to men, but women did control some industries such as textiles.

How did a young person learn a craft during the Middle Ages?

____

____

____

Skilled craftspeople often took on an **apprentice**. Apprentices were just starting to learn a trade. They spent several years with a master, often living with the master and his family. Once trained in a career, the apprentice graduated to **journeyman**. Journeymen either traveled to continue to learn from a variety of masters, or they stayed in one town, working on their craft as they saved money to open their own shops.

DAILY LIFE IN CITIES

Daily life in cities during the Middle Ages could be unpleasant. Cities were small and cramped. Narrow, dark streets were filled with people, animals, and trash. Disease was common because of the numerous rats and insects attracted to the waste. Cooking fires created a lot of smoke and threatened the wooden buildings. There was violence and theft. However, cities also offered inhabitants opportunities for entertainment and sport. Social activities were popular, especially on religious holidays. Plays, festivals, and ball games were a part of city life.

Name 3 things that characterized daily life in a city during the Middle Ages.

____

____

____

Name ______________________ Class ______________ Date ______________

The High Middle Ages

Section 3

MAIN IDEA
During the Middle Ages, great achievements were made in the visual arts, in literature, and thinking and learning.

Key Terms and People

Gothic building style that used advances in engineering to make churches taller and brighter than earlier churches

flying buttresses supports that helped hold up church walls from the outside, allowing for much higher ceilings and an interior that had no columns

illumination the process of decorating a written manuscript with pictures or designs

Hildegard of Bingen a famous medieval nun who was both a poet and a composer

troubadours wandering singers who performed epics and romances

Geoffrey Chaucer English author of the Canterbury Tales

Dante Alighieri Italian author of the Divine Comedy

Thomas Aquinas influential scholar who argued that classical ideas could be used to improve people's understanding of Christian teachings

Scholasticism a combination of Christian faith and rational thought set forth by Aquinas

Taking Notes

As you read, use a graphic organizer like the one below to take notes on the great achievements in visual arts, literature, and learning of the Middle Ages.

Visual Arts	
Literature	
Thinking and Learning	

Section Summary

VISUAL ARTS

Most art in the Middle Ages was symbolic. It was created to glorify God, not to bring fame to the artist. The Cathedral of Notre Dame in Paris is a fine example of the period's artistic advancements. Notre Dame was built in a style called **Gothic** architecture. Gothic churches and cathedrals were taller and felt airier than their predecessors because Gothic architecture used **flying buttresses** on the outside of the structure. They supported walls, making it possible to have larger windows and more interior light. Flying buttresses also made interior columns no longer necessary. Cathedrals were decorated inside and out. Stained glass windows became common. Murals of religious scenes and items made of gold and gems could also be found inside. Many exteriors featured statues of saints and kings. Gargoyles, rain spouts carved to look like beasts, were also common.

What are characteristics of Gothic architecture?

____

____

Religious texts were works of art in their own right. Manuscripts were decorated with pictures or designs in a process called **illumination**. Many medieval tapestries, or woven wallhangings, were made by noble women. Hung on castle walls to prevent drafts, tapestries showed scenes from daily life or mythical creatures such as unicorns and dragons.

What type of scenes typically appeared on medieval tapestries?

____

____

LITERATURE

Literature of the Middle Ages was varied in style and topic. Many of the writings from this era dealt with religion, as few people who were not priests or monks could read or write. Examples include sermons and tales of saints' lives. One famous medieval writer was a nun who created poems and music to go with them. Her name was **Hildegard of Bingen**.

Nonreligious writings included epics, long stories about heroes and villains, such as the Song of Roland. Romances were stories about true love and chivalry, which is the code of honor knights were supposed to live by. It required knights to be generous and courteous, especially to women. Stories that are still familiar today, such as King Arthur and his knights of the Round Table, were featured in some medieval

Circle three themes found in medieval literature.

romances. Because epics and romances were meant to be entertainment, they were not written and sung in Latin, but in vernacular languages. These included English and French, languages people spoke in their everyday lives. **Troubadors**, wandering singers, performed these stories as entertainment.

Two major works of literature from this period are *The Canterbury Tales* and *The Divine Comedy*. *The Canterbury Tales* was written by **Geoffrey Chaucer** and tells the story of a group of religious pilgrims on a journey. The descriptions of characters from a variety of backgrounds give modern readers a good idea of what life was like in the Middle Ages. Chaucer also helped spread English by writing in this language. *The Divine Comedy* was written by **Dante Alighieri** and tells about the poet's imagined journey through the afterlife. This work helped to shape and spread the Italian language.

Why do you think people read the Canterbury Tales today?

____

____

THINKING AND LEARNING

New ways of learning about the world emerged during the Middle Ages. Alchemy, an early type of science, led curious people to experiment to learn about the world. Some alchemists tried to turn lead to gold and find the key to eternal life. Though they did not succeed in these two pursuits, the work of alchemists influenced the later growth of science.

Why was alchemy important?

____

____

At this time, universities were established in Europe. Because they were started by churches, early universities taught religious courses. The universities grew over time to offer a wider variety of subjects for study, such as law, medicine, grammar, astronomy, logic, and music. One influential scholar who lived and taught during the Middle Ages was **Thomas Aquinas** (uh-KWY-nuhs). Aquinas argued that earlier philosophers such as Aristotle should be studied even though they were not Christians. This went against what earlier scholars had believed. In fact, Aquinas said that these classical thinkers' ideas could be used to better understand Christian teaching. He tried to use Aristotle's methods of logic to prove God's existence. His mixture of rational thought and Christian faith became known as **Scholasticism**.

Why was Thomas Aquinas a controversial thinker?

____

____

MAIN IDEA

In the late Middle Ages, Europeans faced many challenges, including religious crises, wars, and a deadly plague.

Key Terms and People

heresy beliefs that oppose the church's official teachings

Inquisitions legal procedures supervised by special judges who tried suspected heretics

friars members of religious orders who took vows of poverty and obedience and lived among the people to whom they preached

Hundred Years' War a war between Britain and France that began as a dispute over the throne of France

Joan of Arc peasant girl who led the French into battle during the Hundred Years' War and won several victories before she was captured, tried, and executed by the British

Wars of the Roses conflict between the York and Lancaster families for the English throne

Henry VII nobleman whose rise to king ended the Wars of the Roses and started a new era in English history

Black Death a devastating plague that swept across Europe between 1347 and 1351

Taking Notes

As you read, use a graphic organizer like the one below to take note of the various challenges faced by people in the late Middle Ages.

Section Summary

RELIGIOUS CRISES

During the high Middle Ages, Europe faced many challenges. These included changes to the religious order, political upheaval, violence, and disease. First, there was religious turmoil, dangerous because Christianity was the element that tied most Europeans together. Beliefs that were contrary to the church's official teaching, also called **heresy**, spread quickly in the 1100s. To combat heresy, the pope and other church leaders used **Inquisitions**. These were special trials for people suspected of heresy. Those found guilty were punished by local political authorities. Another way that leaders dealt with their problem was by establishing new religious orders. **Friars** who belonged to these orders lived and preached among people in cities. Finally, the pope used war to combat heresy. In the 1200s Christian soldiers from throughout Europe fought a twenty-year battle against heretics in France. Religious turmoil in Europe continued in the 1300s when two men claimed to be pope at the same time. One man reigned in Rome and another reigned in Avignon. Although the dispute was eventually resolved, the confusion greatly weakened the Catholic Church's influence.

Name three tactics religious leaders used to combat heresy during the Middle Ages.

____

____

____

WARS AND CONFLICT

Political leaders also fought during this time, which led to two destructive wars, the **Hundred Years' War** and the Wars of the Roses. The Hundred Years' War started when the king of France died and left no clear successor. One claimant to the throne was English; the other was French. The French did not want to be ruled by an English king, so they were glad when the French claimant was crowned King Philip VI. Still intent on ruling France, the British invaded in 1337. They won many victories mostly due to having better weapons than the French, such as the cannon and Welsh longbow. The English marched all the way to Paris.

Circle the names of the two wars that broke out during the high Middle Ages.

In 1429, **Joan of Arc** led the French army, changing the course of the war. This unlikely leader, a young peasant girl, convinced the French prince that the saints wanted her to lead the army. He agreed and at her command, the French won many important victories. She was eventually captured and killed by the English. Inspired by Joan's example, the French king Charles VII rallied the army. They then took back the land they had lost and drove the English out after more than one hundred years of fighting. The war finally ended in 1453.

What did Joan of Arc accomplish?

____

____

____

The **Wars of the Roses** took place in England soon afterward. Two families, each using a rose as their emblem, claimed the throne. The Lancasters and Yorks battled for several years. Edward IV of the York family took the throne and won many victories against the Lancaster family. When Edward died, his young sons disappeared while in custody in the Tower of London. As a result, Edward's brother Richard III became king. Richard died in battle during one of the many uprisings that followed by taking the throne. **Henry VII** of the Tudor family then rose to power and became king. The fact that he was neither a York nor a Lancaster ended the War of the Roses. A new era in English history began.

BLACK DEATH

While the Hundred Years' War raged, another devastating crisis swept Europe. The **Black Death**, a plague that gripped Europe between 1347 and 1351, killed millions. The Black Death was probably a combination of bubonic plague, which was spread by fleas that lived on rats and other animals, and pneumonic plague, an airborne threat spread by coughing and sneezing. The plague was brought to Europe by merchant sailors from Genoa who did not know they were carriers. Infected rats moved from ship to ship while in port, spreading the disease. Victims suffered high fevers, dark splotches on their skin, vomiting, and severe headaches. Most died within days. One third of the population was lost to the plague, about 25 million people. The plague changed Europe forever because those who survived were in high demand as workers. They insisted on being paid wages and later left the manor to live in cities. This ended the medieval manor system.

How did the Black Death spread to Europe?

____

____

How did the Black Death lead to the end of the manor system?

____

____

Chapter Summary

In Italy the growth of wealthy trading cities and new ways of thinking helped lead to a rebirth of the arts and learning. This era became known as the Renaissance. Classical Greek and Roman texts, art, and architecture inspired people like Leonardo da Vinci to create masterpieces.

Renaissance ideas soon spread beyond Italy to Northern Europe by means of trade, travel, and printed material. The northern Renaissance had unique features such as a Christian humanist philosophy and a painting style that showed everyday subjects.

Criticism of the Roman Catholic Church led to a religious movement called the Protestant Reformation, changing religion and politics across Europe. Protestants believed the church was corrupt, and disagreed with some Catholic ideas.

Catholics at all levels recognized the need for reform in the church; their work turned back the tide of Protestantism in some areas and renewed the zeal of Catholics everywhere. At the same time, religious turmoil continued across Europe.

COMPREHENSION AND CRITICAL THINKING

Use information from the graphic organizer to answer the following questions.

1. **Recall** What were two features of the northern Renaissance that differed from the one that took place in Italy?

____

____

2. **Draw Conclusions** Why did reform within the Catholic Church help limit the growth of Protestantism?

____

____

3. **Make Judgments** Since the Catholic Church did reform itself, do you think people still had the right to criticize it? Why or why not?

____

____

Section 1

MAIN IDEA

In Italy the growth of wealthy trading cities and new ways of thinking helped lead to a rebirth of the arts and learning. This era became known as the Renaissance.

Key Terms and People

Renaissance an era of renewed interest and remarkable developments in art, literature, science, and learning in Europe beginning in Italy in the 1300s

secular having a worldly rather than spiritual focus

humanism a movement that emphasized the possibilities of individual accomplishment and the almost limitless potential of the human mind

Baldassare Castiglione Italian aristocrat who wrote *The Courtier,* which became a handbook for how to succeed in society

Niccolò Machiavelli Florentine political philosopher and statesman who wrote *The Prince*, which advised rulers to separate morals from politics

Lorenzo de Medici ruler of Florence who was an important patron of arts and learning

Leonardo da Vinci "Renaissance man" who became famous as a painter, architect, inventor, and engineer; painter of the *Mona Lisa* and *The Last Supper*

Raphael famous painter of both classical and religious subjects and accomplished architect

Michelangelo Buonarroti sculptor and painter famous for works such as the Sistine Chapel, the statue *David*, and the design of the dome of St. Peter's Cathedral

Taking Notes

As you read the summary, take notes on the beginnings of the Renaissance, its ideas, and its art in a graphic organizer like this one.

Beginnings	Art and Ideas

Section Summary

THE BEGINNING OF THE RENAISSANCE

In the 1300s, so many people died of the Black Death, starvation, and warfare that the population declined. Farmers produced so much food that food prices dropped, giving people more money to spend on other things. Various areas of Europe began to specialize in the products that were best suited to their environment, and regional trade increased.

In what is now Italy, several large city-states grew in the north, while the south was made up of several kingdoms and the Papal States. The south was mostly rural. The northern cities of Venice, Milan, and Florence became centers for commerce. The church, nobles, artisans, and merchants dominated society. Venice, which had access to the sea, built its economy on shipbuilding and trading with ports as far as the Near East and Egypt. Milan's economy was built on agriculture, silk, and weapons, while Florence became famous for banking and for cloth.

Why did the price of food drop? How did this affect people?

____

____

____

____

RENAISSANCE IDEAS

As the economy and society changed, new ideas began to appear, and interest in the arts, literature, science, and learning returned and grew stronger. We call this era in history the **Renaissance**, French for "rebirth." The Renaissance first arose in Italy, thanks to its cities, trade, and wealthy merchants.

People began looking to the past for inspiration. They admired the artifacts from ancient Greek and Roman culture. They also became interested in the ideas of the ancient world, which they rediscovered by reading Latin and Arabic texts. These works inspired further advances in science, art and philosophy.

Although religion was still extremely important in European life, the Renaissance movement was more **secular**, that is, focused on this world. A movement called **humanism** developed. This emphasized the achievements of individuals rather than focusing on glorifying God. Many historians date the beginning of the Renaissance to the works of writers Giovanni Boccaccio and Francesco Petrarch. They both wrote in the everyday language of the people instead of Latin.

Why do you think this era is known as a "rebirth"?

____

____

____

____

Why do you think it was important that Bocaccio and Petrarch did not write in Latin?

____

____

____

____

Some humanists focused on society. **Baldassare Castiglione**, (cah-steel-YOH-nay) an Italian aristocrat, wrote a book describing how the perfect Renaissance man or woman should behave. Another Italian, **Niccolo Machiavelli**, was inspired by the political violence of his times to write *The Prince.* It advises rulers to do whatever is necessary to keep in power.

Scientists like Galileo Galilei and Nicholas Copernicus suggested that the Earth was not the center of the universe, which conflicted with the view of the church. Galileo was arrested for expressing his views.

Do you think Machiavelli's advice about politics is controversial? Why or why not?

____

____

____

____

RENAISSANCE ART

The artwork of the Renaissance showed new levels of expertise, and much of this works is still greatly admired. During this period, wealthy people became patrons of the arts and used art as status symbols. In Florence, the ruling Medici family and especially **Lorenzo de Medici** gave artists, intellectuals, and musicians huge sums of money for their works.

Leonardo da Vinci achieved greatness in many areas, among them painting, engineering, science, and architecture. Two of his paintings became extremely famous, *Mona Lisa* and *The Last Supper.* He also came up with ideas for a flying machine, a tank, and a machine gun. Among other things, he designed and built canals and a machine to cut threads in screws.

Underline examples of Leonardo da Vinci's painting, engineering, science, and architecture in the passage.

During this period, artists wanted to paint the real world as realistically as possible. They began to use perspective, a technique for representing three-dimensional objects on flat surfaces. Their artwork looked very different from that of the Middle Ages. A painter and architect still admired today is **Raphael**. He painted both religious and classical subjects.

What was a goal many Renaissance painters and sculptors shared?

____

____

Michelangelo Buonarroti was an accomplished sculptor who was able to make very lifelike human statues. His statue *David* is still unsurpassed. He also painted the ceiling of the Sistine Chapel in Rome, and created many other masterpieces in painting, sculpture, and architecture.

As in other areas, Renaissance building design reflected the renewed love of ancient Greek and Roman ideas. The most famous architect was Donato Bramante, who designed St. Peter's Basilica in Rome.

MAIN IDEA

Renaissance ideas soon spread beyond Italy to northern Europe by means of trade, travel, and printed material, influencing the art and ideas of the north.

Key Terms and People

Johannes Gutenberg German man credited with the invention of movable type in the mid-1400s

Desiderius Erasmus priest and Christian humanist philosopher who wrote about the need for a simple Christian life without the rituals and politics of the church

Sir Thomas More English humanist who wrote *Utopia*, a book that told about a perfect but nonexistent society based on reason

William Shakespeare English playwright and poet; author of such famous works as *Hamlet*, *Romeo and Juliet*, *Macbeth*, and *A Midsummer Night's Dream*

Christine de Pisan Italian-born woman who wrote the first important work focusing on the role women played in society

Albrecht Dürer German artist who visited Italy in the late 1400s, learning techniques of realism and perspective, influencing later German Renaissance artists

Jan van Eyck Flemish painter who focused on landscapes and everyday life

Taking Notes

As you read the summary, take notes in a graphic organizer like this one. In the boxes, list key facts about philosophers, writers, and artists.

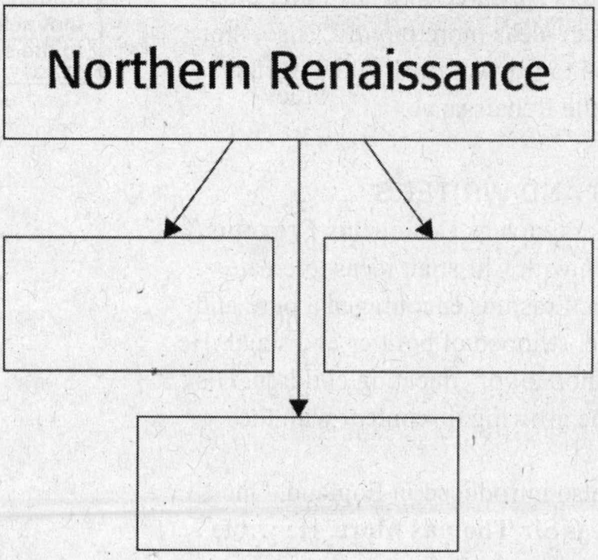

Section Summary

THE RENAISSANCE SPREADS NORTH

In the 1200s and 1300s, most of Europe's cities were in Italy. By the 1500s, however, large cities had also grown in northern Europe. These cities included London, Paris, Amsterdam, and others. Trade, the exchange of artists and scholars, and the development of printing helped spread Renaissance ideas to the newer cities.

Why do you think the Renaissance took longer to get to northern Europe?

____

____

Trade in northern Europe was dominated by the Hanseatic League, a merchant organization that operated from the 1200s to the 1400s. The league worked to protect members from pirates, and made shipping safer by building lighthouses and training ship captains. This group helped spread ideas as well as goods. Ideas were also spread by Italian artists who fled the fighting taking place in Italian cities, as well as by scholars from the north who went to Italy for education and then returned with humanist ideas.

In the mid-1400s, a German named **Johannes Gutenberg** developed movable type, made of metal letter plates locked into a wooden press. This made it possible to quickly print text on both sides of a sheet of paper. Until this time, the only way to produce a book was by hand. Now books and other printed material could be produced much more quickly and cheaply. Soon, printers appeared in many other cities. Scholars had access to ideas more rapidly. Also, more people were inspired to learn to read, which further spread the ideas of the Renaissance.

Underline the ways that movable type contributed to the spread of ideas.

PHILOSOPHERS AND WRITERS

Northern philosophers such as **Desiderius Erasmus** combined humanism with Christian ideas to create Christian humanism. Erasmus encouraged a pure and simple Christian life, stripped of politics and ritual. He also stressed the important of educating children. His writings added to the growing discontent with the Catholic Church.

Humanism was also introduced in England. One English humanist was **Sir Thomas More.** He wrote the famous book *Utopia*, which described a perfect but nonexistent society based on reason. His book also criticized the real society and government of the time. We still call an ideal society a utopia.

The greatest English writer of the Renaissance was the playwright and poet **William Shakespeare**. Shakespeare was inspired by ancient Greek and Roman writers as well as more recent authors. Shakespeare's works displayed complex human emotions and a deep understanding of language. His use of language and choice of themes, however, made his plays appeal even to uneducated people. Through his plays, Shakespeare helped spread the ideas of the Renaissance to a mass audience. His dramatic plays were a shift from the religious morality plays that had become popular during the Middle Ages. By the time of his death in 1616, London was the scene of a thriving theater district.

How was Shakespeare's writing different from that of the writers who influenced him?

____

____

____

Christine de Pisan, an Italian-born woman who grew up in France, focused her writings on the role of women in society. A poet, biographer, and moralist, she encouraged education and equality for women, and was greatly admired even in her own time.

ARTISTS

German artist **Albrecht Dürer** (DOOR-uhr) visited Italy in the late 1400s. There, he learned the techniques of realism and perspective. After returning to Germany, he influenced many German Renaissance painters with this new style. His work also had some features that were unique to the northern Renaissance. For example, like many northern European painters he used oil paints. This allowed a great deal of detail to be added to paintings, such as the texture of fabric, or the tiny image of objects reflected in a mirror.

In the area of the Netherlands known as Flanders, painters developed a unique style known as the Flemish School. This style was perfected by painter **Jan van Eyck**. His work often showed landscapes or everyday domestic scenes. Van Eyck paintings contained symbolism such as a ray of light to stand for God's presence.

In the 1500s Flemish artist Pieter Brughel (BROY-guhl) the Elder used Italian techniques. But he also painted scenes of everyday life, very different from the mythological scenes of Italian paintings.

How was northern European painting similar to that of the Italian Renaissance? How was it different?

____

____

____

____

____

____

> **MAIN IDEA**
> Criticism of the Roman Catholic Church led to a religious movement called the Protestant Reformation and brought changes in religion and politics across Europe.

Key Terms and People

Protestant Reformation a movement beginning in the 1500s to reform the Roman Catholic Church, which led to a split of the church between Catholics and Protestants

indulgences exchange of money for forgiveness of sin

Martin Luther critic of the Roman Catholic Church whose theses sparked discussion about its practices and beliefs and to the founding of Lutheranism

theocracy a government in which church and state are joined and whose officials are considered to be divinely inspired

John Calvin important Protestant reformer whose writings became the basis of Calvinism

predestination religious doctrine that states God has already determined who will be saved and so nothing people do can change their fate

Henry VIII English king who broke with the Catholic Church in order to divorce his first wife

annulled declared invalid based on church laws

Elizabeth I daughter of Henry VIII and queen who firmly established England as Protestant

Taking Notes

As you read, take notes in a graphic organizer like this one. Write the causes of the Protestant Reformation. Add more circles as needed.

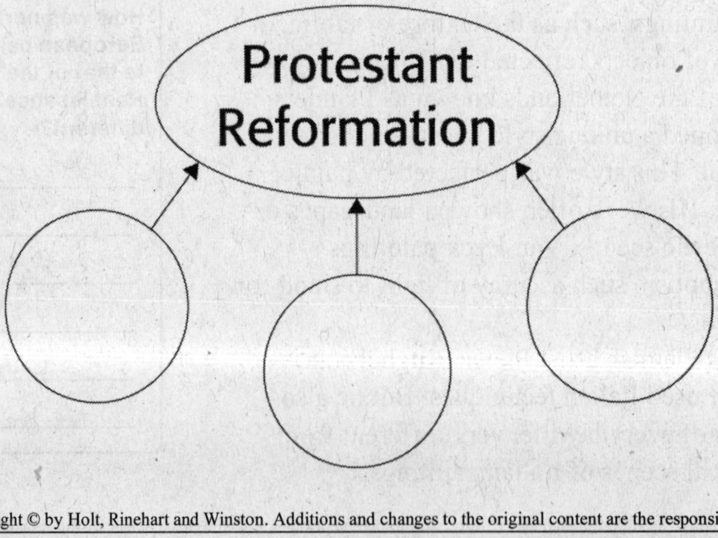

Section Summary

CATHOLICISM IN THE 1400S

By the early 1500s the **Protestant Reformation** had started. This was a movement against financial corruption, abuse of power, and immorality in the Catholic Church. At the time, the church made a practice of selling **indulgences** to help raise money. Indulgences were pardons issued by the pope to reduce the time a soul spent in purgatory. Also, people began to feel loyalty to their nation was more important than loyalty to the church.

Two early challengers of the church were John Wycliffe and Jan Hus. Wycliffe believed that the church should give up its earthly possessions. Hus preached against the immorality and worldliness of the church. Wycliffe lost his teaching job, and Hus was condemned to death for heresy. But their views helped lead to reform.

What did Wycliffe and Hus dislike about the church?

____

____

____

MARTIN LUTHER

In 1517 German monk **Martin Luther** nailed his criticisms of the church to the door of a church in Wittenberg. He condemned the sale of indulgences, which he did not believe had any power to forgive sin. He also criticized the pope's power and the church's wealth. His writings were published and widely read and discussed. Luther believed that faith only, not good works, get someone into heaven, and that Jesus, not the pope, is the only head of the church. He also translated the Bible into German so that people could interpret it for themselves.

In 1521 Luther was called before Emperor Charles V. Luther refused to change his opinions, so Charles declared the Edict of Worms, condemning Luther's writings. But Luther's ideas continued to spread. By 1530, Lutheranism was a branch of Christianity. When Charles tried to suppress Lutherans, princes in his own parliament who were Lutherans issued a protest. This is where the term Protestant comes from.

What were Martin Luther's beliefs?

____

____

____

____

____

____

THE SPREAD OF PROTESTANTISM

New Protestant leaders arose. Ulrich Zwingli founded a church in Switzerland which had **theocracy** at its base. This means that church and state are joined and leaders are believed to be inspired by God. Many, including Luther, opposed Zwingli. The Catholic Church went to war against this group.

John Calvin was a humanist and supporter of Luther's reforms. He is known for preaching the doctrine of **predestination**. This is the belief that God already knows who will be saved, and nothing can change their fate. Calvinism became popular throughout northern Europe. Switzerland became a theocracy under Calvin's leadership. Attending church was required, and there were laws against feasting, dancing, and singing.

John Knox spread Calvinism in Scotland. Eventually his Reformed Church replaced the Roman Catholic Church there. Another group, called Anabaptists, further divided from other Protestants in their belief that adults should be rebaptised.

Underline the names of the Protestant sects described here.

PROTESTANTISM SPREADS TO ENGLAND

In England, a young King Henry VIII was a devout Catholic. But in 1525 he asked to have his marriage **annulled**, or declared invalid by the church, because his wife had not given him a son. The pope would not allow an annulment. Meanwhile, Henry had fallen in love with another woman, Anne Boleyn.

Henry got Parliament to declare that England was no longer under the authority of the pope—that instead, Henry led the English church. Parliament declared Henry's first marriage null and void. They also passed the Act of Supremacy, which required subjects to agree that Henry was head of the church.

Henry had six wives in all, and two daughters and one son. Protestantism continued to grow in England under his son, Edward VI. But he died very young, and Henry's daughter Mary returned England to Catholicism. She became known as Bloody Mary for having Protestants burned at the stake. When she died, her half-sister Elizabeth became queen. A committed Protestant, Elizabeth drafted a new Supremacy Act in 1559, making England Protestant again. Elizabeth persecuted Catholics, some of whom plotted to place her Catholic cousin Mary, Queen of Scots, on the English throne.

Why did Henry VIII break with the Catholic Church? How did he do so?

____

____

____

____

____

____

MAIN IDEA

Catholics at all levels recognized the need for reform in the church. Their work turned back the tide of Protestantism in some areas and renewed the zeal of Catholics everywhere.

Key Terms and People

Counter-Reformation reform movement within the Catholic Church

Jesuits religious order which emphasized reform of the church, spirituality, service to others, education, and the further spread of Catholicism; also called Society of Jesus

Ignatius of Loyola founder of the Jesuits whose search for spiritual peace led him to give up his belongings and practice self-denial

Council of Trent meetings called by Pope Paul III to make a series of reforms to the church and clarify important teachings, took place between 1545 and 1563

Charles Borromeo archbishop of Milan who implemented the reforms decreed by the Council of Trent, such as building schools for priests

Francis of Sales French missionary who returned the French district of Savoy to the Catholic church and founded a religious teaching order for women

Teresa of Avila Spanish nun who reformed the Carmelite order

Taking Notes

As you read the summary, take notes in a graphic organizer like this one on the reforms, effects, and wars related to the Counter-Reformation.

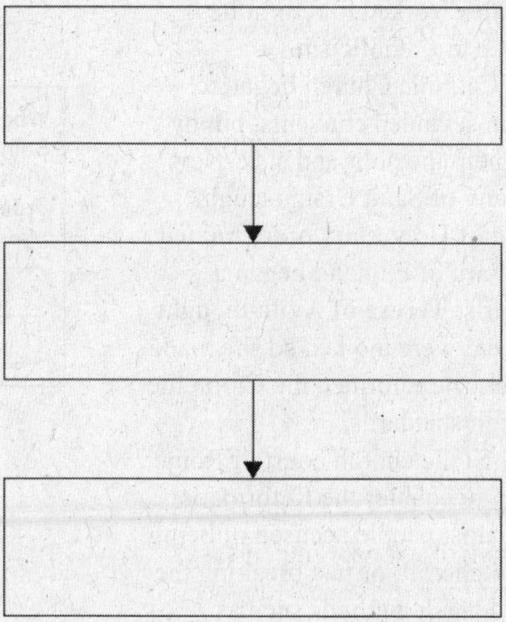

Section Summary

REFORMING THE CATHOLIC CHURCH

In response to the spread of Protestantism, some Catholics worked to reform their church during the **Counter-Reformation**. In the 1400s, Girolamo Savonarola preached in Florence that churches should melt down their gold and silver to feed the poor. The pope praised Savonarola at first, but eventually had him executed. Others reformed the church by founding religious orders. **Ignatius of Loyola** founded the Society of Jesus or **Jesuits**, who focused on spirituality and service. Loyola ran the Jesuits like a military organization, establishing missions, schools and universities. By 1700, the Jesuits operated 769 colleges and universities. These helped the Catholic Church began to regain ground against Protestantism.

Why do you think the pope opposed Savonarola's ideas but accepted the Jesuits'?

____

____

____

____

In 1545, Pope Paul III called the **Council of Trent**. The council met over the next 18 years, addressing problems like corruption of the clergy and the sale of indulgences. The council rejected the emphasis of Protestants on individual faith, arguing that the church could help believers achieve salvation by using mystery and ceremonies. The council also rejected compromise between Catholics and Protestants. After the Council, leaders put the reforms in place. **Charles Borromeo**, archbishop of Milan, built a new school for priests. **Francis of Sales** worked to return the district of Savoy in France to Catholicism.

Women's roles in the Catholic Church began to change. They had lived in secluded convents, but by the 1500s they began to help the poor and sick. New orders arose. The Company of Saint Ursula taught girls, while the Visitation of Holy Mary order trained women to teach. Mary Ward of England began a network of schools for girls. **Teresa of Avila** thought the practices of her convent were too lax, so she made her own strict rules. Later, she reformed the Carmelite order to meet her own high standards.

What did the Company of Saint Ursula and the Visitation of Holy Mary order do?

____

____

____

Pope Paul III established the church court of Rome, known as the Inquisition, to counter the Reformation. The court heard cases against people accused of being Protestants, practicing witchcraft, or just breaking the law. The Inquisition used harsh methods such as torture and execution. People were also warned that reading forbidden books would endanger their souls.

RELIGIOUS AND SOCIAL EFFECTS

The Catholic Church's changing policies caused a renewed enthusiasm for the church, which then spread the religion to North America. Meanwhile, religious turmoil increased. Catholics persecuted non-Catholics, while non-Catholics persecuted Catholics and each other. Many Protestant factions formed, often disagreeing with each others' ideas. In Spain and Portugal, Jews and Muslims were forced to convert to Catholic Christianity or leave Spain. In other areas of Europe, Jews had to live in ghettos, parts of the city surrounded by walls and gates that were closed at night. Fear of witchcraft also increased at this time. Leaders accused witches of causing hardships like bad harvests. From 1580 to 1660, thousands of people, mostly poor or women, were executed for witchcraft.

Over time, the Protestant Reformation indirectly encouraged the formation of independent states and nations by separating political power from churches.

How did the Reformation help the Catholic Church? What problems did it cause for society?

____

____

____

____

RELIGIOUS WARS AND UNREST

In 1494 the Italian Wars began, in which France and Spain vied for control of the Italian peninsula. England and several popes also became involved before the wars ended in 1559. The real significance of the Italian Wars was that troops returned home carrying ideas they had been exposed to in Italy. Also, artists from Italy fled to the north, bringing new techniques and styles with them.

In Germany, Emperor Charles V was Catholic but many of the princes were Lutheran. They fought for years with no clear winner, so in 1555 the Peace of Augsburg was signed, giving each prince the right to decide his subjects' religion—either Catholic or Lutheran. It was a small step for religious freedom.

In France, the Protestant minority fought for years against Catholics. The fighting ended when their leader Henry of Navarre converted to Catholicism. He also issued the 1598 Edict of Nantes, granting religious toleration to Protestants.

What was the real significance of the Italian Wars?

____

____

____

____

Do you think the Peace of Augsburg was fair? Why or why not?

____

____

____

Chapter Summary

Inspired by greed, curiosity, and the desire for glory and aided by new technologies, European explorers sailed to many previously unknown lands in the 1400s and 1500s. Portugal sent the first explorers; other nations, impressed by their wealth, followed.

↓

The countries of Europe established colonies in the lands they had discovered, but in some cases, such as in the Aztec and Inca empires, only after violently conquering the native people who lived there. European diseases also killed many Native Americans.

↓

The creation of colonies in the Americas and elsewhere led to the exchange of new types of goods, the establishment of new patterns of trade, and new economic systems in Europe. Colonies were only valued to the extent they could contribute to the home nation's wealth as it competed with other nations for power.

↓

Millions of Africans were captured, shipped across the Atlantic Ocean, and sold as slaves in the Americas between the 1500s and the 1800s. Their labor helped build the colonies and make them successful, but both the slaves and Africa as a whole suffered terribly as the result of the slave trade.

COMPREHENSION AND CRITICAL THINKING

Use information from the graphic organizer to answer the following questions.

1. **Identify** What was the purpose of a colony to the nation that controlled it?

____

____

2. **Draw Conclusions** Europeans had a fairly easy time establishing colonies in the Americas, conquering people as necessary. Why do you think this is so?

____

____

3. **Make Inferences** How is it that the slave trade could cause not only enslaved Africans, but Africa as a whole, to suffer?

____

____

Name ______________________ Class ______________ Date ______________

Exploration and Expansion

Section 1

MAIN IDEA

Inspired by greed, curiosity, and the desire for glory and aided by new technologies, European explorers sailed to many previously unknown lands in the 1400s and 1500s.

Key Terms and People

caravel a light, fast sailing ship with a rudder and lateen sails

Henry the Navigator son of King John I of Portugal, patron and supporter of explorers

Vasco da Gama Portuguese explorer who traveled to Calicut, India in 1497

Christopher Columbus Italian sailor who traveled west to reach China but discovered islands in the Caribbean instead

Ferdinand Magellan first explorer to attempt the circumnavigate the globe; while he was killed on the way, some of his sailors completed the journey

circumnavigate travel completely around the world

Sir Francis Drake English explorer, second man to circumnavigate the globe

Henry Hudson Dutch sailor who looked unsuccessfully for the Northwest Passage and explored the river that is now named after him

Taking Notes

As you read the summary, use a graphic organizer like this one to take notes about the reasons Europeans explored and where their explorations took place.

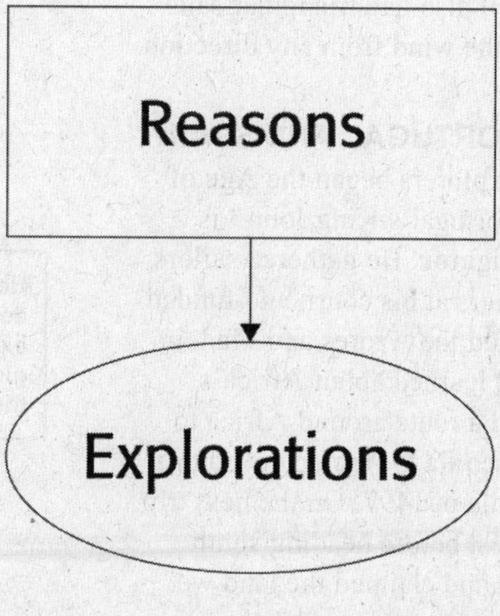

Name ______________________ Class ______________ Date ______________

Exploration and Expansion

Section 1

Section Summary

FOUNDATIONS OF EXPLORATION

In the late 1400s and 1500s, Europeans began looking for new lands and new routes to known places. This period is often called the Age of Exploration. One major reason for exploring was the desire for money. For years, goods from China and India such as silks and spices could only be purchased from Italian merchants at high prices. Explorers looked for faster routes to China and India in hopes of trading directly. Other explorers sought fame. Still others hoped to spread their faith to new people. Curiosity about exotic lands and peoples was also a factor.

List reasons that inspired European explorers in the 1400s and 1500s.

____

____

____

____

These voyages were made possible by advances in technology. Sailors needed to be able to calculate their location accurately. From China, Europeans learned about the compass, which allowed them to know at all times which direction was north. From the Muslims they learned to use an astrolabe, an instrument which allowed navigators to calculate their location based on the position of the sun and stars. Europeans also made advances in shipbuilding. They made ships that sat lower in the water than earlier ships, allowing them to withstand heavier waves and also to carry more supplies. The **caravel**, a new type of light, fast ship, also aided in exploration. It was steered by a rear rudder instead of by oars. It also had triangular sails which allowed it to catch the wind from any direction.

Name two advances in navigation and explain what each helped sailors to do.

____

____

____

____

EXPLORERS FROM PORTUGAL AND SPAIN

Portuguese and Spanish explorers began the Age of Exploration. The son of Portugal's King John I is known as **Henry the Navigator**. He gathered sailors, mapmakers, and astronomers at his court, and funded expeditions. Portugal settled the Azores and Madeira Islands in the Atlantic and learned about Africa's coast. Henry hoped to find a route around Africa to India, but died before **Vasco da Gama** achieved this goal, reaching Calicut, India in 1497. On the next trip, Pedro Cabral sailed far west before heading south around Africa. He spotted and claimed the land we now call Brazil. In India, the Portuguese built trading

Henry the Navigator did not actually make voyages of exploration. So why was he given this name? Underline the answer.

centers. They became one of the richest and most powerful European nations.

In 1492 Spain paid for Italian **Christopher Columbus** to try to sail west to China. Columbus knew the world was round, but believed it was smaller than it actually is. He also had no idea the American continents existed. So when he reached a Caribbean island after two months at sea, he believed he had reached Asia. He called the people living there Indians. He returned to the Caribbean three times, never realizing it was not Asia. Only in 1499 did Amerigo Vespucci conclude that South America was a new land. Mapmakers named the land *America* in his honor. In 1513 Vasco Núñez de Balboa crossed the Isthmus of Panama, becoming the first European to see the Pacific. Europeans realized they would have to cross the ocean to reach Asia. In 1519, **Ferdinand Magellan** tried to sail west all the way around the world. He died in the Philippines, but some of his crew made it back to Spain in 1522. They were the first to **circumnavigate** the globe.

Why do you think Columbus never figured out that he had not found Asia?

____

____

____

____

EXPLORERS FROM THE REST OF EUROPE

In 1497, Englishman John Cabot sailed to the Atlantic coast of what is now Canada, thinking it was Asia. But soon the English realized this was a new land, so the queen sent **Sir Francis Drake** to round the tip of South America and explore its west coast. He stopped in California, then sailed north looking for a passage back to the Atlantic. He gave up, headed west back to England, and became second to circumnavigate the globe. Dutch-born **Henry Hudson** was also sent by England to look for a shorter route to Asia, hoping to find a hidden Northeast Passage around Europe or a Northwest Passage through the Americas. He found neither, but did explore the river we call the Hudson.

Both Giovanni da Verrazzano and Jacques Cartier were sent by France to look for a Northwest Passage. Cartier left France in 1534. He sailed up the St. Lawrence River, claiming the land along it for France.

In 1610 the Dutch paid Henry Hudson to look for the Northwest Passage again. On this voyage he explored what is now Hudson Bay.

Why do you think so many people looked for a Northwest Passage?

____

____

____

Name ______________________ Class ______________ Date ______________

Exploration and Expansion

Section 2

MAIN IDEA
The countries of Europe established colonies in the lands they had discovered, but in some cases only after violently conquering the native people who lived there.

Key Terms and People

encomienda Spanish system in which a colonist received land and Native American workers to whom he was required to teach Christianity

Hernán Cortés Spanish explorer and conqueror of Mexico's Aztec empire

conquistador Spanish term for conqueror; name for Spanish military leaders who fought against the native peoples of the Americas

Moctezuma II Aztec emperor at the time of Cortés's conquest of Mexico

Francisco Pizarro conqueror of Inca Empire in Peru for the Spanish

Atahualpa ruler of Inca Empire killed by Spanish invaders led by Pizarro

viceroys officials who ruled large areas of Spain's American colonies in the king's name

Bartolomé de Las Casas Spanish priest who criticized treatment of Native Americans, suggesting that slaves from Africa be used as laborers instead

Treaty of Tordesillas treaty signed in 1493 dividing the Americas between Spain and Portugal along an imaginary line

Taking Notes

As you read the summary, take notes about each country's colonies in a chart like this one.

Location	Description

Section Summary

SPAIN BUILDS AN EMPIRE

After European explorers reached the Americas, countries scrambled to establish colonies in the lands they had found. First, Spain settled islands in the Caribbean using the ***encomienda*** system to make the islands profitable. This system gave colonists land and Native Americans to work on it. In exchange, the colonists had to teach the workers about Christianity. Under this system Native Americans suffered from overwork, abuse, and worst of all, from diseases brought by the Europeans. Millions of natives died because they had no resistance to diseases like smallpox, tuberculosis, and measles.

Some Spaniards moved to the mainland. **Hernán Cortés**, a conqueror, or **conquistador**, led an expedition to Mexico. At the time, the emperor of the native Aztec people there was **Moctezuma II**. The Aztecs were powerful, but also disliked by many of the people they had conquered. As a result, thousands of Native Americans joined Cortés as he marched to the Aztec capital. New diseases again took their toll. In 1519 Cortés reached Tenochtitlán, the Aztec capital. The Spanish, who had the advantages of metal weapons and horses, killed the emperor. After months of fighting, Cortés took over the Aztec empire.

What contributed to the defeat of the Aztec Empire?

____

____

____

____

Soon after this, **Francisco Pizarro** led an expedition to Peru in search of the wealthy Inca empire. The empire had recently suffered an outbreak of smallpox which led to unrest. In 1532 its new emperor, **Atahualpa**, met with Pizarro, who demanded he accept Christianity and hand over his empire to Spain. Though Atahualpa gave Pizarro gold and silver, the Spanish killed him, then took over.

Spain's king used officials called **viceroys** to rule the colonies. The colonial economy was based on mining and farming. Native Americans were forced to do the work, but disease and mistreatment killed over 90 percent of them. Some Spaniards such as priest **Bartolomé de Las Casas** protested the mistreatment of natives. Instead, he recommended using African slaves. Slaves were soon being used in the Americas.

Which two major Native American empires were conquered by Spain?

____

____

THE PORTUGUESE IN BRAZIL

The 1493 **Treaty of Tordesillas** drew an imaginary line through the Atlantic. Everything to the west of it belonged to Spain, to the east to Portugal. This left Portugal with only Brazil in the Americas. The first colonists to Brazil in the 1530s established farms like those of the Spanish. To do the work they first used Native Americans and then enslaved Africans.

Underline the terms of the Treaty of Tordesillas.

FRENCH, DUTCH, AND ENGLISH COLONIES IN THE AMERICAS

Inspired by the wealth of Portugal and Spain, other countries founded American colonies. New France, or Canada, had been founded by Jacques Cartier. Instead of gold, the French found trade goods there: fish and furs. Small groups of French traders moved to the colony and allied with Native Americans. French explorers also claimed new lands to the south. Samuel de Champlain founded Quebec in 1608. René-Robert La Salle canoed the entire Mississippi River down to the Gulf of Mexico, claiming all the region for France and naming it Louisiana after his king, Louis XIV.

The only large Dutch colony in North America was New Netherland, in the Hudson River Valley. In 1626 the Dutch bought the island of Manhattan, where it founded the city of New Amsterdam, which later became New York City. The settlement remained small because the Dutch were more focused on their more profitable colonies in the Caribbean and southeast Asia than the city of New Amsterdam.

Why did the Dutch colony in North America remain small?

____

____

____

The first English colony was Jamestown, Virginia, established in 1607. In 1620, Pilgrims established a colony in Plymouth, Massachusetts. Both colonies received aid from Native Americans, but English colonists treated them with distrust and violence. The English also angered French settlers by trying to settle in French territory. War broke out in 1754. Native Americans allied with the French, so the English called this the French and Indian War. Eventually, France surrendered Canada and all of their territory east of the Mississippi. When England's king tried to make colonists pay the costs of the war, which colonists resented, helping to spark the American Revolution.

How did the French and Indian war eventually lead to the American Revolution?

____

____

____

MAIN IDEA

The creation of colonies in the Americas and elsewhere led to the exchange of new types of goods, the establishment of new patterns of trade, and new economic systems in Europe.

Key Terms

Columbian Exchange the exchange of plants, animals, and diseases due to contact between the peoples of Europe and the Americas

mercantilism the European economic policy that called for nations to gain wealth in order to build a strong military and expand influence

balance of trade the amount of goods sold by a country against those purchased from other countries; a favorable balance of trade meant selling more goods than were bought

subsidies grants of money given by governments for purposes such as helping people start new businesses

capitalism economic system in which private individuals rather than governments perform most of the economic activity, with the goal of making a profit

joint-stock company a company in which investors buy shares of stock, receiving a portion of the profits, but only losing the amount of their investment if it failed

Taking Notes

As you read the summary, take notes on the Columbian Exchange, mercantilism, and capitalism in a graphic organizer like this one.

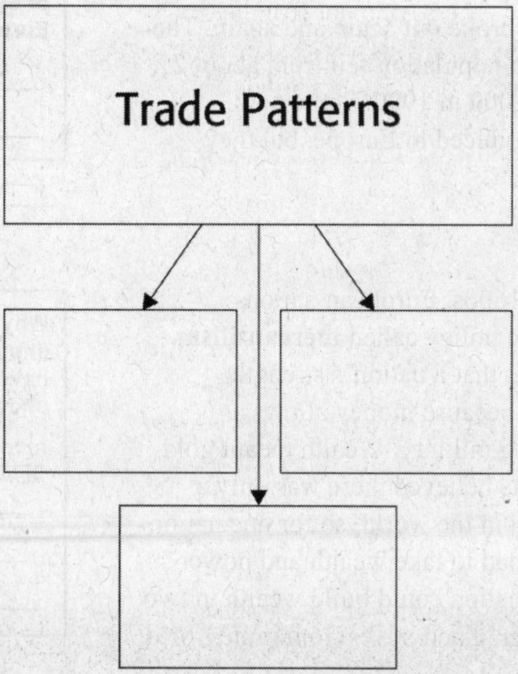

Section Summary

THE COLUMBIAN EXCHANGE

The arrival of Europeans in the Americas led to changes in both Native American and European culture. A widespread exchange of plants, animals, and diseases we call the **Columbian Exchange** took place. New foods from the colonies appeared in Europe, while colonists brought their familiar foods to the New World. Before contact with the Americas, Europeans had not known potatoes, turkey, corn, or chocolate, and Native Americans did not have coffee, rice, oranges, wheat, sheep, or cattle. Europeans also brought horses, which became a new source of labor and transportation for Native Americans.

This exchange affected societies over time. Crops native to the Americas such as potatoes and corn became staples in the European diet. Italians began cooking with tomatoes. And economic activities like cattle ranching in Texas would not have happened without this exchange. It was not entirely beneficial, however. The Irish became so dependent on the potato that when crops failed in the 1840s, millions starved.

Also disastrous was the introduction of new diseases in the Americas. Native Americans had no resistance to European diseases like smallpox, measles, influenza, and malaria. Epidemics following the Europeans' arrival broke out again and again. The North American Indian population fell from about 2 million in 1492 to 500,000 in 1900. Some new diseases were also introduced to Europe, but they were much less deadly.

What were the long-term effects of the Columbian Exchange?

____

____

____

What new diseases appeared for the first time in the Americas as a result of the arrival of Europeans?

____

____

MERCANTILISM

During the 1500s and 1600s, European nations developed an economic policy called **mercantilism**. The basic principle was that a nation's strength depends on its wealth, because money allows a country to have a strong military. Wealth meant gold and silver. Mercantilists believed there was only a fixed amount of wealth in the world, so for one nation to become wealthy, it had to take wealth and power from other nations. A nation could build wealth in two ways: it could extract gold and silver from mines, or it

Why do you think it was important for a country to have a strong military under mercantilism?

____

____

____

____

could sell more goods than it bought from other countries. This created a favorable **balance of trade**, meaning that a country received more gold and silver than it paid out. To achieve this, countries used tariffs, or import taxes, to make these goods more expensive and less desirable to the population. They could also make high-priced goods to sell to other countries. Manufactured goods sold for more than raw materials, so governments paid **subsidies** or grants to help grow industries. Finally, nations could create a favorable balance of trade by controlling sources of raw materials found in their colonies.

Colonies also served as markets for manufactured goods. Mercantilists believed that colonies only existed for the benefit of the home country. Economic activity in the colonies was restricted. Colonists could only sell raw materials to their home nation, and could only buy manufactured goods from there as well. And colonies could not manufacture their own goods.

In Europe, towns grew as business increased. A powerful merchant class emerged. But rural life continued as it had for centuries, and most people remained poor.

What did governments gain from paying subsidies to help industries?

____

____

____

THE RISE OF CAPITALISM

During this period, **capitalism** emerged. In this system, most economic activity is carried out by individuals or organizations in hopes of making a profit. Individuals began to build huge fortunes. Merchants who carried goods between colonies and home nations became rich, allowing them to invest in more ventures. Economic activity increased.

Investors were willing to take these risks because of inflation, the rise in prices of goods. This was caused by two things: the increasing demand for goods as populations grew, and the introduction of more gold and silver into the money supply.

Underline two causes for inflation.

If business ventures were too expensive for individuals, they could buy shares in **joint-stock companies**, earning a portion of the profit if it was successful and only losing as much as they invested if it failed. The Virginia Company was a joint-stock company which paid to establish the colony of Jamestown in 1607.

MAIN IDEA

Between the 1500s and the 1800s, millions of Africans were captured, shipped across the Atlantic Ocean, and sold as slaves in the Americas.

Key Terms and People

plantation estates in the Americas where cash crops were grown on a large scale

triangular trade trading network that brought goods from Europe to Africa to be traded for slaves, took the slaves to the Americas to be sold, then brought American goods back to Europe

Middle Passage name for the second leg of the triangle, bringing captive Africans to the Americas, where they were sold as slaves

Olaudah Equiano African who wrote about the horrific conditions Africans endured on Middle Passage voyages

African Diaspora the spread of people of African descent throughout the Americas and Western Europe as a result of the slave trade, eventually spreading African culture throughout the Western world

Taking Notes

As you read the summary, use a graphic organizer like this one to take notes on the origins, process, and effects of the slave trade.

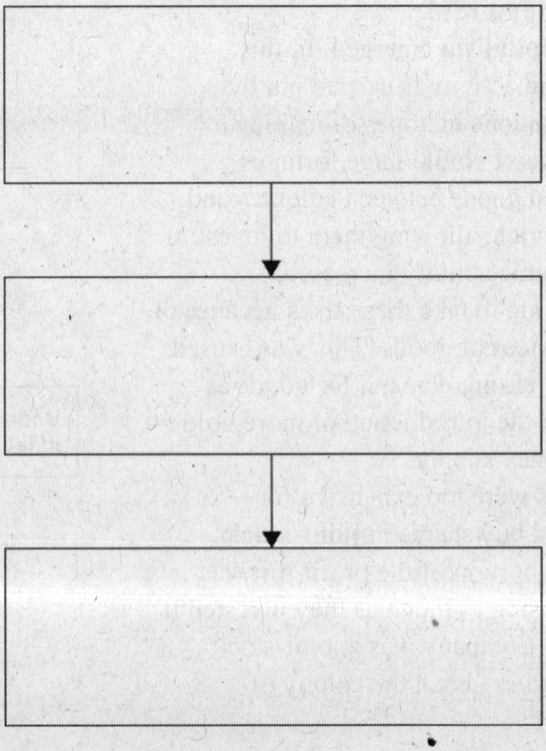

Section Summary

ORIGINS OF THE SLAVE TRADE

Throughout history, slavery has existed in many parts of the world, and the people forced into slavery have come from many walks of life. Slavery in the Americas started because of a shortage of labor. **Plantations**, large farming estates, required many workers. The European planters had first used Native Americans to do the work, but disease and warfare killed millions of them. In the 1600s, planters brought in indentured servants from Europe to work. But they needed even more workers, so they soon turned to enslaved Africans.

Why didn't the use of indentured servants solve the labor problems of plantations?

____

____

Millions of Africans were taken to the Americas before the slave trade ended in the 1800s. Most came from the coast of West Africa. Some were supplied by African rulers in exchange for European goods, while others were kidnapped by Europeans during raids. The Africans who were taken became part of the **triangular trade**, the trading network in which European goods went to Africa in exchange for slaves, slaves were shipped to the Americas, and then American products were brought back to Europe. The step during which Africans were sent to America is referred to as the **Middle Passage**. Some slaves were taken by slave traders from the Americas and were not part of the triangular trade.

What was the third part of triangular trade?

____

____

____

The journey to America was terrifying and miserable for the Africans. They were chained together and forced into dark, cramped spaces below the deck. We know of these conditions thanks to Africans such as **Olaudah Equiano**, who later wrote about the experience. The journey usually took three to six weeks, and as many as one in four of the Africans did not live through the voyage. When those who survived finally arrived in America, their suffering continued.

SLAVERY IN THE COLONIES

Slaves went to many parts of the Americas. Spanish traders took them to the Caribbean to work on sugar plantations. The Portuguese brought millions to Brazil. By the end of the 1600s, England dominated the trade. They brought most of their captives to the West Indies, but also brought many to North America. Most enslaved Africans worked on plantations, but some worked in mines, in towns, and in the country. Those who knew crafts like metalworking often continued using those skills. Sometimes women worked as servants or cooks. Enslaved people had to meet their own basic needs at the end of the long work day.

What jobs did slaves do?

____

____

____

Because slaveholders lived in fear that the slaves would rebel, they used brutal punishment for even minor offenses. Slaves had no rights or freedoms because by law, they were considered property. Slaveholders controlled the conditions under which slaves lived, and often abused them. The enslaved Africans coped in different ways. Some tried to keep their cultural traditions alive, while others turned to religion for strength. Some slaves resisted by working slowly or destroying equipment. At times, some slaves revolted, attacking the people holding them captive. Others ran away, forming their own communities in remote areas.

EFFECTS OF THE SLAVE TRADE

The Atlantic slave trade continued for 400 years, devastating West African society. About 20 million Africans were shipped to the Americas; millions more went to other places around the world. Unknown numbers of people died while being forced from Africa's interior or during the overseas voyage. Millions lost their freedom, and so did their descendants.

The effects of the slave trade in Africa were severe. Many of the captured were the strongest young people—potential future leaders. The slave trade also turned Africans against each other, as rulers waged wars to gain captives to sell to the Europeans. The forced labor of these Africans helped to build the American colonies instead of helping Africa.

How might the slave trade have affected the way Africans viewed their leaders?

____

____

____

____

The slave trade led to the **African Diaspora**, the spread of people of African descent throughout the Americas and Western Europe. This helped spread African culture—art, music, religion, and food—throughout the Western world.

Name ______________________ Class ______________ Date ______________

New Asian Empires

Chapter Summary

Ottoman Empire	
Strength Sultans practiced religious and cultural tolerance to conquered peoples.	**Weakness** The strict social hierarchy gave citizens few freedoms.

Mughal Empire	
Strength The first shahs were generous and tolerant to conquered peoples.	**Weakness** Later rulers' cruelty and intolerance led to ethnic and religious conflict.

Ming Dynasty	
Strength Emperors had absolute rule and no challenge to their authority.	**Weakness** Absolute rule led to lazy emperors and government corruption.

Japanese Shogunates	
Strength Shoguns ruled following a strict code of ethics, leading to unity and peace.	**Weakness** Strict social system and high taxes led to revolts by farmers and urban dwellers.

COMPREHENSION AND CRITICAL THINKING

Use information from the graphic organizer to answer the following questions.

1. **Identify** What titles were given to rulers in each of the four empires?

____

____

2. **Cause and Effect** How did Japanese shoguns' strict rule have both positive and negative effects on Japanese society?

____

____

3. **Elaborate** How do you think life changed for ethnic and religious minorities under later Mughal shahs?

____

____

4. **Predict** How might the Ming Dynasty have changed in order to survive?

____

____

Name ______________________ Class ______________ Date ______________

MAIN IDEA
The Ottoman and Safavid empires flourished under powerful rulers who expanded the territory and cultural influence of their empires.

Key Terms and People

ghazis nomadic, militaristic "warriors for the Islam faith"

Ottomans Western name for Osman I and his descendants

sultan the Arabic term for "ruler"

Janissaries enslaved Christian boys who were converted to Islam and trained as elite soldiers, loyal only to the sultan

Mehmed II sultan at the time of the Ottoman Empire's spectacular phase of expansion, conquered Constantinople and made it his capital

Suleyman I sultan whose rule brought the Ottoman Empire to its height

shah Persian title for "king," leader of the Safavid Empire

'Abbas greatest shah of the Safavid Empire

Taking Notes

As you read the summary, take notes in a graphic organizer like this one to record key facts about the Ottoman and Safavid empires.

Ottoman	Safavid

Section Summary

THE OTTOMAN EMPIRE

In the early 1300s, Anatolia was flanked by the Byzantine and Muslims empires. The warlike, nomadic Muslim Turks of Anatolia were Muslim. They thought of themselves as ***ghazis***, or "warriors for the Islam faith." By 1300, the *ghazi* leader Osman I built a strong state in Anatolia. He and his descendants were called **Ottomans** by Westerners.

Osman's son Orhan I declared himself **sultan**, an Arabic term for "ruler." Ottoman forces attacked the Byzantine Empire in the Balkans, then in 1361 they took the important Byzantine city Adrianople and made it their capital, Edirne. Soon, the Ottomans became a true empire and a European power.

Identify the reasons for the Ottomans' military success.

____

____

____

The Ottomans succeeded due to their military, which contained enslaved Christian boys converted to Islam and trained as elite soldiers called **Janissaries**. The Ottomans also used gunpowder cannons, which enabled them to invade heavily walled cities.

Timur (TEEM-uhr), also known as Timur the Lame because of an old leg injury, was a great Central Asian conqueror who attacked the Ottomans in 1402. His army crushed Ottoman forces at the Battle of Ankara, then withdrew, leaving the empire in shambles.

Following this decline, Sultan **Mehmed II** conquered Constantinople, the great Byzantine capital, in 1453. In 1514, the Ottomans defeated the Safavids in Persia, then swept through Syria, Egypt, and the holy Islamic cities of Mecca and Medina.

The Ottoman Empire reached its height under **Suleyman I** (soo-lay-MAHN), known in the West as Suleyman "the Magnificent." During his reign, from 1520 to 1566, Ottoman forces pushed through Hungary up to Vienna and gained control of the eastern Mediterranean and the North African coast. Suleyman reformed the tax system and government bureaucracy, improving the court system and issuing laws to reduce corruption. Architects built grand mosques and palaces, and culture reached its peak.

Why do you think Westerners called Suleyman "the Magnificent"?

____

____

____

Two classes existed in Ottoman society, the privileged ruling class that included the sultan, and everyone else. Non-Muslims had to pay heavy taxes, but they did not have to serve in the military. Non-Muslims also formed millets, or religious communities where they could follow their own religious laws.

After Suleyman's reign, the Ottoman Empire gradually declined, in part because of the practice of new sultans killing their brothers to eliminate rivals. After the 1600s, they locked up princes in the royal palace instead. But when the prince was finally released to become sultan, he had no experience with governing. Despite a series of weak sultans, the empire lasted until the early 1900s.

What did the Ottomans require of non-Muslims in the empire?

____

____

THE SAFAVID EMPIRE

The founder of the Safavid Empire was a 14-year-old boy named Esma'il (is-mah-EEL). In 1501, he led an army of supporters on a sweep of conquest in Persia. A series of victories gave him control of what is now Iran and part of Iraq. Esma'il then took the Persian title of **shah**, or "king," of the Safavid Empire. He made Shiism the official Safavid religion even though most people in the empire were Sunnis.

Circle the official Safavid religion. Were most of the people in the Safavid empire Shia or Sunni Muslims?

____

____

____

The blending of Shia religion and Persian tradition gave the Safavid state a unique identity and laid the foundation for the national culture of present-day Iran. Shiism also separated the Safavid state from its Sunni neighbors, the Ottomans and the Uzbeks.

The Ottomans defeated Esma'il at the Battle of Chaldiran in 1514 by using gunpowder weapons. Later Safavid shahs struggled to keep the empire together. Then in 1588 the greatest Safavid leader, **'Abbas**, became shah. He reformed the government, strengthened the military, and acquired modern gunpowder weapons. He also had slave youths captured in Russia trained to be soldiers. Under his rule, the Safavids defeated the Uzbeks and gained back land lost to the Ottomans.

Why was 'Abbas considered the greatest Safavid leader?

____

____

____

____

'Abbas's achievements produced a golden age in Safavid culture. Glazed tiles and ceramics, graceful arches, lush gardens, and domes were created. Products like hand-woven Persian carpets brought wealth that helped establish the empire as a major Muslim civilization. The empire lasted until 1722.

Name ______________________ Class ______________ Date ______________

MAIN IDEA
Mughal rulers created a powerful empire in which military might and artistic culture flourished.

Key Terms and People

Babur conqueror who defeated the rulers of Delhi and established the Mughal Empire

Mughal Empire India's first Muslim empire, widely known for its wealth and power

Akbar the Great Babur's grandson, greatest of all Mughal rulers

Sikhism religion founded in the late 1400s, blending elements of Islam and Hinduism

Shah Jahan Mughal ruler during the empire's cultural golden age

Taj Mahal greatest example of Mughal architecture

Aurangzeb Shah Jahan's son; Mughal leader known for expanding the empire and imposing his strict Sunni Muslim views on society

Taking Notes

As you read the summary, take notes in a graphic organizer like the one on the growth, government, arts, and society of the Mughal Empire.

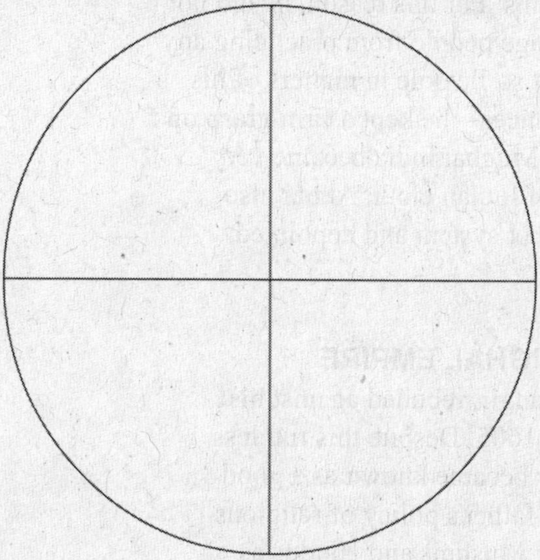

Section Summary

MUSLIM RULE IN INDIA

After the fall of the Gupta Empire in the late 500s, small kingdoms emerged. Over time, Muslim traders settled peacefully in Indian towns. By the early 700s, Muslim raiders began to conquer Indian. Those who took control of north India called their government the Delhi sultanate. A new culture formed that blended Muslim and Indian elements.

Which two religious groups were in contact before and during the Mughal Empire?

____

A NEW EMPIRE

By 1526, the young Central Asian conqueror **Babur** defeated the rulers of Delhi and established the **Mughal Empire**. It was India's first Muslim empire and one of the great civilizations of history.

Babur's grandson **Akbar the Great** rose to power in 1556 at age 13. Akbar would become the greatest of all Mughal rulers. By about 1600, Akbar ruled most of India. Akbar's policy of religious tolerance came from his belief that no single religion—including Islam, which he grew up practicing—could provide all the answers to life's problems. For this reason, he did not discriminate or discourage people from practicing any religion. But he was not so flexible in matters of his government and its finances—he kept a firm grasp on both. During his reign, Mughal India became very wealthy from the sale of Indian cloth. Akbar also reformed the empire's tax system and appointed officials to monitor it.

Summarize the policies that made Akbar the greatest Muslim ruler.

____

____

HEIGHT OF THE MUGHAL EMPIRE

Akbar's oldest son, Jahangir, rebelled against his father to gain power in 1605. Despite this ruthless path to power, Jahangir became known as a good ruler. He continued his father's policy of religious tolerance by appointing Muslims and Hindus as officials. He also supported writers and artists and adopted many Persian customs into Indian society that were inspired by his Persian wife.

Despite his religious tolerance, Jahangir came into conflict with a religious group known as the Sikhs (SEEKS), some of whom had supported a rebellion that tried to overthrow him. **Sikhism**, which had been founded in the late 1400s, blended elements of Islam and Hinduism. Like Muslims, Sikhs believe that there is only one God who created the world. But unlike Muslims, Sikhs believe in the Hindu concept of reincarnation. They also do not practice rituals from earlier religions such as pilgrimage and yoga.

How is Sikhism similar to Islam? How is it different?

____

____

____

Jahangir's son **Shah Jahan** succeeded him. During his reign, the Mughal Empire entered a golden age of art and architecture. The greatest example of Mughal architecture, the **Taj Mahal**, was built as a tomb for his beloved wife. It displays elements of Indian, Persian, and Muslim architectural styles.

The cost of building monuments such as the Taj Mahal was enormous. To pay for them, Shah Jahan imposed heavy taxes on the people of India. He demanded half of all crops grown in the country, which led to widespread hardship and famine. Adding to Shah Jahan's need for money was a series of wars he launched against India's neighbors. Many of these wars were fought in the name of Islam against Christians and Hindus. Unlike his father and grandfather, Shah Jahan was a Muslim who did not believe in tolerance.

Why did Shah Jahan impose heavy taxes on the people of India?

____

____

____

Shah Jahan's son **Aurangzeb** seized power in 1657, after jailing his father and killing his brother. Aurangzeb expanded India's borders and imposed his strict Sunni Muslim views on society. He issued decrees about morality and personal behavior and appointed officials to enforce them. He also persecuted Hindus and Sikhs, taxing them, forbidding them high positions in government, and destroying their temples.

Although Aurangzeb had enlarged the Mughal Empire, his actions marked the beginning of its end. Due to his restrictions and persecution of his subjects, frequent rebellions broke out in the later 1600s. When he died, rival claims to the throne led to civil war. Soon, invaders poured into India from the north.

Despite this disorder, the Mughals held on to power for about 150 more years. Eventually, India fell to the British—it became a colony in their empire.

Approximately how long did the Mughal Empire last?

____

Name ______________________ Class ______________ Date ______________

MAIN IDEA

During the Ming and Qing dynasties China prospered, but the empire entered a period of isolation in response to increasing European contact.

Key People

Hongwu name taken by the founder of the Ming dynasty, meaning "vastly martial"

Yonglo Hongwu's son, the Ming emperor who moved the capital to Beijing

Zheng He Chinese Muslim admiral who led seven journeys around the Indian Ocean

Matteo Ricci Italian Jesuit priest who introduced Christianity and European learning in mathematics and science to the Chinese

Kangxi Qing emperor who expanded the empire to its largest size by conquering Taiwan, Mongolia, and Tibet

Qianlong grandson of Kangxi who brought the Qing dynasty to its height

Lord George Macartney British official who failed to establish a trading relationship with China in 1793

Taking Notes

As you read the summary, use a graphic organizer like the one below to take notes on the Ming and Qing dynasties and their culture.

Ming	Qing

Section Summary

THE MING DYNASTY

After the death of emperor Kublai Khan, the Mongol dynasty in China weakened. In 1368, a peasant overthrew the last Mongol emperor, took the name **Hongwu** (meaning "vastly martial"), and founded the Ming Dynasty. It lasted for nearly three centuries.

Hongwu reduced taxes and passed reforms to improve agriculture and trade. In addition, he worked to revive traditional Chinese values and practices, such as Confucian principles. He also improved the civil service examination system and fought to end corruption.

What actions did Hongwu take that may have pleased the Chinese people?

____

____

____

Hongwu expanded his power as emperor by eliminating the positions of some high-level officials and taking greater control of the government. In 1402 Hongwu's son **Yonglo** (yung-loh) became emperor. Yonglo made Beijing the new capital of China, and built a vast imperial complex within the city. This complex, which was surrounded by high walls, became known as the Forbidden City because most people were not allowed to enter it.

Which Ming emperor moved the Chinese capital to Beijing?

____

To extend China's influence, Yonglo directed Chinese Muslim admiral **Zheng He** (juhng HUH) to lead seven voyages around the Indian Ocean as far as Africa. In the 1500s, however, the Ming heavily restricted foreign trade and travel to limit outside contacts. One reason for this decision to isolate China was the arrival of European traders and Christian missionaries. Still, a few Europeans such as **Matteo Ricci** (mah-TAY-oh REE-chee) were allowed to visit the royal court. Ricci was an Italian Jesuit priest who introduced Christianity and European learning in mathematics and science to the Chinese.

A renewed Mongol threat led the Chinese to restore and extend the Great Wall. They also developed better irrigation methods, and planted new crops such as corn and sweet potatoes from the Americas. As a result, their farm output increased. Plentiful food and stability led to population growth. Though its cities grew, China remained primarily an agricultural society.

What led to population growth in China?

____

____

In the late 1500s, several weak rulers took the throne. As defense efforts drained the treasury, the rulers raised taxes. High taxes combined with crop failures in the 1600s led to famine and hardship. Rebellions broke out. As Ming China weakened, the Manchu, a people from the northwest, in Manchuria, seized Beijing. In 1644 they formed their own dynasty—the Qing (ching).

What events caused the Ming Dynasty to weaken? List at least three.

____

____

____

THE QING DYNASTY

The Manchu rulers used most of the Ming government structure. To win the support of the Chinese, the Manchu respected Chinese customs and traditions, and equally distributed government positions to the Chinese and Manchu. Some rules, however, were put in place to keep the two people separated.

Qing China flourished under two outstanding emperors: **Kangxi** (kahng-shee) and his grandson **Qianlong** (chyahn-lung). Kangxi reduced taxes for peasants and expanded the empire into parts of Central Asia. He also supported the arts and learned about science and other areas from Jesuit priests.

Qianlong brought the Qing dynasty to its height. From 1736 to 1796, he expanded the Chinese empire to its largest size by conquering Taiwan, Mongolia, and Tibet. During his reign, agricultural production continued to rise; and China's population boomed.

Circle the name of the Qing emperor who expanded the Chinese empire to its largest size. Underline the territories this emperor conquered.

Qianlong continued to restrict foreign trade, demanding that trade occur on their terms. Agreeing with these terms, Dutch traders obtained Chinese porcelain, silk, and teas. However, the Chinese sent away a British official named **Lord George Macartney**. In the 1800s this policy of isolation prevented the Chinese from keeping up with European advances. European efforts to open China's closed society eventually toppled the Qing dynasty.

MING AND QING CULTURE

The arts and literature grew under Ming and Qing rule. Exquisite porcelain that became a valuable trade item was produced, and rising literacy rates contributed to the growth of short stories and the first Chinese novels.

MAIN IDEA

During the medieval period, a feudal warrior society developed in Japan, while Korea's rulers endured invasion and turned to isolation.

Key Terms and People

samurai a trained professional warrior during Japan's feudal age

Bushido "the way of the warrior," samurai code of ethics

Zen Buddhism form of Buddhism that stresses discipline and meditation

shogun supreme military leader who ruled in the name of Japan's emperor

daimyo Japanese lord who held large estates, controlled their own territories, and battled for power

Tokugawa Ieyasu was made shogun in 1603, after winning complete control of Japan

haiku Japanese form of poetry that consists of three lines with 17 syllables

kabuki type of Japanese theater that had singing, dancing, and audience interaction

Yi Song-gye general who gained control of Korea and established the Choson kingdom

Taking Notes

As you read the summary, use a graphic organizer like the one below to take notes Japan's warrior society, the Tokugawa shogunate, and medieval Korea.

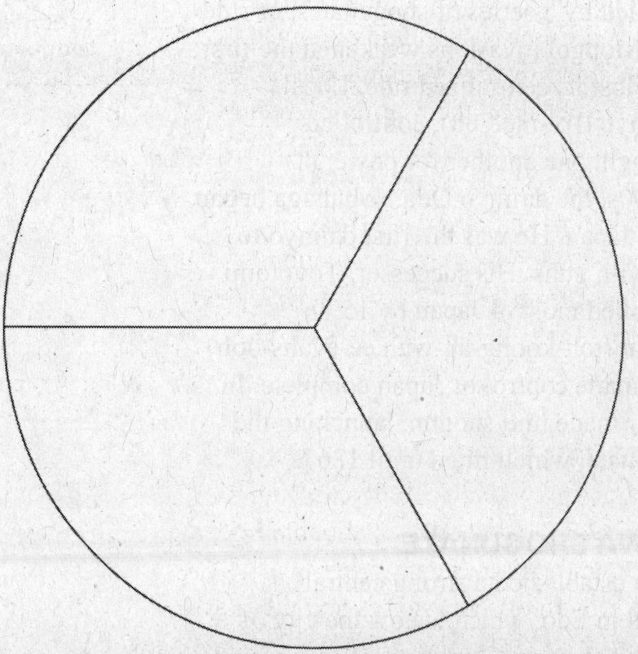

Section Summary

JAPAN'S WARRIOR SOCIETY

By the 1100s Japan's central government had begun to lose control of the empire. Local clans began to fight each other for power and land. Law and order gave way to conflict and chaos, and bandits roamed the countryside. For protection, large landowners hired armies of **samurai** (SA-muh-ry), trained professional warriors. Samurai had to follow a strict code of ethics known as **Bushido** (BOOH-shi-doh). Bushido required samurai to be courageous, honorable, obedient, and most of all loyal. Samurai who failed to obey or protect their lord were expected to commit suicide rather than live with their shame.

Why did landowners hire samurai?

____

____

The Samurai practiced **Zen Buddhism**, a form of Buddhism that spread from China to Japan in the 1100s. It stressed discipline and meditation to focus the mind and gain wisdom. Women in the samurai class were trained in the martial arts and followed Bushido. Women could also inherit property and participate in business.

What were the duties and privileges of women in the samurai class?

____

____

From the late-1100s to the mid-1800s, the real power in the Japanese government was held by the **shogun** rather than the emperor. The shogun was the supreme military leader who ruled in the emperor's name. Japan was led by a series of shogunates, or rule by shoguns. The Mongol invasions weakened the first shogunate. Japan lost its centralized rule. Local warlords, or **daimyo** (DY-mee-oh), controlled territories and fought one another for power.

During the 1500s, the daimyo Oda Nobunaga began to take control of Japan. He was the first daimyo to arm his soldiers with guns. His successor, Toyotomi Hideyoshi, controlled most of Japan by 1590. **Tokugawa Ieyasu** (toh-koohg-ah-wuh ee-eyahs-ooh) won a battle that made control of Japan complete. In 1603, the emperor made him shogun, launching the Tokugawa Shogunate, which ruled until 1867.

THE TOKUGAWA SHOGUNATE

Tokugawa Ieyasu established a strong central government based in Edo, which is now the city of Tokyo. Under the Tokugawa, Japan enjoyed a period of relative unity and peace. To keep daimyos loyal, they were required to live from time to time in Edo, but their families had to live there year-round.

Japan's population and cities grew, and economic activity increased. New roads further improved trade. The Tokugawa rulers created a strict social structure. The warrior class was the emperor (mostly a figurehead), shogun, daimyo, and samurai. Below the warrior class were three classes: peasants, artisans, and merchants. Members of these classes could not rise in status, nor serve in the military or government.

Underline the four social classes under Tokugawa rule. Which class included farmers?

____

Most Japanese were peasant farmers. They enjoyed a relatively high social position but lived with hardship due to high taxes. Artisans had higher status than merchants because they made things. During this period, women's status declined. Many ronin, or masterless samurai, learned to get by in peacetime as farmers, warriors-for-hire, or bandits.

Japan made greater contact with Europeans, who brought new ideas, products, and technologies. Christian missionaries began converting some Japanese, which so worried the shoguns that they restricted foreign trade and travel. Shunning European influence, Japan shut its doors to all Europeans except the Dutch by the 1650s. The country remained isolated for more than 200 years.

How was Japan affected by contact with Westerners?

____

____

Culturally, a form of poetry called **haiku** became popular. A haiku consists of three lines with 17 syllables. Many haiku deal with themes of nature and harmony. In theater, Japanese audiences turned to **kabuki**. Actors in kabuki plays sang, danced, and interacted with audience members.

MEDIEVAL KOREA

In 1392 a powerful general named **Yi Song-gye** gained control of Korea and established the Choson kingdom, also called the Yi dynasty. In the late 1500s the Choson defeated two Japanese invasions with the help of Ming China. Then, in the early 1600s, the Chinese invaded Korea and made it a vassal state. The Choson kings increasingly isolated Korea from the world except for trade with China. Still, Korea prospered and produced cultural achievements, such as the creation of a Korean alphabet.

Who helped the Choson defeat the Japanese?

____

Name ______________________ Class ______________ Date ______________

The Monarchs of Europe

Chapter Summary

Spain experienced a golden age in the 1500s, largely due to the wealth from its American colonies. Spanish art and culture thrived. But economic problems and military struggles, such as the Dutch revolt and the destruction of the Spanish Armada, decreased Spanish power by the 1600s.

The first three Bourbon kings gradually strengthened **France's** monarchy, with Louis XIV setting the example of an absolute monarch for the rest of Europe. At the same time, France experienced conflict between the Catholic majority and the Huguenots, French Protestants.

Europe's Monarchies

Parliament's power and influence increased as absolute monarchy declined in **England**. Parliament demanded more and more control over the government. Monarchs resisted, leading to civil war and the end of monarchy. Parliament later restored the monarchy but maintained power.

The czars of **Russia** ruled with absolute power, while the Hapsburg and Hohenzollern families battled for control of Central Europe. The great Russian rulers expanded their lands and made reforms. After the Thirty Years' War, Prussia rose as a power to challenge the Hapsburgs of Austria.

COMPREHENSION AND CRITICAL THINKING

Use information from the graphic organizer to answer the following questions.

1. **Explain** What happened to the monarchy in England?

____

____

2. **Make Inferences** Why do you think Spain's power decreased even though it was wealthy?

____

____

3. **Rank** Which of these monarchies would you most want to live in? Explain why.

____

____

Section 1

MAIN IDEA

Spain experienced a golden age in the 1500s, but economic problems and military struggles decreased Spanish power by the 1600s.

Key Terms and People

absolute monarch ruler whose power was not limited by having to consult with anyone before making decisions

divine right the belief that monarchs received their power directly from God

Charles V member of the Hapsburg family, king of Spain, and Holy Roman Emperor

Peace of Augsburg treaty signed by Charles in 1555, which gave each German prince the right to decide whether his state would be Catholic or Protestant

Philip II son of Charles I, king of the Netherlands, Spain, Sicily, and Spain's American colonies

El Greco Greek painter who often painted religious subjects

Diego Velázquez Spanish painter whose impressionistic style influenced other artists

Miguel de Cervantes Spanish author of *Don Quixote de la Mancha*

Sister Juana Ines de la Cruz Mexican nun who wrote poetry, prose, and plays

Spanish Armada Spain's fleet of about 130 ships and over 20,000 soldiers

Taking Notes

As you read the summary, take notes in a graphic organizer like the one below. Record examples of Spain's strengths and weaknesses during the 1500s and 1600s.

Strengths	
Weaknesses	

Section Summary

THE KING BECOMES EMPEROR

In 1516, a member of the powerful Hapsburg family became King Charles I of Spain. Like many other European rulers from 1500 through the 1700s, Charles was an **absolute monarch**—a ruler whose power was not limited by having to consult with anyone before making decisions. These rulers believed that they ruled by **divine right**, meaning that their power came from God.

Charles also ruled Belgium and the Netherlands, and in 1519 he decided he wanted to be Holy Roman Emperor. This position was elected, so he paid people for their votes. He became Holy Roman Emperor as **Charles V**. Now, he held an even larger empire, including Spain, parts of Italy, Austria, the German states, and colonies in the Americas. Charles also had enemies: Ottoman Turks, the French, and rebellious German princes. He fought, unsuccessfully, to keep Europe Catholic. After years of devastating war, Charles signed the **Peace of Augsburg** in 1555. It gave German princes the right to decide whether their states would be Catholic or Protestant.

At the same time, Spanish explorers like Cortés and Coronado were conquering vast areas in the Americas. This would eventually bring Spain great wealth. In 1556, Charles stepped down from his thrones, frustrated by his failures in Europe. His brother took over the Hapsburg holdings in Austria, while his son, **Philip II**, became king of Spain, the Netherlands, Sicily, and the colonies in the Americas.

How did Charles I of Spain become Holy Roman Emperor Charles V?

____

____

____

Why do you think Charles divided his empire between his brother and his son?

____

____

____

____

ARTISTIC ACHIEVEMENTS

The mid-1500s to the mid-1600s is known as the Golden Age of Spanish art, a time when Spanish artists were influential across Europe. The work of the Greek painter **El Greco** was mostly religious, and reflected Spain's central role in the Counter-Reformation. The Spanish painter **Diego Velázquez** painted masterpieces portraying people of all social classes. **Miguel de Cervantes** was a famous writer who wrote the masterpiece *Don Quixote de la*

What was the Golden Age of Spanish art?

____

____

Mancha. Mexican nun **Sister Juana Ines de las Cruz** wrote poetry, prose, and plays.

SPAIN UNDER PHILIP II

The Spanish empire reached its peak under Philip II. The American colonies sent gold and silver home, making Spain very rich and powerful. However, money could not solve Spain's problems.

Philip II was a devout Catholic and leader of the Counter-Reformation. He saw a chance to spread Catholicism when he married Queen Mary I of England, who was also Catholic. She died, though, before she could give birth to an heir who could have returned England to the Catholic faith. Philip also wanted to secure the position of Catholicism in his European territories. But his faith clashed with the Calvinist Protestantism that was spreading through the northern provinces of the Netherlands, Belgium, and Luxembourg. A bloody revolt began in the 1560s when the Dutch refused to declare allegiance to Philip. The revolt dragged on for decades, until a truce was reached in 1609. The seven northern provinces formed the independent nation of the Netherlands, while the southern provinces remained in Spanish hands.

Why did the Dutch revolt in the 1560s? What was the outcome of the revolt?

____
____
____
____
____
____

Conflict between Spain and England grew in the 1500s. England supported the Dutch rebels and Elizabeth I allowed her ship captains to attack Spanish ships returning from the colonies with treasure. Philip decided to invade England, both to stop the raids and to return Catholicism to England. He built the **Spanish Armada**, a fleet of about 130 ships and 20,000 soldiers. In 1588, they sailed into the English Channel. Philip thought they could not be defeated. Instead, a series of accidents followed by English attacks scattered the Armada, sinking some ships and damaging others. When the remaining ships left in defeat, many of them were sunk in a storm.

The defeat of the Armada symbolized both Spain's decline and England's rise in power. But there were other reasons for Spain's decline. The king managed his government poorly and spent the wealth from the Americas on constant warfare. Also, Spain did not develop industries, and its economy lagged behind that of other countries.

Underline the reasons for Spain's decline in power.

Name ____________________ Class ____________ Date ____________

The Monarchs of Europe

Section 2

MAIN IDEA

Henry IV, Louis XIII, and Louis XIV strengthened the French monarchy, with Louis XIV setting the example of an absolute monarch for the rest of Europe.

Key Terms and People

Huguenot French Protestant

Saint Bartholomew's Day Massacre fighting begun on Saint Bartholomew's Day in 1572 between Catholics and Protestants, in which many Huguenots were killed

Henry IV Huguenot who converted to Catholicism in order to be accepted as king

Edict of Nantes proclamation by Henry IV that gave certain rights to French Huguenots but stressed that Catholicism was the official religion of France

Louis XIII French king who took the throne after Henry IV was assassinated; Cardinal Richelieu served as his adviser

Cardinal Richelieu prominent Catholic priest who became chief minister and adviser of King Louis XIII

Louis XIV French king who held absolute power, became known as "the Sun King"

War of the Spanish Succession costly war fought by Louis XIV over the successor to the Spanish throne

Treaty of Utrecht ended the War of the Spanish Succession; forced Louis XIV to give up territory and forbid France and Spain from being ruled by the same monarch

Taking Notes

As you read the summary, use a graphic organizer like the one below to take notes on how Henry IV, Louis XIII, and Louis XIV increased the power of absolute monarchy in France.

Henry IV	
Louis XIII	
Louis XIV	

Section Summary

RELIGIOUS WARS AND HENRY IV

By the 1560s, one in 10 people in France had become a **Huguenot** (HYOO-guh-NAHT), or French Protestant. In 1562, Huguenots and Catholics began a long-lasting civil war. Ten years later, hostilities took a horrible turn when the Catholic queen of France ordered the killing of Huguenots in Paris. Her assassins started with the Huguenot nobles who were in the city for the wedding of Henry of Navarre, a French nobleman. The event became known as the **Saint Bartholomew's Day Massacre**. From Paris, the violence spread to other parts of France. The final Huguenot death toll ranged from 10,000 to 70,000.

What set off the St. Bartholomew's Day Massacre?

____

____

____

____

Henry of Navarre escaped death by denying his religion. Years later, he fought to become king **Henry IV** of France. In order to be accepted, he converted to Catholicism in 1593. However, he believed the Huguenots needed certain rights in order to restore peace, so he issued the **Edict of Nantes** (NAHNT) in 1598. This allowed Huguenots limited freedom to worship as they pleased. It also stressed that Catholicism was the official religion of France.

Underline the purpose of the Edict of Nantes.

LOUIS XIII AND RICHELIEU

In 1610, Henry IV was assassinated, and the next king, **Louis XIII**, was very young. His mother served as regent. Later, **Cardinal Richelieu** (REESH-uhl-oo) became Louis XIII's most trusted adviser. One of Richelieu's goals was to strengthen the monarchy.

Richelieu's forces held the Huguenots inside the city of La Rochelle in a siege that lasted over a year. When the Huguenots finally surrendered, Richelieu ordered the walls destroyed and all churches to become Catholic. Richelieu's spies uncovered a series of planned revolts against the king by nobles, and punished those involved harshly. By such actions, Richelieu and Louis XIII worked to reduce the power of the Huguenots and the French nobles.

Why do you think Cardinal Richelieu worked so hard to strengthen the monarchy, even though he was not the king?

____

____

____

____

THE MONARCHY OF LOUIS XIV

The son of Louis XIII, **Louis XIV**, led France during a time of great power and prosperity. He became known as the Sun King. Like his father, he became king at a young age, and his mother was regent. She received advice from Cardinal Mazarin after the death of Cardinal Richelieu. But Louis XIV was more confident than his father in his own ability to rule. When Mazarin died in 1661, Louis declared that he would run the government himself, as an absolute monarch. This began a tradition of absolute monarchy in France that would last for well over a century. Louis demanded that he be in charge of all military, political, and economic initiatives. He also wanted his subjects' religion to be under his direct control.

How were Louis XIII and Louis XIV alike? How were they different?

____

____

____

____

____

____

By drawing so much power to himself and the central government, Louis deprived the nobles of influence. Their influence declined further when Louis built an enormous palace at **Versailles** (ver-SY), outside Paris, and required the nobles to visit him there. In time, about 10,000 officials, servants, and courtiers came to live in the palace.

Louis's grand lifestyle cost a great deal of money. Fortunately, France's wealth grew, largely because of the policies of Jean-Baptiste Colbert, the minister of finance. He called for limiting imports and increasing exports in order to build wealth. Colbert also changed the tax policy to maximize money coming to the government.

Another way that Louis established absolute monarchy was by smashing the power of the Huguenots once and for all. In 1685 Louis made his move. He canceled the Edict of Nantes that had protected the Huguenots, and outlawed Protestantism in his realm. Over 200,000 Huguenots fled France.

Louis wanted increased power as well as wealth. He went to war in Europe to reclaim territory that had formerly been ruled by France. His most famous war was the **War of the Spanish Succession**. The Spanish king had no heir so he had named Louis XIV's grandson, Philip V, to succeed him. But the other European powers did not want France and Spain to be so closely connected, so they went to war against both countries. After many years of fighting, Philip remained king of Spain, but in the **Treaty of Utrecht**, France had to give up much of the territory it had wanted to claim.

Did the War of the Spanish Succession allow Louis XIV to increase his power and wealth? Why or why not?

____

____

____

Name ______________________ Class ______________ Date ______________

The Monarchs of Europe

Section 3

MAIN IDEA
In contrast to the absolute monarchies of Spain and France, the English monarchy was limited by Parliament; following a civil war, Parliament became even more powerful.

Key Terms and People

Puritans Protestant religious group that demanded reforms in the Church of England

Charles I son of James I, became king in 1625

Royalists supporters of the king during the English Civil War

Oliver Cromwell commander of Parliament's army in the Civil War, later Lord Protector

commonwealth republican government based on the common good of all people

Restoration the return of the monarchy to England in 1660

Charles II son of Charles I, became king of Great Britain when monarchy was restored

Glorious Revolution bloodless transfer of power from James II to William and Mary

William and Mary James II's Protestant daughter and son-in-law, who succeeded him

constitutional monarchy a monarchy limited by law

Taking Notes

As you read the summary, take notes in a graphic organizer like the one below about the decreasing power of the monarchy and increasing power of Parliament.

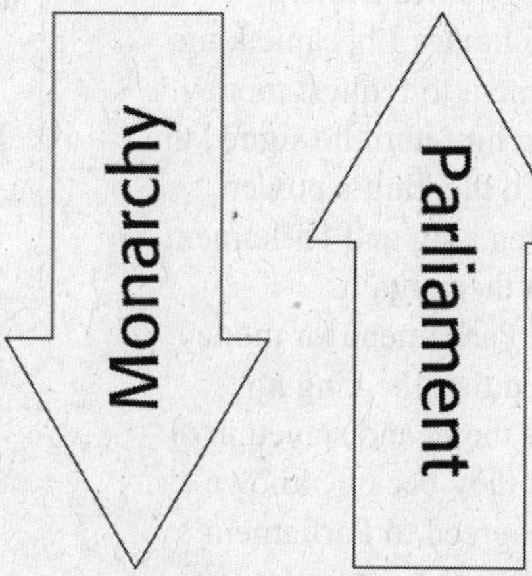

Section Summary

THE TUDORS AND PARLIAMENT

To convert England to Protestantism, Henry VIII had teamed up with Parliament. In 1534, the Act of Supremacy named the king the head of England's official church, the Church of England.

Henry's daughter Mary briefly returned England to Catholicism. When her sister Elizabeth became queen, Elizabeth had to re-establish the Church of England. She worked well with Parliament, but she strongly believed in her divine right to be queen. In 1601, a noble rebelled against her authority. He was quickly brought to trial, but this showed a growing tendency to question the monarchy.

THE ENGLISH CIVIL WAR

In 1603 Elizabeth died, and the Scottish king became James I of England. He believed in the divine right of kings, but he needed money from Parliament, who rarely gave him what he wanted. Religious tensions also troubled him. The **Puritans**, a group of strict Calvinists, wanted to lessen the power of church officials. James, who depended on the support of the church leadership, refused to pass most Puritan reforms. However, he did authorize an English version of the Bible, known as the King James Bible.

Why did the English rulers deal with Parliament even though they believed in the divine right of kings to rule?

____

____

____

____

When James died, his son **Charles I** became king. In 1628, he summoned Parliament to request money. Parliament refused to give it to him until he signed the Petition of Right, which limited the king's power. Still, conflict continued between king and Parliament. Charles decided not to consult them again.

In 1640, Charles had to ask Parliament for money again. This Parliament declared that the king no longer had the right to dismiss them, and stayed in session for so many years that they became known as the Long Parliament. Charles agreed to Parliament's demands, but planned to overturn the new rules.

In 1642, Charles interrupted Parliament in session, intending to arrest five members for treason. The men fled, but Charles's plan to take back power was revealed. Some members of Parliament decided to rise against the king, and the English Civil War began.

Supporters of the king were called **Royalists**. Parliament's army, called Roundheads, consisted of Puritans, merchants, and some gentry. Their leader was **Oliver Cromwell**, an army general and Puritan member of Parliament. After his army took control of London, he sent troops to dismiss members of Parliament who disagreed with him. The group left behind was called the Rump Parliament. They charged the king with treason and put him on trial. Charles refused to recognize the authority of the court, but he was sentenced to death, and beheaded in 1649.

The House of Commons abolished the House of Lords and the monarchy and England became a **commonwealth**, a republican government based on the common good of all people. At first, Cromwell ruled England as Lord Protector. Then in 1658 he dismissed Parliament to rule alone. He also affected English social life by closing theaters and other forms of entertainment.

Conditions during the English Civil War inspired philosopher Thomas Hobbes to write *Leviathan*, in which he described people as naturally selfish and fearful and in need of a powerful leader to rule them.

What led some members of Parliament to rise up against the king?

____

____

____

____

Why did the influence of Puritanism increase under Cromwell?

____

____

THE MONARCHY RETURNS

When Cromwell died in 1658, his son took power, but he was not a strong leader. In 1660, Parliament voted to bring back the monarchy. The **Restoration** brought **Charles II**, son of Charles I, back from exile. He supported religious toleration, reopened the theaters, and passed the Habeas Corpus Act guaranteeing that those accused of crimes had the right to appear in court. Charles's brother, a Catholic, became King **James II** in 1685. However, James was unpopular and in 1689, Parliament asked James's Protestant daughter and son-in-law to take power. James fled to France. This bloodless transfer of power was known as the **Glorious Revolution**. Parliament made the couple, **William and Mary**, agree to a new English Bill of Rights. Among other things, it kept the monarch from overruling Parliament's laws. England was now a **constitutional monarchy**, a monarchy limited by law.

Why do you think Parliament did not want James II to become king? Why do you think Charles II ignored Parliament's request?

____

____

____

____

____

____

Name ______________________ Class ______________ Date ______________

The Monarchs of Europe

Section 4

MAIN IDEA

The czars of Russia struggled with the westernization of their empire, while powerful families battled for control of Central Europe.

Key Terms and People

czar title for Russian rulers; adaptation of "caesar," used by Romans to mean "emperor"

Ivan IV Russian czar also known as Ivan the Terrible

boyars wealthy Russian landowners

Peter the Great czar who transformed Russia into a modern state

westernization the introduction of western European culture into other countries

Catherine the Great German-born wife of czar Peter III who became empress after her husband's murder

Thirty Years' War war between Catholics and Protestants in Europe, 1618–1648

Treaty of Westphalia 1648 treaty that ended the Thirty Years' War

Maria Theresa heir of Holy Roman Emperor Charles VI

Frederick the Great title earned by Frederick II as he doubled the size of Prussia

Taking Notes

As you read the summary, use a graphic organizer like the one below to take notes on Russia, including changes in territory, key people, and key events. Create a similar chart for Central Europe.

Russia
• changes in territory • key people • key events

Section Summary

THE MONARCHY OF IVAN IV

When he was 16, prince Ivan declared himself **czar** (ZAHR) or emperor of Russia. In time, he became known as **Ivan the Terrible**. At first, although an absolute ruler, he made several military and legal reforms. These reforms reduced the power of the **boyars**, the landowners. Ivan also expanded Russia's western borders by conquering the Tatars.

During the 1560s, Ivan changed. He became suspicious of his advisers. When his wife died, he believed she was murdered. He created a police force to brutally punish anyone who spoke against him, and seized land from 12,000 boyars. He also ordered the killing of thousands in the city of Novgorod. He even killed his own son and heir. When Ivan died, the lack of a successor led to chaos until 1613, when a relative of Ivan's wife became the first Romanov czar.

Why did Ivan IV become known as Ivan the Terrible?

____

____

____

PETER THE GREAT

Russia's next great czar, **Peter the Great**, worked to modernize Russia. In 1697, he traveled in disguise through western Europe. Back home, he made several changes based on what he learned; he strengthened the Russian navy, and he started to bring elements of Western culture to Russia in a process known as **westernization**. He brought the church under his control, built up industry, started the first newspaper, sponsored new schools, modernized the calendar, and promoted officials based on service. Unfortunately, he also allowed factory owners to buy and sell workers.

Peter fought the Great Northern War against Sweden with the goal of gaining a warm-water port. The war lasted from 1700 to 1721, when Peter won the land on which he built St. Petersburg, his new capital designed with western style architecture.

Name two changes Peter made based on what he learned during his travels in western Europe.

____

____

____

CATHERINE THE GREAT

Russia's next major monarch was a German princess named Sophia. She married Peter the Great's grandson Peter III, changed her name to Catherine, and converted to the Russian Orthodox religion. But Peter was soon murdered, and **Catherine the Great** was declared empress. She supported Western writers and thinkers, but ruled with absolute power.

Under Catherine, Russia fought and won a war in Poland. Catherine divided Poland between Russia and Austria. She faced a crisis when a man named Pugachev declared himself to be Peter III, not dead after all. The serfs supported him. After his capture, Catherine strengthened her authority in rural areas by reorganizing local governments and putting their administration in the hands of landowners and nobles.

Why do you think serfs supported Pugachev?

____

____

____

MONARCHY AND CONFLICT IN CENTRAL EUROPE

In 1555, the Peace of Augsburg temporarily solved the Protestant question in Central Europe. But in 1618 in Prague a Catholic official ordered the destruction of a Protestant church. Protestants reacted by throwing the Emperor's representatives out the palace windows. This began the **Thirty Years' War**, which involved most of Europe for either political or religious reasons. For example, France entered the war on the Protestant side to weaken the alliance of Spain and the Holy Roman Empire. The war ended in 1648 with the **Treaty of Westphalia**. The treaty was in general a Protestant victory that extended religious toleration. It also diminished the power of the Holy Roman Empire and strengthened the states within it.

The Hapsburgs, who had ruled Austria and the Holy Roman Empire for centuries, now had rivals—the Hohenzollern family. They began to claim towns deserted after the war, and in 1701 Frederick I became the first to take the title King of Prussia. In 1740, the Hapsburg emperor Charles VI died. Charles had planned to leave his throne to his daughter, **Maria Theresa**. Frederick II of Prussia fought the War of the Austrian Succession to prevent this. In the end, the popular Maria Theresa remained empress. But Austria had lost territory. Frederick II was known as **Frederick the Great** because he doubled the size of Prussia with his army.

In 1756 the Seven Years' War began. Prussia and Great Britain fought against Austria, France, and Russia. The war ended with both sides exhausted. However, they continued to struggle for many years.

Name three wars fought in Central Europe, who fought them, and what the outcomes were.

1. ______________________

____

____

2. ______________________

____

____

3. ______________________

____

____

Chapter Summary

New discoveries and new ways of thinking during the Scientific Revolution lead to changes in society. Scientists use reason to make important advances in the knowledge of human life and about the solar system. This challenges traditional beliefs based on the teachings of ancient Greeks and the Church.

↓

New ideas about government and society spread during the Enlightenment. Important thinkers write about human rights, equality, and the people's right to rebel against governments that do not serve them well enough. Many, including some rulers, are inspired by Enlightenment ideas.

↓

Enlightenment ideas lead to independence and a new government in the United States. The colonists, frustrated with Britain's rule, declare independence and fight for Britain to give it to them. A new form of government is created. The Constitution combines state and federal governments and a system of checks and balances.

COMPREHENSION AND CRITICAL THINKING

Use information from the graphic organizer to answer the following questions.

1. **Identify** List two important ideas introduced during the Enlightenment.

____

____

2. **Make Inferences** How do you think Enlightenment ideas contributed to the colonists' decision to fight for their independence?

____

____

3. **Make Judgments** If you had been a colonist, do you think you would have wanted to fight for independence, not knowing whether or not you would win? Explain your answer.

____

____

Enlightenment and Revolution

Section 1

MAIN IDEA
New ways of thinking led to remarkable discoveries during the Scientific Revolution.

Key Terms and People

geocentric theory the theory that earth is the center of the universe, and the sun, moon, and planets revolve around earth

Scientific Revolution the posing and testing of theories about the natural world that began in the mid-1500s in Europe

scientific method a five-step process used to investigate scientific hypotheses

René Descartes French scholar who used reason – logic and math – to prove basic truths

Nicolaus Copernicus Polish astronomer who recognized the inaccuracy of the geocentric theory; his complete model of the solar system supported the heliocentric theory

heliocentric theory the theory that the sun is near the center of the universe and the earth rotates around the sun

Galileo Galilei Italian astronomer who built the first telescope and published a book that supported Galileo's heliocentric theory, and stood trial for heresy

Isaac Newton English scientist, developed the universal laws of gravity and motion

Taking Notes

As you read the summary, use a chart like this one to record details about new discoveries made during the Scientific Revolution.

New Discoveries
astronomy
telescope
physics
math

Section Summary

DAWN OF MODERN SCIENCE

For a long time, people had turned to church teachings or the writings of ancient scholars to learn about the natural world. For example, the Greek philosopher Aristotle proposed the **geocentric theory**, the idea that the earth is the center of the universe, in the 300s BC. The church agreed with this idea and it was accepted as truth for centuries.

In the mid-1500s, however, scholars began to challenge traditional beliefs. Historians call this change the **Scientific Revolution**. Exploration had introduced Europeans to places, people, and animals that the ancient scholars and the church had not known about. Exploration also required very accurate information so that people could travel across oceans without getting lost. As scientists examined the natural world more closely, they found that their discoveries did not match ancient teachings.

What was the Scientific Revolution?

____

____

____

____

Scientists invented the **scientific method**, a five-step process. First, scientists identify a problem. Next, they form a hypothesis or theory about the problem that can be tested. They then experiment to test the hypothesis. They record the results of the experiment, and finally, analyze their results to determine whether or not their hypothesis is correct. One of the developers of this method was **René Descartes** (day-KAHRT). He used math and logic to prove basic truths. Scientists use the scientific method to this day.

Underline the five steps of the scientific method.

DISCOVERIES IN ASTRONOMY, PHYSICS, AND MATH

Many early scientists focused on learning about the planet and the solar system. **Nicolaus Copernicus**, a Polish astronomer, noticed that the geocentric theory was not accurate. After years of observation, he developed a **heliocentric theory**. In it, he stated that the earth rotates in circles around the sun and that the sun is near the center of the universe. Copernicus did not publish his findings until shortly before he died. He knew that the church would not approve. Also, his mathematical formulas were not perfect. But later scientists improved on his ideas. The work of Tycho

Brahe (brah) of Denmark convinced the king to fund an observatory. Later, Brahe's assistant Johannes Kepler used Brahe's measurements of Mars's orbit to show that planets orbit in ellipses, not circles. This proved Copernicus's heliocentric theory correct.

The Italian scientist **Galileo Galilei** built the first working telescope in 1609. This tool helped him to discover the rings of Saturn and the makeup of the Milky Way. He was also the first to the craters on the moon, sunspots, and the moons of Jupiter.

Isaac Newton is perhaps the most important scientist of this era. An English scientist, he published works correctly explaining the movements of the planets and the law of gravity. He also invented calculus at the same time as Gottfried von Leibniz.

What events happened after Copernicus's heliocentric theory that enabled Kepler to confirm that it is correct?

____

____

____

DISCOVERIES IN BIOLOGY AND CHEMISTRY

For hundreds of years, no progress had been made in understanding the human body. The Flemish doctor Andreas Vesalius dissected the bodies of criminals and published drawings of what he found. The English doctor William Harvey explained how the human heart and circulatory system worked.

The invention of the microscope resulted in new information about bacteria, cells, yeast, and other microorganisms. The study of elements, atoms, and the properties of matter advanced modern chemistry. The metric system of measurement and the periodic table were also both introduced during this time.

What advancements in science were made during this time?

____

____

____

SCIENCE AND SOCIETY

For centuries, the Catholic Church was the main source of knowledge and learning. The new and progressive views of scientists challenged this. Conflicts between the church and scientists, most of whom were Christians, grew. Galileo was put on trial because his work showed that Copernicus's heliocentric theory was correct. However, religious leaders eventually accepted that reason could help rather than hurt the church. In fact, scientific experiments contributed to the great works of artists and architects during this time—most of which was created to glorify God.

MAIN IDEA

European thinkers developed new ideas about government and society during the Enlightenment.

Key Terms and People

Enlightenment the time during which philosophers emphasized the use of reason to understand truth, also known as the Age of Reason

salons social gatherings at which writers, artists, and thinkers discussed their ideas

social contract the arrangement between individuals and their government: people give up some of their personal freedoms in exchange for order, peace, and safety

John Locke political philosopher whose ideas about government later influenced the writers of the Constitution

Jean-Jacques Rousseau thinker who believed people were naturally good but that society corrupts

Baron de Montesquieu writer who argued in favor of separation of power and checks and balances in government

philosophes French term for the philosophers of the Enlightenment

Voltaire Witty French writer who supported justice, liberty, and religious tolerance

enlightened despots rulers inspired by Enlightenment ideas to make social reforms

Taking Notes

As you read the summary, use a graphic organizer like this one to record the changes that the Enlightenment brought to society.

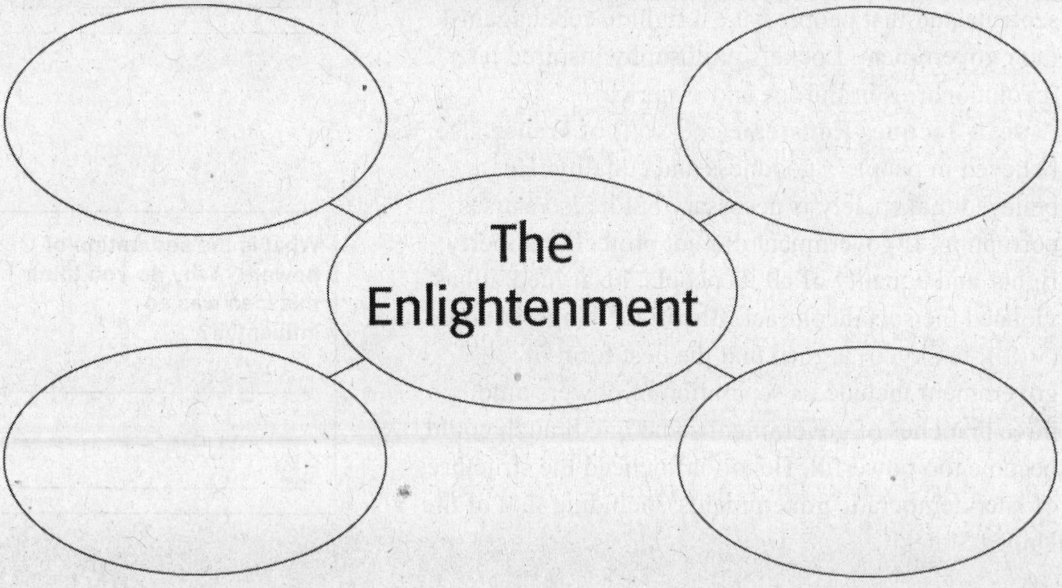

Section Summary

THE AGE OF REASON

The many about the physical world during the Scientific Revolution convinced some European thinkers about the power of reason. In the 1600s a new generation of philosophers began to view reason as the best way to understand human nature and society. This exciting time of optimism and possibility is now called the **Enlightenment**, or the Age of Reason. It reached its peak in Paris in the 1700s. There, wealthy women began hosting social gatherings called **salons** where scientists, philosophers, artists, and writers met to discuss their ideas.

NEW VIEWS ON GOVERNMENT

Many Enlightenment thinkers applied reason to understanding the organization of government. Thomas Hobbes of England believed that people are not naturally good. So they must exchange some freedoms for the order, peace and safety that come from having a government. Hobbes called this exchange the **social contract**. Hobbes favored a strong monarchy to impose law and order.

Underline the definition of the social contract.

Another English thinker, **John Locke**, disagreed. He believed that people are naturally good, reasonable, and born equal, and that the role of government is to protect citizens' rights. Locke believed government and the church should be separate and that people have a right to rebel against their government. Locke's philosophy inspired later revolutionaries in Europe and America.

Jean-Jacques Rousseau (roo-SOH) of France also believed in people's goodness and equality. He believed that society is necessary but it also causes corruption. If government did not protect the liberty, rights, and equality of all its people, he argued, it has violated the social contract. **Baron de Montesquieu** (MOHN-tes-kyoo) argued that the best form of government included a separation of powers among three branches of government so no one branch could become too powerful. He too influenced the structure of later democratic governments, including that of the United States.

What is the separation of powers? Why do you think this idea was so influential?

____

____

____

NEW VIEWS ON SOCIETY

One of the best known **philosophes**, or French philosophers, was a writer known as **Voltaire** (vohl-TAYR). He used his sharp wit and writing skills to speak for justice, religious toleration, and liberty. In the process, he made many enemies.

Other well-known Enlightenment figures included Denis Diderot (DEE-de-roh), who wrote a 28-volume encyclopedia; and Mary Wollstonecraft, who argued for equal rights for women. Wollstonecraft argued that if women had the same education as men, they could hold the same place in society. Other thinkers applied reason to the economy. Scotsman Adam Smith argued for a free market, that is, allowing the law of supply and demand to regulate the economy without government interference.

Choose one of the people described here, and explain his or her contribution to the Enlightenment.

____
____
____
____
____

ENLIGHTENMENT IDEAS SPREAD

Enlightenment ideas inspired some European monarchs to reform their governments. These rulers are known as **enlightened despots**.

Frederick the Great of Prussia was a strict ruler but he used Enlightenment ideas to strengthen his nation. He tried to establish elementary education for all, and supported religious toleration. However, opposition from the aristocracy prevented him from going as far as he liked; for example, he was unable to abolish serfdom. Catherine the Great of Russia was also inspired by Enlightenment ideas. She established some reforms, but she too was unable to go as far as abolishing serfdom, as she needed the support of landowners to stay in power. Joseph II of Austria actually did abolish serfdom, requiring that laborers be paid for their work. He also established toleration of religion, and provided food and medicine for the poor. But again, reforms were resisted by the nobility as well as the church.

During the Enlightenment, long-held beliefs about government, religion, and society were challenged. This process inspired future leaders. People began to believe that human reason could solve any problem. The Enlightenment inspired not only reform but revolution.

Why do you think there was such strong opposition among Europe's nobility to abolishing serfdom?

____
____
____
____

MAIN IDEA

Enlightenment ideas led to revolution, independence, and a new government for the United States.

Key Terms and People

Stamp Act act requiring colonists to pay a tax for an official stamp for letters and most paper goods

Thomas Jefferson Declaration of Independence writer

George Washington Commanding General of the Continental Army and later President of the United States

Benjamin Franklin colonist who convinced the French king to support American independence

Treaty of Paris treaty in which Great Britain officially recognized the United States' independence

James Madison primary writer of the U.S. Constitution

federal system system governing the United States as a whole

Taking Notes

As you read the summary, use a diagram like this one to record the steps in the American colonies' rise as a new nation. Add more ovals as needed.

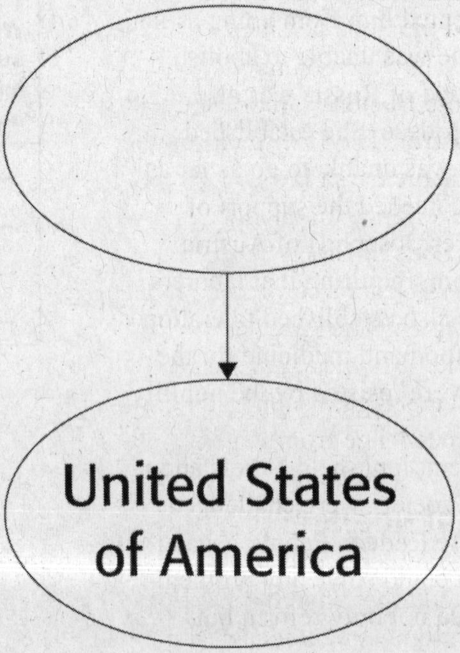

Section Summary

CHANGE AND CRISIS

In the American colonies, ideas of the Enlightenment began to spread. At the same time, differences between the colonies and their homeland increased. Since the first English settlement was established in the early 1600s, the British colonies expanded rapidly along the east coast. Each colony had its own government and made most of its own laws. Over time, the colonists began to identify more closely with the colonies and less with Britain itself.

Britain defeated France in the French and Indian War in 1763, causing France to give up its North American colonies. The war had been very expensive for Britain, so Britain decided to make the colonies pay part of the cost in the form of new taxes. The **Stamp Act** of 1765 forced colonists to pay a tax for an official stamp on letters and most paper goods. After colonists boycotted English goods, the Stamp Act was repealed. But in 1767, the British passed a series of new taxes on glass, paper, paints, and tea. Boston boycotted, so the British sent troops to control the city. In 1770, some troops shot and killed five men, an event known as the Boston Massacre.

Most of the acts were repealed, but not the tax on tea. In 1773, a group called the Sons of Liberty boarded ships holding tea. They then dumped hundreds of crates of tea into Boston Harbor, an event known as the Boston Tea Party. The British closed the port of Boston and passed more harsh laws.

In 1774, colonists held the First Continental Congress. Meanwhile, the Sons of Liberty prepared for war. In April 1775, British troops confronted rebel American soldiers in Lexington. The American Revolution had begun. Writer Thomas Paine's pamphlet Common Sense helped gain support among American patriots for independence from Britain.

Why did the British government need money in 1763? Who did they think should give them this money?

____

____

____

Name four items that the government taxed.

____

____

____

STRUGGLE FOR INDEPENDENCE

In June 1775, the Second Continental Congress decided to declare that the colonies should be free. **Thomas Jefferson** used Enlightenment ideas from Locke and Rousseau and the English Bill of Rights as

Underline two of Jefferson's influences while writing the Declaration of Independence.

he wrote the Declaration of Independence. On July 4, 1776, it was adopted.

The rebels had little money, but they had a great general in **George Washington**. The British left Boston and went to New York, where they were joined by many British ships. They sent the rebel army into New Jersey, where the British defeated Washington twice. Eventually, Philadelphia was taken by the British. In October 1777, however, the British were defeated at the Battle of Saratoga. This helped **Benjamin Franklin** convince France to support the Americans. Over the next two years, the American forces strengthened. In October 1781, Lord Cornwallis was forced to surrender at Yorktown, Virginia, ending the war. In 1783, the **Treaty of Paris** the British recognized American independence.

Why do you think the American victory at Saratoga helped convince France to support the American side in the war?

____

____

____

FORMING A NEW GOVERNMENT

The Articles of Confederation established the first government of the new United States. It intentionally made the central government weak. All measures had to be passed unanimously by all states. However, the government was too weak to do its job. In 1787, a Constitutional Convention was called to revise the Articles of Confederation. **James Madison** came to the convention ready to write a draft of a constitution that would give most of the power to the people, who would then transfer it to elected officials. After a series of compromises, a constitution was adopted which called for a two-house legislature, a President, and a judiciary as part of the **federal system**. While some powers were kept for state governments, others were reserved for the federal government. Its power, in turn, was regulated by checks and balances.

Opponents to the Constitution called for the addition of protections for individual rights. Congress passed ten amendments to the Constitution, known as the Bill of Rights, to protect freedoms of speech and religion and guarantee due process of law.

Underline the rights and freedoms guaranteed by the Bill of Rights.

News of the American colonies' successful revolution had a huge impact on other governments, especially in France. Beginning in 1789, France experienced its own revolution, due in part to the example of the American Revolution.

Name ______________________ Class ______________ Date ______________

The French Revolution and Napoleon

Chapter Summary

Causes and Effects of the French Revolution	
Causes	**Effects**
• Poor harvests; food shortages	• France adopted written constitution
• Weak leadership from Louis XVI	• End of the monarchy
• Massive government debt	• Reign of Terror
• King Louis XVI's refusal to accept financial reforms	• European alliance against France
• Spread of Enlightenment ideas	• Napoleon seizes power
• Inequalities in society	• Growth of nationalism
• Fall of Bastille	• Revolutionary ideas spread

COMPREHENSION AND CRITICAL THINKING

Use information from the graphic organizer to answer the following questions.

1. **Recall** Who was king of France during the French Revolution? Describe his leadership.

____

____

2. **Identify Cause and Effect** Was Napoleon's rise to power a cause or effect of the revolution? Explain.

____

____

3. **Evaluate** Why do you think the Revolution caused other European nations to oppose France?

____

____

____

____

MAIN IDEA

Problems in French society led to a revolution, the formation of a new government, and the end of the monarchy.

Key Terms and People

Old Order France's social and political structure that places the king at the top and three estates below him

King Louis XVI ruler during early years of the French Revolution

Marie-Antoinette Austrian wife of King Louis XVI, serving as queen during his reign

First Estate small, privileged class made up of Roman Catholic clergy in France

Second Estate the class in France that was made up of the nobility

Third Estate the class of 97% of France, made up of the bourgeoisie, artisans, merchants, and peasants

bourgeoisie city-dwelling merchants, factory owners, and professionals

sansculottes "without knee breeches"; a nickname for workers of the Third Estate

Declaration of the Rights of Man and of the Citizen document written by the National Assembly advocating equality, freedom of speech, and freedom of religion

radicals people favoring extreme change

Taking Notes

As you read the summary, use the graphic organizer below to record events that occurred before and after the revolution.

Events Before the Revolution

↓

Events After the Revolution

Section Summary

CAUSES OF THE REVOLUTION

The structure of French government and society, called the **Old Order**, caused resentment among the poor and working class. At the top was **King Louis XVI**. His wife, **Marie-Antoinette**, spent money lavishly and was disliked by many, perhaps because she was from Austria, France's long-time rival.

The rest of French society was divided into estates. The **First Estate** was made up of the Roman Catholic clergy, about 1 percent of the population. They had special rights and did not have to pay taxes. Some were very wealthy.

Name a privilege of the First Estate.

____

____

The **Second Estate** was the nobility, accounting for about 2 percent of the population. They held important positions in government and the military, and paid few taxes. Most lived on large estates or in the king's court.

The **Third Estate** was the largest—97% of the population. At the top of the Third Estate was the **bourgeoisie** (BOOR-zhwah zee)—merchants, factory owners, and professionals, some of whom were wealthy and well-educated. This did not, however, give the bourgeoisie influence with the king and his court. This estate also included city-dwelling artisans and workers. They were nicknamed **sansculottes** (san KOO laht) because they wore long pants instead of the knee breeches worn by the nobility. At the bottom were the peasants who farmed the nobles' fields. Peasants had to pay many taxes and fees and perform labor without pay. Poor and miserable, they had no hope for a better future.

Circle the estate that contained the most people.

Resentment and anger about social inequalities played a large role in inspiring the French Revolution. Enlightenment ideas did too. The French noted that in Great Britain, the king's power was limited, and that American colonists successfully rebelled against their king during the American Revolution.

Economic problems also contributed to the revolution. France was deeply in debt, though the king and his court continued to spend wildly. The king unsuccessfully tried to tax the Second Estate. Soon, France was almost bankrupt. When record low temperatures brought food production to a halt, people began to starve. The poor, hungry French citizens got angry. People in the First and Second Estates were also angry as they lost power to the monarchy.

Circle two events that contributed to the French Revolution.

FIRST EVENTS OF THE REVOLUTION

In early 1789, the king called a meeting of the Estates General for the first time in 175 years. Seeking reforms, each group of representatives brought a list of grievances to Paris with them. In the past, each estate cast one vote, regardless of the number of representatives present. The Third Estate, having the most representatives, wanted to change the rule so that each person had a vote. The king disagreed, so the Third Estate formed a group called the National Assembly. When the king locked them out of their own meeting, they met in an indoor tennis court and took an oath, later called the Tennis Court Oath, stating that they wouldn't leave until they created a new constitution. The king relented, allowing all representatives a vote. He also brought troops to Paris and Versailles in case they were needed. Seeing the troops, members of the National Assembly and Parisian stormed an old prison, the Bastille, to get weapons. This event became a powerful symbol of the French Revolution.

Which estate became the National Assembly?

____

CREATING A NEW NATION

The National Assembly removed the First Estate's privileges, sold church land to pay France's debts, made clergy public employees, and downgraded the king and queen to commoners. The Assembly adopted the **Declaration of the Rights of Man and of the Citizen**, which laid out the basic principles of the Revolution. It declared that all men were equal and made more people able to vote. Mob violence increased and foreign troops entered France to protect the monarchs. The National Assembly, now controlled by **radicals**, elected a new legislature called the National Convention. The new government abolished the monarchy and declared France a republic.

MAIN IDEA

An extreme government changed French society and tried through harsh means to eliminate its critics within France.

Key Terms and People

Maximilien Robespierre Mountain member and a leader of the National Convention

guillotine an execution device that drops a sharp, heavy blade through the victim's neck

counterrevolution a revolution against a government established by a revolution

Reign of Terror series of accusations, arrests and executions started by the Mountain

Taking Notes

As you read the summary, use a chart like the one below to record changes in French government and society as well as those brought about by the Reign of Terror.

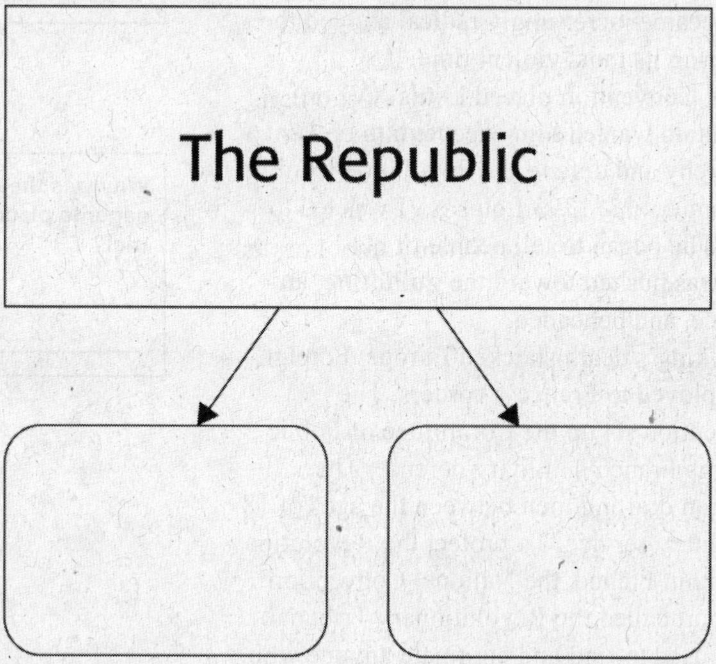

Section Summary

A RADICAL GOVERNMENT

Although everyone in the new National Convention supported the Revolution, they were divided into three political groups. The Mountain or Montagnards were the most extreme. They were mostly made up of the lower middle class and poor. The Girondins were the moderates who did not want the Paris mob to have too much influence. They supported the idea of a constitutional monarchy. The third group, the Plain, initially supported the Girondins, but later switched its support to the Mountain.

Three men played important roles in the new government. They were all members of the Mountain. Jean-Paul Marat, a radical, was in favor of violent methods. George-Jacques Danton, a violent agitator in the Revolution's early days, in time favored compromise. The intensely dedicated **Maximilien Robespierre** became increasingly radical and led the Convention during its most violent time.

What did Marat, Danton, and Robespierre have in common?

____

____

The National Convention placed Louis XVI on trial. The Mountain wanted him executed, to prevent a return to monarchy and defend the Revolution from its enemies. On January 23, 1793 Louis XVI was led to the scaffold. As he began to tell people of his innocence, he was pushed toward the **guillotine**, an execution device, and beheaded.

Why was the Mountain eager to place the king on trial?

____

____

News of the king's death shocked Europe. Foreign troops were deployed to France's borders. The National Convention set up the Committee of Public Safety to manage France's military defense. The Committee began drafting men between the ages of 18 and 45 into military service. To protect the Revolution from threats within France, the National Convention also set up a court called the Revolutionary Tribunal. This court was used to find and eliminate anyone who threatened the goals of the Revolution.

France was transformed during the Revolution. The monarchy ended and new governments formed. French society changed too. The National Convention tried to eliminate all connections to the old ways of life. Churches were shut down and clergymen lost their positions. Robespierre created a new religion,

Underline the ways French society changed during the Revolution.

replacing worship of God with enthusiasm for the Revolution. To further cut ties to the past, the months of the year were renamed. A metric system replaced the old system of weights and measures, one change that was kept.

THE REIGN OF TERROR

By the middle of 1793, France was at war with several European nations. Within the country, many were criticizing the Revolution. Revolutionary leaders feared a possible **counterrevolution**, or backlash against the new government. The Mountain began to accuse, try, and execute anyone who opposed them. These actions were known as the **Reign of Terror**.

Peasants were especially angry. They opposed the draft and remained devoutly Catholic. Resistance to the Revolution was so strong in a region in western France called the Vendée that civil war broke out. After fierce fighting that destroyed much of the region and the people who lived there, government forces defeated the Grand Royal and Catholic army.

Why were peasants angry?

____

____

Back in Paris, the Mountain went after anyone who criticized the Revolution. The accused people had few rights and at one point, they were not even allowed to defend themselves. Punishment was swift. Executions, mostly by guillotine, drew crowds and became a daily activity. Robespierre even sent Dalton and other member of his own party to death.

The Reign of Terror spared no one. Nobles, peasants, and revolutionaries died. In the end, about 17,000 people were executed. The ten-month Reign of Terror finally ended when Robespierre and his followers were taken into custody and executed. France began again with a new constitution written by the National Convention, and a weak and corrupt governing board called the Directory. In time, its rule shared many characteristics of the Old Order such as high prices, bankruptcy, and unhappiness among the people. With no one in firm control, something had to change.

Why did France still have problems after the Reign of Terror ended?

____

____

____

MAIN IDEA

Napoleon Bonaparte rose through military ranks to become emperor over France and much of Europe.

Key Terms and People

Napoleon Bonaparte ambitious military leader who became emperor of France

Admiral Horatio Nelson British naval commander who won the Battle of the Nile

coup d'état a forced transfer of power

plebiscite a question put before all voters

Continental System a blockade that stopped French and allied ships from trading with Great Britain to prevent that nation from funding the rebellion against Napoleon

nationalism a sense of identity and unity as a people

Taking Notes

As you read the summary, use a graphic organizer like the one below to record the steps in Napoleon's rise to power. Add more boxes as needed.

Section Summary

NAPOLEON'S RISE TO POWER

As a young man, **Napoleon Bonaparte** achieved several military victories, including stopping an uprising in Paris in 1795. As a reward he was promoted and given increased responsibility over French troops. He protected France's interior and led the invasion of Italy, winning new territory for France.

Napoleon next set his sights on Egypt. He wanted to weaken the valuable trade route between Great Britain and India. In 1798, his troops won control of most of Egypt. However, **Admiral Horatio Nelson**, commander of the British navy, trapped Napoleon's ships in Egypt. During the long Battle of the Nile, the British destroyed most of the French fleet.

Napoleon returned to France. He covered up his defeat by keeping reports out of the newspaper. The attention he drew to his successes made him a national hero. Napoleon wanted to take political power from the weakening Directory at a time when many feared the monarchy would return to power. In 1799, Napoleon's supporters took control of the weak French government in a **coup d'état** (koo day-TAH). In name, a consulate led France, but its members elected Napoleon First Consul. Though France was still set up like a republic, Napoleon ruled as a dictator. He promised to restore order and stability to people who, exhausted by the Revolution and the warfare that followed, were willing to trade some freedoms for peace, prosperity, and glory for France.

Why do you think Napoleon was given more and more responsibility?

____

____

____

How did Napoleon handle his defeat in Egypt?

____

____

____

Why didn't the French people mind that Napoleon ruled as a dictator?

____

____

____

EMPEROR NAPOLEON

In order to make his power permanent and able to be passed on to his descendents, Napoleon submitted a **plebiscite** that asked all voters if they wanted an empire. They voted yes and so Napoleon became Emperor Napoleon I in 1804. Napoleon wanted to rule Europe and the Americas. Even though France controlled Louisiana, Florida, and Saint Domingue (now Haiti), his campaigns were unsuccessful in the Americas. Napoleon sold the Louisiana Territory to the United States and focused once more on Europe.

During these Napoleonic Wars, Great Britain was France's greatest enemy. Napoleon was often successful on land. However, the British navy under Admiral Nelson prevented Napoleon from conquering all of Europe. Just two months after a combined French and Spanish navy at the Battle of Trafalgar, Napoleon bounced back with a great victory over Russia and Austria at the Battle of Austerlitz. France was not going to give up on its desire to expand its empire, at least not with Napoleon in control.

To weaken Great Britain, he planned a blockade called the **Continental System**, in which French and allied ships were not allowed to trade with Britain. This would cut down on Britain's ability to fund other nations' efforts to stop him. Britain responded by requiring all ships to get British permission before trading with the French Empire. Conflicts in other places kept the two nations from enforcing these laws. However, Napoleon sent troops to Portugal, a nation that refused to comply with the Continental System. He then took control of Spain, placing his brother Joseph on the throne taken from the king. In 1808, Britain joined Spain to fight the Peninsular War against Napoleon. After he won the war, peasant-led guerrilla fighting forced France out of Spain. Even with these setbacks, by 1812 he ruled nearly all of Europe. Only Great Britain, Sweden, Portugal, and the Ottoman Empire were free from Napoleon's control.

Which nation helped Spain in the Peninsular War?

____

Circle the nations that were not part of the French Empire.

NAPOLEON'S POLICIES

Napoleon wanted a strong central government. His plans changed several aspects of French society. He officially recognized the influence of the Roman Catholic Church. He established the Bank of France and set up an efficient way to collect taxes. Under his leadership, French law was reorganized as the Napoleonic Code. The code ended some unfair laws but restricted some basic rights. Napoleon set up high schools, universities, and technical schools to educate young men. This prepared them for careers in government and the military.

All over Europe, Napoleon's actions increased feelings of **nationalism**. People developed a sense of identity, unity, and allegiance to France.

List two ways that Napoleon changed French society.

____

____

____

Name ______________________ Class ______________ Date ______________

MAIN IDEA
After defeating Napoleon, the European allies sent him into exile and held a meeting in Vienna to restore order and stability to Europe.

Key Terms and People

Czar Alexander I Russian ruler during Napoleon's failed invasion of Russia

Hundred Days brief period of renewed glory for Napoleon

Duke of Wellington head of the British troops during the Battle of Waterloo

indemnity payment to other countries to compensate for damages caused during war

Charles Maurice de Talleyrand French diplomat who attended the Congress of Vienna on behalf of King Louis XVIII and helped ensure fairness as the new map was drawn

Prince Klemens von Metternich Austrian prince who strongly influenced policy decision-making at the Congress of Vienna

reactionary opposing progress in hopes of conditions returning to those of earlier times

Taking Notes

As you read the summary, use the graphic organizer below to record key events during the last years of Napoleon's rule.

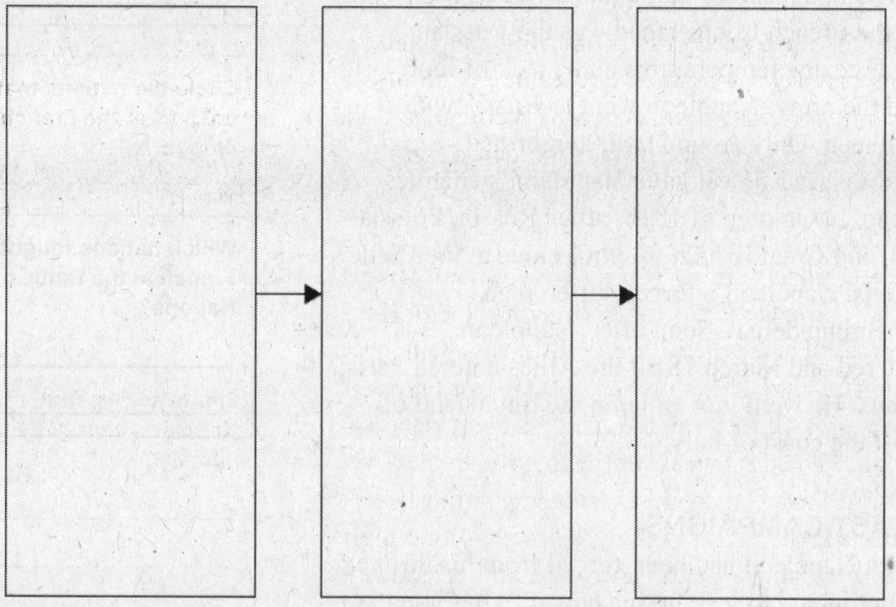

Section Summary

DISASTER AND DEFEAT

Napoleon was soon to lose control of his empire. Concerned about Russia's increasing military power and decreasing support for the Continental System under its leader, **Czar Alexander I**, Napoleon decided it was time to attack. The Russian campaign of 1812 was a disaster for Napoleon. His soldiers were mostly new recruits who did not feel loyalty to him. Many army supplies were lost or spoiled as French troops marched east along rough roads in the intense heat.

The soldiers found there was no one to fight—and nothing to eat. The Russian army was moving away from the French. So were the peasants who burned their fields, leaving nothing the French could use. When they finally did meet the Russian army, the French won a battle at the town of Borodino but lost many soldiers. When they reached Moscow, the deserted city was in flames. Because Napoleon knew his troops could not survive winter in Moscow, they turned back toward France. Disease, desertion, hunger, and Russian peasants attacking small groups of soldiers had inflicted damage. However, the worst enemy the French troops faced was the Russian winter. Freezing temperatures and a lack of food crushed the army. Napoleon went to Russia with 600,000 men. Only around 94,000 returned.

The disastrous defeat gave Napoleon's enemies new hope. In October of 1813, allies Russia, Prussia, Austria, and Great Britain fought France at the Battle of Nations. Napoleon's forces suffered an overwhelming defeat. Soon after, Napoleon surrendered and March 1814, the Allies entered Paris, victorious. He went into exile on the tiny island of Elba, off the coast of Italy.

What problems did French soldiers face as they traveled to Russia?

____

____

What was the worst enemy for Napoleon's troops?

____

Which nations fought the French at the Battle of Nations?

____

____

THE LAST CAMPAIGNS

Although Napoleon had been forced from his throne, he did not intend to give up his power. After about a year, he returned to France and headed for Paris. In that time, the allies had returned the monarchy to power. When word of Napoleon's return reached King Louis XVIII, the unpopular new French ruler, he fled to Belgium in fear. Many citizens hated Napoleon. Still, he had a large number of supporters in France, including the soldiers sent to arrest him who pledged their loyalty to him instead. His return to Paris on March 20, 1815, marked the start of the **Hundred Days**. This was a very brief return to his former glory. Napoleon's final stand took place at the Battle of Waterloo. Led by the British **Duke of Wellington**, who also had Dutch and German troops working with his army, the battle waged fiercely. When the Prussian army joined the Allies, together they drove the French army off the field by day's end. After a failed attempt to escape to America, Napoleon was exiled to Saint Helena, a remote volcanic island in the South Atlantic. He remained there until he died at the age of 51.

Underline the king's response to Napoleon's return.

THE CONGRESS OF VIENNA

Before Napoleon's escape from Elba, 700 diplomats had met at the Congress of Vienna to create a plan to restore order to Europe. They decided to change boundaries across Europe to strengthen the nations surrounding France. France gave up all of its conquered territory and paid a fee called an **indemnity** to countries it had damaged during the wars. **Charles Maurice de Talleyrand** attended the Congress on behalf of the French king. He worked hard to make sure each country traded territory fairly as the new map of Europe was drawn. **Prince Klemens von Metternich** of Austria was a major force at the Congress. He had **reactionary** views; he wanted Europe to return to how it had been before Napoleon's rule.

What was the goal of the Congress of Vienna?

____

____

____

THE REVOLUTION'S LEGACY

The French Revolution changed Europe even though some things returned to how they had once been. The nobility realized that Enlightenment ideas about human dignity, personal liberty, and the equality of all people would not go away. Common people learned that change could make their lives better. These ideals inspired political movements around the world.

Chapter Summary

Effects of the Industrial Revolution

Inventions
- seed drill
- cotton gin
- spinning frame

Factory Workers
- moved to cities from the countryside
- worked long hours with poor conditions
- organized unions and strikes

New Economic Theories
- laissez-faire economics
- socialism
- communism

COMPREHENSION AND CRITICAL THINKING

Use information from the graphic organizer to answer the following questions.

1. **Explain** How did new inventions help to start the Industrial Revolution?

____

____

____

2. **Cause and Effect** What caused working conditions to improve in Great Britain and the United States?

____

____

____

3. **Evaluate** How did industrialization change the lives of people who had worked in cottage industries such as weaving and farming?

____

____

____

4. **Elaborate** What do you think about the idea of a utopian community? Do you think it is possible? Why or why not?

____

____

Name ______________________ Class ______________ Date ______________

The Industrial Revolution

Section 1

MAIN IDEA

In the 1700s, conditions in Great Britain led to the rapid growth of the textile industry, which in turn led to huge changes in many other industries.

Key Terms and People

Industrial Revolution the time period when power-driven machinery was developed

enclosure movement the combining of many small farms by wealthy landowners

factors of production the essential elements that a nation needs for economic success

cottage industry a craft occupation performed in the home

factory a building that housed machine-driven industry

industrialization the process of changing to power-driven machinery

Jethro Tull gentleman farmer who invented the seed drill for planting grain

Richard Arkwright inventor of the spinning frame, which spun stronger, thinner thread

James Watt British inventor who made steam engines faster and more efficient

Robert Fulton developed and operated the steamship *Clermont* on the Hudson River

Taking Notes

As you read the summary, add information about the Industrial Revolution to this chart.

Beginnings	Textiles
Steam	Spread

Section Summary

A REVOLUTION IN GREAT BRITAIN

During the 1700s, the world was transformed by the development of power-driven machinery. This movement, which began in Great Britain, is called the **Industrial Revolution**.

British farmers experimented with agriculture to find ways to produce more food. Around 1701, **Jethro Tull** invented the seed drill to plant grain. During the **enclosure movement**, wealthy landowners bought and combined smaller farms.

Britain possessed natural resources such as water and coal to generate power; a growing population of workers; and the money and skills of prosperous investors. These elements, called **factors of production**, are essential for economic success.

List Britain's three factors of production. Underline the definition of this term.

____

A REVOLUTION IN TEXTILES

The Industrial Revolution began with the British cloth-making, or textile, industry. Weaving cloth was a **cottage industry** – a craft occupation performed in the home. The old ways of making cloth were transformed by **industrialization**, or the process of changing to power-driven machinery.

During the 1700s, inventors built new machines to handle Britain's growing supply of wool and cotton fibers. **Eli Whitney** developed the cotton gin to pull seeds from raw cotton. **Richard Arkwright** invented the spinning frame, which spun stronger, thinner thread. These large, power-driven weaving machines were operated in buildings called **factories**. Out of this flurry of invention, an industry was born. In 1770, England produced about 50,000 bolts of fabric; by 1800, production had increased to about 400,000 bolts.

Circle the names of two machines used in the textile industry. What two fibers were used?

STEAM POWERS THE REVOLUTION

British inventors learned how to harness the force of steam to drive machines that transformed the world. **James Watt** made the steam engine efficient, fast, and better able to power machinery. The steam engine also made it possible to build factories anywhere because the engines ran on coal, not power from streams and rivers. Soon factories and towns sprung up near Britain's northern coal mines and near roads and ports. Being able to build factories anywhere changed the landscape. Farmlands disappeared as busy, noisy boomtowns took their place.

Steam engines also produced a revolution in transportation. Steam-powered trains and steamships made possible the fast shipment of goods to faraway markets. Like the steam engines in factories, those that powered ships also ran on coal. Though England had huge supplies of coal, mining it was dangerous, and in its early days, even brutal. Mine explosions, coal dust, collapsing shafts, and the sheer hard labor of mining caught the public's attention, as did the fact that many workers were children. Reforms, however, were slow in coming.

List three uses of the steam engine.

____

____

____

INDUSTRIALIZATION SPREADS

Britain attempted to protect its industrial discoveries, but the Industrial Revolution eventually spread to the United States and other countries. People wanted to compete and were rewarded for their innovation. Mill worker Samuel Slater was known as the Father of American Industry after he copied, from memory, Richard Arkwright's design and opened what is today known as Slater's Mill in Rhode Island. By 1850, the mill city of Lowell, Massachusetts, had over 10,000 workers using looms.

Who was known as the Father of American Industry?

____

Though Britain's new technologies were soon used in Belgium, the Industrial Revolution reached other places in Europe much later. Rebellion followed by the Napoleonic Wars kept France from industrializing until after Napoleon was defeated in 1815. France did not become an industrial power until 1848. Germany's lack of central government delayed industrialization until the 1850s. Industry also spread to Japan after 1868, and in China, India and Russia in the twentieth century.

Name ______________________ Class ______________ Date ______________

The Industrial Revolution

Section 2

MAIN IDEA
The transition from cottage industries changed how people worked in factories, what life was like in factory towns, labor conditions, and eventually, processes within factories.

Key Terms and People

labor union organizations representing workers' interests

strike work stoppages

mass production the system of manufacturing large numbers of identical items

interchangeable parts identical machine-made parts

assembly line system in which workers stay in one place, adding parts as items go by

Taking Notes

As you read the summary, use this chart to compare factors in pre-industrial and industrial production.

Differences in . . .
where work was done
working conditions
towns
labor conditions
factory processes

Section Summary

PRODUCTION BEFORE FACTORIES

Before the Industrial Revolution, most people worked in cottage industries, such as weaving and farming. Family life revolved around the business, and people decided how much to produce and when. Weaving families, for example, worked from their homes, transforming the raw materials they purchased from merchants into finished goods.

Working in a cottage industry also had disadvantages. A business could be ruined by fire, flood, the loss of livestock, or the death of an older, highly skilled family member. Factory work offered the end of these drawbacks, as the owners knew.

List two types of cottage industries. Underline the disadvantages people working in them faced.

FACTORIES AND FACTORY TOWNS

Working in factory-based industries known as the factory system helped people support their families, but it also caused hardships. Each factory worker was assigned a simple task to be done repeatedly. Though most factory workers were adult men, owners preferred hiring children because they could be paid lower wages. Factory workers worked 12 to 18 hours each day in dreadful, dangerous conditions. Many workers had left the countryside to find factory work and found themselves living nearby in poor quality, factory-owned housing. They endured pollution created by the factories, especially the dangerous soot and smoke from burning coal. These unsanitary conditions caused disease to spread rapidly.

Underline the hardships faced by factory workers. Why were children hired?

____

THE FACTORY SYSTEM AND WORKERS

The factory system needed three levels of workers. Business people invested in and owned the factories, mid-level employees supervised day-to-day operations, and workers ran the machines.

Some cottage industry workers resorted to violence to protest that their goods could not compete with the less expensive versions produced in factories. Their actions, called the Luddite Movement included burning factories and smashing machines. It was short-lived, however, as several Luddites were caught and hanged.

Circle the three types of factory employees. Who owned the factories?

____

Factory workers were also unhappy. In the 1800s, first in Britain and then in America, many of them formed **labor unions** that represented their interests. Unions organized **strikes**, or work stoppages, to protest low wages and poor working conditions.

Change happened slowly. Reports told the public about abuses in the factories. Britain passed laws that limited work hours and kept children under nine from working. Some people became more prosperous. Increased productivity created more jobs for managers, accountants, salespeople, and transporters.

FACTORIES AND MASS PRODUCTION

Many new methods of improving industry began in the United States. American industry became expert in **mass production**, the system of manufacturing large numbers of identical items. Many goods produced this way were made of **interchangeable parts**—all the exact same size and shape, creating a standard of measurement that made it easy to replace broken parts later. This is much different from cottage industry production, in which every part was handmade, and therefore slightly different. Henry Ford used a new system called the **assembly line** to speed production. Instead of moving around a product as they worked, workers stayed in place while products moved on belts. This saved time and forced people to work as fast as the belt brought the items to them. Because of these factors mass production increased the amount of goods available for sale and made products more affordable.

How was working on an assembly line different from working in a cottage industry?

____

____

MAIN IDEA

The Industrial Revolution inspired new ideas about economics and affected society in many ways.

Key Terms and People

laissez-faire the idea that governments should not interfere in business

Adam Smith the leading advocate of laissez-faire economics

Thomas Malthus thinker whose beliefs about poverty were used to justify low wages

entrepreneur someone who starts a business

Andrew Carnegie industrialist who led the expansion of the American steel industry

socialism the theory that society, not individuals, should own all property and industry

Karl Marx German thinker who put forth a radical view of socialism

communism a system in which the government controls the economy

standard of living level of material comfort experienced by a group of people

Taking Notes

As you read the summary, use the chart below to show results of the Industrial Revolution. Add ovals as needed.

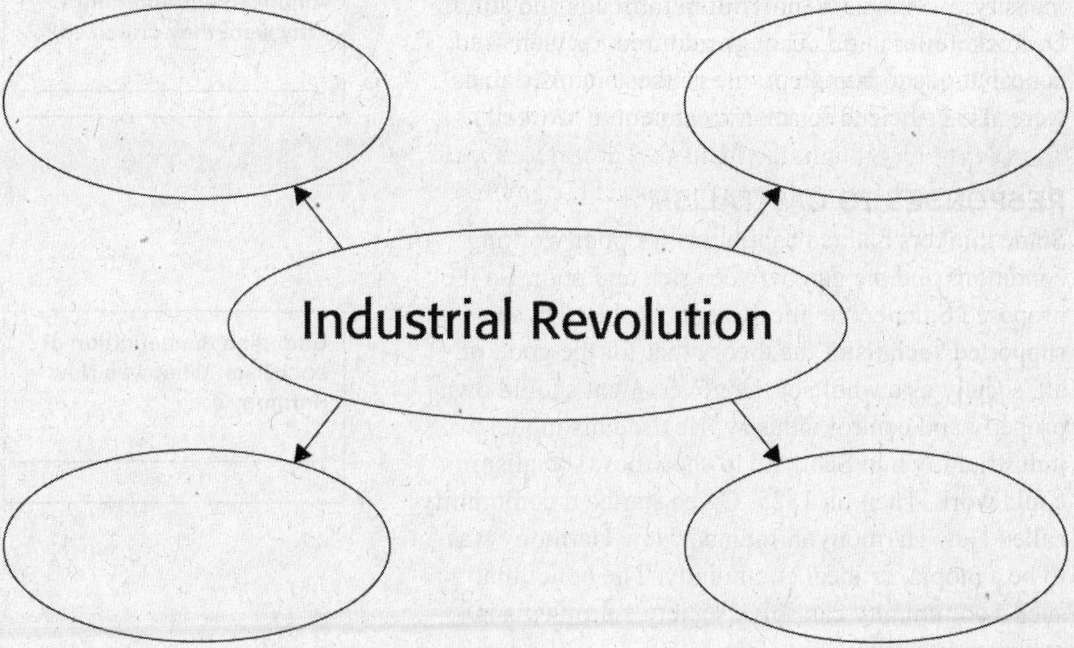

Section Summary

NEW IDEAS ABOUT ECONOMICS

Starting in the late 1700s, people began supporting **laissez-faire** (LEHZ-ay fehr) economics, or the idea that governments should not interfere in business. **Adam Smith** described and advocated this economic system in The Wealth of Nations. Supporting Smith, the British government ended most regulations by the 1840s.

Smith's ideas influenced **Thomas Malthus**, who believed that poverty and misery would never go away because the population would always grow faster than food production. With this in mind, many people believed that trying to help the poor was a waste of time, as poverty would persist no matter what. In time, Malthus was proved wrong.

The Industrial Revolution also highlighted the role of the **entrepreneur**, someone who starts a business. Financiers, bankers, and investors pooled their money to create large corporations. Some industrialists acquired vast wealth by creating the largest corporate empires ever seen. These included "rags to riches" Scottish immigrant **Andrew Carnegie** in the steel industry, Cornelius Vanderbilt in railroads and John D. Rockefeller in oil. Though admired for their contributions to human progress, these industrialists were also criticized for their treatment of workers.

Underline the definition of laissez-faire economics. Who wrote about this idea?

____

Circle the names of American entrepreneurs. Why were they criticized?

____

RESPONSES TO CAPITALISM

Some thinkers blamed capitalism for poor working conditions and the gap between rich and poor. So they proposed other economic systems. Robert Owen supported **socialism**, the theory that for the good of all, society as a whole or the government should own property and control industry. He used his model industrial town in Scotland to show how socialism could work. Then, in 1825, Owen started a community called New Harmony in Indiana. New Harmony was to be a utopia, or ideal community. The belief that such a community can solve society's problems is called utopianism.

Germans Friedrich Engels and **Karl Marx** put forth a more radical view of socialism. Marx believed that

Underline the definition of socialism. What was New Harmony?

____

capitalism would fail and eventually cause a revolution led by workers who would change society to one of cooperation and equal distribution of wealth. Fearing this would not happen quickly enough under socialism, Marx thought workers should control the government, so that it in turn could control the economy. He therefore supported **communism**, a system in which the government owns almost all the means of production and controls the economy. It also ignores basic human rights and freedom of choice.

EFFECTS ON SOCIETY

The Industrial Revolution brought countless changes, large and small. As industry drew workers away from home, middle-class women usually stayed home to care for children. This led to men and women being seen as occupying "separate spheres." Women and the home were thought of as the moral center of society.

For countries such as Great Britain, France and Germany, industrialization brought great power. These nations became leaders in the global economy. Mass production made it possible to make more weapons and build more ships. With increased military strength, some countries conquered and controlled places that could supply raw materials. This practice could also eliminate competition, such as Britain's taking control of cotton cloth-producing India. The United States also gained global political power by industrializing. It benefited from the arrival of immigrants who could work with the nation's vast natural resources. These factors, plus the spirit of independence led to the success of capitalism in the United States and its cultural variety.

Overall, the **standard of living**, or level of material comfort, for people in industrialized countries improved. Though much of the wealth created by industrialization made only a few individuals wildly wealthy, it did help create a large middle class. For the first time, people in the middle class enjoyed leisure activities such as sports and vacations. They also had the time to become more educated or participate more deeply in politics.

How did industrialization affect family life?

____

____

Chapter Summary

Leaders of the Industrial Age

Innovators	Scientists	Musicians and Writers
Thomas Edison: first usable, practical light bulb	Charles Darwin: theory of evolution	Ludwig van Beethoven: expressed love of nature in symphonies
Wilbur & Orville Wright: first sustained flight of a powered airplane	Louis Pasteur: studied germs, made vaccines, and pasteurization	William Wordsworth: poet who wrote about nature
Samuel Morse: invented telegraph and Morse code	Albert Einstein: theory of relativity	Charles Dickens: wrote about poor in cities
Alexander Graham Bell: telephone		Leo Tolstoy: wrote about cruelties of war

COMPREHENSION AND CRITICAL THINKING

Use information from the graphic organizer to answer the following questions.

1. **Recall** What notable achievements was Samuel Morse known for?

____

____

2. **Compare** Nature was the subject of which writer and which musician? Compare their work with the work of the innovators and scientists in the chart. How did they differ?

____

____

3. **Evaluate** Why was the work of Louis Pasteur important to the field of medicine?

____

____

4. **Rank** Which person on the chart above changed life in the 1800s the most? Why do you think so?

____

____

Name ______________________ Class ______________ Date ______________

Life in the Industrial Age

Section 1

MAIN IDEA
The technological breakthroughs of the Industrial Age included advances in electric power, transportation, and communication.

Key Terms and People

Michael Faraday English chemist who invented the dynamo

Thomas Edison developer of the first usable and practical light bulb; invented phonograph

Bessemer process steel-making process which made steel both stronger and cheaper

Henry Ford developer of mass-production factory methods; produced affordable Model T cars

Wilbur and Orville Wright brothers who were the first people to succeed in flying a powered airplane in sustained flight

Samuel Morse inventor of the telegraph and the code used to send telegraph messages

telegraph a machine that sends messages instantly over wires with electricity

Alexander Graham Bell inventor of the telephone

Guglielmo Marconi developer of the wireless telegraph, or radio

Taking Notes

As you read, take notes on key technological advances of the Industrial Age.

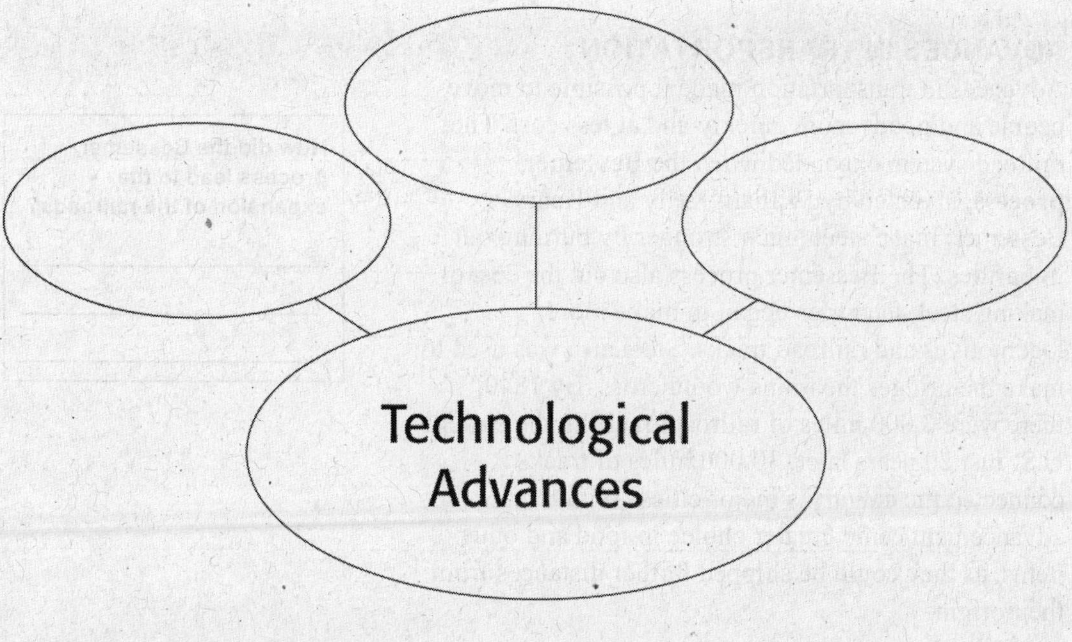

Section Summary

ELECTRIC POWER

By the late 1800s scientists began to find alternatives to water, coal, and stream. These sources had powered industry but they did not work very efficiently. Electric power changed things more than any other invention. It started in 1831 when the English chemist **Michael Faraday** found a practical use for electric power. He created the dynamo, a machine that generated electricity by moving a magnet through a copper coil. Faraday used the electricity from the dynamo to invent the first electric motor.

In 1879, **Thomas Edison** developed the first light bulb that had a practical use. Later, he and his team made generators, motors, light sockets, and other electrical devices. Edison also worked to bring electricity to several city blocks when he created the world's first permanent central power plant in New York. Electricity allowed factories to stop depending on large steam engines and the water sources that powered them. This gave factory owners the freedom to locate their factories in other places. No longer relying on sunlight, workers could work later, producing more goods. Electricity also allowed people to light their homes more safely than with the gas or oil lamps they had used earlier.

Name three ways electricity changed how people lived or worked.

____

____

____

ADVANCES IN TRANSPORTATION

Advances in transportation made it possible to move people and goods more quickly and at less cost. The railroad system expanded when the **Bessemer process**, invented by William Kelly and Henry Bessemer, made steel much stronger by burning out impurities. The Bessemer process also cut the cost of making steel. Factories began to make more locomotives and railroad tracks. Steel also was used to make the bridges the trains would cross. By 1840, there were 3,000 miles of railroad tracks in the eastern U.S. Just 20 years later, 30,000 miles of tracks connected the country's major cities. With this advancement came greater choice in food and other items, as they could be shipped farther distances from their origin.

How did the Bessemer process lead to the expansion of the railroads?

____

____

____

Life in the Industrial Age

Section 1

People began thinking about other forms of transportation in addition to trains. Instead of sailing ships that depended no wind, ocean vessels were now powered by steam. The first practical car was built in Germany when Gottlieb Daimler and Carl Benz put an internal combustion engine on a horse carriage. Americans followed with their own automobiles. **Henry Ford**, however, was responsible for making cars so popular. He built the Model T using the assembly line, which made the car affordable for many Americans to purchase. Free to travel anywhere at any time, roads soon covered more miles than rail lines. Brothers **Orville and Wilbur Wright** turned their attentions to the sky. They studied aerodynamics, or how forces act on solid surfaces moving through the air. They used this knowledge to help them build the first powered airplane to achieve sustained flight. Their successful first flight happened on December 17, 1903.

Circle the names of the first two inventors to build a practical automobile.

ADVANCES IN COMMUNICATIONS

The 1800s and early 1900s brought many changes in the ways people communicate. In 1837, **Samuel Morse** used electricity to send messages with his invention, the **telegraph**. Telegraphs used a code Morse also invented to transmit pulses over wires. These long and short pulses represented letters. By putting telegraph wires along railroad lines, people were able to send messages at train stations.

How did telegraphs work?

____

____

____

The invention of the telegraph led to **Alexander Graham Bell**'s creation of the telephone. The telephone became widely used during the 1880s thanks to the thousands of miles of phone lines that stretched across every region of the country. By 1900 almost 1.5 million telephones were in American homes and offices.

Thomas Edison recorded sound with the phonograph, which became the record player. Now, music became available to everyone. In 1896, Italian physicist **Guglielmo Marconi** developed a telegraph that did not need wires. Also called the radio, the device was first used on ships for communication. By the 1920s, radio was a popular medium for news and entertainment.

Why was the radio a communication breakthrough?

____

____

____

Name ______________________ Class ______________ Date ______________

MAIN IDEA
Advances in science, medicine, and the social sciences led to new theories about the natural world and human mind, an improved quality of life, and longer life spans.

Key Terms and People

Charles Darwin scientist who developed the theory of natural selection

Marie and Pierre Curie Married French chemists who discovered the elements polonium and radium and described the process of radioactivity

radioactivity the process through which certain elements break down, releasing energy

Albert Einstein German scientist who developed the theory of relativity to describe the relationship between space, time, and motion

Louis Pasteur French chemist who showed the link between germs and disease and developed the process of pasteurization

pasteurization heating liquids to high temperatures to prevent fermentation

anesthetic something given to a medical patient to reduce pain or cause unconsciousness

Ivan Pavlov Russian physiologist who proved that dogs could be conditioned to have certain reflex actions

Sigmund Freud Austrian doctor who introduced the concept of the unconscious mind

Taking Notes

Record basic information on new ideas in the sciences, medicine, and the social sciences in a graphic organizer like this one.

Sciences	
Medicine	
Social Sciences	

Section Summary

NEW IDEAS IN SCIENCE

A number of scientific breakthroughs changed the way many people viewed the world in the late 1800s. **Charles Darwin** took a voyage during which he studied variations among plants and animals. He developed the concept of natural selection that said the strongest, best-adapted creatures were those that lived long enough to reproduce. Darwin said that over time the species would evolve or change to improve its survival chances. This idea became known as the theory of evolution. It was controversial because it says that humans evolved from other animals. It changed how many people looked at the world, even though some thought it was ridiculous or contradicted the creation story in the Bible.

Why was Darwin's theory of evolution controversial?

____

____

____

The fields of chemistry and physics also saw new discoveries during the 1800s. A scientist in England named John Dalton developed modern atomic theory. Atoms are the small particles that make up all matter. Dmitri Mendeleyev arranged the periodic table of elements in 1871. It showed all the known elements but left spaces for elements that were not yet discovered. Two of these elements, polonium and radium, were revealed by **Marie and Pierre Curie** in 1898. The Curies were chemists in France who also concluded that certain elements release energy as they break down. Marie Curie called this process **radioactivity**.

What are atoms?

____

____

What achievements are Marie and Pierre Curie known for?

____

____

Albert Einstein offered his groundbreaking theory of relativity in 1905. It said that particles of matter cannot move faster than the speed of light, and that motion is measured relative to a particular observer. His work changed the field of physics forever.

What theory did Albert Einstein develop?

____

____

MEDICAL BREAKTHROUGHS

Medicine saw great advancements during this time. French chemist **Louis Pasteur** was the first to show that bacteria, or germs, can cause disease. He also showed that bacteria are always present in the air around us and that they cause fermentation. An example of fermentation is milk going sour. By heating liquids and foods to a high temperature, the bacteria is killed so that fermentation will not happen. This process is called **pasteurization**. In addition to these breakthroughs, Pasteur developed the first vaccines, for anthrax and rabies.

What are three of Louis Pasteur's accomplishments?

The new understanding of disease and infection led to changes in how medicine was practiced. Doctors began to use **anesthetic** in order to reduce pain or make patients unconscious so they could perform pain-free surgeries. In the 1860s, English surgeon Joseph Lister developed antiseptic to clean wounds and equipment, greatly reducing hospital deaths. More hospitals were built and the need for nurses and doctors increased. Millions of American and European women attended nursing school. Some women also attended medical school. One result from these advances was a huge decrease in infant mortality, or deaths in infancy.

How did the treatment of medical patients change?

NEW IDEAS IN SOCIAL SCIENCES

New fields of science developed in the late 1800s to study people's minds and human societies. These included psychology, archaeology, anthropology, and sociology. **Ivan Pavlov**, a Russian physiologist, worked with dogs. By ringing a bell each time he fed his dogs, he found that in time, they salivated when they heard the bell, with or without the sight or smell of food. Pavlov concluded that human behaviors are also linked reflexes. **Sigmund Freud** developed a new therapy called psychoanalysis. He argued that people have unconscious minds, which means thoughts we are not aware that we have. To find out what they contained, Freud encouraged patients to talk about dreams or go under hypnosis.

What two ways did Freud propose for learning more about the unconscious mind?

Other sciences studied societies or communities with a shared culture. Archaeologists studied past civilizations and the objects left behind, while anthropologists studied humanity and human ancestors. Finally, sociologists worked to understand why large groups of people behave as they do.

Name ______________________ Class ______________ Date ______________

Life in the Industrial Age

Section 3

MAIN IDEA
During the late 1800s, cities grew and changed, while education, leisure time activities, and the arts reflected those changing times.

Key Terms and People

urbanization growth in the proportion of people living in towns and cities

romanticism art movement that was a reaction to the cold, impersonal nature of Enlightenment rationalism and the Industrial Age

William Wordsworth English romantic poet who wrote about the natural world

Ludwig van Beethoven German composer who expressed a love of nature and passionate emotion in his symphonies

realism style of writing or art in which everyday life is portrayed, as a reaction to romanticism

Charles Dickens English writer whose novel *Hard Times* described the miseries caused by industrialization

Leo Tolstoy Russian writer of *War and Peace*

Henrik Ibsen Norwegian playwright who wrote *A Doll's House*

impressionism a style of painting in which artists show brilliant color and motion

Taking Notes

As you read, take notes to list ways in which cities and daily life changed. Add more boxes as needed.

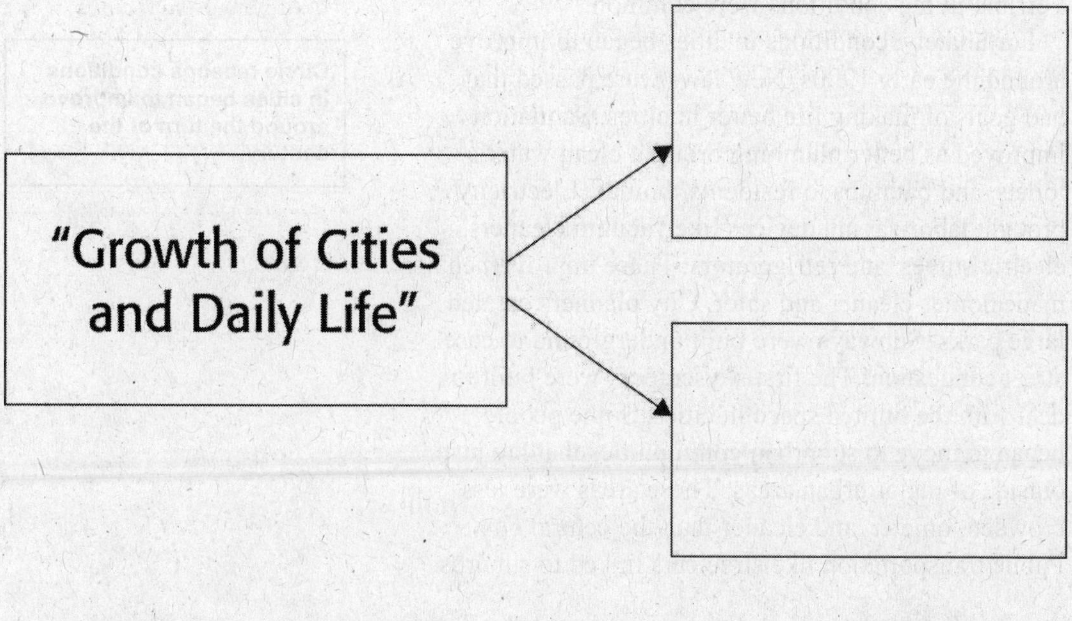

Section Summary

CITIES GROW AND CHANGE

During the 1800s, many people moved away from the countryside. The growth in the proportion of people living in cities and towns is called **urbanization**. Cities like New York, London, and Paris grew rapidly. In addition to population growth, cities began to look different and to serve a new purpose: the production and distribution of goods. Transportation networks and warehouses were built to serve the new industries. Some cities became known for specific products. For example, the meatpacking industry thrived in Chicago, while Pittsburgh became a center for the steel industry.

How did cities change in the 1800s?

____

____

Cities were loud, crowded, busy places. Cities were also becoming polluted with the smoke from the coal used to run steam engines and to warm homes. In London, smoke mixed with the fog that is very common there. This smog made it difficult for people to breathe. Despite these problems, people kept moving to cities. Whether they came from within the United States or from other countries, new city-dwellers sought jobs, but also an escape from hunger, political oppression, and discrimination. About 12 million Europeans came to the United States between 1870 and 1900. American cities such as New York, Chicago, and Boston became popular destinations. Terrible living conditions were common.

Why were cities in the 1800s unhealthy?

____

____

____

Fortunately, conditions in cities began to improve around the early 1900s. New laws were passed that had goals of making life better in cities. Sanitation improved as better plumbing brought clean water, toilets, and bathtubs to residents' homes. Electricity brought labor-saving devices like vacuum cleaners, electric stoves, and refrigerators. These improvements made homes cleaner and safer. City planners created large parks. Subways were built underground to ease street congestion. The first skyscrapers were built to deal with the limited space in cities. Some people began to move to suburban communities that lay just outside of major urban areas. These areas were less crowded, quieter, and cleaner than the central city. Public transportation like streetcars linked to suburbs.

Circle reasons conditions in cities began to improve around the turn of the century.

EDUCATION, LEISURE, AND ARTS

The growth of cities led to new art forms. People also began to earn enough money to afford leisure activities. Professional sports such as football, soccer, rugby, and baseball became popular. In Britain, railroad lines allowed working class people to travel to see soccer games and enjoy seaside resorts.

City governments began building new concert halls and theaters and supporting more orchestras, bands, and choral groups. Museums such as the Louvre (loov) in Paris made great works of art available to all. Public libraries also opened their doors.

New art forms appeared during this time. A movement called **romanticism** was the result of artists who were unhappy with the rationalism that defined the Industrial Age. Poets such as **William Wordsworth** and composers like **Ludwig van Beethoven** created works that showed their love of nature and their emotions. **Realism** was a style of writing and art that portrayed everyday life. It was a reaction to romanticism. Examples of realist writers were Englishman **Charles Dickens**, who wrote about the struggles of London's poor, and Russian **Leo Tolstoy**, who described war as chaotic and horrible. Norwegian playwright **Henrik Ibsen** revealed the unfair treatment of women within families in A Doll's House. A new style of painting called **impressionism** also appeared. Its artists tried to capture bright color and motion.

How did realism differ from romanticism?

____

____

____

The new industries of the 1800s needed an educated workforce. Governments responded by requiring education for all children. New schools that taught specific skills were built, such as Booker T. Washington's private vocational school that trained African American teachers. As more and more people learned to read, newspapers appeared in many towns. New technology improved newspaper printing processes. Journalism developed as a profession.

Why did governments start to require that all children attend school?

____

____

____

Chapter Summary

Country/Colony	Event or Situation	Reforms and Results
Great Britain	unequal representation in Parliament	Reform Act of 1832 expanded voting rights
	Chartists seek universal suffrage for men	Parliament eventually passes many voting reforms
	Women's Social and Political Union	women's suffrage
	Irish potato famine	demands for Irish independence
France	Revolution of 1830	Louis Phillipe becomes king, suffrage expanded
	1870, Third Republic	trade unions made legal, two-house legislature, president, universal manhood suffrage, universal education
Hispaniola	fighting led by Toussaint L'Ouverture	independence for Haiti
Mexico	conflicts between creoles and peninsulares	fight for Mexican independence
	spread of Enlightenment ideas	fight for South American independence; individual nations created
Brazil	Portuguese ruler flees to Brazil	Brazil granted independence
United States	Louisiana Purchase and War of 1812	Belief in manifest destiny; increased westward expansion
	colonization of Texas by American settlers	Texas independence
	war between Mexico and United States	Mexico gives up territory to United States
	Civil War	abolition of slavery

COMPREHENSION AND CRITICAL THINKING

Use information from the graphic organizer to answer the following questions.

1. **Identify** List the names of the areas that demanded independence.

____

2. **Make Inferences** How many of the above reforms or results do you think were influenced by Enlightenment ideas?

____

____

Section 1

MAIN IDEA
During the 1800s Great Britain passed many democratic reforms that changed the way people lived and worked.

Key Terms and People

suffrage the right to vote

Queen Victoria British monarch who ruled from 1837 to 1901

Victorian Era the years of Queen Victoria's reign, which were characterized by the British Empire growing increasingly democratic

Benjamin Disraeli Victorian Era British prime minister, extended voting rights of men

Emmeline Pankhurst woman who fought for women's suffrage and organized the Women's Social and Political Union (WSPU)

Taking Notes

As you read the summary, take notes on social, political, and voting reforms. Use a graphic organizer like the one below to record key points.

Reforms	
Social	
Political	
Voting	

Section Summary

SOCIAL AND POLITICAL REFORMS

The Industrial Revolution brought some prosperity to the working and middle class, groups that were not well-represented in Britain's government. Only wealthy land-owning men in England could vote. There were few political offices for minorities, such as Jews and Catholics. Representatives in Parliament were not paid, limiting political life to the wealthy. The Reform Act of 1832 gave some new industrial towns representation for the first time. The act also increased the number of men eligible to vote by about 50 percent. Many others were still kept from voting.

That same year, Parliament member Michael Sadler investigated the treatment of children in textile factories. The Sadler Report revealed harmful working conditions such as physical abuse, long hours, and low wages. Based on Sadler's findings, Parliament passed the Factory Act in 1833. This law limited the working hours of women and children in textile factories and required that children 9 to 13 years of age receive two hours of schooling a day. Also in 1833, Parliament passed the Slavery Abolition Act and new health and crime laws.

A group called the Chartists worked for all men to have **suffrage**, or voting rights. The group got its name from the People's Charter, a petition sent to Parliament in 1839. The charter also demanded vote by secret ballot, annual elections, and payment of representatives of Parliament. This last demand would make it possible for representatives to come from the working class. Parliament rejected the People's Charter, sparking public support for the Chartists. A large revolt and many uprisings followed. By the end of the 1800s, Parliament had passed many of the reforms demanded in the People's Charter.

Underline the demands sought in the People's Charter. When were many of these demands met?

____

VICTORIAN ERA VOTING REFORMS

Queen Victoria became the ruler of the British Empire in 1837. The years from her crowning until her death in 1901 are called the **Victorian Era**. Great Britain had been a constitutional monarchy for centuries. During the Victorian Era, it became more democratic. Two important prime ministers of the era were **Benjamin Disraeli** and William Gladstone. Disraeli introduced a bill that in 1867 extended voting rights to more working men. He also helped the secret ballot come into use. In 1885, Gladstone helped to extend voting rights even farther.

Some members of Parliament wanted to add women's suffrage to the 1867 bill, but it was not passed. Many women had sought the right to vote, hoping this would lead to more power for women in society. Instead, they faced a 40-year struggle, during which government leaders ignored their requests. Tired of these efforts bringing no progress, **Emmeline Pankhurst** organized the Women's Social and Political Union (WSPU) in the early 1900s. The group eventually used vandalism and arson to call attention to the suffragist cause. Parliament granted suffrage to some women in 1918, and in 1928, women had the same voting rights as men.

Why did suffragists work so long to gain the right for women to vote?

____

____

CHANGES IN THE BRITISH EMPIRE

The Act of Union created the United Kingdom in 1801, bringing together England, Scotland, and Wales with Ireland. British policies hurt Irish farmers, a situation that grew worse when the Irish potato crop failed in the mid-1800s, causing famine. Irish farmers were left without food and income. Unable to pay rent to their British landlords, many Irish were evicted from their land. Ireland continued to export food, as the British insisted that the economy not be disrupted. About 1 million people starved to death; 1.5 million others emigrated, many to the United States. The experience led many Irish to demand independence or home rule.

What events led to the death by starvation of 1 million Irish and 1.5 million more emigrating.

____

____

____

Canada, another British colony, was ruled by a governor-general starting in 1838. In 1867 the united Canadian colonies became a dominion, or a self-governing colony. Australia and New Zealand followed the Canadian example, receiving self-rule while still part of the British Empire. New Zealand became the first country to give women the right to vote in 1893.

Circle the names of nations that gained self-rule during the 1800s and 1900s.

MAIN IDEA

During the 1800s opposing groups in France struggled to determine what kind of government France would have—a republic, a constitutional monarchy, or an absolute monarchy.

Key Terms and People

Louis Philippe aristocrat called the "citizen king" whose reign was the result of the Revolution of 1830

Louis Napoleon nephew of Napoleon, elected president of France at the start of the era known as the Second Republic, later elected emperor Napoleon III

Dreyfus Affair court case in which a Jewish French army officer Alfred Dreyfus was falsely accused and convicted of spying for Germany

anti-Semitism prejudice toward Jews

Zionism movement to create a Jewish state in the original homeland of the Jews

Taking Notes

As you read the summary, use a graphic organizer like the one below to record details about the different eras in French history during the 1800s.

Years	
Leader	
Key events and policies	

Section Summary

THE REVOLUTION OF 1830

In 1830, France's King Charles X tried to rule as an absolute monarch. The people of Paris revolted in an uprising known as the Revolution of 1830. Within days, Charles gave up the throne and fled to England.

Louis Philippe became the new king. He was an aristocrat by birth but was popular with the middle-class. He dressed like them and appeared to live simply. People called him the "citizen king," but not for long. During his reign, more men received the right to vote, but voting was still limited to wealthy landowners. Louis Philippe limited freedom of the press. The gap between rich and poor grew deeper. When an economic depression surfaced in 1848, France faced another revolution.

Why did the French initially call Louis Philippe the "citizen king"?

____

____

BIRTH OF A REPUBLIC

During the Revolution of 1848, angry protesters built barricades in the street. Louis Philippe stepped down and protesters formed a new government. They called the government a republic because it was to be led by a president instead of a monarch. Voters elected **Louis Napoleon**, nephew of Napoleon. The era that followed was known as the Second Republic. The First Republic had existed during the years between the French Revolution and the reign of Napoleon. Effects of the Revolution of 1848 included permanent suffrage for all men and the start of a new women's rights movement. The Revolution also inspired others across Europe.

Not content with being president because he could not run for re-election, Louis Napoleon in 1851 sent his troops to Paris. They arrested National Assembly members who opposed him. Then Louis Napoleon called for a national vote to decide whether he should be allowed to write a new constitution. Voters gave him this power, and a year later elected him Emperor Napoleon III.

Underline phrases that explain how Louis Napoleon gained control of the French government.

Napoleon III's rule ended in 1870 after he surrendered to the Prussians during the Franco-Prussian War. Shamed, the French Assembly overthrew the king and proclaimed the Third

Republic. Despite the immediate crisis caused by the Prussian siege of Paris, the Third Republic went on to make important reforms. These included legalizing trade unions, reducing working hours, and making primary education available for children between the ages of 6 and 13.

THE DREYFUS AFFAIR

The divisions that split France came to the surface over a court case known as the **Dreyfus Affair**. A French army officer named Alfred Dreyfus (DRAY-fuhs) was falsely accused and convicted of spying for Germany. Dreyfus was Jewish. After Dreyfus was publicly humiliated, evidence revealed that another officer was found not guilty even though that officer, who was not Jewish, may have been the spy.

The incident sharply divided France into those who sided with Dreyfus and those who did not. After writer Émile Zola published a letter in which he accused the French government of **anti-Semitism**, or prejudice toward Jews, the courts reopened the Dreyfus case. Anti-Semitic riots broke out around France. Zola himself was convicted of libel.

An Austrian journalist named Theodor Herzl began a movement called **Zionism**. This movement sought to create a Jewish nation in the original homeland of the Jews. Herzl believed that the root of the problem of anti-Semitism was the lack of a Jewish homeland. By the early 1900s, settlers had created a few Jewish settlements in the eastern Mediterranean area known as Palestine. Zionism was a growing movement.

What divisions in French society were revealed by the Dreyfus affair?

____

____

What problem did Theodor Herzl believe Zionism would solve?

____

____

MAIN IDEA

Revolutionary ideas took hold in Latin America as colonies fought for independence from Europe.

Key Terms and People

Toussaint L'Ouverture a former enslaved African who led the Haitian independence movement against the French in Saint Domingue

creoles people of European descent who were born in the colonies

peninsulares colonists born in Spain

Miguel Hidalgo creole priest who was the first to call for Mexican independence

José María Morelos creole priest who led the revolutionary movement in Mexico

Simón Bolívar revolutionary leader known as the Liberator because of his key role in liberating Spain's colonies in South America

José de San Martín revolutionary leader who fought for independence from Spain in Argentina, Chile, and Peru

Pedro I prince from Portugal who declared Brazil independent then became its emperor

Taking Notes

As you read, use a graphic organizer like the one below to record details about independence movements in Latin America in the 1800s.

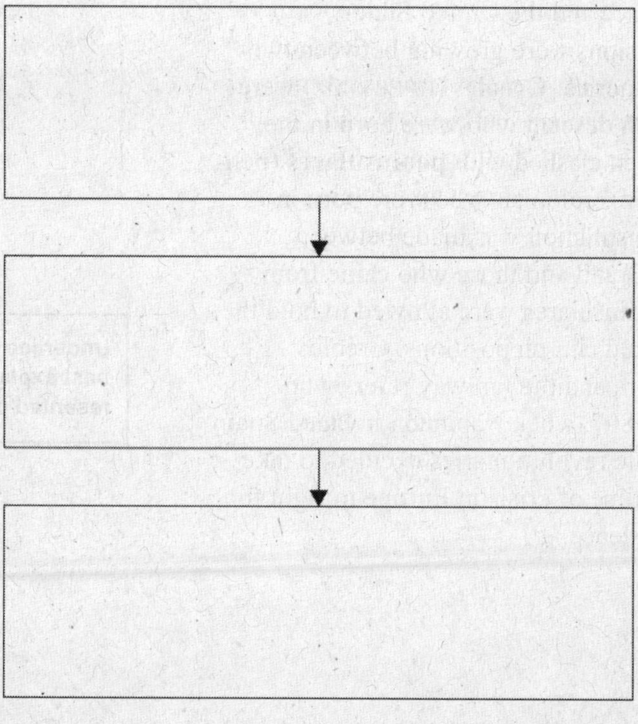

Section Summary

EARLY STRUGGLES IN LATIN AMERICA

Tensions between ethnic and social groups and colonial reforms led Europe's Latin American colonials to demand greater freedom. Born into slavery, **Toussaint L'Ouverture** (TOO-san loo-vehr-TOOR) became a military leader in Saint Domingue, the western half of the Caribbean island of Hispaniola, a French colony. He led a bloody revolt against French settlers there, making him a hero to many.

Worried that L'Ouverture had too much power, Napoleon sent a French general to take control of the island. After months of struggle, L'Ouverture agreed to an armistice, which France broke when troops captured him and sent to prison, where he died. The island continued to fight for independence. In 1804, the revolutionaries of Saint Domingue declared their independence from France and named their new nation Haiti.

What nation did Saint Domingue become?

____

While Saint Domingue sought freedom from France, colonists in Mexico and South America sought independence from Spain and Portugal. Spanish colonies had grown wealthy. Their people had access to education and to new ideas like Enlightenment philosophy and information about revolutions in France and the United States.

Meanwhile, tensions were growing between two groups in Latin America. **Creoles** (KREE-ohlz) were people of European descent who were born in the colonies. They often clashed with **peninsulares** (peh-neen-soo-LAHR-ayz), colonists who were born in Spain. A similar distinction was made between colonists born in Brazil and those who came from Portugal. Only peninsulares were allowed to hold the best government and church positions. Creoles resented this system and the faraway rulers who maintained it. In 1807, when Napoleon invaded Spain and Portugal, creole revolutionaries decided to take advantage of this time of crisis in Europe to fight for their own independence.

Underline the sentence that best explains why creoles resented peninsulares.

INDEPENDENCE IN MEXICO

In 1810, a creole priest named Father **Miguel Hidalgo** called for peasants to revolt against the peninsulares. It was the first call for Mexican independence. Hidalgo was captured and executed by Spanish authorities, but the fight for Mexican independence had just begun. Another creole priest, **José María Morelos** took Hidalgo's place. He organized a Mexican congress and led the troops that took control of parts of Mexico. He too was captured and executed.

A creole military officer named Agustín de Iturbide (ah-goos-TEEN day ee-toor-BEE-day) had remained loyal to Spain. In 1820 Spanish authorities asked Iturbide to lead a battle against the revolutionaries. When another liberal revolution in Spain threatened to take some of his power, Iturbide switched sides and fought with the revolutionaries. Mexico declared its independence in 1821. Iturbide was named Emperor Agustín I of Mexico.

In what year did Mexico declare its independence from Spain?

____

REVOLUTIONARY LEADERS IN SOUTH AMERICA

In northern South America, **Simón Bolívar** (see-MOHN boh-LEE-vahr) led military campaigns that gained independence for Spain's colonies. Bolívar's wanted to turn the former colonies into the Federation of the Andes. Instead, Venezuela, Colombia, Panama, and Ecuador became the state of Gran Colombia. Other leaders set up separate countries in Peru, Bolivia, and elsewhere.

While Bolívar was fighting in the north, **José de San Martín** led independence movements in parts of present-day Argentina, Chile, and Peru. After helping to liberate Argentina and Chile, he met Bolívar in Gran Colombia, resigned, and returned to Europe.

Brazil's path to independence was very smooth, by comparison. After Napoleon invaded Portugal, the Portuguese King John VI and his family fled to Brazil. Rio de Janeiro became capital of the Portuguese empire. Brazil was able to trade directly with the rest of the world. When John VI returned to Portugal, his son Pedro ruled Brazil. At the Brazilian colonists' request, Prince Pedro declared Brazil independent in 1822. He became Emperor **Pedro I**.

How did Brazil gain its independence from Portugal?

____

____

MAIN IDEA

As the United States began to expand westward, conflicts erupted over territory and slavery.

Key Terms and People

Louisiana Purchase agreement with France that gave the United States a huge territory in central North America

Monroe Doctrine U.S. President James Monroe's declaration that the Americas were off-limits to further European colonization

manifest destiny term for some Americans' belief that they had a God-given right to settle land all the way to the Pacific Ocean

Trail of Tears Cherokee march from their homes to Indian Territory

abolition end of slavery

Abraham Lincoln president whose election led to the secession of South Carolina and the start of the Civil War

secession separation from a union

Emancipation Proclamation Lincoln's declaration that freed all slaves in some areas of the Confederate states

Taking Notes

As you read the summary, use a graphic organizer like the one below to note the causes and effects of westward expansion and civil war in the United States.

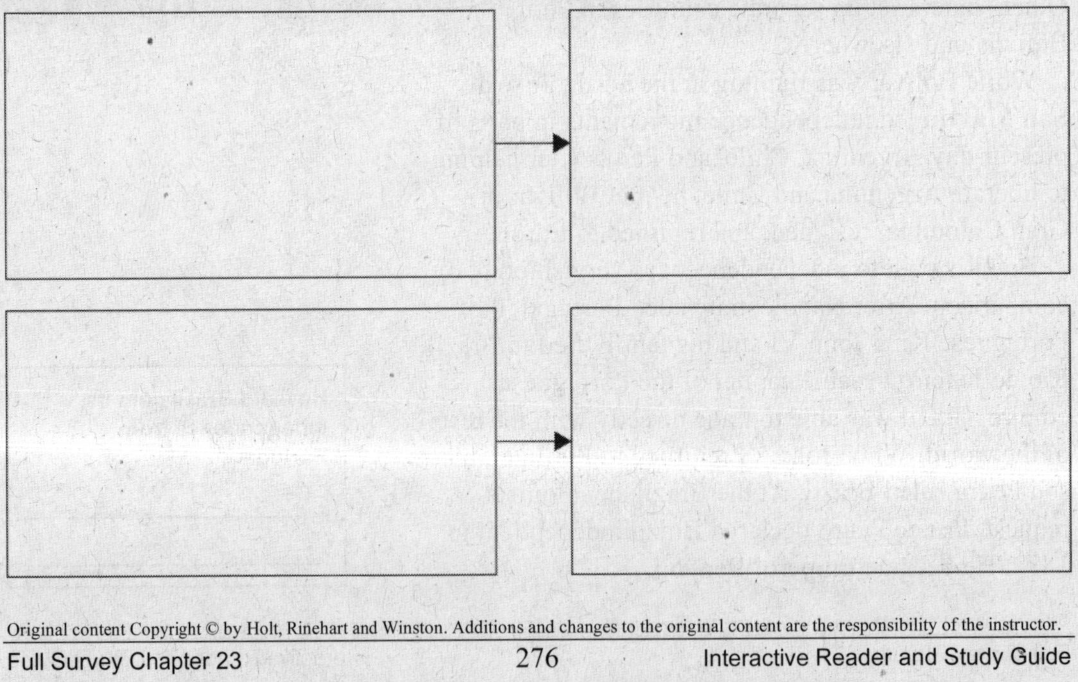

Section 4

Section Summary

GROWTH OF THE UNITED STATES

In 1803 the United States obtained from France a huge territory in central North America in the **Louisiana Purchase**. Westward expansion continued for the rest of the 1800s. Great Britain still claimed parts of Canada. Conflicts between Britain and the United States were frequent. Britain had begun seizing American sailors and forcing them to serve in British navy battles against Napoleon. The British government also helped Native Americans fight American settlers. In 1812 these conflicts led to war between Great Britain and the United States. No territory changed hands when the fighting ended, but Americans felt they had shown their independence in the conflict. President James Monroe later proclaimed that the Americas were off-limits to further European colonization in the **Monroe Doctrine**.

What conflicts between the United States and Great Britain led to the War of 1812?

____

____

____

In 1820 an American named Moses Austin received permission from Spain to start small settlements in Texas. After Mexico gained independence from Spain, Texans fought for and won independence from Mexico. Texas became part of the United States in 1845. However, the Mexican government still claimed Texas was part of Mexico. The United States and Mexico went to war over this dispute and others. The Mexican-American War ended in 1848. Mexico accepted defeat and the United States gained a large territory that is now the southwestern United States.

Why did the United States and Mexico go to war?

____

____

In 1830 the Indian Removal Act forced five Native American nations to move to territory in the Great Plains. The Cherokee's march there was so deadly it became known as the **Trail of Tears**. Later laws moved Native Americans into specific areas called reservations. By 1850, the United States had claimed territory all the way to the Pacific Ocean. Some Americans felt it was their God-given right to settle this land. This belief is called **manifest destiny**. As they moved west, white settlers often moved onto land that was inhabited by Native Americans. Conflict was frequent. Many white settlers believed the Native Americans should simply be moved farther west.

THE CIVIL WAR

Slavery had helped the American economy since its earliest days. The South especially relied on slave labor. In the 1800s, however, some people sought **abolition**, or the end of slavery. They felt it was wrong to deny the enslaved people their freedom.

As settlers moved west, Americans had to decide whether the new states and territories would allow slavery. For the first half of the 1800s, a series of compromises in Congress kept the balance between slave states and free states. In 1854 the Kansas-Nebraska Act gave the people of these two new territories the power to decide whether to allow slavery. This set off a bitter debate between antislavery and proslavery Americans.

Underline the name of the act that allowed voters in two new territories to determine whether slavery would be allowed there.

Just a month after **Abraham Lincoln** was elected president, South Carolina announced its **secession**, or separation, from the Union. Other southern states followed. Together these states called themselves the Confederate States of America. They wrote a new constitution and elected their own president, Jefferson Davis. Soon the northern and southern states were fighting a civil war. The war lasted four years and was the deadliest in American history.

In January 1863, as fighting continued, Lincoln issued the **Emancipation Proclamation**. It freed all slaves in some areas of the Confederate states. Slaves fled to the North, hurting the Southern economy. Union soldiers were encouraged because now their cause had another purpose than preserving the Union: the end of slavery. The South lost support from European nations after the proclamation was issued.

The turning point of the war came later in 1863, with the Union victory at the Battle of Gettysburg. Union soldiers finally saw they could win the war. Two years later, Confederate general Robert E. Lee surrendered. The Civil War was over.

What Civil War battle was a major turning point?

____

After the war, much of the South lay in ruins. Congress and the president had to decide how to deal with the former Confederate states and how to rebuild them. This era is known as Reconstruction. Congress passed laws and constitutional amendments to protect formerly enslaved people which became the foundation for later civil rights legislation.

Name ______________________ Class ______________ Date ______________

Nationalism in Europe

Chapter Summary

NATIONALISM IN EUROPE		
Region	**Positive Effects**	**Negative Effects**
ITALY	• Italian states freed from Austrian rule • Italian states unified as kingdom	• Ethnic conflicts continued • Catholic Church refused to recognize Italy as a nation
AUSTRIAN EMPIRE	• Dual Monarchy gave Austria and Hungary equal status • Laws passed to end ethnic discrimination	• Ethnic conflicts continued • Anti-discrimination laws were ineffective
OTTOMAN EMPIRE	• Many territories gained independence	• Series of wars destroyed population and resources
GERMANY	• Germany unified • Federalist government developed with power shared between state and national governments • Economy improved	• Conflict between Catholic Church and government • Formed European alliances that would ultimately lead to war
RUSSIA	• Nicholas II passed democratic reforms • New constitution promised individual liberties	• Protesters killed in Bloody Sunday attack • Pogrom of Jews claimed 150,000 lives

COMPREHENSION AND CRITICAL THINKING

Use information from the graphic organizer to answer the following questions.

1. **Identify** How did nationalism negatively affect both Italy and Austria?

____

____

2. **Interpret** What two factors most likely caused nationalist uprisings in Russia?

____

3. **Evaluate** Do you think the positive effects of nationalism in Europe justified the negative effects? Why or why not?

____

____

Name ______________________ Class ______________ Date ______________

Section 1

MAIN IDEA
In the 1800s, Italian states rebelled against Austria and unified as the Kingdom of Italy.

Key Terms and People

Giuseppe Mazzini founder of Young Italy, a nationalist group that fought for unification

Camillo di Cavour leader of the Italian unification movement

Giuseppe Garibaldi military leader who unified the southern states, joined them to the north, eventually forming the united Kingdom of Italy

Red Shirts Garibaldi's small, loyal army of volunteer troops

Victor Emmanuel the first king of the united Italy

Taking Notes

As you read the summary, take notes in a graphic organizer like the one below. Record details that show how nationalism in Italy led to unification and, later, challenges.

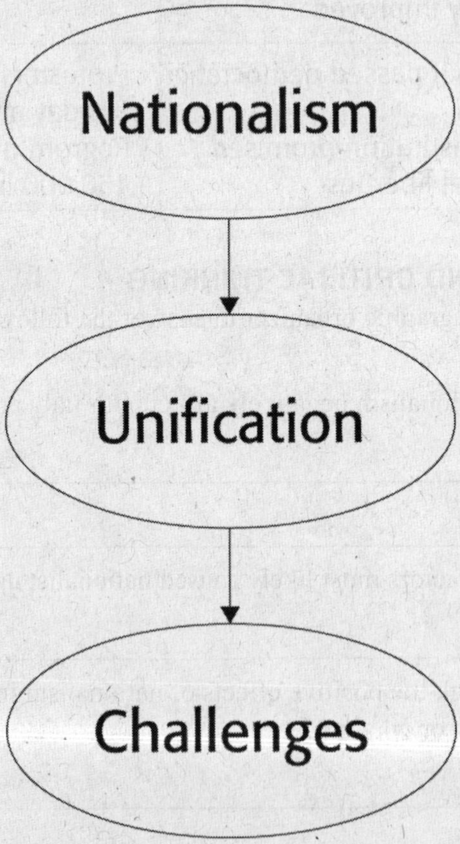

Name ______________________ Class ______________ Date ______________

Section Summary

STIRRINGS OF NATIONALISM

Nationalism, or devotion to one's national group, was an important force in Europe during the 1800s. Greece, Belgium and Poland all fought for independence early in the century, sparking nationalist movements in Italy, Germany, Austria, and Russia.

One cause of the growth of nationalism was Europe's political boundaries. Most nations did not share a common language or culture. Instead, large empires included people of very different backgrounds. When the Congress of Vienna divided Italy, some parts falling under Austrian rule, nationalism grew. Some Europeans believed that people of the same background should form separate nation-states. **Giuseppe Mazzini** formed a nationalist group called Young Italy. Mazzini's group attracted tens of thousands of supporters who wanted to fight for the unification of the Italian states.

Underline factors that led to the growth of nationalism in Europe in 1950.

THE PATH TOWARD UNITY

Politician **Camillo di Cavour** was a leader of the Italian unification movement. In 1847 Cavour founded a nationalist newspaper called Il Risorgimento, which means "resurgence" or "rebirth." Cavour believed that the Italian nationalist movement was strong enough to unite Italy, despite differences between the many Italian states.

In 1848 nationalist uprisings in France and Britain inspired a revolution in Italy. Some Italian states declared themselves republics. In other places, kings were forced to outline the people's rights in constitutions. In Piedmont, the king declared war against Austrian rule. Though the war ended in defeat, it was an important step toward unification. The leaders of the Italian states realized they needed to unite to defeat Austria.

What did Italian leaders learn from the revolution in Piedmont?

____

____

Cavour became prime minister of the Kingdom of Sardinia in 1852. He formed an alliance with France during France's war against Russia. France, in turn, agreed to support Sardinia in its planned war against Austria. By 1860 the northern Italian states were liberated from the control of the Austrian Empire.

GARIBALDI AND THE RED SHIRTS

An important member of Young Italy, **Giuseppe Garibaldi**, unified the southern Italian states and joined them to the north. Together, the states formed the Kingdom of Italy. In addition to military campaigns in central and southern Italy, Garibaldi is best known for his followers, the **Red Shirts**, who were named after their colorful uniforms.

Though Garibaldi wanted to establish a republic on conquered territory in Sicily, he instead offered it to King **Victor Emmanuel** of Sardinia. In 1860 all Italian territories except the Prussian state of Venetia and the French-supported Papal States voted for unification. By 1870, though, Prussia gave Venetia to Italy, and France withdrew their troops from Italy. All of Italy was now unified.

Why do you think Venetia and the Papal States did not vote for Italian unification in 1860?

____

____

CHALLENGES AFTER UNIFICATION

In the following years, Italy faced many challenges. People in the south resented that the government was located in the north. Rome became the new capital of Italy in 1871, but the Catholic Church did not recognize Italy as a legitimate nation. Catholics were forbidden from voting.

Voting rights increased and most Italian men could vote by the late 1800s. However, in the 50 years following unification, some 4.5 million Italians left Italy to escape widespread poverty. Working class Italians began to fight for change in a growing labor movement. Working conditions improved and production increased.

In 1882 Italy formed a military alliance with Austria-Hungary and Germany known as the Triple Alliance. Similar alliances brought most of Europe to war in 1914. Italy also tried to expand its influence elsewhere in the world. In 1911, Italy fought the Ottoman Empire and won territory in Africa.

Why did the Catholic Church forbid Italian Catholics from voting?

____

____

Name ______________________ Class ______________ Date ______________

MAIN IDEA

In the late 1800s, Otto von Bismarck transformed Germany from a loose confederation of separate states into a powerful empire.

Key Terms and People

Frederic Wilhelm IV Prussian king during the revolution of 1848

Zollverein an economic alliance that allowed for free trade between the German states

Wilhelm I king of Prussia who appointed Bismarck prime minister

Otto von Bismarck Prussian prime minister, leading force behind German unification, later first chancellor of Germany

realpolitik "politics of reality," philosophy based on practical goals, used by Bismarck

Austro-Prussian War war between Prussia and Austria from June to August 1866

Franco-Prussian War war between France and Prussia from 1870 to 1871, unification of Germany resulted

Taking Notes

As you read the summary, take notes in a graphic organizer like the one below. Record details about the steps toward unity, the wars of unification, and the establishment of the German empire after 1871.

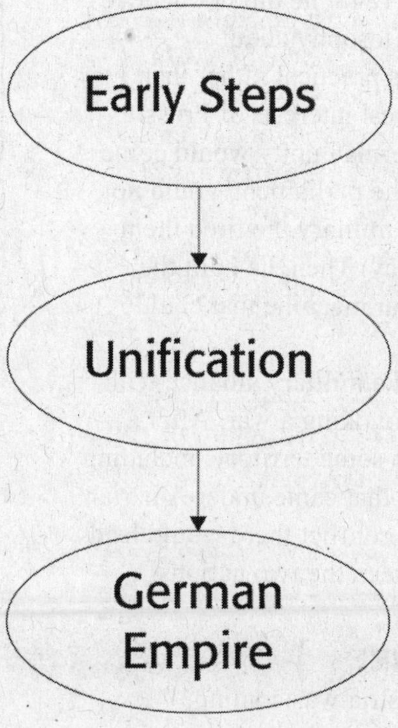

Section Summary

STEPS TOWARD UNIFICATION

Like Italy, Germany was not a unified nation in 1848. The German Confederation was made up of 39 separate states that shared a language and culture. These states included Austria and Prussia. As revolution swept through Europe in 1848, liberal Germans protested for increased democracy. Prussian king **Frederick Wilhelm IV** promised a constitution, and other reforms. However, by the end of 1848, the king went back on his promises.

Another early step toward creating a unified Germany was the **Zollverein** (TSOHL-fer-yn) in 1834. This economic alliance allowed for removal of taxes on products traded between the German states. The Zollverein encouraged the growth of railroads to connect the states. It helped join Germans economically, if not politically.

What was the purpose of the Zollverein?

____

____

BISMARCK'S PLAN FOR GERMANY

In 1862, King **Wilhelm I** chose **Otto von Bismarck** to be Prussia's prime minister. Bismarck became the leading force behind German unification, though unlike the revolutionaries of 1848, he did not believe in liberal democracy. His philosophy about government, **realpolitik**, was practical rather than idealistic, and based on the best interests of Prussia.

Underline the definition of realpolitik. Who supported this philosophy?

____

Bismarck declared that German unity would come by "blood and iron." When the parliament would not approve funds to expand the military, he fired them and collected his taxes anyway. Then, he built the Prussian army into a great war machine that could force Germany to unite.

In 1864, Bismarck formed a military alliance with Austria against Denmark, provoking a war. After a brief fight, Denmark gave up some territory, including a small bit of land in Prussia that came under Austrian control. Bismarck knew that conflict there would lead to what he desired: war between the two nations.

UNIFICATION AND EMPIRE

Convinced that war with Austria was coming, Bismarck promised territory to the Italian prime minister in return for his support. He also persuaded France to remain neutral in the upcoming war. Bismarck then provoked a war with Austria that lasted only seven weeks. Called the **Austro-Prussian War**, it resulted in a major victory for Prussia and the joining together of the North German states. It was the first step toward German unification.

In 1870, a conflict was brewing with France over the territory of Alsace and Lorraine. This issue sparked feelings of nationalism in the south German states.These states supported Prussia and the north German states in the **Franco-Prussian War** against France. Prussia won the war, and the peace treaty declared the unification of Germany. Wilhelm I became its first kaiser, or emperor. He appointed Bismarck as his first chancellor. The German victory brought more power to the new empire, while France's power decreased.

Circle the two wars that led to the unification of Germany. Who became Germany's first emperor?

____

THE EMPIRE'S GROWTH AND CHANGE

In the years after 1871, Germany became a strong empire. This period was known as the Second Reich. Each of Germany's 25 states wanted to retain some power. As a result, a federalist government developed so that power could be shared between state and national governments.

Germany also experienced economic growth after its unification. France paid reparations, money for damages, after the Franco-Prussian War. Germany used some of the money to build railroads to link the German states. Over the next 50 years, the German empire quickly caught up with the other industrial countries of Europe. However, German socialists protested against harsh factory conditions and within a few years Bismarck pushed for laws providing benefits for health, accidents, old age, and disability.

Bismarck believed that Germany was threatened by France. In response, he formed alliances with Austria-Hungary, Italy, and Russia. He also passed laws known as Kulturkampf, or "the struggle for culture," to limit the power of the Catholic Church in Germany.

In 1890, Bismarck was fired as prime minister after a disagreement with the kaiser. The kaiser continued to make alliances with other European nations.

List the two groups that Bismarck believed threatened Germany after its unification.

____

____

MAIN IDEA
Nationalism broke down two old European empires—the Austrian Hapsburg Empire and the Ottoman Empire.

Key Terms and People

Franz Joseph I emperor of Austria in 1848

Magyars an ethnic group that fought for independence in Hungary

Dual Monarchy the joining of Austria and Hungary to create Austria-Hungary, two separate, equal states under one ruler, the Austrian emperor

Crimean War war in which Britain, France, and Ottoman Turks fought Russia

Young Turks nationalist group that began a revolution in Turkey in 1908

Balkan Wars war involving many European nations that began in 1912, resulted in the Ottoman empire losing most of its land in Europe

Taking Notes

As you read the summary, take notes in a graphic organizer like the one below. Record details about nationalism in Austria, Hungary, and the Ottoman Empire.

Nationalism	
Austria	
Hungary	
Ottoman Empire	

Section Summary

THE AUSTRIAN EMPIRE

After the Congress of Vienna, the Austrian emperor, Franz I, and his foreign minister, Prince Metternich, worked together to maintain the power of the Austrian Empire and the Hapsburg monarchy. One way they did this was through laws known as the Carlsbad decrees that created a system of censorship and investigation of nationalist groups. In 1820, Metternich held the Congress of Troppau with several other European nations. Austria, Prussia, and Russia agreed to work together against nationalist revolutions in Europe. Great Britain and France refused.

In 1848 revolutions in France, Italy, and the German states set off revolts in the Austrian Empire. Metternich resigned due to rebellions in Vienna, and by the end of 1848, the emperor was replaced by **Franz Joseph I**.

Meanwhile, a revolution was raging in Hungary, another part of the Austrian empire. An ethnic group known as the **Magyars** fought for independence. The Russian czar sent troops to help Austria crush the revolt. Franz Joseph I then abolished the reforms enacted in 1848, including the new constitution. The revolutions stopped for a while.

How did Franz Joseph I end the revolutions in the Austrian empire?

____

____

THE DUAL MONARCHY

As nationalist movements continued in Europe, Austria lost one of its provinces to Italy in 1859. When Prussia defeated Austria in 1866, Franz Joseph I decided to reach an agreement with Hungarian leaders. Called the Compromise of 1867, it created the **Dual Monarchy** of Austria-Hungary. In this agreement, Austria and Hungary became two separate, equal states, both ruled by the Austrian emperor. The Dual Monarchy remained until 1918.

Circle the name of the agreement that created Austria-Hungary.

The Dual Monarchy had both benefits and problems. Hungary provided raw materials and food to Austria. Austria provided industrial products to Hungary. Ethnic divisions remained among the countries, who did not even speak the same language.

THE OTTOMAN EMPIRE

Many European powers were concerned about the declining Ottoman Empire. If it fell, other nations' territorial interests and the balance of power in Europe would be affected. The future of the Ottoman Empire became known as "The Eastern Question."

Why were European nations concerned about the future of the Ottoman Empire?

____

____

In 1854, the **Crimean War** erupted over a religious dispute between Catholics and Orthodox Christians in Palestine. Britain, France and the Ottoman Turks fought Russia in this deadly war that did not provide answers about the Ottoman Empire's future, however.

In 1865 and 1866 nationalist groups began revolutions in a small area of the empire called the Balkans. The rest of Europe became involved, and war broke out. The war lasted about two years and resulted in about 500,000 deaths. In the end, the Ottoman Empire suffered a major defeat and lost most of its territory.

In 1908, a nationalist group called the **Young Turks** began a revolution in Turkey. They fought against the absolute power of the sultan, the ruler of the Ottoman Empire. Their revolution resulted in a more representative, liberal government and more individual liberties for the Turkish people.

Russia became involved in several conflicts against the Ottomans in the Balkans, hoping to gain territory. Great Britain, France, Germany, and Austria became involved in the **Balkan Wars**. By the end of these wars, the Ottoman Empire had lost most of its land in Europe.

During which conflict did the Ottoman Empire lose most of its European territories?

____

MAIN IDEA

In the 1800s and early 1900s, Russians rebelled against the absolute power of the czar and demanded social reforms.

Key Terms and People

autocracy government by one ruler with unlimited power

serfs people who were considered part of the land they worked on

Alexander II Russian czar who came to power in 1855, believed reform was necessary

pogroms widespread violent attacks by ethnic Russians against Jews

Trans-Siberian Railroad railroad linking western Russia to Siberia in the east

Russo-Japanese War war that started in 1904 between Japan and Russia

socialist republic a form of government in which the state owns and distributes all goods to the people and there is no private property

Vladimir Lenin Marxist who published a work supporting the overthrow of the czar

Bloody Sunday massacre of Russian protesters by their government on January 22, 1905

Duma a representative assembly for approving all laws

Taking Notes

As you read the summary, take notes in a graphic organizer like the one below on government and society, reform and repression, and war and revolution in Russia.

Section Summary

GOVERNMENT AND SOCIETY

Russia's social system and government differed from western European society. For centuries, Russian monarchs maintained absolute control over most aspects of Russian life. Most czars believed in **autocracy**, or government by one ruler with unlimited power. Russia's large size made this sort of rule effective. Its size also made Russia slower to industrialize than the rest of Europe. It had a mostly agricultural economy and most of the population was peasants. Many of these peasants were **serfs**, people who were considered part of the land they worked on and were ruled by lords, the wealthy nobles who owned the land. Serfs were not slaves, but their living conditions sometimes resembled slavery. Some czars had tried unsuccessfully to improve life for the serfs. The institution of serfdom was a major problem in Russian society.

Why did Russia industrialize slower than the rest of Europe?

____

____

REFORM AND REPRESSION

Some Russians formed secret societies to fight against the czar. When Czar Alexander I died in 1825, a revolutionary group called the Decembrists rebelled against the government. Czar Nicholas I, who replaced Alexander I, crushed the rebellion and sent many of the Decembrists to Siberia. Although the revolt failed, it began a revolutionary movement that would not be stopped.

The next czar, **Alexander II**, believed that reform was necessary after Russia's defeat in the Crimean War. In 1861, he freed the Russian serfs, allowing them to buy the land on which they worked with their own money or with government help. Alexander II also set up a new judicial system, allowed some local self-government, and reorganized the army and navy.

The next czar, Alexander III, ended the reforms of his father and claimed absolute power for himself. At the same time, mobs of people were attacking and killing Jews in widespread violent attacks known as **pogroms**. Several waves of pogroms occurred in Russia.

How did Alexander II improve life for Russian serfs?

____

____

Name ____________ Class ____________ Date ____________

Nationalism in Europe

Section 4

The next czar, Nicholas II, led Russia in an era of great industrialization and expansion. The **Trans-Siberian Railroad** was built in the 1890s, linking western Russia with Siberia in the east. This expansion provoked a war with Japan known as the **Russo-Japanese War**, which began in 1904. The Japanese eventually defeated Russia.

What provoked the Russo-Japanese War in 1904?

____

____

WAR AND REVOLUTION

Russians who followed the communist theories of Karl Marx wanted a **socialist republic**. Under this society, there would be no private property, and the state would own and distribute all goods to the people. In 1902 a young Marxist named **Vladimir Lenin** published a work supporting the overthrow of the czar. Lenin became a leader of the growing revolutionary movement against the czars.

By 1905 many Russians were ready to rebel. On January 22, 1905, Orthodox priest Father Gapon led a group bringing a list of demands to the czar. As the protesters neared the Winter Palace, troops fired at the group, and hundreds died. The day became known as **Bloody Sunday**. This event inspired other Russians to rise up against the czar. Workers went on strike, university students formed protests, and peasants rebelled against their landlords. This was the Russian Revolution of 1905.

At first the Czar Nicholas II did not respond. Then he promised reform but did not follow through. Finally, a widespread worker's strike convinced him that something had to be done. He issued the October Manifesto, an official promise for reform and a more democratic government. It promised a Russian constitution that gave individual liberties to all Russians. He also gave voting rights to more Russian citizens who would elect representatives to the **Duma**, an assembly that would approve all laws.

What reforms were promised in the October Manifesto?

____

____

Name ______________________ Class ______________ Date ______________

The Age of Imperialism

Chapter Summary

Nation	Experience with Imperialism
India	British East India Company controls trade and rules country, changes Indian society; nationalist movement grows
China	British sell opium to Chinese to try to balance trade; fight war to continue selling opium; China forced to sign humiliating treaties with several nations; lose war to Japan takes control of Korea
Japan	agrees to open ports to U.S. trade; Emperor Meiji modernizes country, especially military and education; Japan takes control of Korea
Indochina	tried to expel French missionaries; French overthrow Vietnamese government and take control
Egypt	British build Suez Canal, then occupy Egypt to protect their interests
African nations	European nations divide Africa based on their own interests; rebellions ultimately unsuccessful
Ethiopia	Menelik II modernizes military and keeps nation independent
Mexico	continuing political upheaval; French emperor Napoleon III overthrows government and makes Austrian archduke emperor; U.S. supports some rulers and helps end civil war
Cuba	nationalists fight for independence; United States declares war on Spain, makes Cuba protectorate
Philippines	U.S. buys from Spain, makes colony; granted independence in 1946
Panama	United States helps nation win independence from Columbia and gets land to build Panama Canal

COMPREHENSION AND CRITICAL THINKING

Use information from the graphic organizer to answer the following questions.

1. **Recall** How did the imperialism of the 1800s differ from the colonialism of the 1500s and 1600s?

____

____

2. **Make generalizations** In what ways did European imperialism lead to the growth of nationalism in Africa and Asia?

____

____

3. **Evaluate** Do you think Africans might have been more accepting of European control if Europeans had respected traditional cultural and ethnic boundaries?

____

____

Name ______________________ Class ______________ Date ______________

The Age of Imperialism

Section 1

MAIN IDEA
One of the first examples of European imperialism in Asia, the British rule over India changed Indian politics, economics, and society and led to the rise of Indian nationalism.

Key Terms

British East India Company British company created to control trade between Britain, India, and East Asia, which ruled India in the name of Great Britain

Sepoy Mutiny rebellion by Indian soldiers who fought in the British army against their officers, set off by the introduction of a new type of British rifle

Raj Hindi word for "rule"; term used for the era of British rule in India

Indian National Congress first Indian nationalist organization, established in 1885 by English-speaking Indians, most of whom were Hindu

Muslim League organization that sought to protect the interests of Indian Muslims

Taking Notes

As you read the summary, use a graphic organizer like the one below to take notes on the development and effects of British rule in India.

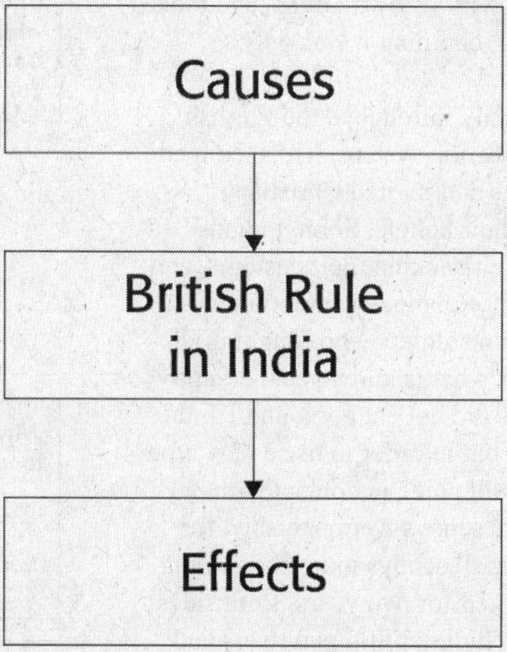

Name ______________________ Class ______________ Date ______________

Section Summary

SETTING THE STAGE

The arrival of the British in India was an example of European imperialism, the process of one people ruling or controlling another. European states in the 1700s sought to expand their influence around the world. As empires in Asia and Africa declined, and European military technology advanced, European faced little resistance as they claimed new territories.

BRITISH EAST INDIA COMPANY

Early British imperialism in India was carried out by the **British East India Company**. The company had been created to control trade between Britain, India, and East Asia. By 1800, however, it had come to rule much of India in Great Britain's name.

What was the purpose of the British East India Company?

____

When the Mughal Empire weakened, leaders of the East India Company convinced regional rulers they needed British support. This led to chaos as the company manipulated the rulers, keeping them from cooperating with one another. The East India Company then swept in with its own armies and took control of much of India, claiming it was only restoring order.

Underline the ways in which the East India Company was able to take control of India.

The East India Company introduced the English language and a new education system. It also banned some traditional customs and invited Christian missionaries to spread their beliefs. Some Indians believed the British were attacking their customs, and the practice of Hinduism. Relations grew strained.

In 1857, sepoys, Indian soldiers who fought in the British army, rebelled in what is known as the **Sepoy Mutiny**. Muslim sepoys did not eat pork, and Hindu sepoys did not eat beef, but in order to use a new type of British rifle, they would come in contact with pork and beef fat. When some sepoys were punished for refusing to use the rifles, all sepoys in northern India rose up. The fighting lasted for two years. Both sides committed atrocities, including killing civilians and burning villages. When it was over, the British government took over direct rule of India. Though they ended some of the social regulations that had

Why did the sepoys refuse to use the new type of rifle?

____

____

____

angered many, distrust continued between the British and the Indians.

INDIA AS A BRITISH COLONY

The era of British rule in India is often called the British **Raj** (RAHZH), a Hindi word meaning "rule." The administration of India was handled by a government agency called the Indian Civil Service. Most officials were British and held prejudiced opinions, such as Indians could not govern themselves without British help.

To help move troops more easily and help sell British goods throughout India, Britain built railroads, roads, and canals. An important market for British manufactured goods, India was also a source of raw materials, such as cotton, tea, indigo, and jute. Taxes collected from Indian landowners paid for the government and the Indian army. To prevent competition with British companies, officials closed Indian factories. The textile industry was especially hard hit. Many groups in India were deeply disturbed by the changes the British made. The educated and elite resented having little say in government.

Why did the British build roads, railroads, and canals in India?

____

____

During the 1800s, Indians began to see themselves as having the same rights as Europeans—and as having rights like free speech and religion routinely violated. This led to the growth of a nationalist movement. The first Indian nationalist organization, the **Indian National Congress**, was founded in 1885 by English-speaking Indians, many of whom were Hindu. At first, their requests were modest.

When Britain announced plans to partition Bengal, nationalist feelings increased. Some nationalists saw the partition as an attempt to break up Bengal's Hindu population, not, as the British said, to make the region easier to govern. Radicals in the Congress called for a boycott of British goods. The three-year boycott forced the British to make concessions.

What incident led to a three-year boycott of British goods and the creation of the Muslim League?

____

____

Another result of the boycott was the formation of the **Muslim League**. Many Muslim leaders feared that Hindus had opposed the partition of Bengal to preserve the power of Hindus at the expense of Muslims. The Muslim League sought to protect the interests of Indian Muslims.

Name ______________________ Class ______________ Date ______________

MAIN IDEA
While Western nations focused their imperial ambitions on East Asia, the reactions and results differed in China, Japan, and Southeast Asia.

Key Terms and People

unequal treaties treaties that benefited European countries at the expense of China

extraterritoriality the right of British citizens accused of crimes to be tried in British courts

Taiping Rebellion movement led by Hong Xiuquan that opposed the Qing dynasty after many believed it had lost the mandate of heaven

Boxer Rebellion rebellion by a secret society that began when its members, also called the Harmonious Fists, started attacking Christians

Sun Yixian radical who called for the overthrow of the Qing dynasty and creation of a ruling national party and, eventually, democracy

Treaty of Kanagawa agreement between Japan and the United States in 1854 that allowed American ships to stop at two Japanese ports

Emperor Meiji Japanese emperor who took control after the shogun was forced to step down in 1868, believed Japan needed to modernize and reform

Sino-Japanese War war between Japan and China over control of Korea in 1894

Taking Notes

As you read the summary, use a graphic organizer like the one below to take notes on the actions of Western nations and the responses of nations in East Asia.

	Western Actions
China	
Japan	
Indochina	
Siam	

Name ______________________ Class ______________ Date ______________

The Age of Imperialism

Section 2

Section Summary

WESTERN NATIONS GAIN POWER

Chinese rulers restricted Western trade to a single city. The British wanted to balance its trade with China, but the Chinese would only buy silver. So Britain began to smuggle opium, which was banned, into China. When the Chinese government destroyed a cache of smuggled British opium, the British responded militarily. British forces captured Shanghai in 1842 and forced the Chinese to sign the Treaty of Nanjing.

Circle the products that the Chinese bought from British traders. Which product was illegal?

____

This was the first of several **unequal treaties** that benefited European countries at the expense of China. The Treaty of Nanjing opened five more ports to Western trade and gave **extraterritoriality** to the British. This meant that any British citizen accused of a crime had the right to be tried in British, rather than Chinese, courts. Over the next several decades, the Qing dynasty was forced to sign more treaties with Britain, France, the United States, and Russia.

As the Qing rulers lost control to foreign powers, some Chinese believed the dynasty had lost the mandate of heaven. In the 1850s a movement called the **Taiping Rebellion** captured large territories and the city of Nanjing. Qing soldiers, helped by the British and French, fought the rebellion for more than a decade. By the time the Qing were victorious, more than 20 million Chinese had died in the fighting.

After China lost a war to Japan, Western nations took more parts of China for themselves. By the 1890s, U.S. officials feared it would lose profits from trade with China. It proposed the Open Door Policy, allowing free trade in ports under European control.

What was the goal of the Open Door Policy?

____

____

China's humiliation by Western nations sparked several nationalist movements. The most important was a secret society called the Harmonious Fists, or Boxers. The **Boxer Rebellion** began in 1899 with attacks on Christians. Boxers next held foreigners hostage for 55 days. Foreign troops suppressed the uprising and fined the Chinese government for secretly supporting the Boxers.

After the Boxers' defeat, Qing officials finally began to enact reforms. However, Chinese radicals living abroad called for the overthrow of the Qing dynasty. The most prominent of these radicals was **Sun Yixian**. He wanted to create a nationalist party that would rule until the Chinese people were ready for democracy. The Qing dynasty fell in 1911.

THE RISE OF MODERN JAPAN

The Tokugawa regime that ruled Japan from 1600 to 1868 at first resisted Western contact. In 1853, the U.S. Navy sent war ships to Edo (Tokyo) Bay as a show of American military power. That convinced Japanese officials to sign the **Treaty of Kanagawa**. This treaty allowed American ships to stop at two Japanese ports. A later treaty allowed trade at more ports and established extraterritoriality for Westerners. Many Japanese found these treaties humiliating.

How was the United States able to intimidate Japan into opening its ports to trade with Americans?

____

____

After the shogun, who was Japan's supreme military ruler, agreed to Western demands, the Japanese people forced him to step down. **Emperor Meiji** took power. He made reforms to strengthen Japan, including mandatory education for all children, modernization of the military, and rapid industrialization. Japan forced Korea to open ports to its merchants. When rebellion broke out in Korea in 1894, China and Japan both sent troops. Japan defeated China in the **Sino-Japanese War** and became the most powerful state in Asia. Japan took control of Taiwan, and in 1910, annexed Korea.

EUROPEANS IN SOUTHEAST ASIA

European nations had begun establishing colonies in Southeast Asia in the 1500s to obtain valuable spices. Later, they developed plantations to produce raw materials. The Dutch controlled trade in Malaysia and grew sugar and coffee. In the 1800s, the British gained control of part of Malaysia and grew rubber trees.

The Dutch controlled the spice trade from Southeast Asia for several centuries. Underline the other products the Dutch produced in Southeast Asia.

French missionaries and traders were active in Indochina in the early 1800s. When Vietnamese rulers tried to expel French missionaries, French emperor Napoleon III sent his navy. France eventually gained control of the entire country. Siam (called Thailand today) was the only Southeast Asian country to retain its independence in the 1800s. However, even Siam gave up some territory to Western nations.

Name ______________________ Class ______________ Date ____________

MAIN IDEA

In the late 1800s and early 1900s, European powers claimed land in much of Africa.

Key Terms and People

Social Darwinism philosophy that applies Charles Darwin's theory of natural selection to groups of people and states certain nations or races are more "fit" to rule the "less fit"

Cecil Rhodes English advocate of Social Darwinism who believed that a railway connecting Britain's Cape Colony to Cairo, Egypt, would bring the benefits of civilization to all Africans

Suez Canal waterway connecting the Mediterranean and Red seas, shortening the voyage from Europe to the Indian Ocean

Berlin Conference meeting during which European leaders established rules for dividing Africa among them

Leopold II Belgian king who claimed the Congo Free State in Central Africa for himself

Shaka Zulu leader who created a strong kingdom by defeating neighboring peoples

Menelik II Ethiopian emperor who undertook a program of modernization and defeated an Italian invasion

Taking Notes

As you read the summary, use the graphic organizer below to take notes on new imperialism in Africa, European nations in Africa, and resistance to imperialism.

Section Summary

THE NEW IMPERIALISM

Before the early 1800s, some European nations had profited from the slave trade in Africa. Later, some nations outlawed the slave trade. Africa then became a source for raw materials such as rubber and cotton for Europe's factories. European businesspeople established mines, plantations, and trade routes in Africa. Sometimes these Europeans asked their home nations to protect their businesses from competitors. These ambitious individuals drove colonization.

European expansion in Africa reflected power struggles in Europe. As France expanded control over West and Central Africa, its old rival Britain tried to block the French by expanding its own colonial empire. Germany and Italy sought to establish colonies in Africa to show their status as great powers.

The new imperialism was also fueled by cultural attitudes. Some Europeans felt they were superior and believed they were helping Africans by teaching them good government, European customs, and Christian values. Defenders of imperialism often applied Charles Darwin's theory of natural selection to the struggle between groups of people. **Social Darwinism** stated that certain nations or races are more "fit" than others and should rule over the "less fit" nations. One advocate of Social Darwinism was Englishman **Cecil Rhodes**. Rhodes believed that a railroad linking Britain's Cape Colony in southern Africa with Cairo, Egypt, would bring what he believed was the benefits of civilization to all Africans.

Describe the cultural attitudes of some Europeans toward Africans.

____

____

EUROPEAN CLAIMS IN AFRICA

Advances in medicine, travel, communication, and weaponry made it easier for Europeans to conquer Africa. New technologies enabled Europeans to travel more easily, avoid disease, defeat African fighters, and overcome communication problems.

In 1869, the British opened the **Suez Canal** in Egypt. This waterway connected the Mediterranean with the Red Sea and dramatically shortened the trip from Europe to India and Asia. The British occupied

Why was the Suez Canal important to European traders?

____

____

Egypt in 1882 and later established Egypt as a protectorate to ensure British access to the canal.

In 1884 European leaders met in Berlin, Germany, to divide African territory. Leaders at the **Berlin Conference** decided that when a European nation claimed a new African territory, it had to tell other European countries and prove it could control the territory. Africans' traditional ethnic boundaries were ignored as the Europeans proceeded.

What did the people at the Berlin Conference overlook? Why do you think they did this?

____

____

In southern Africa, Dutch settlers known as Boers opposed British claims to the territory. War broke out in 1899. The British eventually won and made South Africa a self-governing union under British control.

Unlike most of Africa, the Congo Free State in Central Africa was claimed by a single individual. Belgian king **Leopold II** exploited the natural resources of the Congo for his own personal gain until international outcry over Leopold's cruelty toward his Congolese subjects caused the Belgian government to take control of the Congo in 1908.

AFRICAN RESISTANCE

Africans did not passively accept European claims to rule over them. The Zulu people in South Africa resisted colonialism for more than 50 years. Their leader **Shaka** built a strong kingdom by subduing neighboring peoples in the early 1800s. The British invaded Zulu territory in 1879, eventually annexing the kingdom as a colony.

Circle the groups of African peoples who fought against European imperialism.

Only Ethiopia remained independent because it matched European firepower. In 1889 the emperor of Ethiopia, **Menelik II**, modernized his nation and his army. This modern army defeated Italian forces that invaded Ethiopia in 1895.

In West Africa, Samory Touré, the leader of the Malinke people, created his own army. They were able to fight off French rule for 15 years. He was overthrown in 1898. This ended the resistance to French rule in West Africa.

In German East Africa, several groups of people united against the Germans' order to grow cotton for export. That rebellion, however, was put down quickly as the Germans killed tens of thousands of Africans.

MAIN IDEA

Imperialism in Latin America involved the United States and European nations seeking to strengthen their political and economic influence over the region.

Key Terms and People

Antonio López de Santa Anna popular leader who dominated politics for 30 years after Mexico's independence

Porfirio Díaz Mexican leader who ruled with an iron fist and modernized Mexico's economy, largely to the benefit of the rich and elite

Francisco "Pancho" Villa revolutionary who led a band of peasants against the Mexican government, capturing the city of Juárez in 1911

Emiliano Zapata rebel who led a group of indigenous peasants against the government and called for land reform

Venustiano Carranza political rival of Pancho Villa, became Mexican president in 1916

José Martí exiled Cuban nationalist who founded the Cuban Revolutionary Party and used his writings to urge Cubans to continue to fight for independence

Spanish-American War war between Spain and the United States in Cuba

Emilio Aguinaldo Philippine rebel leader who felt betrayed when the United States did not grant the Philippines independence

Roosevelt Corollary declaration by President Theodore Roosevelt that the United States would use military might to keep Europeans out of the Americas

Taking Notes

As you read the summary, take notes on the sequence of events in Latin America from 1820 to 1920. Use the graphic organizer below, or make one yourself on a separate sheet of paper, to record key points.

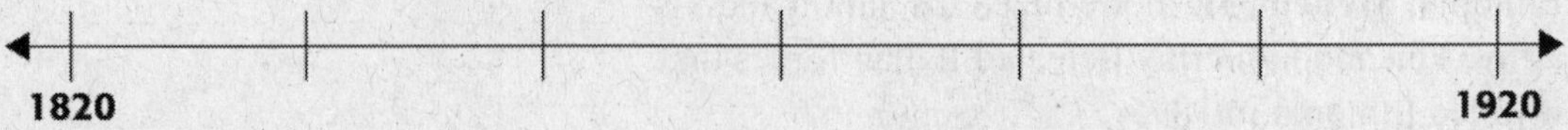

Section Summary

POWER STRUGGLES IN MEXICO

Mexico won independence from Spain in 1821. It became a republic in 1823. For the next 30 years, **Antonio López de Santa Anna** dominated Mexican politics. He was president seven times. He was exiled then returned to power several times before being overthrown by reformers in 1855. The leader of those reformers was Benito Juárez. He reduced the power of the Catholic Church and the military. These changes angered conservatives, and civil war erupted. Juárez won with the help of the United States.

Conservatives turned to French emperor Napoleon III, who wanted to restore a French empire in the Americas. In 1861, he sent troops to overthrow the Mexican government. Napoleon made Austrian archduke Maximilian emperor of Mexico. When French troops later withdrew, Maximilian did not have enough support to stay in power. In fact, he was executed by Republican troops. Considered a national hero for fighting against Maximilian and the French, Juárez became president again.

How did Austrian archduke Maximilian become emperor of Mexico?

____

____

After the death of Juárez, **Porfirio Díaz** came to power. He maintained law and order and modernized Mexico's economy. Discontent grew, however, because few Mexicans benefited from the modernization. Díaz controlled the outcome of the election of 1910, then jailed his opponent, Francisco Madero. Madero later fled to the United States. While in Texas, he declared himself president of Mexico and called for a revolution against Díaz.

A year later, rebellion was spreading in Mexico. **Francisco "Pancho" Villa** led a band of rebels who supported Madero's ideas. They captured the city of Juárez in 1911. Meanwhile, **Emiliano Zapata** led a group of indigenous peasants calling for land reforms. Díaz was soon forced to resign. Madero was elected president in 1911. Within months he was overthrown by army chief Victoriano Huerta then executed. Villa and Zapata revolted, United States Marines were sent to occupy the city of Veracruz, and in 1914 Huerta fled to Spain.

What two men led uprisings against the rule of Díaz?

____

____

Venustiano Carranza declared himself president. Villa and Zapata refused to support him. Civil war erupted again. Carranza won, but Villa and his army continued to attack the government. When the United States recognized Carranza as president, Villa led an attacked across the U.S. border. American forces pursued Villa, but were never able to capture him.

GROWING U.S. INFLUENCE

In the 1860s nationalists in Cuba began fighting for independence from Spain. **José Martí** was an exiled rebel leader. Through his writings, he encouraged Cubans to fight for independence. He was killed when he returned to Cuba in 1895 to join an uprising that was brutally stopped by the Spanish.

U.S. newspapers printed sensational stories and illustrations about events in Cuba and urged the United States to enter the war. This kind of reporting is known as yellow journalism. When the U.S. battleship *Maine* exploded in Havana's harbor in 1898, Congress declared war on Spain. The United States easily won the **Spanish-American War**. Spain gave up Puerto Rico and Guam. The United States agreed to buy the Philippines for $20 million. The United States made Cuba a protectorate.

What part may yellow journalism have played in starting the Spanish-American War?

____

____

In the Philippines, some nationalists believed independence would come next. However, the United States made the Philippines a colony. Rebel leader **Emilio Aguinaldo**, who had cooperated with U.S. forces against Spain, felt betrayed. Rebels fought the U.S. occupation for three years, but the Philippines did not win independence until 1946.

In Latin America, the United States wanted to build a canal across the Isthmus of Panama. Columbia would not allow it. U.S. president Theodore Roosevelt supported an uprising against Columbia. Panama was declared independent and signed a treaty giving the United States land to build the canal.

Circle the country that at first blocked U.S. efforts to build the Panama Canal.

In 1904, Roosevelt announced the **Roosevelt Corollary** to the Monroe Doctrine. This policy stated that the United States would use its military might to keep Europeans out of the Americas. In the early 1900s the United States used this policy to justify sending troops to several Latin American countries.

Chapter Summary

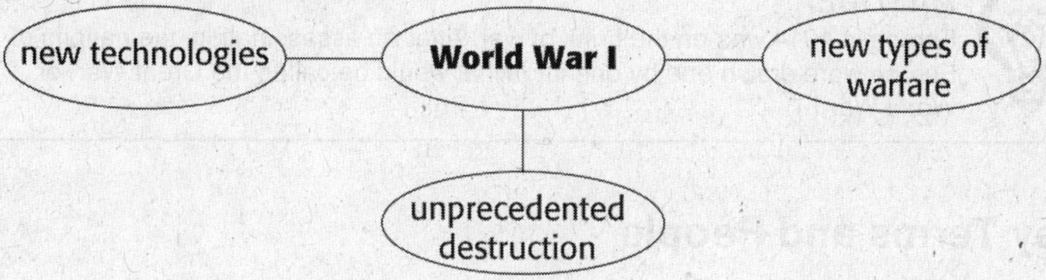

COMPREHENSION AND CRITICAL THINKING

Use information from the graphic organizer to answer the following questions.

1. **Explain** Why was poison gas sometimes dangerous to the army who had launched it against an enemy?

____

____

2. **Analyze** In what ways was World War I different from wars that had come before it?

____

____

3. **Elaborate** In some European nations, almost all the young men died in World War I. How do you think this loss affected those nations in the years to come?

____

____

4. **Rank** Which of the new technologies and new forms of warfare used in World War I do you think was the most effective? Explain.

____

____

MAIN IDEA

Europe in 1914 was on the brink of war. After an assassination, the nations of Europe were drawn one by one into what would be called the Great War, or World War I.

Key Terms and People

Triple Alliance partnership that united Germany, Austria-Hungary, and Italy

Triple Entente alliance between France, Russia, and Great Britain

Franz Ferdinand archduke of Austria-Hungary whose assassination led to World War I

Gavrilo Princip young Serbian who assassinated Franz Ferdinand and his wife Sophie

neutral taking no side in a conflict

Central Powers term for Germany and Austria-Hungary in World War I

Allied Powers term for Great Britain, France, Russia, and Serbia in World War I

Western Front series of trenches dug by both the Allied Powers and Central Powers in northern France, resulting in a deadlock

Taking Notes

As you read the summary, take notes on the events leading up to the outbreak of war in a graphic organizer like this one. Add boxes as needed.

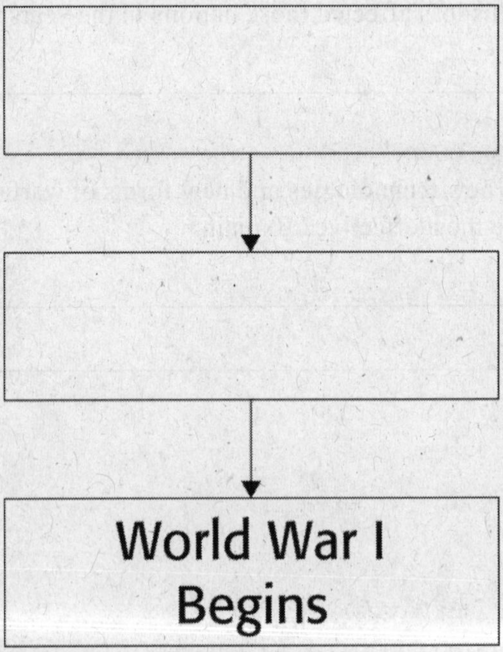

Section Summary

EUROPE ON THE BRINK OF WAR

In 1914, four factors led to rising tensions in Europe. Militarism, alliances, imperialism, and nationalism combined to put the continent on the brink of war.

Throughout the previous decades, European countries had built up their armies and navies. They wanted to protect their overseas colonies from attack by other nations. Germany in particular had greatly increased the size of its military.

This military build-up made nations nervous about the power of their neighbors. Many sought alliances for protection. In the late 1800s, Germany, Austria-Hungary, and Italy united as the **Triple Alliance**. Each nation pledged to defend the others in the event of an attack. In response, France and Russia formed their own alliance. Great Britain then made an agreement, or entente (ahn tahnt), with France and Russia. These three nations became known as the **Triple Entente**. Across Europe, leaders hoped these alliances would prevent any nation from attacking another.

Underline the nations that were part of the Triple Alliance. Circle the nations that were part of the Triple Entente.

At the same time, rivalries over empires were growing. Germany, France, Russia, and Great Britain had all built foreign empires and sought to keep other nations from gaining greater imperial power.

How were military alliances related to imperialism in pre-war Europe?

____

____

Another cause of rising tensions was an increase in nationalism, a strong pride in one's country. In Europe, nationalism had led to the creation of countries such as Germany and Italy. It also led to struggles for power, especially on the Balkan Peninsula in southeastern Europe. Serbia wanted to expand its borders and unite all the Serbs living in the Balkans in a "greater Serbia." Austria-Hungary to the north opposed Serbian expansion because it feared rebellion by other Slavic groups in Austria-Hungary.

WAR BREAKS OUT

As tension grew, the archduke of Austria-Hungary, **Franz Ferdinand**, visited the Bosnian city of Sarajevo (SAR-uh-YAY-voh). Serbian rebels had plotted to assassinate the archduke. As Ferdinand's car rolled through the city, one of those rebels,

Gavrilo Princip, shot and killed the archduke and his wife Sophie.

After Princip was identified as a Serb and the murder weapon was found to be supplied by the Serbian government, the Austrian-Hungary government threatened war against Serbia. Russia, which had promised to support the Serbs, prepared for war. Germany saw Russia's war preparations as a threat and declared war on Russia. Germany later declared war on Russia's ally, France.

Which nation was first to declare war in 1914?

____

Germany's army first attacked Belgium, planning to travel through that nation on the way to France. Belgium, however, was a **neutral** country that had promised to take no side in the conflict. Because Germany had attacked a neutral country, Great Britain declared war on Germany. The war became a conflict between two groups of nations. Germany and Austria-Hungary became known as the **Central Powers**. France, Russia, Serbia, and Great Britain were called the **Allied Powers**.

FIGHTING IN 1914

German troops quickly advanced through Belgium, meeting a combined force of French and British soldiers in mid-August 1914. The first major battle, the Battle of the Frontiers, ended with a clear German victory. Meanwhile, however, Russia attacked German territory from the east. In the Battle of Tannenberg, German forces crushed the Russian army. However, the Russian attack had given Great Britain and France time to reorganize their forces. In early September, the Allied Forces succeeded in driving back German forces at the Battle of the Marne. After retreating, German soldiers dug a series of trenches along the Aisne (AYN) River. When the allies attacked again, Germany won the Battle of the Aisne. Allied forces dug trenches of their own. Despite a series of battles that followed, German and Allied forces gained little ground in the coming months. This deadlocked region in northern France became known as the **Western Front**.

Underline the names of the major World War I battles of 1914.

MAIN IDEA
With the introduction of new types of warfare and new technologies, World War I resulted in destruction on a scale never before imagined.

Key Terms and People

trench warfare war fought from trenches

total war war that requires the use of all of society's resources

propaganda information designed to influence people's opinions

Battle of Verdun battle in which Germany tried to kill as many French soldiers as possible, believing the French could not bear to see this historic city captured

Gallipoli Campaign Allied effort to destroy the Central Powers' guns and forts that lined the Dardanelles

genocide the deliberate destruction of a racial, political, or cultural group

Taking Notes

As you read the summary, take notes on the weapons and technology of the battlefield and the events of the war in a graphic organizer like this one.

Section Summary

THE WORLD WAR I BATTLEFIELD

By the end of 1914, the war had become one of **trench warfare**, or fighting from trenches. Both sides had dug hundreds of miles of trenches along the Western Front. Neither could make significant advances. Trenches were muddy, unsanitary, and crowded. When troops were ordered "over the top" of their trench to attack the enemy, many were gunned down. Often, their bodies could not be recovered.

In an effort to gain an advantage in the war, both sides sought new technologies and weapons. Poison gas was developed to injure or kill enemy soldiers. However, the wind sometimes blew the gas back toward the soldiers who had launched it. Gas became even less effective when both sides developed gas masks to protect soldiers. Other technologies were more effective, such as machine guns and tanks. Aircraft quality improved, and in time, airplanes were not just observing enemy positions: they were equipped with machine guns and dropping bombs. Even with these innovations, neither side gained a battlefield advantage. The war raged on.

Underline the new technologies that were developed and used in World War I. Why were these technologies developed?

____

____

WAR ON THE HOME FRONT

World War I required all of society's resources. This is called **total war**. Governments took control of important industries and the economy. They also censored newspapers. **Propaganda**, or information created to influence people's opinions, helped maintain public support for the war.

Women on the home front took over jobs men had left. In some cases, they worked in factories making weapons and munitions. Other women served as nurses to wounded soldiers. These efforts helped transform people's idea of what women could do. In the United States, this new view helped women finally win the right to vote.

What actions by women during World War I helped them finally gain the vote in the United States?

____

____

BATTLES ON THE WESTERN FRONT

In May 1915, Italy entered the war by joining the Allied Powers. In a long series of battles against Austria-Hungary on the Italy-Austria border, Italy made little progress. German leaders planned to attack Verdun, believing that the French could not bear to see the historic city captured. The German army's goal in the **Battle of Verdun** was to kill as many French soldiers as possible. In 1916, German troops killed some 400,000 French soldiers. However, a similar number of German soldiers died. Both sides were badly weakened.

Partly in an effort to push the Germans back from Verdun, the British launched an attack at the Somme River area in France. Like the Battle of Verdun, the Battle of the Somme resulted in massive casualties on both sides, but no major breakthrough. In July 1917, the British started the Third Battle of Ypres (ee-pruh) in Belgium. The Germans held the high ground in an otherwise flat area, easily defeating the British.

What was the total number of soldiers killed in the Battle of Verdun, from both France and Germany?

____

WAR AROUND THE WORLD

With the stalemate in Europe continuing, nations turned to other regions to seek an advantage. After the Ottoman Empire joined the Central Powers in 1914, the Allies attacked the Ottoman-controlled Dardanelles (dahr-den-ELZ). The region is a sea passage that connects the Black Sea and the Mediterranean. The Allies relied on the passage to ship supplies to Russia. The **Gallipoli Campaign** in 1915 was an unsuccessful Allied effort to destroy the guns and forts in the Dardanelles.

Underline the name of the area the Allies sought to control through the Gallipoli Campaign. Why was this area important?

____

____

As the Ottoman Empire fought off the Allies in Gallipoli, Russia attacked the Caucasus (KAW-kuh-suhs) region on Turkey's northern border. The area was home to millions of Armenians. Turkish leaders, accusing the Armenians of helping the Russians, forcibly removed them from the area. After some 600,000 Armenians died from neglect and violence, Turkish leaders were accused of **genocide**, the deliberate destruction of a racial, political, or cultural group. Later, when Ottoman subjects in Arabia began to rebel, the British sent officer T.E. Lawrence to help them win their independence.

Other battles were fought in Asia and Africa as armies attacked their enemies' colonies abroad. Colonists from all over the world took part in the fighting.

Name ______________________ Class ______________ Date ______________

World War I

Section 3

MAIN IDEA

The war and social unrest combined to push Russia to the edge of a revolution. The events that followed led to Russia's exit from the war and became a major turning point in world history.

Key Terms and People

Bolsheviks Marxist group that sought to lead a revolution against the Czar's government

Grigory Rasputin self-proclaimed holy man and healer, advisor to Czarina Alexandra

Marxism-Leninism another term for Bolshevism

Leon Trotsky top Bolshevik official who negotiated for peace with the Central Powers

New Economic Policy 1921 plan that permitted some capitalist activity in Russia in order to increase food production

Taking Notes

As you read the summary, take notes on Russia during the war, during the Revolution, and after the Revolution in the graphic organizer like the one below. Add more causes and effects as necessary.

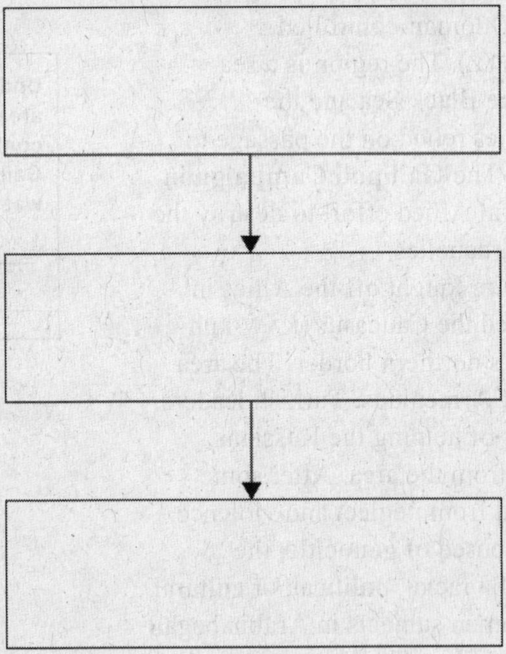

Section Summary

RUSSIA AND WORLD WAR I

Before World War I, poor economic conditions in Russia made Czar Nicholas II increasingly unpopular. A small group of Marxists who called themselves **Bolsheviks** (BOHL-shuh-viks) sought to lead a revolt against the government. In 1914, conditions were so bad that government officials hoped the war would unify the Russian people's trust in its leadership.

In 1914, Russia had a huge army, but it was not prepared for war. The army was led by weak and inexperienced officers and still used out-of-date equipment. Factories could not produce supplies quickly enough. In addition, Russia's transportation system was inadequate for moving troops and equipment.

Underline the problems the Russian army faced in 1914.

Millions of Russian soldiers died or were wounded in the first year of the war. In 1915, Nicholas decided to personally take command of the army. However, he knew little about warfare and could not lead the army to victory. The soldiers lost faith in their leaders and the army was nearly ruined.

Back in Russia, Nicholas had left his unpopular wife, Czarina Alexandra, in control when he went to war. Alexandra relied on the advice of self-proclaimed holy man and healer **Grigory Rasputin**, who many Russian people saw as corrupt and immoral.

THE RUSSIAN REVOLUTION

On March 8, 1917, unhappy Russians took to the streets of the capital, Petrograd, to protest the lack of food and fuel. Soldiers refused to shoot the rioters as ordered. Czar Nicholas II ordered the Russian legislature, known as the Duma, to disband. They too refused. No longer in control, Nicholas abdicated, or stepped down, on March 15. The monarchy in Russia had ended.

What events led Czar Nicholas II to abdicate in 1917?

____

____

____

The Duma established a temporary government under the leadership of Aleksandr Kerensky. The new government planned to continue fighting the war. This plan was unpopular with the people.

The Bolsheviks opposed Kerensky's government. They pushed for a Marxist revolution that would bring economic and social change. Because the Bolsheviks were led by Vladimir Lenin, Bolshevism was also known as **Marxism-Leninism**.

In mid-1917 the exhausted Russian army collapsed while fighting a final battle against the Central Powers. In November, armed factory workers known as the Red Guard attacked the provisional government. Kerensky's government was quickly overthrown; the Bolsheviks took control. Lenin became the nation's leader. He established a radical Communist program. The program made private land ownership illegal and gave workers control over factories.

What was the Red Guard? Underline the phrase that tells what the Red Guard did.

____

AFTER THE REVOLUTION

After the revolution, Lenin sent **Leon Trotsky**, a top Bolshevik official, to negotiate for peace with the Central Powers. The weakness of the Russian army gave Trotsky little to bargain with. Under the terms of the treaty, Russia had to give up huge chunks of its empire.

Why was Russia forced to accept the unfavorable terms of the treaty?

____

____

Many Russians were upset by the treaty. Some of the Bolsheviks' opponents came together to form the White Army. They went on to fight a three-year civil war against the Bolshevik government's Red Army. By the time the Bolsheviks won, millions of Russians had died and famine had swept the country.

Lenin introduced the **New Economic Policy** in 1921. This plan permitted some capitalist activity, such as peasants selling their food for profit. The goal was to increase food production in Russia. By 1922 the economy was improving, and Russia reunited with neighboring lands that had been part of the Russian empire before 1917. The country then became known as the Union of Soviet Socialist Republics, also called the Soviet Union. Lenin's death in 1924 brought about a struggle for control of the nation.

Name ______________________ Class ______________ Date ______________

MAIN IDEA

After several years of bloody stalemate—and the entry of the United States into the conflict—the Allied Powers finally prevailed. The peace, however, proved difficult to establish.

Key Terms and People

Woodrow Wilson United States President during World War I

U-boats German submarines that threatened ships in the waters around Great Britain

Zimmermann Note German diplomat's secret message to Mexico urging an attack on the United States

armistice truce

Fourteen Points Woodrow Wilson's plan for world peace, proposed in 1918

Treaty of Versailles treaty that ended World War I and punished Germany severely

League of Nations organization of nations created with the hope of ending future wars

mandates territories to be ruled by European powers

Balfour Declaration statement issued by Britain in 1917 favoring the creation of a Jewish state in Palestine

Taking Notes

As you read, take notes on the events that led to the war's end, the peace process, and the war's costs in the graphic organizer like the one below. Add more causes and effects as necessary.

Section Summary

THE UNITED STATES ENTERS THE WAR

Many Americans agreed with President **Woodrow Wilson**'s decision to keep the United States out of other nations' affairs. America remained neutral at the beginning of World War I. However, events eventually brought the United States into the war.

As part of its strategy of unrestricted submarine warfare, Germany used **U-boats**, or submarines, to attack any ship traveling around Great Britain. Germany hoped this would weaken Britain's ability to get supplies needed for the war. Germany believed this would help defeat the British navy. However, attacks on passenger ships such as the Lusitania angered the American public.

Underline the sentences that explain why the German navy attacked passenger ships.

The **Zimmermann Note** further angered Americans. This was a secret message in which a German diplomat asked Mexican officials to attack the United States. German leaders hoped such an attack would keep the United States out of the war in Europe. Instead, the United States joined the Allies.

THE END OF THE FIGHTING

In 1917, as the United States prepared to fight in Europe, Russia accepted defeat. Germany was then able to focus all its resources on the Western Front. In March 1918, Germany launched its final attack on the Western Front, forcing the Allies back. However, the German army suffered huge losses. After fresh American troops arrived, the Allies started the Second Battle of the Marne. Pushed back, the German army collapsed. Germany and the Allies agreed to an **armistice**, or truce, on November 11, 1918.

Why was Germany able to focus its military resources on the Western Front in 1918?

____

A DIFFICULT PEACE

Before the end of the war, Woodrow Wilson had announced a plan for world peace that he called the **Fourteen Points**. It asked all countries to reduce weapons and give their people the right to choose their own governments. To prevent future wars, Wilson proposed forming an international organization of nations to protect each other from aggression. The other Allied leaders had different goals. The French wanted to punish Germany and destroy its ability to fight war. The British wanted to punish Germany, but preferred to keep Germany strong enough to stop the spread of communism from Russia. Italy wanted to gain land.

The Allies eventually compromised on the **Treaty of Versailles**. Germany was forced to take responsibility for starting the war and pay huge sums of money to the Allies. The treaty limited the size of Germany's military. Germany was also required to give up its colonies and to give back conquered lands to France and Russia. The treaty was humiliating, but Germany had no choice but to accept it.

The treaty also called for creation of the **League of Nations**, the international body Wilson had sought in his Fourteen Points. However, Germany was excluded from membership. The organization was not as strong as it could have been because Wilson was not able to convince the U.S. government to join.

The other Central Powers negotiated separate treaties with the Allies. Austria-Hungary and the Ottoman Empire were broken up into the new nations of Austria, Hungary, Yugoslavia, Czechoslovakia, and Turkey. Middle Eastern lands formerly ruled by the Ottoman Empire were turned into **mandates**, or territories to be ruled by European powers. In 1917, Britain issued the **Balfour Declaration**, which favored establishing a Jewish state in Palestine, the ancient Jewish homeland.

Underline the phrases that describe the differing goals of the Allied Powers' leaders.

Why was the Treaty of Versailles humiliating for Germany? Why was Germany forced to accept the terms of the treaty?

____

____

____

THE COSTS OF THE WAR

World War I was the most devastating conflict the world had ever seen. Nearly nine million soldiers were killed. The next year, the world's suffering continued. In the spring of 1919, a deadly outbreak of influenza killed up to 50 million people around the world.

In Europe, the war devastated farmland, cities, and national economies. While Europe rebuilt, Japan and the United States emerged as economic powers.

Monarchies were overthrown in Austria-Hungary, Germany, the Ottoman Empire, and Russia. In far-off colonies, colonists who had fought in the war began to demand rights for themselves and their nations. The age of great empires was coming to its end.

Underline the number of soldiers killed in World War I. Circle the number of people killed by the 1919 influenza outbreak.

Chapter Summary

Challenges of the Interwar Years, 1919-1939

Leadership Changes	The Great Depression	Rise of Nationalism
• Mussolini is Italy's dictator • Military leaders control Japan • Stalin rises to power in the USSR, Hitler in Germany	• U.S. stock market crashes • worldwide trade slows and stops • widespread unemployment • banks close • political instablilty	• Mao Zedong leads Chinese communists • Turkey and Iran created • Gandhi leads Indian fight for independence

COMPREHENSION AND CRITICAL THINKING

Use information from the graphic organizer to answer the following questions.

1. **Recall** What were three effects of the Great Depression?

____

____

2. **Contrast** What are the differences between nationalism and fascism?

____

____

3. **Draw conclusions** How did the Great Depression contribute to the rise of dictators such as Adolf Hitler?

____

____

4. **Rank** What do you think was the most serious challenge faced by people who lived during the interwar years? Why?

____

____

MAIN IDEA

During the chaotic years following World War I, nationalist feeling increased in Asia and Africa. The resulting unrest continued into the 1930s.

Key Terms and People

Jiang Jieshi leader of the nationalist Guomindang party in China, he was also known as Chiang Kai-Shek

Mao Zedong leader of the Communist party in China

Long March a 6,000 mile trek through China traveled by Communists to find a safe place beyond Guomindang control

Amritsar Massacre 1919 incident in which British soldiers opened fire on unarmed Indian demonstrators, killing 400 people and convincing many Indians that British rule must end

Mohandas Gandhi leader of nonviolent movement in India against British rule

Kemal Atatürk leader of the military effort to claim Anatolia for ethnic Turks, which led to the establishment of the Republic of Turkey

Taking Notes

As you read the summary, use a graphic organizer like the one below to record details about the rise of nationalism in the years after World War I.

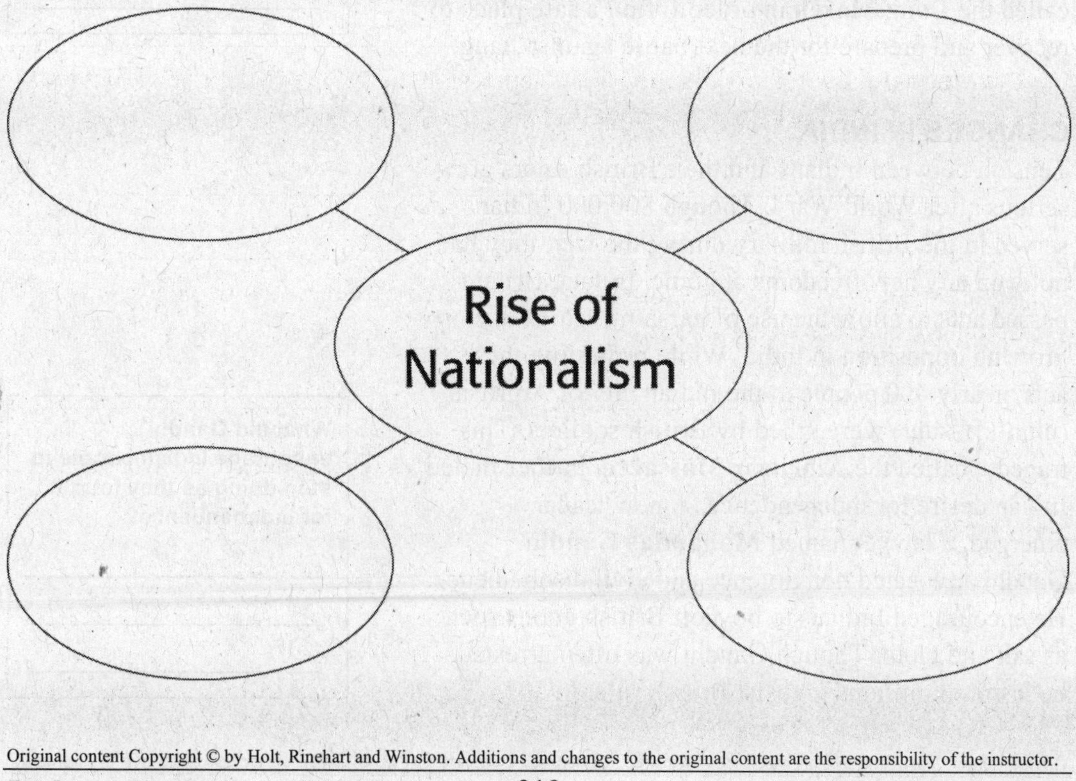

Section Summary

CHINA AFTER WORLD WAR I

China faced unrest after World War I. The Treaty of Versailles gave Germany's Chinese territory to Japan instead of returning it to China. Many Chinese believed other nations viewed China as weak and unimportant, and that changes had to be made. Thousands of angry students demanded change on May, 4, 1919, an event that led to a series of strikes and protests called the May Fourth Movement.

The Communists and Chinese nationalists known as the Guomindang formed an uneasy partnership to fight the warlords who controlled many areas of China. The head of the Guomindang party was **Jiang Jieshi** (jee-AHNG-jee-ay-SHEE), also known as Chiang Kai-Shek. The Guomindang continued to fight until they controlled much of China. Eventually, Jiang turned against his Communist allies, attacking them in several cities and killing thousands. This action marked the beginning of the Chinese Civil War.

What were the two political parties in China after World War I?

____

____

Surviving members of China's Communist Party, led by **Mao Zedong,** worked to rebuild their organization. In 1934 Mao led thousands of Communist supporters on a brutal 6,000 mile journey called the **Long March** in order to find a safe place to recover and prepare for the next battle against Jiang.

Why did Mao Zedong and his followers embark on the Long March?

____

____

CHANGES IN INDIA

Tension between Indians and their British rulers grew serious after World War I. Though 800,000 Indians served in the British military during the war, they had not won any new freedoms at home. In fact, Britain passed acts to allow the use of harsh measures to stop growing opposition in India. While protesting these acts, nearly 400 people in the Indian city of Amritsar (uhm-RIT-suhr) were killed by British soldiers. This tragedy, called the **Amritsar Massacre**, further fueled Indian desire for independence. A new leader emerged, a lawyer named **Mohandas Gandhi**. Gandhi advocated nonviolence and civil disobedience. He encouraged Indians to boycott British goods such as salt and cloth. Though Gandhi was often arrested, he inspired millions to resist British rule. In 1935

What did Gandhi encourage Indian people to stop doing as they fought for independence?

____

____

____

British Parliament granted India some self-rule, but the struggle for complete independence continued.

THE MIDDLE EAST

The breaking apart of the Ottoman Empire after World War I offered ethnic Turks an opportunity for independence. Instead of accepting Allied plans to give their territory to Greece and other nations, Turks under the leadership of **Kemal Atatürk** defeated Greek forces and established the Republic of Turkey in 1923. Atatürk founded a modern nation with a nonreligious government.

Similar reforms took place in Persia. Reza Kahn led an overthrow of the shah and created the modern nation of Iran. Arab nationalists in other parts of the Middle East hoped for the creation of an independent Arab state. Instead, the French and British continued to control the region, offering no Arab state. With the Balfour Declaration, the British officially supported Zionism, or the creation of a Jewish homeland in the Middle East. Anger among Arabs led to violence as tens of thousands of Jews moved to Palestine in the 1920s and 1930s. The struggle for control of this land would continue through the rest of the century.

Circle the names of two modern nations created in the Middle East after World War I.

Why did many Jews move to Palestine?

____

____

____

NATIONALISM IN AFRICA

Like people in India, many thousands of Africans supported the war effort. They, too, expected their nations to be granted independence but were denied, as the Versailles Treaty gave their lands to other nations. Africans were not involved in the negotiations. The end of World War I brought economic struggle when trade between Africa and Europe slowed. Europe invested little money in its African colonies. In response, people of African heritage around the world organized meetings known as Pan-African Congresses to demand independence. Protests broke out in Egypt and many people were killed. Though Egypt was granted independence from Great Britain in 1922, the majority of the continent did not follow. It would be several more decades before African nationalism would lead to major change on the continent.

Which African nation won independence in 1922?

____

Name ______________ Class ______________ Date ______________

Section 2

MAIN IDEA

In the late 1920s an economic depression started in the United States and quickly spread around the globe, causing great hardship and creating ideal conditions for political unrest.

Key Terms and People

credit an arrangement in which a purchaser borrows money from a bank or other lender and agrees to pay it back over time

Black Tuesday October 29, 1929, a day when investors sold off 16 million shares of stock, leading to a massive stock market collapse

Great Depression severe downturn in the American economy that followed the 1929 stock market crash

Franklin Delano Roosevelt U.S. President elected in 1932 who increased the government's role in the economy and in the daily lives of Americas

New Deal a government program that created jobs, spent more money on welfare and other relief programs, and regulated banking and the stock market

John Maynard Keynes British economist who believed governments could limit or prevent economic downturns by spending money even if this caused an unbalanced budget

Smoot-Hawley Tariff Act a 1930 act that placed heavy taxes on goods imported to the United States in order to encourage Americans to buy goods made in the United States

Taking Notes

As you read the summary, use a graphic organizer like the one below to take notes on the causes and spread of the Great Depression.

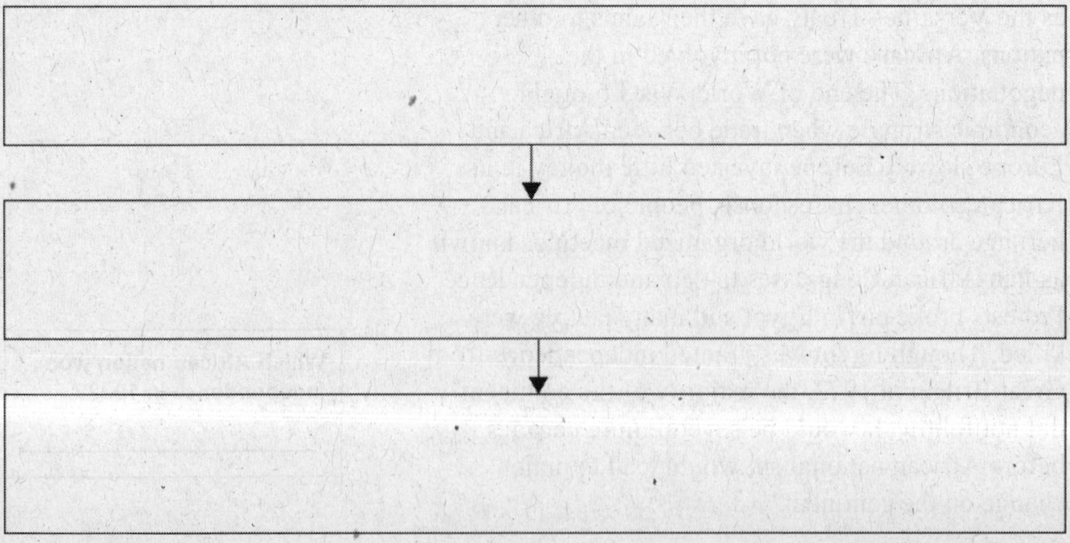

Section Summary

THE U.S. ECONOMY IN THE 1920S

American farms and factories supplied most of the goods needed to fight World War I. After the war, the American economy experienced a brief downturn but was booming again by 1921. Growth was steady due to factories producing automobiles and consumer goods such as washing machines. The value of stocks traded on the stock market rose quickly and many people wanted to buy them, which drove the prices higher still. However, hidden economic problems would soon emerge.

The wealth created by the stock market was distributed unevenly. The richest 1 percent of the population earned 19 percent of the nation's income. Also, some investors bought stock with **credit**, an arrangement in which a person borrows money from a bank or other lender and agrees to pay it back later. When people reached the limit of how much they could borrow, spending slowed. Stockholders began to worry about the downturn in the economy. They started to sell their shares. On October 29, 1929, known as **Black Tuesday**, stock market prices plummeted when investors sold off 16 million shares. Since few people were buying, stock prices collapsed. People sold shares for less than they had paid for them just to pay back their loans. The stock market's crash ruined American investors, banks, and industry. Then the effects of the crash reached other places.

What happened on Black Tuesday?

____

____

____

THE DEPRESSION SPREADS

The economic downturn that followed the 1929 stock market crash is called the **Great Depression**. Many factors contributed to the crisis. First, industrial production of goods slowed because people no longer bought as much. Workers lost their jobs. Banks failed because businesses and investors could not pay off their loans. Many people withdrew their money from banks, fearing they would lose it. As a result, thousands of banks went out of business.

Circle factors that contributed to the spread of the Great Depression.

At first, the government did little to help. President Herbert Hoover and his advisors believed that the government should limit its role in business affairs.

Some of them believed the economy would correct itself and that the Depression was a normal, healthy adjustment to the economy.

Many Americans, however, felt that more needed to be done. **Franklin Delano Roosevelt** was elected president in 1932. He involved the federal government more in helping people. Roosevelt introduced the **New Deal**, a government program designed to fight the Great Depression through increased government spending. The New Deal consisted of public works programs to create jobs for the unemployed, new regulations for the stock market and banking system, and government spending on welfare and other relief programs. The New Deal centered on the idea that massive government spending could help limit or even prevent economic downturns. This theory was supported by **John Maynard Keynes**, a British economist. Though this policy did seem to help at first, the Great Depression did not end quickly. It lasted through the 1930s.

What was the theory behind New Deal spending?

____

____

____

THE WORLDWIDE DEPRESSION

Because the United States in the 1920s had produced much of the world's industrial output and was a leading importer and money lender, the Great Depression soon spread to other countries. As many European nations continued to struggle with financial problems caused by World War I, the Depression brought another crisis.

The **Smoot-Hawley Tariff Act** of 1930 put a heavy tax on goods imported to the United States. President Hoover had hoped that the act would encourage Americans to buy goods made in the United States at a cheaper cost. Instead, the act backfired. Foreign nations increased their own tariffs on American goods, resulting in a worldwide trade standstill. Without foreign trade fueling industry, many nations suffered further economic peril, remaining unable to recover from World War I. Nations became politically unstable. France and Great Britain stayed democratic, but as unrest grew, people turned to dictators in Germany and Italy. These dictators promised their people a return to former glory, but their rise to power would eventually lead to crisis.

What impact did the Smoot-Hawley Tariff Act have on world trade?

____

____

____

What happened in Germany and Italy as a result of the Great Depression?

____

____

Name ______________ Class ______________ Date ______________

MAIN IDEAS

A modernized Japan emerged from World War I as one of the world's leading powers. Dreams of empire, however, led the country in a dangerous direction.

Key Terms and People

Manchurian Incident plot in which Japanese military leaders, acting independently of the civilian government, took over the Chinese region of Manchuria

Manchukuo a new state under Japanese control, formerly Manchuria

Anti-Comintern Pact agreement between Germany and Japan to work together to oppose the spread of communism and aid each other in the event of attack by the Soviet Union

Nanjing Massacre event in which Japanese soldiers murdered 300,000 Chinese men, women, and children after capturing the city of Nanjing

Taking Notes

As you read the summary, use a graphic organizer like the one below to record details about changes in Japan in the years following World War I.

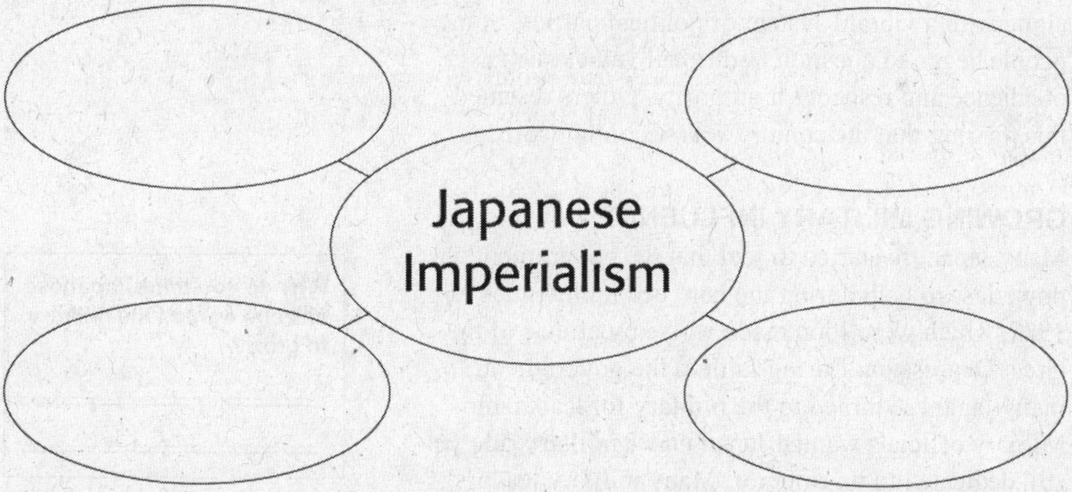

Section Summary

JAPAN IN THE 1920S

Despite Japan's emerging from World War I as a strong nation, its postwar years were not easy. Some of its problems were economic. Peasants and rural workers did not share in the nation's new prosperity. As industrial output slowed after the war, many people lost their jobs. Strikes, labor disputes, and unrest were common.

Name reasons for Japan's economic troubles in the 1920s.

____
____
____

Japan did not have enough natural resources to keep its industries supplied. Instead it had to import materials, paid for with money from the sales of goods to other countries. As those countries passed tariffs to protect their own goods from competition, trade slowed. Expanding Japan's land holdings seemed to be the only way it could get the natural resources it needed. Japan's shift from a feudal, agricultural nation to a more urban, industrial country also brought changes to its society during the 1920s. Education and new ideas from the West helped democracy flourish, along with a vibrant system of political parties. Some people began to question traditional values such as obedience and respect for authority. Others resented this, fearing that the country was becoming corrupt.

GROWING MILITARY INFLUENCE

Many Japanese started to feel that the government was powerless to help during the hard economic times of 1927, which were soon made worse by effects of the Great Depression. Losing faith in the government, many Japanese turned to the military for leadership. Military officials wanted Japan under military rule yet still dedicated to its emperor. Many military leaders were unhappy with the civilian government's approach to foreign policy. They felt the government was too cooperative with major Western powers, especially in its promise to limit the size of the Japanese navy. This action ended the possibility of overseas expansion. Many Japanese were offended when the United States banned Japanese immigration in 1924. More people questioned why the Japanese government was so agreeable with the West's

Why do you think Japanese citizens wanted the military to grow?

____
____

requests. The nationalist spirit grew, as people put their faith in a military that promised a strong Japan.

JAPANESE AGGRESSION

As Japanese society grew more military-oriented, military leaders began to focus on creating brave soldiers who would never surrender. They hoped these soldiers would make up for the military's lack of modern weapons. Military leaders tried to instill a fighting spirit in the public, even visiting Japanese schools. Some civilian leaders were even assassinated. In time, the government became dominated by the military.

How did Japanese military leaders try to make up for not having modern weapons?

____

____

____

The Japanese's military's growing power is seen in the **Manchurian Incident**. The army decided to conquer Manchuria, a region in China that had rich natural resources. Many felt these resources could help the growing empire depend less on trade with the West and compete better with other nations. Because the Japanese public supported the invasion, the government could not stop it. Manchuria became **Manchukuo**, a state under Japanese control. The military set up a government in the region.

Japan faced disapproval from the League of Nations for its actions in Manchuria. As a result, Japan withdrew from the league in 1933. Military leaders announced that they would determine the size of the navy. In 1936, Japan signed an agreement with Germany. The **Anti-Comintern Pact** held that the two nations would work together to oppose communism and help each other if the Soviet Union attacked them. Italy joined the pact a year later.

What was the purpose of the Anti-Comintern Pact?

____

____

Hostilities grew between China and Japan, leading to war in 1937. An early battle took place in the Chinese city of Nanjing, also called Nanking. The Japanese captured this city and then killed about 300,000 people, many of them civilians, in what became known as the **Nanjing Massacre**.

Japan needed resources to continue the war. It turned to Southeast Asia, calling for the creation of a plan in which a group of nations in the region would combine resources to keep from depending on the West. In reality, the plan was simply Japan's attempt to grow its empire.

Why did Japan become interested in Southeast Asia?

____

____

Name ______________________ Class ______________ Date ______________

The Interwar Years

Section 4

MAIN IDEA

The political and social unrest that followed World War I helped totalitarian dictators rise to power in Europe.

Key Terms and People

Benito Mussolini Italian dictator whose ideas led to drastic change in government and its view of Italy's role in the world

fascism authoritarian form of government that places the good of the nation above all else, including individual needs and rights

totalitarianism the attempt by a government to control all aspects of life

Joseph Stalin leader who worked to turn the Soviet Union into a totalitarian state in order to strengthen communism

Gulag a system of labor camps in the Siberian region of the Soviet Union

Adolf Hitler dictator in Germany who rose to power in the 1930s

Nazi Party Germany's National Socialist Party, the political party of Adolf Hitler

anti-Semitism hostility toward or prejudice against Jews

Nuremberg Laws laws that created a separate legal status for German Jews, eliminating their citizenship and many civil and property rights

Kristallnacht Night of the Broken Glass, an attack against Jews across Germany that occurred on November 9 and 10, 1938

Taking Notes

As you read the summary, use a graphic organizer like the one below to take notes on the rise of totalitarian dictators in Italy, the Soviet Union, and Germany in the 1920s and 1930s.

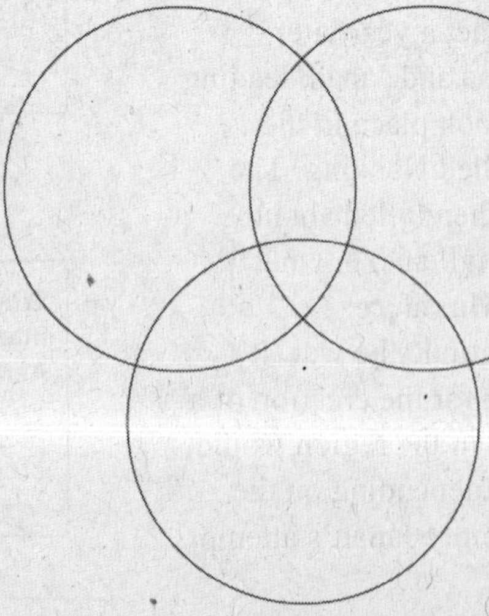

Section Summary

MUSSOLINI'S ITALY

Benito Mussolini promoted new ideas about government power in Italy in the years after World War I. Hoping to build a great Italian empire, he founded the National Fascist Party in 1919. **Fascism** is an authoritarian form of government led by an all-powerful dictator. In fascism, the good of the nation is more important than anything else, even individual needs and rights. Mussolini took control of the government after his followers convinced Italy's king to place him at the head of the parliamentary government. Once in power, Mussolini tried to influence all aspects of Italian life. This is called **totalitarianism**. He used propaganda, festivals, and holidays to encourage pride in Italian heritage. Then in 1935, Mussolini conquered Ethiopia. Though the world condemned the action, other nations did nothing to stop Mussolini. Still recovering from World War I, they did not want to risk another conflict. Even the League of Nations only placed some economic sanctions on Italy.

List two traits of fascist governments.

____

____

____

STALIN'S SOVIET UNION

Soviet leader Vladimir Lenin died in 1924. At the end of the power struggle that resulted, **Joseph Stalin** became the new leader. Stalin believed totalitarianism was needed so that communism could grow stronger. He also wanted to modernize the Soviet economy. In 1928, he started the first Five-Year Plan. Factories and mines were given production goals by the government as part of its system of central planning. This is different from capitalism, which uses market forces to determine the type and number of goods to make.

What happened under collectivization?

____

____

Stalin brought collectivization to Soviet farms. Small farms were combined to make them more productive. Land given to Russian peasants by Lenin was taken away from them. Those who protested faced violence. Many thousands of Russian citizens were killed or sent to the coldest region of Siberia to work in a system of labor camps called the **Gulag**. Many died there. In the republic of Ukraine, people resisting collectivization were starved to death when

What happened to people who opposed Joseph Stalin?

____

____

Stalin cut off all food supplies to punish them. Fearing a political plot against him, Stalin began a program of terror called the Great Purge, or the Great Terror, in the mid-1930s. Civilians and military officers suspected of opposing the Communist Party were killed or sent to the Gulag. Stalin's rule dominated every aspect of daily life. Places were renamed in his honor, churches were closed, and his portraits appeared all across Russia.

Circle three ways in which Stalin dominated daily life in the Soviet Union.

HITLER'S GERMANY

Adolf Hitler rose to power during a time when Germany was unstable, both politically and economically. After serving in the first World War, Hitler became involved in politics. In the National Socialist Party, also known as the **Nazi Party**, he emerged as a leader. Wanting more power, he led a failed attempt to overthrow Germany's government in 1923. This landed him in prison, where he wrote a book that described his political ideas. These included nationalism and the racial superiority of the Germans.

Why was Hitler sent to prison in 1923?

____

____

Hitler's power grew as the effects of the Great Depression worsened in the 1930s. He promised to make Germany strong and rebuild its military, even though this defied the Treaty of Versailles. Desperate for life to improve, Germans elected Hitler Chancellor in 1933. He removed opposition to his leadership through arrests and intimidation. Hitler bullied the German legislature to give him total power.

Explain how Hitler was able to gain power in the 1930s.

____

____

____

A key part of the Nazi system was **anti-Semitism**, prejudice against Jews, whom Hitler blamed for Germany's problems. The Nazis encouraged people to believe that Jews were a separate race. The Nazis passed the **Nuremberg Laws** in 1935. The goal of these laws was to exclude Jewish people entirely from mainstream German life. They gave Jews a separate legal status, eliminated their citizenship, and took away many rights. On November 9 and 10, 1938, Nazis attacked Jewish people, their property, and their places of worship in riots across the country. This event, **Kristallnacht**, resulted in the death of 100 Jews and much damage. This destruction was only a preview of the terrible years yet to come as Hitler led his nation into another world war.

What difficulties did Jews in Germany face as a result of Hitler's power?

____

____

____

Name ______________________ Class ______________ Date ______________

Chapter Summary

Axis Powers	Role in World War II
Hitler	Chancellor of Nazi Germany
Rommel	Leader of German forces in North Africa, called the Desert Fox
Allies	
Churchill	British prime minister, inspired the British with his fighting spirit
Eisenhower	Supreme commander of the Allied forces in Europe
Roosevelt	President who ended U.S. isolationism by entering the country into war
Truman	U.S. president who made the decision to use the atomic bomb

COMPREHENSION AND CRITICAL THINKING

Use information from the graphic organizer to answer the following questions.

1. **Recall** What role did Dwight D. Eisenhower play in World War II?

____

____

2. **Identify** Which people in the chart represent Axis countries? Which people represent Allied countries?

____

____

____

3. **Make a Judgment** President Roosevelt led the United States through most of the war. President Truman brought the war to an end with the decision to use the atomic bomb. Which president had the more difficult task? Explain your position.

____

____

____

____

Name ______________________ Class ______________ Date ______________

World War II

Section 1

MAIN IDEA

In the late 1930s Germany and Japan used military force to build empires. Their aggressive actions led to the outbreak of World War II.

Key Terms and People

appeasement giving in to aggressive demands in order to maintain peace

Axis Powers military alliance made up of Germany, Japan, and Italy

nonaggression pact an agreement between parties not to attack one another, such as the 1939 pact made between Germany and the Soviet Union in which each side agreed not to attack the other

blitzkrieg German word for "lightning war," a type of assault that emphasized speed and close coordination between airplanes and ground forces

Allies military alliance between Great Britain, France, and later the United States and the Soviet Union

Winston Churchill Prime Minister of Great Britain during World War II

Battle of Britain German campaign to bomb Britain

Hideki Tojo general and leader of Japanese government during World War II

isolationism desire to stay out of the affairs of other nations

Taking Notes

As you read the summary, keep track of events that led to the start of World War II on a graphic organizer like the one below.

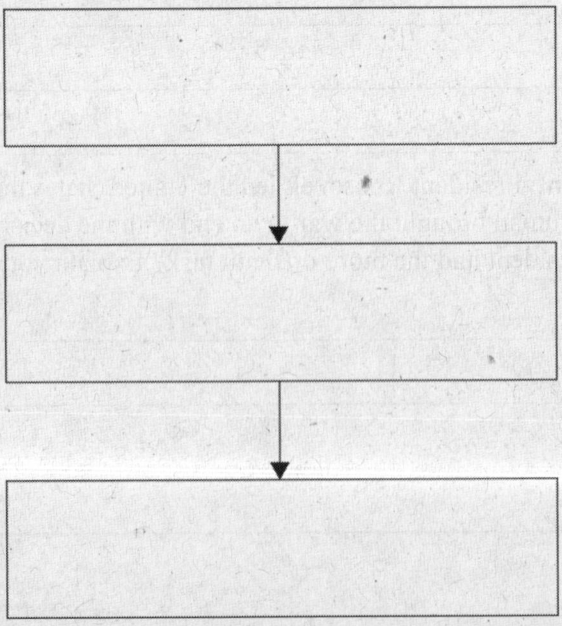

Section Summary

GERMANY EXPANDS

After World War I, the terms of the Treaty of Versailles left Germany economically damaged and its people feeling humiliated. Adolf Hitler promised to restore Germany to greatness. He rose to power in 1933 and secretly started rebuilding Germany's military. His goal was to gain more territory for Germany. Soon, he was speaking publicly about re-arming Germany, a violation of the treaty. Tired of war, leaders of other European nations did little to stop him. Hitler took advantage of this. In 1936 he sent armed forces to the Rhineland, a German territory that bordered France. In 1938 he annexed Austria, a German-speaking country that had many Nazi party supporters, and made it part of Germany.

Convinced that no one would stop him, Hitler made plans to invade Czechoslovakia. The Czechs who opposed annexation believed that France would help them fight Germany. However, leaders of France and Britain, following a policy of **appeasement**, agreed not to block Hitler's way. They felt that in staying out of the way, they would prevent an unnecessary war.

Why didn't European leaders stand up to Hitler in the 1930s?

____

____

____

Who did the Czechs think would help if Germany invaded? What actually happened?

____

____

____

ALLIANCES AND CIVIL WAR

Germany formed military alliances with Japan and Italy. These three nations were known as the **Axis Powers**. They also agreed to fight the spread of communism and to oppose the Soviet Union. Germany and Italy also aided the fascist leader Francisco Franco in the Spanish Civil War, which started in 1936. His victory brought the fascist dictator to power.

Concerned about Hitler's actions, British and French officials began to discuss an alliance with the Soviet Union. Soviet leader Joseph Stalin felt threatened by Hitler's military actions. Stalin did not think the British or French would protect his country. In 1939 the Soviet-German **nonaggression pact** was revealed. Each side agreed not to attack the other, shocking the British and French, who were counting on the Soviets' support if Germany attacked them.

Why did Britain and France want an alliance with the Soviet Union?

____

____

____

THE WAR BEGINS

Just a few days later, on September 1, 1939, World War II began when Germany attacked Poland. German forces used planes and fast-moving troops in a tactic called **blitzkrieg**, or “lightning war.” Great Britain and France, now known as the **Allies**, declared war on Germany. They did little to help Poland, however, and that country fell to Germany’s army within weeks.

Next, Hitler turned his attention to France. He knew that better access to the Atlantic Ocean would help, so he first took Denmark and Norway. On the way to France, he captured Belgium and the Netherlands. Allied forces were no match for Germany. On June 22, 1940, France surrendered to Germany.

Between August and October of 1940 German planes bombed Great Britain. The British people, led by Prime Minister **Winston Churchill**, would not surrender. They also had a new technology called radar which helped locate and create images of distant objects, such as German aircrafts. The **Battle of Britain** was a failure for Hitler, who called off his invasion there in 1941. In June, Hitler broke the nonaggression pact by invading the Soviet Union. German troops, unprepared for the harsh winter and outnumbered by the Soviet’s Red Army, did not reach the capital city. Though the Soviets had lost many troops, they were ready to fight back.

List the nations that Hitler invaded.

____

____

____

JAPAN ATTACKS

Japanese expansion in Asia was also on the rise. In 1941, led by General **Hideki Tojo**, Japan invaded the French colony Indochina. This area was rich in natural resources Japan could use as it continued its military action. In response, American leaders banned the sale of oil to Japan. Relations between the two nations fell apart. Japan bombed the U.S. naval base at Pearl Harbor in Hawaii on December 7, killing 2,400 people and destroying nearly 200 aircrafts and all eight battleships in the harbor. With this, the United States abandoned its policy of **isolationism**, or staying out of the affairs of other nations. On December 8, the U.S. Congress declared war on Japan, joining the Allies in the fight against the Axis Powers.

What event caused the United States to enter World War II?

____

____

MAIN IDEA

The early years of World War II went poorly for the Allies. But after the United States joined the war, the Allies soon recovered and began making gains against the Axis.

Key Terms and People

Erwin Rommel German general who lead the German-Italian force in North Africa

Battle of El Alamein key battle in North Africa won by the British in October 1942

Dwight D. Eisenhower commander of American forces, defeated Rommel in Africa

Siege of Leningrad German blockade in the winter of 1941–42 which resulted in the deaths of one million Russian civilians

Battle of Stalingrad crushing defeat of German forces, led to a turning point in the war

Douglas MacArthur commander of American forces in the Pacific

Bataan Death March brutal forced march of American and Filipino prisoners of war by their Japanese captors

Battle of Midway key Allied victory in the Pacific which weakened Japan's navy

Battle of Guadalcanal lengthy battle in the Pacific resulting in an Allied victory

kamikaze any Japanese pilot who loaded his plane with explosives and crashed into an Allied ship, sacrificing his own life

Taking Notes

As you read the summary, use a graphic organizer like this one to record the main instances of Allied success in the war in 1942 and 1943.

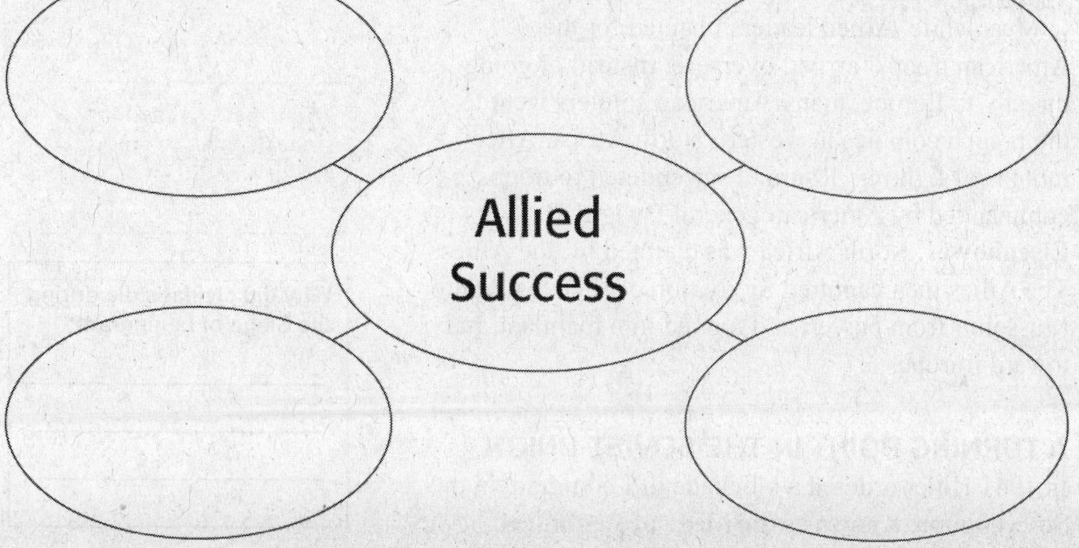

Section Summary

EARLY AMERICAN INVOLVEMENT

One key factor in winning World War II was control of the Atlantic Ocean. The Allies depended on supplies shipped by sea. German U-boats sank hundreds of Allied ships. The American people got involved. Millions of men volunteered or were drafted to serve and U.S. factories produced goods and weapons for the war. As a result, many women and African Americans had new job opportunities. However, those of German, Italian, and Japanese descent lost some rights. By 1943, the Allies had more ships and planes with more firepower. They were also able to break German codes to locate German U-boats. This kept Allied supply lines open on the Atlantic.

Why was control of the Atlantic Ocean important?

____

____

____

WAR IN NORTH AFRICA AND ITALY

Another important battleground during the war lay in North Africa, because the Suez Canal was a vital link to oil from the Middle East. After defeating Italian forces in Egypt, the British were on the verge of controlling all of North Africa. Hitler sent troops to help Italy there; the joined forces were called the Afrika Corps. German general **Erwin Rommel** earned the nickname the Desert Fox for pushing British forces out of Libya. However, British troops weakened Axis power with their victory at the **Battle of El Alamein** (el-a-luh-MAYN) in Egypt.

Circle the name of an important North African link to oil from the Middle East.

Meanwhile, Allied leaders planned for the American troops' arrival overseas. Instead of going directly to Europe, many American soldiers went to the French colonies in western North Africa. After months of fighting, Rommel surrendered to troops commanded by American general **Dwight D. Eisenhower**. North Africa was claimed for the Allies. The Allies then captured Sicily, forced dictator Benito Mussolini from power, and moved into mainland Italy toward Europe.

A TURNING POINT IN THE SOVIET UNION

In 1941 Hitler ordered a blockade of Leningrad, in the Soviet Union. Known as the **Siege of Leningrad**, it

Why did civilians die during the Siege of Leningrad?

____

____

____

was designed to weaken the city by preventing supplies from entering. A million Russian civilians died, with as many as 4,000 people starving to death each day. In 1942 German forces seemed to be on the verge of taking Stalingrad, a large port city where military equipment was made and shipped, along with other goods, throughout the Soviet Union. The **Battle of Stalingrad** was one of the war's most brutal. A million Russian soldiers died defending the city. In the end it was a defeat for Hitler. It was an important turning point in the Allies' favor, and the beginning of the end for Hitler.

Why would the loss of Stalingrad have been a major threat to the Allies?

____

____

A TURNING POINT IN THE PACIFIC

In the Pacific, the Allies were at first outmatched, as they had to rebuild the fleet lost at Pearl Harbor and were focused mostly on Europe. The better-equipped Japanese forced American troops led by **Douglas MacArthur** out of the Philippines in 1942. Following the American surrender of the Philippines, the Japanese forced 70,000 prisoners to march up the Bataan Peninsula to a distant prison camp. During this **Bataan Death March**, heat, lack of food and water, and violence from their captors killed thousands of American and Filipino prisoners.

The Japanese easily conquered Hong Kong, Singapore, Burma, and many islands in the Pacific. Japan had a strong navy and the advantage of fighting close to home. But this advantage did not last for long.

Americans had broken the secret Japanese code used to send messages. With information on the date and location of Japanese attacks, the Allies won important victories at the **Battle of Midway** and the **Battle of Guadalcanal**. The Battle of Midway changed the balance of power in the Pacific. The Allies went on the offensive.

Why was the Battle of Midway important?

____

____

____

Allied forces used a strategy that became known as "island hopping." They captured weak targets and attempted to isolate Japanese strongholds. The Allies would then use these areas as bases as they moved closer and closer to Japan. Japanese forces, in turn, sank many Allied ships using **kamikaze** pilots to crash planes loaded with explosives into the ships. Before long, Japan's navy was nearly destroyed.

What is island hopping?

____

____

____

MAIN IDEA

During World War II, Germany's Nazi government deliberately murdered some 6 million Jews and 5 million others in Europe. These actions became known as the Holocaust.

Key Terms and People

deported forced to leave a country

Final Solution deliberate, mass execution of Jews

ghettos confined areas within a city

concentration camps labor camps meant to hold the people Hitler called enemies of the state

Holocaust campaign of mass murder that the Nazis waged against the Jews

Taking Notes

As you read the summary, use a graphic organizer like this one to record notes about Nazi anti-Semitism during the 1930s and 1940s.

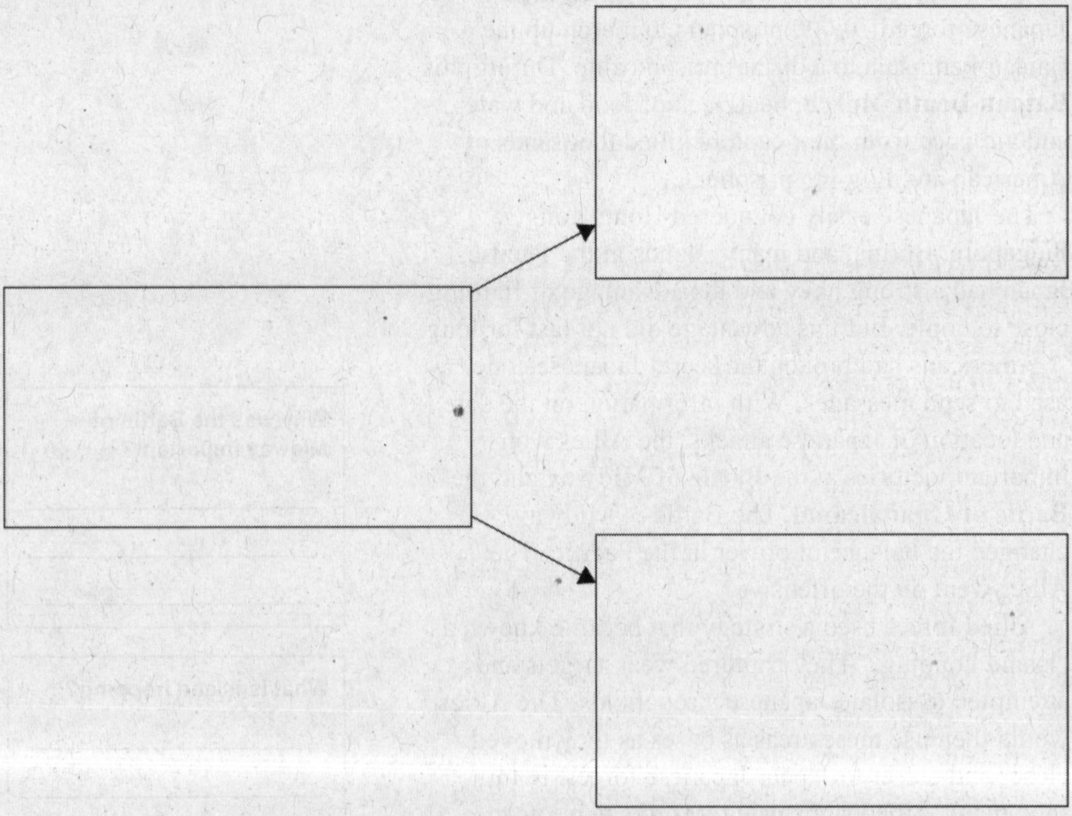

Section Summary

NAZI ANTI-SEMITISM

At the end of World War I, Germany faced serious economic troubles. Many people were suffering and out of work. Hitler blamed Jewish people for Germany's problems, even though there was no factual basis for this. He broadcasted his feelings of anti-Semitism, or discrimination against Jews. He also encouraged the belief that Germans were racially superior to all other people.

The Nazi regime began severely limiting the rights of Jewish citizens in the 1930s. Jews' citizenship was taken away, they could not hold government jobs, and their right to own property or hold *any* job was limited. Thousands of Jews were **deported**, meaning they were forced to leave the country. Others chose to leave the country on their own. However, leaving Germany was difficult. Jews were stripped of money and property. The United States and many European countries still recovering from the Great Depression would either limit or not accept the poor newcomers because jobs were scarce. The outbreak of World War II also made travel difficult. By late 1941, thousands of Jews were trapped in the country because, by then, leaving Germany had been outlawed.

Why do you think many German citizens accepted Hitler's anti-Semitism?

____

____

____

How did Jews end up trapped in Germany during the war?

____

____

THE "FINAL SOLUTION"

Millions of Jewish people in Europe came under Nazi control as German forces conquered new territory. Hitler's plan for these people was called the **Final Solution**—mass killing of all Europe's Jews. At first, some Jews were forced to live in **ghettos**. These were small, confined areas within a city. Conditions were terrible and thousands died of starvation. Walls, barbed wire fences, and armed guards kept people from escaping. Many others were sent to **concentration camps**, or labor camps meant to hold what Hitler called enemies of the state. There they were forced into slave labor or used for cruel medical experiments. Many starved to death.

Thousands of Jews and other civilians were gunned down in Polish and Soviet villages when Nazi soldiers arrived. Finally the Nazis decided that the killing was

Why didn't Jews leave the ghettos?

____

____

not taking place fast enough. They built more concentration camps, this time with gas chambers that could kill large numbers of people quickly.

Ultimately 6 million Jews, or two-thirds of Europe's Jewish population, died during the Nazi regime. Five million others were also killed for being what the Nazis felt were "inferior." These included people with disabilities, homosexuals, the Romany (an ethnic group also known as Gypsies), Slavs, and Poles. This campaign of killing is known today as the **Holocaust**.

How many people died in the Holocaust?

____

THE WORLD REACTS

For most of World War II, other countries were unaware of the extent of Hitler's brutality, although they had known of his anti-Semitism in the 1930s. The other nations were also fighting for their own survival. The United States and Great Britain investigated the mass murders when their governments received reports in 1942.

In 1944, the U.S. helped to rescue 200,000 European Jews by creating the War Refugee Board. However, winning the war itself was still the Allies' main goal. As Allied forces pushed back the German armies, they saw the concentration camps for themselves. In the camps, they found thousands of dead, as well as prisoners who were too ill or starved to survive. They also found evidence that many more people had once been held there.

Though the Germans tried to cover up what they had done, the scenes at the death camps shocked the world. Soviet soldiers found the Auschwitz camp, and American troops reached the Buchenwald camp. Sadly, many of the Jewish prisoners were too sick to survive their rescue. The world now knew what Adolf Hitler had done. Fortunately, the Nazi hopes of controlling the world were about to end.

Why didn't the Allied Powers do more to stop the Holocaust as it occurred?

____

____

____

MAIN IDEA

In 1945 the Allies finally triumphed over the Axis Powers in Europe and the Pacific, but the war left many nations in ruins.

Key Terms and People

D-Day June 6, 1944, the day Allied forces invaded France on the beaches of Normandy

V-E Day Victory in Europe Day, May 8, 1945, the day Allied victory was declared

Battle of Iwo Jima brutal battle in which the Allies captured a strategic island close to Japan

Battle of Okinawa Pacific battle that claimed 12,000 American lives for an Allied victory

Harry S Truman U.S. President who made the decision to use the atomic bomb

Hirohito Japanese emperor who surrendered to Allies

V-J Day August 15, 1945, the day Japan surrendered to the Allies, ending World War II

Yalta Conference meeting held by the Allied nations to plan postwar Europe

Potsdam Conference meeting of Allied leaders in which tension between the Soviet Union and the other Allies surfaced

United Nations world organization meant to encourage international cooperation and the prevention of war

Taking Notes

As you read the summary, take notes about the end of the war, using a graphic organizer like the one below.

Europe	Pacific

Section Summary

WAR ENDS IN EUROPE

Toward the end of 1943 and beginning of 1944, Soviet troops were able to push Axis forces back into central Europe. Axis forces had lost over two million troops. They were unable to stop the Soviet advance. American and British military leaders began to plan a major invasion of Western Europe. They felt that opening a second front might end the war.

What weakened the Axis forces?

____

____

American generals Marshall and Eisenhower led the Allied preparations. They knew the operation would be hard. Allied forces would have to invade by sea. The Allies needed special equipment to get tanks and troops across open water. They also misled Hitler about where the invasion would land.

D-Day, June 6, 1944, marked the beginning of the campaign. Allied forces landed nearly 150,000 troops on the beach at Normandy, France. There, despite high casualties, they defeated strong German forces. Then they moved inland. Over 1 million Allied soldiers would come ashore by July. The Allies crushed a German counterattack in Belgium, known as the Battle of the Bulge. This victory for the Allies marked the end of major German resistance. Soon, the Allies raced to Berlin. There they found the body of Adolf Hitler. He had committed suicide.

How did the Soviets and other Allies stop Hitler?

____

____

____

With Hitler dead and Berlin surrounded, Germany surrendered on May 7, 1945. The Allies celebrated the victory in Europe by proclaiming May 8, 1945 as **V-E Day**. After six years of brutal fighting, the war in Europe was over.

WAR ENDS IN THE PACIFIC

Though they had achieved victory in Europe, the Allies still faced Axis powers in the Pacific. In order to effectively bomb Japanese targets such as Tokyo and other cities, Allied forces needed island bases closer to Japan. The **Battle of Iwo Jima** and the **Battle of Okinawa** were fought to secure such locations for the Allies. Both battles were extremely brutal. During the month-long fight at Iwo Jima (EE-who JEE-muh), nearly 7,000 Americans and 19,000 Japanese died as they fought for the tiny island. In

Okinawa (OH-kee-NAH-wah), Japanese troops fought to the death. In that battle, 12,000 Americans died, as did 100,000 Japanese soldiers.

The invasion of mainland Japan looked very risky. The Allies feared that up to a million of their soldiers would be killed or wounded during the invasion. Instead, President **Harry S Truman** made the difficult decision to use the atomic bomb. It had been successfully tested in 1945, after six years of development. Truman and his advisers hoped that using the bomb would lead to Japan's surrender, ending the war quickly and saving American lives. Two bombs were dropped in August of 1945. One was dropped over the Japanese city of Hiroshima. When that did not led to surrender, the other was dropped over Nagasaki. Tens of thousands of Japanese civilians were killed by the bombs and the resulting radiation. Japanese emperor **Hirohito** surrendered to the Allies on August 15, 1945. This became known as **V-J Day**. World War II was over.

What did the battles of Iwo Jima and Okinawa teach the Allies about how the Japanese waged war?

____

____

Where did American forces drop atomic bombs in Japan?

____

____

THE POSTWAR WORLD

The Allies still faced many challenges after the war ended. Tens of millions of people had died. Entire countries had to be rebuilt because their economies were collapsing. Many cities, villages, and farms were destroyed or very damaged. Poland, Yugoslavia, the Soviet Union, and also Germany, Japan, and China suffered these conditions. Millions of people whose lives had been uprooted during the war faced the enormous challenge of starting over.

In 1945, the **Yalta Conference** and **Potsdam Conference,** however, revealed divisions between the Soviet Union and the other Allies. Stalin agreed to be part of the **United Nations**, an international peacekeeping organization. Still, American and British leaders worried that communism and Soviet influence would spread in Eastern Europe. Soon, the end of World War II would signal the dawn of a new conflict. The Cold War was about to begin.

What challenges faced the Allies after the war?

____

____

____

What did American and British leaders worry about after the war?

____

____

____

Chapter Summary

Post-War Conflicts and Changes

1950s The **Cold War** begins. The U.S. forms **NATO** and begins a policy of **containment** in Korea. The **Marshall Plan** helps rebuild Western Europe and protect it from communism.
1960s The **arms race** heats up and conflicts break out in **Vietnam**, South America, and elsewhere. The **Berlin Wall** goes up. The **civil rights movement** makes gains.
1970s The **counterculture** that opposed U.S. involvement in Vietnam sees forces leave in 1975. More laws support racial and gender-based equality.
1980s–2000s The Cold War ends as the Soviet Union disintegrates. The United States faces threats from the Middle East. The **Persian Gulf War** occurs and the **war on terror** begins.

COMPREHENSION AND CRITICAL THINKING

Use information from the graphic organizer to answer the following questions.

1. **Explain** In what ways did the Cold War grow fiercer during the 1960s?

____

____

2. **Recall** What brought about the end of the Cold War at the end of the 1980s?

____

____

3. **Make Judgments** How did the Marshall Plan protect Western Europe from communism?

____

____

____

4. **Predict** What do you think the challenges of the near future will include?

____

____

____

Section 1

MAIN IDEA

Once partners in war, the Soviet Union and the other former Allies found it much more difficult to cooperate in peace. The result was an era of conflict and confrontation called the Cold War.

Key Terms

Nuremberg trials trials at an Allied military court that brought several dozen Nazi military leaders to justice for crimes committed during World War II

Cold War a post-World War II era of open hostility and high tension between the United States and the Soviet Union

iron curtain Winston Churchill's term for the division of Europe created by Soviet actions

Truman Doctrine U.S. pledge to provide economic and military aid to oppose the spread of communism

Marshall Plan a massive program of U.S. economic aid to help Western Europe make a rapid recovery from the war and remain politically stable

containment a policy of resisting Soviet aggression to contain the spread of communism

Berlin airlift a massive effort to supply West Berlin by air after the Soviets blockaded it

NATO North Atlantic Treaty Organization, a military alliance between the United States, Canada, and Western Europe designed to counter Soviet power in Europe

Warsaw Pact an alliance formed between the Soviet Union and the Communist nations of Eastern Europe

Taking Notes

As you read the summary, take notes on the problems, containment effects, and confrontations of the beginning of the Cold War. Use a graphic organizer like this one.

Problems
Containment
Confrontations

Section Summary

THE PROBLEMS OF PEACE

After World War II, the question of how to rebuild Europe created tension between the Allied powers. To govern the shattered nation of Germany, the Allies agreed to split it into four temporary zones of occupation. The Soviet Union controlled about one-third of the country. The United States, France, and Great Britain each had a zone in the remaining two-thirds. Berlin, the capital, was located deep within the Soviet zone. It was also divided into four zones of occupation, one for each of the four powers.

What did the Allies do in order to govern Germany after WWII?

____

____

____

To bring Nazi military leaders to justice, the Allies conducted the **Nuremberg trials** in Germany between 1945 and 1949. Some Nazis were executed for their role in the Holocaust and in other war crimes. Next, the Allies enacted a plan in which Germany paid reparations for the damage it had caused during the war. The Soviets received the largest share, because they had suffered the most damage in the war.

Circle two ways in which the West dealt with Germany in the aftermath of World War II.

The Soviet Union was in conflict with Great Britain and the United States when it came to Eastern Europe. The Soviets wanted friendly Communist governments there to prevent future attacks on their own country. U.S. leaders worried that Soviets would try to expand their power beyond Eastern Europe.

THE CONFLICT WORSENS

Relations between the Soviet Union and the West continued to get worse. An era of hostility and tension called the **Cold War** began. The Cold War was a struggle between two different economic systems, forms of government, and lifestyles. The Soviet Union directly controlled many Communist governments in Eastern Europe soon after the war. The conflict worsened when the Soviet Union failed to remove its troops from northern Iran. Both sides believed war was likely. Winston Churchill described the division of Europe as an **iron curtain** created by Soviet actions. He, too, felt that Soviet actions were a threat to peace. In early 1947, the United States decided to give financial aid to the governments of Greece and Turkey. Both governments were threatened by Soviet-

What was the Cold War?

____

____

____

backed Communists. President Truman used this event to announce a pledge to provide economic and military aid to oppose the spread of communism. This 1947 pledge became known as the **Truman Doctrine**. Fearing that worsening conditions might make communism more appealing to other European nations, the U.S. government also launched the **Marshall Plan.** It provided $13 billion in aid, helping Western Europe recover and stay stable after the war.

COLD WAR CONFRONTATIONS

The Truman Doctrine and the Marshall Plan were established to resist Soviet aggression and to contain the spread of communism. This policy is known as **containment**. Confrontations between East and West became more severe. Western leaders planned to create a democratic German nation from the three western occupation zones. They also wanted to create a democratic government in West Berlin. The Soviets opposed this plan. They started a blockade in 1948 that prevented all supplies, even food, from entering the city. In response, the West organized the **Berlin airlift**, using planes to bring supplies to the city. After almost a year, the Soviets called off the blockade.

What was the goal of the Truman Doctrine and the Marshall Plan?

____

____

____

Days later, the western zones became the Federal Republic of Germany. The Soviet zone became the nation of East Germany. The United States, Canada, and most nations in Western Europe formed the North Atlantic Treaty Organization, **NATO**, a military alliance to resist Soviet power. The Soviet Union and the Communist nations of Eastern Europe formed an alliance called the **Warsaw Pact**.

How did the West respond to the Soviet blockade of Berlin?

____

____

New troubles emerged in Asia, specifically in Korea, which had been divided after World War II. In 1950, Communist North Korea invaded non-Communist South Korea. The United States, with the support of the United Nations, sent forces to help South Korea. At first, the North Koreans nearly conquered the South. Then, American forces pushed the North Koreans back. Communist China helped North Korea drive the UN-South Korean troops back. The war settled into a stalemate and both sides agreed to an armistice in 1953. North Korea stayed Communist and South Korea remained a western ally.

List important events in the war in Korea.

____

____

____

____

Name ______________________ Class ______________ Date ______________

MAIN IDEA

As the Cold War continued, the world's two superpowers—the Soviet Union and the United States—competed for power and influence around the world.

Key Terms

hydrogen bomb an immensely destructive weapon powered by nuclear fusion

deterrence the development of or maintenance of military power to deter an attack

arms race a struggle between nations to gain an advantage in weapons

Sputnik the world's first satellite, a human-made object launched in 1957 by the Soviet Union that flies in orbit around the Earth

Bay of Pigs invasion unsuccessful invasion of Cuba by a secretly trained force, which U.S. leaders believed would result in a massive uprising to overthrow Fidel Castro

Cuban missile crisis a tense standoff between the United States and the Soviet Union that occurred after the Soviets installed nuclear missiles in Cuba

nonaligned nations countries that refused to support either side during the Cold War and tried to promote the interest of poorer countries

détente reduced tension between the superpowers

Taking Notes

As you read the summary, take notes on the major events of the Cold War from the 1940s to the 1980s. Use a graphic organizer like this one.

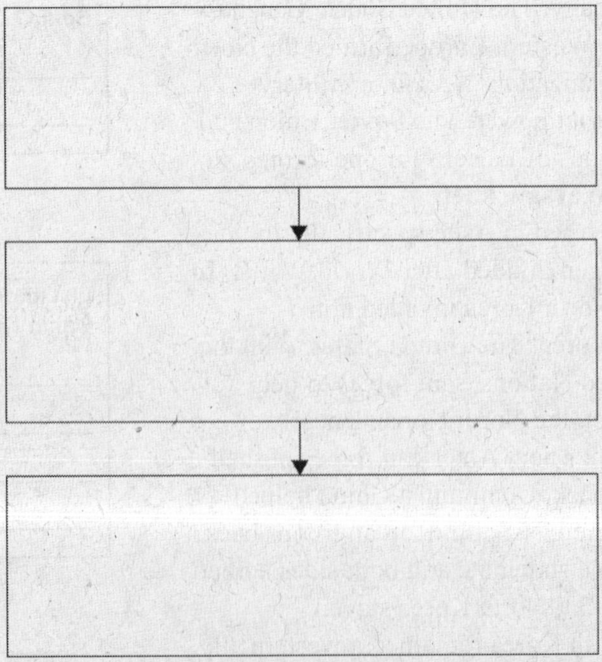

Section Summary

THE ARMS RACE BEGINS

Through the 1950s and 1960s the Soviet Union and the United States competed to develop superior weapons. The Soviets successfully tested an atomic bomb in 1949. In 1952 the United States developed the deadlier **hydrogen bomb**, powered by nuclear fusion. Less than a year later, the Soviets had tested their own hydrogen bomb. The development of new weapons was part of a strategy of deterrence. **Deterrence** is the development of or maintenance of military power to deter, or prevent, and attack. The **arms race** continued as the two nations tried to gain a weapons' advantage. Both built missiles that could carry nuclear weapons thousands of miles. The rivalry spread into space in 1957, when the Soviet Union launched ***Sputnik***, the world's first satellite. In response, the United States launched its own satellite and established NASA to focus on space research.

Why did both sides work to develop nuclear weapons during the Cold War?

____

____

____

The fear of nuclear war affected many aspects of American society. People built bomb shelters, schools led air-raid drills, and books and movies were filled with stories centered on the dangers of nuclear war. The Cold War led to a Red Scare in the 1940s and 1950s. Many Americans feared Communist influence on the U.S. government.

COLD WAR AROUND THE WORLD

The Cold War created conflict far from the United States or Soviet Union. In Vietnam, Communist rebels fought the French, who had wanted to restore their colonial power in Southeast Asia. When the rebels won, Vietnam was divided—half controlled by Communists, the other half by an anti-Communist regime. When Communist North Vietnamese tried to unite the nation, the United States gave military aid to the South, leading to long-term involvement there.

In Berlin, German citizens began crossing from the Communist East into democratic West Berlin. To stop the flow of as many as 1,000 people per day, East Germany built a barrier in 1961 known as the Berlin Wall. Crossing it was forbidden and the wall became a symbol of brutality of the Communist system.

Why was the Berlin Wall built?

____

____

____

Closer to the United States, Fidel Castro came to power in Cuba. He established government control of the economy and developed a close relationship with the Soviet Union. These actions upset the United States. In 1961, a group of 1,500 Cubans trained by the United States invaded Cuba. The **Bay of Pigs invasion** quickly failed. The **Cuban missile crisis** followed the next year, when U.S. leaders learned that the Soviet Union had installed missiles in Cuba. Two weeks of tense negotiations ended with the Soviet Union removing the missiles.

In 1956 Britain, France, and Israel fought Egypt for control over the Suez Canal. After the Soviet Union said it would support Egypt, the United States asked its allies to withdraw, to prevent all-out war. In Africa, the West supported a corrupt dictator in the Congo because they believed he was a good ally against the Soviets. In South America, as Soviet-friendly regimes rose to power, the United States supported efforts to overthrow them, ousting Salvador Allende in Chile and the Communist government on the island of Grenada. Some nations tried to avoid being part of the Cold War rivalry by refusing to support either side. These **nonaligned nations** sought to promote the interests of poorer countries.

Why do you think American leaders were opposed to having an ally of the Soviet Union in Cuba?

____

____

List two examples of Cold War conflicts throughout the world.

____

____

____

ATTEMPTS AT ARMS CONTROL

Attempts at East-West cooperation during the Cold War centered on reducing the threat of nuclear war. President Eisenhower proposed an open skies treaty in 1955 that would allow each side to gain information about the other. The Soviets rejected it. The United States rejected Soviet calls for arms limitations. President Kennedy focused on trying to limit nuclear testing. This led to the 1963 Test Ban Treaty. President Nixon pursued a policy of **détente** (day-TAHNT), or reduced tension between the superpowers. Strategic Arms Limitations Talks, known as SALT I and SALT II, and arms treaties resulted. Though President Ronald Reagan took an aggressive stance against the Soviet Union, he also conducted talks with Soviet leader Mikhail Gorbachev and forged an agreement that called for reductions of weapons on both sides.

Circle three examples of attempts at arms control during the Cold War.

MAIN IDEA

The Cold War brought tremendous economic and social change to North America, Western Europe, and Eastern Europe and the Soviet Union.

Key Terms and People

Martin Luther King Jr. leader of a civil rights campaign that exposed racial injustice and won reforms

counterculture a youth movement that rebelled against mainstream American society

Solidarity a movement of Polish workers who united to protest against the Communist government and Soviet control

Mikhail Gorbachev Soviet leader who came to power in 1985 and made changes in the nation's economy and government

glasnost "openness," a willingness to discuss the problems of the Soviet Union

perestroika "restructuring," a concept for the reform of the Soviet economic and political system

Velvet Revolution a peaceful revolution that removed Communists from power in Czechoslovakia

Taking Notes

As you read the summary, take notes on the changes that occurred in North America, Europe, and the Soviet Union during the postwar years. Use a graphic organizer like this one.

North America	
Europe	
Soviet Union	

Section Summary

NORTH AMERICA

The American economy grew rapidly during the postwar era, fueled by consumer spending on goods like cars and appliances. By the 1970s, however, inflation and unemployment had slowed the economy. When the cost of energy spiked in the 1970s, the cost of other goods rose, too. The nation's debts grew as the federal government spent more money than it took in. Heavy industry companies struggled to compete with companies from other countries. Many Americans lost their jobs when factories closed.

Society changed during the postwar era as the American standard of living rose. Former soldiers used the G.I. Bill to buy homes and pay for college. Many started families, leading to a baby boom. Segregation ended in the armed forces and in public schools. A civil rights campaign led by **Martin Luther King Jr.** exposed racial inequities and won reforms, including the Civil Rights Act of 1964 and Voting Rights Act of 1965. These victories inspired a renewed woman's movement. In the 1960s the **counterculture**—a rebellion of young people against mainstream society—spread around the country. Many young people questioned the Vietnam War.

Canada experienced similar changes. Although some Canadians supported U.S. involvement in Vietnam, Canada sheltered Americans who fled the military draft. In the 1960s, the Quiet Revolution spread across Quebec as nationalism and calls for separation from the rest of Canada increased among the province's French-speaking residents.

Why do you think the postwar economy in the United States was strong?

____

____

Describe how U.S. society changed during the 1960s and 1970s.

____

____

____

____

What was the Quiet Revolution?

____

____

WESTERN EUROPE

Western Europe made a strong economic recovery after the devastation of World War II. This was due in part to the Marshall Plan, U.S. aid that helped farms and factories produce more than they had before the war. Some countries continued to struggle. In others, the availability of jobs attracted immigrants from former European colonies. This influx strained some societies. The nations of Western Europe worked to end their rivalries and band together. NATO members that were once rivals protected each other. The European Economic Community and the European Free Trade Association aided economic cooperation.

Circle the names of organizations that helped Western European nations work together.

EASTERN EUROPE AND THE SOVIET UNION

Eastern Europe and the Soviet Union faced even greater challenges in the postwar years than Western Europe did. Tens of millions of Soviet citizens died in World War II, and cities and farms were devastated. Soviet dictator Joseph Stalin rebuilt quickly and the country was soon producing goods at prewar levels.

Nikita Khrushchev took control after Stalin's death in 1953. Khrushchev loosened some economic restrictions. Soviets remained limited in their personal freedoms and hostility toward the West continued. Changes in the Soviet Union led to hopes that the Soviets would end their control over Eastern Europe. Instead, revolts in Germany, Poland, Hungary, and Czechoslovakia were crushed. In 1980 Lech Walesa led hundreds of thousands of Polish workers in an anti-government protest movement known as **Solidarity**. Poland's Communist government forcefully suppressed the movement.

Underline the countries where citizens revolted against Soviet control.

The Soviet economy began to slow in the 1960s. By the 1980s, industry had grown too large and complex for the government to control. Too few consumer goods were made because the government had focused on heavy industry. **Mikhail Gorbachev** came to power in 1985, knowing that change was needed. He proposed the concepts of ***glasnost***, which means "openness" or willingness to discuss the problems, and ***perestroika***, or "restructuring," the reform of the Soviet economic and political system. Gorbachev pursued arms control agreements, reduced central planning of the economy, and pulled troops out of Eastern Europe. In 1989 revolution spread across Eastern Europe as citizens overthrew their Soviet-backed governments. Most transitions were peaceful, such as the **Velvet Revolution**, which removed Communists from power in Czechoslovakia. In East Germany in 1989, the government opened the gates of the Berlin Wall. Joyful Berliners immediately started tearing down the symbol of the Soviet regime.

Why did Gorbachev propose *glasnost* and *perestroika* in the 1980s?

____

____

____

MAIN IDEA

The Soviet Union collapsed in 1991 and the Cold War came to an end, bringing changes to Europe and leaving the United States as the world's only superpower.

Key Terms and People

Boris Yeltsin leader of the republic of Russia who favored more radical change than Gorbachev did

ethnic cleansing elimination of an ethnic group through killing or forced emigration

Internet a system of networks that connects computers around the world

Saddam Hussein dictator of Iraq who invaded neighboring Kuwait in August 1990

Persian Gulf War war in which a UN-authorized multinational force led by the United States forced the Iraqi military to leave Kuwait

al Qaeda Islamist terrorist organization that launched a series of attacks against U.S. targets

Osama bin Laden al Qaeda leader who aims to unite Muslims and destroy the United States

Taliban Islamist government of Afghanistan that supported and protected members of al Qaeda

Taking Notes

As you read the summary, take notes on the important events in the Soviet Union, Europe, and the United States after the Cold War ended. Use a graphic organizer like this one.

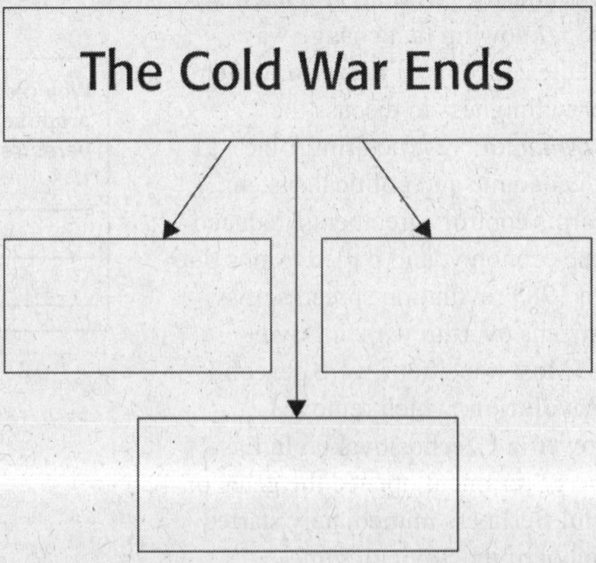

Section Summary

THE BREAKUP OF THE SOVIET UNION

In the late 1980s independence movements in Eastern Europe and within the 15 Soviet republics grew stronger. A failed coup attempt by Communist hard-liners in 1991 opened the door to change. Gorbachev lost power and many republics declared independence. Russia's independence movement was led by **Boris Yeltsin**. The Cold War ended when the Soviet government stopped operating on December 31, 1991.

As communism disintegrated, Yeltsin began a campaign to make Russia's economy more capitalistic. He allowed people to own businesses and land, but lost the guarantee of a government-backed job. Prices of goods rose so high that many people could not afford them. The economic crisis stabilized somewhat by the early 2000s, but ethnic unrest plagued the nation. Chechens in southwest Russia and ethnic Armenians in Azerbaijan faced violence as they sought independence. A 2004 vote in Ukraine led to widespread charges of fraud. The election had to be repeated and left the country deeply divided.

List three events that led to the end of the Cold War.

____

____

____

Name challenges faced by the republics of the former Soviet Union.

____

____

EUROPE AFTER COMMUNISM

Strict Communist control had long suppressed ethnic tensions in Yugoslavia. As communism collapsed, those tensions surfaced. Serbia tried to prevent the breakup of Yugoslavia, and conflict soon broke out in several republics. The worst violence took place Bosnia and Herzegovina. Serbs used a policy of **ethnic cleansing**, or elimination of an ethnic group through killing or forced emigration, against Bosnian Muslims. U.S.-led diplomatic efforts eventually ended the bloodshed in Bosnia. Fighting also erupted between Serbs and Albanians in Kosovo. In an attempt to stop the conflict, NATO planes bombed Serbia in 1999 and NATO peacekeepers moved in.

Market reforms in Eastern Europe allowed people to start new businesses, but unemployment was high in some places. The European Union (EU) was created in 1992 to build an economic and political union among European nations. In recent years a number of Eastern European nations and former

Why was the European Union established?

____

____

Soviet republics have joined the EU. Others are scheduled to join in 2007.

THE UNITED STATES TODAY

The 1990s brought strong economic growth and low unemployment to the United States. Budget deficits disappeared. Increased use of computers made businesses more efficient. Information technology, or IT, became a growing industry while it helped other industries improve productivity. The **Internet**, a system of networks that links computers around the world, created new opportunities for buying and selling. New "dot-com" businesses attracted investors, but the boom ended by the end of the decade. In the early 2000s, high energy costs, increased government spending, and a rising national debt remained areas of concern. The poverty rate also increased, becoming higher than in most other industrialized nations.

What industry helped other industries grow in the United States in the 1990s?

____

New threats emerged during this time in the Middle East. Iraq, led by dictator **Saddam Hussein**, invaded Kuwait in 1990. The United States led a UN-authorized force in the **Persian Gulf War**. Kuwait was liberated. The United States also led peace-keeping efforts in Kosovo, Somalia, Haiti, and Israel.

Circle places the American military helped with peace-keeping efforts during the 1990s.

A series of terrorist attacks against U.S. targets began in the 1990s. The attacks were planned by an Islamist group called **al Qaeda**. Its leader, **Osama bin Laden**, sought to unite Muslims and destroy the United States. The most deadly attack occurred on September 11, 2001, when terrorists hijacked and crashed four airplanes, destroying the World Trade Center towers and damaging the Pentagon. Nearly 3,000 people died. U.S. leaders responded by targeting al Qaeda and the **Taliban**, the group that was governing Afghanistan. The Taliban had been supporting al Qaeda and protecting its leadership. The United States forced the Taliban out of power in 2001. President George W. Bush then focused on Iraq, which he believed possessed biological and chemical weapons. A U.S.-led invasion began in March 2003. U.S. and coalition forces then occupied Iraq and began a rebuilding program. Although Iraqis elected a new government and approved a new constitution, the nation faced ongoing violence.

How did the United States respond to the terrorist actions of al Qaeda?

____

____

Chapter Summary

Nation	Transition	Current Government
INDIA	"Quit India" campaign, partition by Great Britain	Democracy
VIETNAM	War with France, split into halves, war with the U.S.	Communist government
CAMBODIA	Civil war	Communist government, then democracy
CHINA	War between Guomindang and Communists; government exiled	Communist government
JAPAN	War with U.S.; occupation by U.S.	Democracy

COMPREHENSION AND CRITICAL THINKING

Use information from the graphic organizer to answer the following questions.

1. **Recall** What nation ruled Vietnam before World War II? What was this nation's goal after World War II?

____

____

2. **Identify Cause and Effect** What was the effect of Great Britain's decision to partition South Asia into India and Pakistan?

____

____

3. **Make Judgments** Japan retained its emperor after its defeat in World War II. Do you think a nation can be an effective democracy if it has a monarch? Why or why not?

____

____

4. **Evaluate** Why do you think Mao Zedong tried to eliminate all "enemies of the state"? Do you believe such an effort is possible? Why or why not?

____

____

____

MAIN IDEA
India gained its independence from Great Britain, but the region entered an era of conflict and challenges.

Key Terms and People

Muhammad Ali Jinnah leader of the Muslim League who believed India's Muslims needed a separate nation to protect their rights

partition division, such as the one that separated India into Muslim and Hindi countries

Jawaharlal Nehru India's first prime minister

Indira Gandhi daughter of Jawaharlal Nehru and second Indian prime minister

Pervez Musharraf army general who gained power in Pakistan in 1999 by overthrowing the elected government

Taking Notes

As you read the summary, use a graphic organizer like the one below to take notes about the events in India and Pakistan that followed partition.

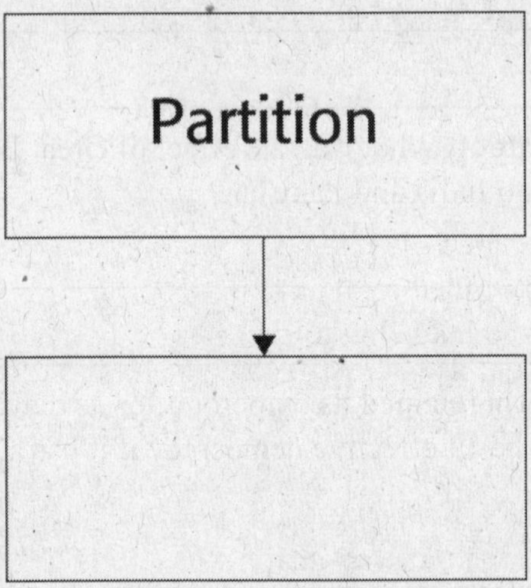

Section Summary

INDEPENDENCE AND CONFLICT

Great Britain controlled India for nearly 200 years. In the early 1900s, Indian calls for independence grew. The Indian National Congress and Mohandas Gandhi won some self-rule for India by the 1930s.

However, when World War II began the British demanded that Indians fight for the Allies. The Indian National Congress was furious because they were being denied democracy, yet being forced to fight for democracy for others.

Gandhi started the nonviolent "Quit India" campaign to drive the British out. After Gandhi and thousands of Indian National Congress officials were jailed, bloody riots broke out. The British decided that controlling India was too costly. After World War II ended, Great Britain made plans to leave India.

India had two main religious groups. The majority were Hindus. Muslims were a large minority. A smaller number of Indians were Sikhs (SEEKS), Christians, and Buddhists. As hopes for independence rose, some Muslims feared that Hindus would dominate the country's government. **Muhammad Ali Jinnah**, who led the Muslim League in the mid-1930s, argued that the only way to protect Muslims' rights was for them to have their own, separate nation. In 1940 the league formally called for a **partition**, or division, of India into Muslim and Hindu countries.

When British rule ended in August 1947 two nations were created: Muslim East and West Pakistan and Hindu India. **Jawaharlal Nehru** (juh-WAH-huhr-lahl NAY-roo) became India's first prime minister.

Although Pakistan had been mostly Muslim and India had been mostly Hindu, many people of both religions lived in both areas. Millions of people moved. Violence between religious groups increased. More than a million people, including Gandhi, died.

Not all border questions had been settled by the British. Soon after the partition, India and Pakistan started fighting for control of an area called Kashmir. They reached a cease-fire in 1949, with India controlling one part of Kashmir, and Pakistan the other.

What action by the British led to the "Quit India" campaign?

____

____

Circle the names of the three major religious groups in India and Pakistan. How were these groups affected by the partition?

____

INDIA AFTER INDEPENDENCE

Nehru as India's first prime minister emphasized unity and economic and social reforms. He worked to increase the rights of women, help the poor, and prevent discrimination based on caste. During the Cold War, India did not take sides. Instead, the new nation focused on economic development.

Nehru died in 1964. His daughter **Indira Gandhi** became prime minister two years later. In 1984, a small group of antigovernment Sikhs occupied a holy temple. Gandhi ordered troops to drive them out. In the process, hundreds were killed. The incident enraged Sikhs. In October 1984, Indira Gandhi was assassinated by her Sikh bodyguards. Anti-Sikh riots broke out, killing thousands and straining relations between the Indian government and the Sikhs.

In the 1990s India undertook reforms that have led to significant economic gains. Areas such as information technology and customer service have expanded rapidly. However, prosperity has come only to a small percentage of India's population. Millions continue to live in poverty in overcrowded cities.

Circle the decade in which India began to make economic changes that led to growth.

CHALLENGES IN SOUTH ASIA

When Pakistan was created in 1947 it had two parts. West Pakistan had a smaller population but controlled the country's government. East Pakistan, hundreds of miles away, remained very poor. In 1971, East Pakistan started a civil war for independence. India sent troops to support East Pakistan. West Pakistan gave up control of East Pakistan, which became the independent nation of Bangladesh. One of the poorest nations in the world, Bangladesh has in recent years tried to build a stable democracy.

What nation was formerly known as East Pakistan?

____

In Pakistan, ethnic and religious tensions have remained. The nation has had a number of different governments. Most recently, General **Pervez Musharraf** in 1999 overthrew the elected government and took control.

Tensions between India and Pakistan remain today. Both nations have successfully tested nuclear weapons. Ethnic fighting also plagues India's neighbor, Sri Lanka. That nation has seen fighting between Buddhists and Hindus since the 1980s.

MAIN IDEA

Long under colonial domination, many Southeast Asian nations achieved independence in the postwar years. The transition, however, was not always a smooth one.

Key Terms and People

Vietminh a group that fought for Vietnamese independence from the French

Ho Chi Minh Communist leader of the Vietminh

domino theory the belief that communism in one nation would quickly spread to surrounding nations

Vietcong literally "Vietnamese Communist"; group that tried to overthrow Ngo Dihn Diem and reunite Vietnam

Sukarno leader of Indonesian independence movement against Dutch rule

Suharto Indonesian general who fought against an attempted coup d'état and then led an authoritarian regime

Khmer Rouge Communist group that gained control of Cambodia in 1975

Pol Pot leader of the Khmer Rouge

Aung San Suu Kyi leader of the opposition to the military dictatorship in Myanmar

Taking Notes

As you read the summary, use a graphic organizer like the one below to take notes about the struggles for independence and the political changes in Southeast Asia after World War II.

Vietnam	
Indonesia	
Cambodia	
Other Nations	

Section Summary

INDEPENDENCE IN SOUTHEAST ASIA

Before World War II, much of Southeast Asia was controlled by colonial powers such as Great Britain, the United States, and the Netherlands. When the war ended, some nations gave up their colonies. Others did not. In Vietnam, a group known as the **Vietminh** fought for independence from the French. The group was led by **Ho Chi Minh**, a Communist who received assistance from China and the Soviet Union.

After what war did colonies in Southeast Asia try to gain independence?

____

THE VIETNAM WAR

After the Vietnamese defeated the French, representatives from several nations met in 1954 to discuss Vietnam's future. Western powers did not want Communists to control Vietnam, so the country was divided in half. The plan was for Vietnam to be reunited in 1956 with a new, elected government.

What did Western nations want to avoid as they discussed the future for Vietnam?

____

____

U.S. president Dwight Eisenhower feared that if Communists won the election, other nations in the region would also fall to communism. This belief was called the **domino theory**. The United States supported Ngo Dihn Diem (NGOH DIN dee-EM) as leader in southern Vietnam with money and military advisers. His rule was corrupt and brutal. By the late 1950s, many of Diem's enemies had formed a group called the **Vietcong**, a term meaning "Vietnamese Communist." The group's goal was to overthrow Diem and reunite Vietnam.

In August 1964, after a report that American navy ships had been attacked by the North Vietnamese, the U.S. Congress to pass the Gulf of Tonkin Resolution. This bill gave President Lyndon B. Johnson the power to expand U.S. involvement in South Vietnam. Soon hundreds of thousands of American troops were fighting in Vietnam.

In 1968, North Vietnam and the Vietcong struck numerous targets in South Vietnam in an attack called the Tet Offensive. The attack showed that the United States was not going to win quickly, as leaders had claimed. American support for the war weakened.

After Tet, the U.S. military expanded the war into Laos and Cambodia to try to destroy a North

Vietnamese supply route. The effort largely failed. In 1973, the United States ended its war with North Vietnam. Vietnam reunited officially in 1976. The United States formally recognized the Communist nation of Vietnam in 1995.

Circle the year in which North and South Vietnam were reunited.

CHANGES IN SOUTHEAST ASIA

Before World War II the 13,000 islands that make up Indonesia had been known as the Dutch East Indies. After the war an independence movement led by **Sukarno** fought against Dutch control, winning independence in 1949.

Sukarno became Indonesia's first president. He gradually took almost total control of the government. His economic policies pushed Indonesia close to bankruptcy. In 1965, a group of army officers and Communists tried to seize power. The army, led by General **Suharto**, fought back. After a great deal of fighting, Suharto took control of the country.

Suharto's regime was authoritarian and corrupt, but revived Indonesia's economy. By the 1980s, however, he was losing support. When the Indonesian economy collapsed in 1997, Suharto was forced to step down.

What forced Suharto to step down in 1997?

____

____

Today, there are more than 300 ethnic groups in Indonesia. This diversity has sometimes led to fighting and terrorist attacks.

In 1975, Indonesia seized control of the former Portuguese colony East Timor, which had declared independence just days earlier. The East Timorese fought for nearly three decades before winning independence in 2002.

In Cambodia, a Communist group called the **Khmer Rouge** (kuh-MER roozh) gained control of the country. This group was led by **Pol Pot**. The Khmer Rouge destroyed all opposition—real or imagined—and killed at least 1.5 million Cambodians. In 1979, Vietnam invaded Cambodia and drove Pol Pot from power. However, civil war raged on until the 1990s.

Burma, now known as Myanmar, has been ruled by a military dictatorship since the 1960s. The leading opposition figure is **Aung San Suu Kyi** (AWNG SAHN SOO CHEE). She has been held in prison or under house arrest since the late 1980s. She won the Nobel Peace Prize in 1991 for her efforts to promote democracy.

MAIN IDEA

China has undergone many changes since becoming a Communist nation in 1949. Today, after making many market reforms, China has a rapidly growing economy.

Key Terms and People

Great Leap Forward a plan to speed China's economic development that involved creating thousands of self-supporting communes

Cultural Revolution a 1960s program that sought to end opposition to Mao and his teachings

Red Guards groups of young men who traveled through China looking for possible offenders during the Cultural Revolution

Gang of Four group that wielded power during Mao's final years, responsible for many of the worst features of the Cultural Revolution

Deng Xiaoping China's leader after Mao's death, helped put in place far-reaching reforms in the Chinese economy

Tiananmen Square Massacre event in the spring of 1989 when tanks and troops fired on pro-democracy protestors occupying Beijing's Tiananmen Square

Taking Notes

As you read the summary, use a graphic organizer like the one below to take notes about the changes that have taken place in China since World War II.

Takeover

↓

Under Mao

↓

After Mao

Section Summary

COMMUNISTS TAKE OVER CHINA

After World War II, civil war resumed in China. Mao Zedong's Communist Red Army was outnumbered by Guomindang forces. However, Mao had the support of many Chinese people. Mao had promised to take land from landowners and give it to the peasants. In 1949, the Guomindang set up a separate government on the island of Taiwan. Mao proclaimed the formation of the People's Republic of China on October 1, 1949.

Some countries, such as the United States, refused to recognize Mao's rule. They recognized the government on Taiwan as China's true government.

Underline the sentence that explains why many Chinese peasants supported Mao and the Communists.

CHINA UNDER MAO

Mao quickly began to create a Communist China. He discouraged religion and, as promised, took land from landowners and gave it to peasants. Mao also sought to increase China's industrial output. His first plans, based on Soviet programs, were successful. The economy improved and rural poverty decreased.

To consolidate Communist control over China, the government began to get rid of people considered "enemies of the state." Anyone suspected of disloyalty or of speaking against the government's policies was executed or sent to a labor camp.

Underline phrases that explain changes Mao made to establish a Communist China.

China had received aid from the Soviet Union and sought guidance from that country. However, during the 1950s, disputes over territory and ideology pushed China and the Soviet Union apart.

In 1958, Mao launched a program called the **Great Leap Forward** to increase China's industrial and agricultural production. The government created thousands of communes. Each commune was supposed to produce its own food and industry. Instead, farm and industrial production fell. Millions of people died in the famine that followed.

The failure of the Great Leap Forward led to a split with the Soviet Union in 1960. China was now almost entirely alone in the world.

After the Great Leap Forward, Mao launched the **Cultural Revolution**. This campaign sought to rid China of its old ways and to create a society in which peasants and physical labor were the ideal. The government eliminated intellectuals such as teachers, skilled workers, and artists. Mao shut down China's schools. Militant high school and college students known as **Red Guards** were encouraged to criticize intellectuals and traditional values. In many cases, the Red Guards killed or tortured people they believed to be politically corrupt.

What program involved getting rid of teachers and artists, and shutting down schools?

____

____

CHINA AFTER MAO

In the 1970s China's isolation began to end. U.S. president Richard Nixon visited China in 1972 and met with Mao. During the last years of his life, Mao suffered bad health and a group known as the **Gang of Four** held much of the power. The group, which included Mao's wife Jiang Qing (jee-AHNG ching), was responsible for many of the worst features of the Cultural Revolution.

After Mao's death in 1976, **Deng Xiaoping** (DUHNG SHOW-ping) eventually became China's leader. He launched reforms in agriculture, industry, science and technology, and national defense.

Seeing economic reforms, as well as democratic reforms in other countries, many Chinese began to demand political freedoms. In the spring of 1989, more than a million pro-democracy protestors occupied Tiananmen (tee-AN-uhn-men) Square in Beijing. China's leaders repeatedly asked the protestors to leave the square, then responded with force. In an event now known as the **Tiananmen Square Massacre** the government sent in tanks and troops that fired on the crowd, killing many.

What were the protestors in Tiananmen Square demanding?

____

China's market reforms have led to rapid economic growth. Today, China's economy is the second largest in the world. Only the United States economy is bigger. Many Chinese continue to live in poverty, but the standard of living is rising for millions of others.

China faces other challenges. Its growing population and industry put strain on its natural resources and environment. Air and water pollution are widespread. Human rights abuses are another concern. The Chinese government continues to limit speech and religion, and strictly controls the media.

MAIN IDEA

The nations of the Asian Pacific Rim underwent remarkable economic growth in the years after World War II, but significant challenges remain.

Key Terms and People

Ferdinand Marcos Philippine president who became an authoritarian dictator in the 1970s

Corazon Aquino president of the Philippines, elected in 1986 after her husband, a rival of Marcos, was assassinated

Kim Il Sung Communist dictator who ruled North Korea after the end of the Korean War

Kim Jong Il son of Kim Il Sung, became ruler of North Korea after his father's death

Asian Tigers Asian nations that made great economic gains by following Japan's example

Taking Notes

As you read the summary, use a graphic organizer like the one below to take notes on the causes and effects of Asian economic growth.

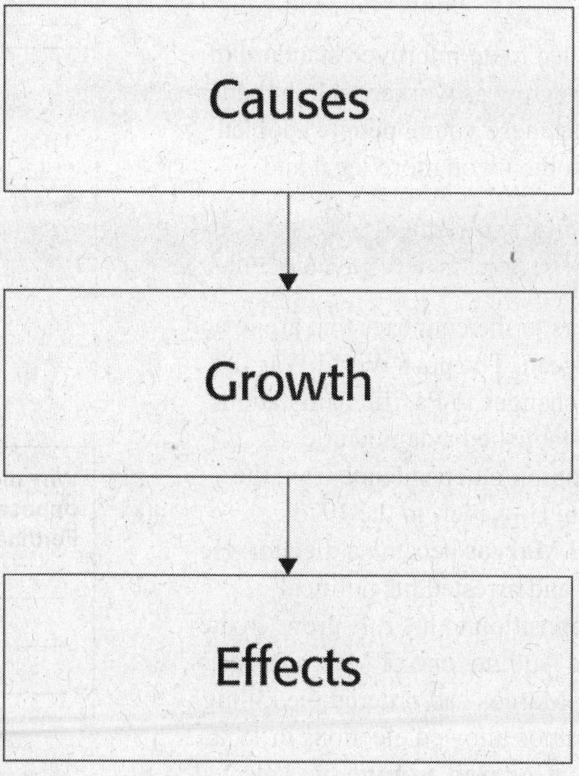

Section Summary

POSTWAR JAPAN

After World War II, U.S. forces occupied Japan. General Douglas MacArthur led U.S. efforts to rebuild the nation. His first goal was to dismantle Japan's military. MacArthur did this by removing all wartime leaders from power and trying many for war crimes.

Circle the name of the U.S. general who led the efforts to rebuild Japan after World War II.

To create a democratic Japan, MacArthur had a new constitution written. It brought Western-style democracy and civil rights to Japan. The emperor became no more than a symbolic leader.

MacArthur made numerous economic reforms, such as breaking up organizations that had dominated Japanese industry. When the Korean War started, Japan got a boost by supplying U.S. and UN military forces.

Postwar rebuilding focused on industries such as steel and auto manufacturing, allowing Japan to export goods to many nations. After the U.S. occupation ended in 1952, Japan's economy continued to grow. By 1968, it was the second largest in the world.

When did the U.S. occupation of Japan end?

____

Economic growth led to an improved standard of living. Japanese cities grew as workers sought better-paying jobs. Many Japanese young people adopted American culture. Women won more legal and social freedoms.

THE PACIFIC RIM

The Pacific Rim refers to the countries that are in and around the Pacific Ocean. The post-World War II years brought many changes to Pacific Rim nations.

The Philippines established a democratic government after winning independence from the United States in 1946. However, in the 1970s President **Ferdinand Marcos** became a dictator. He imposed martial law and arrested his political opponents. Public opposition to his rule grew. In the early 1980s, Benigno Aquino, one of Marcos's rivals, was killed. Thinking Marcos had ordered the killing, the people rioted. Marcos allowed elections in 1986 and Aquino's widow, **Corazon Aquino**, was elected

Why did the Filipino people oppose the rule of Ferdinand Marcos?

____

____

____

president. Afterward, the Philippines struggled to return to democracy and build its economy.

The Korean War ended in 1953 with Korea still divided. North Korea was ruled by Communist dictator **Kim Il Sung**. Aid from the Soviet Union and China helped build up industry and the military. When that aid was cut, poverty and hunger became widespread. When Kim Il Sung died in 1994, his son, **Kim Jong Il**, took power. North Korea's economy has continued to deteriorate and the military has continued to grow. In 2006, North Korea tested a nuclear weapon for the first time.

Circle the name of the nation that tested a nuclear weapon for the first time in 2006.

South Korea received significant aid from the United States after the Korean War. South Koreans enjoyed economic gains but had little political freedom. The country experienced several uprisings and military coups until the late 1980s, when it adopted a more democratic constitution.

In Taiwan the government of the Guomindang built a successful economy based on international trade and production of consumer goods. The Guomindang ruled under martial law until the 1980s.

THE ASIAN TIGERS

Other Asian nations made gains by following Japan's model for economic development. South Korea, Hong Kong, Taiwan, and Singapore became known as the **Asian Tigers** because of their fast economic growth.

Governments in Asian Tiger nations promoted education. This created a skilled workforce. The United States sent economic aid to many nations. The Asian Tigers also benefited from access to major shipping routes. They grew by exporting consumer goods, and by keeping production and labor costs low.

Underline phrases that describe strategies leading to economic growth in Pacific Rim nations.

These economies suffered when a severe financial crisis swept the region in 1997. Asian banks, free from strict banking laws, borrowed more money than they needed. When banks in Thailand began to fail, panic spread through the region. Stock and real estate prices fell, and currencies lost value.

Over the following decade, the region began to recover. Other nations, such as Indonesia, Malaysia, Thailand, and the Philippines, also began to emerge as economic powers.

Chapter Summary

Nationalism in Africa and the Middle East

Africa	Israel	Arab nations
• Decolonization took place after World War II. • New nations often faced poverty, civil wars, and ineffective governments. • Some nations sought better government by holding democratic elections.	• Zionist movement led to the creation of a Jewish state. • UN created Israel as the Jewish homeland after World War II. • Israel faced years of conflict with neighoring Arab countries over its right to exist.	• Islamists argued that Arab nations should follow Islamic laws, not Western ways. • Arab-Israeli conflict arose over territory in and around Israel. • Iranian nationalists fought for Iran to control its own oil.

COMPREHENSION AND CRITICAL THINKING

Use information from the graphic organizer to answer the following questions.

1. **Recall** What challenges did new African nations face after gaining independence?

____

____

2. **Compare and Contrast** How did the Zionist movement differ from nationalist movements in Africa?

____

____

3. **Elaborate** How did the presence of oil reserves affect nationalism in Arab nations?

____

____

4. **Evaluate** Describe one strategy that you think could help resolve the conflict between Israel and its neighbors. Why do you think this strategy would work?

____

____

Section 1

MAIN IDEA

After World War II, almost all countries in Africa gained independence from ruling European powers.

Key Terms and People

Kwame Nkrumah leader of the Gold Coast nationalist movement, founded the Convention People's Party and later, became first prime minister of Ghana

Jomo Kenyatta leader of the nationalist movement in Kenya

Mau Mau violent movement in Kenya to take land back from white farmers

apartheid "apartness;" a policy that divided South Africans into four racial groups

Taking Notes

As you read, use a graphic organizer like the one below to take notes on African independence movements.

British and French	
Portuguese and Belgian	
South Africa	

Section Summary

BRITISH AND FRENCH COLONIES

After World War II, Great Britain and France were the first to begin decolonization,the withdrawal of colonial powers from their colonies and areas of influence. The Gold Coast in Ghana, West Africa was the first British colony to achieve independence. Leaders in the Gold Coast had wanted greater participation in government. They established a convention with goals of cooperating with the British and gain influence through peaceful means.

Another, nationalist movement started in the Gold Coast, but it was less cooperative. **Kwame Nkrumah** led this group, called the Convention People's Party (CPP). Nkrumah was jailed for leading strikes and demonstrations, but the CPP still became a major political party. In 1951, the British allowed national elections. The CPP won. When Britain granted the Gold Coast full self-government in 1957, Nkrumah became its first prime minister.

The path to independence did not go as smoothly in Kenya. White Kenyan farmers and the native Kikuyu people clashed over ownership of the Kenyan highlands. The farmers feared that with independence, they would lose large tracts of valuable cash crops to the Kikuyu, who considered the land their ancestral homeland. **Jomo Kenyatta** supported the Kikuyus and led Kenya's nationalist movement. Many Kikuyu farmers formed a violent movement called the **Mau Mau**, terrorizing the highlands and murdering anyone who opposed them. Though the British fought back against the Mau Mau, it was clear that they should decolonize. In 1963, Jomo Kenyatta became the first prime minister of independent Kenya.

How did Kenya's nationalist movement differ from Ghana's?

____

____

____

____

After World War II, France's prime minister, Charles de Gaulle, tried to make the African colonies part of France itself. He also supported the call for greater African participation in colonial government. Some African leaders wanted self-rule, but others wanted a continuing relationship with France. In 1958, most of the colonies joined a new organization called the French Community, which kept ties with France but gained independence a few years later.

Circle the name of the colonial organization created by France in 1958.

PORTUGUESE AND BELGIAN COLONIES

The transition to independence was difficult for the Belgian and Portuguese colonies in Africa. In the 1950s, African nationalists in the Congo demanded self-government right away. In the 1960s, the Belgians suddenly announced that they would withdraw completely from the Congo. This led to violence against Belgian settlers and a civil war.

As Portugal held on to its colonies, African leaders organized armies to fight for independence in Angola, Portuguese Guinea, and Mozambique. This led to long years of bloody warfare in the colonies. Years of war and a military coup back in Portugal ruined its economy. By 1974, Portugal could no longer support its colonies, and it withdrew completely from Africa.

Explain one similarity between the nationalist movements in the Belgian and Portuguese colonies.

____

____

SOUTH AFRICA

In the early 1900s, South Africa was run by white Afrikaners, descendents of the original Dutch settlers. South Africa has been independent since 1910, but nonwhites had limited freedom under the restrictive Afrikaner government. In 1948, the National Party, dominated by Afrikaners, came to power in South Africa. The party created a policy of **apartheid**, which means "apartness" in the Afrikaans language. This policy divided people into four racial groups: White, Black, Colored (mixed ancestry), and Asian. It imposed harsh controls over nonwhites, banned interracial marriages, and restricted African land and business ownership.

Under apartheid, only white South Africans could vote or hold political office. Blacks, who made up nearly 75 percent of the population, were denied citizenship and could only work certain jobs for very little pay. Blacks were forced to live in poor areas called townships. The government made sure the townships remained poor by restricting their businesses. In the 1950s, the government created "homelands" for African tribes or groups, which did not include good farmland or resources. The government used the homelands as an excuse to deny citizenship to millions of South Africans. Black men had to travel far from their families to work in mines, factories, and farms.

What determined the rights of people living under apartheid in South Africa?

____

What aspects of life on homelands show the South African government was not really helping Blacks by granting them this land?

____

____

____

Name ______________________ Class ______________ Date ______________

MAIN IDEA

Newly independent African nations struggled with poverty, conflict, and ineffective governments. In recent years some countries sought better government by holding democratic elections.

Key Terms and People

African National Congress (ANC) group that protested apartheid in South Africa

Nelson Mandela organized ANC campaign to urge blacks to break apartheid laws; after his long imprisonment, he became the first black president of democratic South Africa

Sharpeville Massacre 1960 killing of 60 ANC protesters by police, turning point in the anti-apartheid movement

Soweto Uprising 1976 student protest in which over 600 people were killed while protesting decree that black schools must teach Afrikaans, the language of most whites

F.W. de Klerk president of South Africa who began negotiations for a new constitution that would end apartheid

one-party system a system in which one political party controls the government and elections are rarely competitive

patronage system used by dictators to keep power by giving loyal followers well-paying government positions

Mobutu Sese Seko corrupt dictator of the Congo who robbed his country of wealth

desertification the spread of desert areas caused by planting crops in poor soil and grazing animals in extremely dry regions

negritude movement efforts of a group of writers living in Paris that focused on African culture and identity while rejecting European culture

Taking Notes

As you read, use a graphic organizer like the one below to take notes on the challenges Africa faced after independence and the challenges it faces today. Enlarge boxes as needed.

Political Challenges
Economic Challenges
Environmental Challenges

Section Summary

POLITICAL CHALLENGES

In the early 1900s a group of blacks in South Africa formed the **African National Congress** (**ANC**). The ANC held peaceful protests against apartheid. In the 1940s, a young lawyer named **Nelson Mandela** joined the ANC, along with other younger and more radical members. In 1952, Mandela urged blacks in South Africa to break apartheid laws, and the ANC gained many followers. In 1960, police killed more than 60 ANC protesters during the **Sharpeville Massacre**. This event became a turning point in the anti-apartheid movement, convincing Mandela and others that the ANC must use violence. In response, the government banned the ANC and jailed Mandela.

How did the ANC change after the Sharpeville Massacre?

____

____

In 1976, students held a major protest of the decree that black schools must teach Afrikaans, the language of most whites. Called the **Soweto Uprising**, the protest turned into a violent revolt. More than 600 people were killed. This led to violent uprisings in many other townships. Many foreign countries refused to trade with South Africa until it ended apartheid.

In 1990, under President **F.W. de Klerk**, South Africa legalized the ANC and began creating a constitution that would end apartheid. De Klerk released Mandela from prison, abolished the homelands, and held South Africa's first democratic election. In the election, Nelson Mandela became the first black president of a democratic South Africa.

Circle the names of two presidents of South Africa. Which president ended apartheid?

____

By the end of the 1960s almost all independent African nations had a **one-party system**. In this system, a single political party controls the government. Elections are rarely competitive. Dictators maintained their power through **patronage**, giving loyal followers well-paying government positions. Corrupt leaders, such as **Mobutu Sese Soku** of the Congo, robbed their countries of wealth, living lavishly while their people lived in poverty.

In many colonies, rival ethnic groups competed for control. Some conflicts led to destructive civil wars. In Nigeria and Somalia, millions died from fighting and starvation. In the 1990s, ethnic conflict led to the

Why did many colonies experience civil war after gaining independence?

____

____

killing of over 1 million people in Rwanda in a mass genocide. Many others fled to refugee camps.

By 2005, more than 30 African countries had abandoned one-party systems and held elections. However, some former dictators used fraud or intimidation to stay in power.

ECONOMIC AND ENVIRONMENTAL CHALLENGES

After independence, the economies of most African nations were fragile. To support themselves, many nations received help from international organizations. However, bad planning and corrupt leaders left many nations disorganized and in debt.

African nations were also challenged by deadly diseases such as malaria. In the 1980s, acquired immune deficiency syndrome (AIDS), spread rapidly through Africa. Today, it continues to devastate many African nations.

African farmers today struggle with poor soil and few pastures for their livestock. When soil dries out, grasses cannot grow. As a result, desert areas are expanding, a process called **desertification**. This process contributes to cycles of drought and famine.

Underline problems caused by desertification.

REVIVAL OF AFRICAN CULTURE

During colonial rule Africans preserved their culture and used it to express dissatisfaction with their rulers. African writers maintained a strong tradition of poetry, plays, and novels written in Swahili. In the 1930s, African and Caribbean students in Paris founded the **negritude movement**. Their writings rejected European culture and instead focused on African culture and identity.

How did some Africans protest colonial rule?

____

____

African artists also used a mix of traditional and new ideas and materials to express their identity. They created masks, musical instruments, and sculptures. This art became highly valued on the world market. Africans also used music and dance to honor their history and mark special occasions. In the 1960s, African musicians blended African and Western music. Later, in the 1980s, African popular music, or Afro-Pop, became popular throughout the world.

Name ______________________ Class ______________ Date ______________

Africa and the Middle East

Section 3

MAIN IDEA

The rise of nationalism in North Africa and the Middle East led to independence for some countries and to conflicts with the West.

Key Terms and People

David Ben-Gurion Israel's first prime minister

Gamal Abdel Nasser Egyptian colonel who lead a military coup in 1952 that abolished the monarchy and existing political parties to create a single government party

Suez Crisis confrontation that led to Nasser gaining control of the Suez Canal

Baghdad Pact U.S.-led alliance against communism in the Middle East

Pan-Arabism Arab unity

Mohammad Reza Pahlavi shah of Iran whose reforms were opposed by conservatives and who used intimidation and torture to stop opposition

Taking Notes

As you read, use a graphic organizer like the one below to take notes on key events and dates in the history of North Africa and the Middle East.

French North Africa	
Israel	
Egypt	
Iran	

Section Summary

FRENCH NORTH AFRICA

After World War II, France faced nationalist movements in its North African protectorates of Morocco, Tunisia, and Algeria. France's attempt to stop these movements, lead to unrest, demonstrations, and wars. Algeria was most important to the French because of its large French settler population. France could not fight wars in Algeria, Morocco, and Tunisia at the same time, so in 1956, France granted independence to Morocco and Tunisia.

In 1954, Algerian nationalist leaders formed the National Liberation Front (FLN). The FLN waged war against French settlers, who owned the best land, and dominated the economy and politics. The French responded with mass arrests and attacks on Muslims that killed thousands. By 1957 the FLN had been mostly defeated in Algiers, the capital. French settlers seized control and demanded more support from the French government. When Charles de Gaulle was appointed prime minister in 1958, he tried to give some self-government to Algeria. When the French settlers reacted violently, de Gaulle decided that France could not rule Algeria, and in 1962 he granted the nation independence.

Circle the name of the nationalist group in Algeria. When did Algeria gain independence?

____

____

THE CREATION OF ISRAEL

Nationalism also led to the creation of Israel. The Jewish nationalist movement, known as Zionism, called for an independent state in their ancient homeland. After World War II, the horrors of the Holocaust were revealed to the world, and many leaders supported the Zionist cause. In 1947, the United Nations divided Palestine into a Jewish state and an Arab state, with the city of Jerusalem to remain under international control. This plan was supported by Jewish leaders, but not Arab leaders.

David Ben-Gurion and other Jewish leaders declared the birth of the democratic state of Israel on May 14, 1948. The next day, Israel was invaded by armies from several Arab countries in the first Arab-Israeli war. The Arab armies were defeated but refused to sign permanent peace treaties.

Why did the UN divide Palestine into two states after World War II?

____

____

Because of the war, the Arab state proposed by the UN was never created. Instead, the lands were seized by Israel and some Arab countries. By the end of the war, around 700,000 Palestinian Arabs became refugees when Israel took control of their lands.

CHANGES IN EGYPT AND IRAN

Israel's victory in the first Arab-Israeli war had effects throughout the Arab world. Egypt had gained independence from Britain in 1922, but the British still occupied the Suez Canal Zone and its monarch was seen as dependent on the British for his power. Egypt's leaders were blamed for Egypt's loss in the war against Israel. Military colonel **Gamal Abdel Nasser** led a coup in 1952, forcing King Farouk I out of power and eliminating the existing political parties. Nasser's group formed a single government party.

After Nasser came to power, he confronted Britain, France, and Israel during the **Suez Crisis**. The conflict began when Nasser refused to sign the **Baghdad Pact**, a U.S.-led alliance against communism in the Middle East. Nasser then signed an arms deal with Czechoslovakia. In response, the U.S. and Britain refused to loan Egypt money to build a dam at Aswan.

Why did the U.S. and Britain refuse to loan money to Egypt for the Aswan dam?

____

____

Nasser decided to take control of the Suez Canal, which was owned by Britain and France. Britain, France, and Israel attacked and defeated Egypt in October 1956. The U.S. did not support these actions and pressured Britain, France, and Israel to withdraw. They did, and Nasser was left in control of the Suez Canal. Nasser became a hero of the Arab world. He promoted **Pan-Arabism**, or Arab unity.

Mohammad Reza Pahlavi became shah of Iran in 1941. Iranian nationalists wanted to take control of the country's oil resources, which were run by Britain. In 1951 the Iranian parliament voted to overthrow the shah and take control of the Iranian oil industry. In response, Britain and the U.S. called for a boycott of Iranian oil. They also supported a coup that returned the shah to power.

Which country controlled Iran's oil in 1941?

____

After the shah returned to power, he improved Iran's industry, education, and health care. However, he ruled with an iron fist. Many believed his reforms moved Iran away from traditional Islamic values.

Name ______________________ Class ______________ Date ______________

MAIN IDEA
Regional issues in the Middle East have led to conflicts between Israel and its neighbors and to conflicts in and between Iran and Iraq.

Key Terms and People

Organization of Petroleum Exporting Countries (OPEC) an organization of mostly Middle Eastern countries that attempts to regulate oil production to maximize revenues

Six-Day War 1967 war between Arab nations (Egypt, Jordan, and Syria) and Israel

Yom Kippur War 1973 surprise attack by Egypt and Syria against Israel to regain territory, named for the Jewish holy day when the attack began

Golda Meir prime minister of Israel during the Yom Kippur War

Anwar Sadat Egyptian president who declared that Egypt wanted peace with Israel

Menachem Begin Israeli prime minister who signed peace agreement with Egypt

Camp David Accords 1978 peace agreements between Egypt and Israel that led to the 1979 treaty in which Egypt recognized Israel's right to exist and Israel returned the Sinai Peninsula to Egypt

intifada rebellion by Palestinians in the West Bank and Gaza strip

Ayatollah Ruhollah Khomeini Shia religious leader who inspired protests against Iran's shah in 1978; he was named leader when Iran became an Islamic republic

Iranian Revolution rebellion during which Iran became an Islamic republic

Taking Notes

As you read, use a graphic organizer like the one below to take notes on regional issues and conflicts in the Middle East.

Regional Issues	
Conflicts	

Section Summary

REGIONAL ISSUES

About two-thirds of the world's known oil reserves are in the Middle East. Oil has brought wealth to Saudi Arabia, Iran, Iraq, Kuwait, and other countries, most of whom belong to the **Organization of Petroleum Exporting Countries (OPEC)**. OPEC tries to regulate oil production in order to increase profits. Money from selling oil has allowed many countries to modernize and improve their economies. However, some countries have used it to build up their militaries and threaten neighbors. Oil has also led to conflicts within the Middle East and with outside nations.

Islamism has also led to conflict. This movement seeks to organize government and society according to Islamic laws. Islamists believe that Muslim countries have strayed from Islam by modeling politics and economies on Western nations. Some extreme Islamists have used violence to bring about the changes they want.

Conflict has also grown between Israel and its neighbors. Most Middle Eastern countries have refused to recognize Israel's right to exist. Also, a series of wars has led to the expansion of Israel. As a result, many Palestinian Arabs live under Israeli control, another source of conflict.

List the three regional issues that have caused conflict in the Middle East.

____

____

____

THE ARAB-ISRAELI CONFLICT

The Arab-Israeli conflict that began in 1948 has continued through the years. In 1967 Egypt and Israel fought the **Six-Day War**. Israel gained control of land in the West Bank and Gaza which had a large Palestinian population. To regain their lands, Egypt and Syria launched the **Yom Kippur War** against Israel on a Jewish holy day in 1973. Israel's government, led by **Golda Meir**, was not prepared. With U.S. support, Israel pushed back Egyptian and Syrian forces and both sides signed a cease-fire.

Circle the name of the Egyptian leader who worked for peace with Israel.

In 1977, Egyptian president **Anwar Sadat** declared that Egypt wanted peace with Israel. U.S. President Jimmy Carter invited Sadat and Israeli prime minister **Menachem Begin** to Camp David in Maryland. In 1978, Sadat and Begin reached an agreement known as the **Camp David Accords**. This ended 30 years of hostility between Egypt and Israel.

Israel continued to face conflict with Palestine. In 1987, Palestinians began a rebellion, called the **intifada**, in the West Bank and Gaza. A second intifada began in 2000. In 2005, Israeli troops withdrew from Gaza and parts of the West Bank. However, conflict began again in 2006.

REVOLUTION IN IRAN

In Iran, Shah Mohammad Reza Pahlavi had close ties to Western governments and oil companies. Under his rule, Iran became industrialized and more like the West. Many Iranians, especially Islamists, opposed the shah. In 1978 **Ayatollah Ruhollah Khomeini**, a Shia religious leader, inspired protests against the shah, who fled to Iran in 1979 during the **Iranian Revolution**. Iran became an Islamic republic ruled by Khomeini. Iran also grew strongly anti-Western, and attacked the U.S. embassy in Tehran in 1979.

Why did Islamists oppose the shah of Iran?

____

____

____

CONFLICT IN IRAQ

In 1980 Iraq, led by Saddam Hussein, used chemical weapons as part of a long and costly war against Iran. In 1988, Iran and Iraq agreed to a cease-fire, but Hussein continued to build up Iraq's military. Then, in 1990 Iraq invaded Kuwait, accusing Kuwait of stealing Iraqi oil. The UN attempted to force Iraq to withdraw from Kuwait. When this failed, the U.S. led an attack against Iraqi forces and freed Kuwait. After the war, the UN insisted that Iraq destroy its chemical weapons and agree not to develop nuclear weapons. Iraq did not fully cooperate with weapons inspectors.

Underline the names of three countries that have experienced conflict with Iraq since 1980.

After the attacks of September 11, 2001, some U.S. leaders believed that Saddam Hussein was hiding deadly weapons that he would give to terrorists. As a result, the U.S. led a 2003 invasion of Iraq that forced Hussein from power. In 2004, power was transferred to the Iraqis. In 2005, Iraq held its first multiparty election in 50 years and approved a new constitution that would make Iraq an Islamic federal democracy. However, continuing violence by armed rebels made the country's future highly uncertain.

Chapter Summary

Latin American Dictatorships

Origins
- Dependence on foreign countries for goods, investments, and military aid
- Economic problems create huge gaps between rich and poor
- Military groups able to seize power

Effects
- Social reforms, such as literacy and free health care
- Some land given to peasants
- Few civil liberties
- Death squads killed people who opposed the goverment

Downfall
- Failed to bring about lasting change
- Slowing economies drew criticism
- International groups applied pressure to make changes
- Voters elected moderate leaders

COMPREHENSION AND CRITICAL THINKING

Use information from the graphic organizer to answer the following questions.

1. **Identify** What were positive effects of Latin American dictatorships?

____

____

2. **Interpret** How did the lives of Latin American citizens improve after the fall of military dictatorships?

____

____

3. **Evaluate** What is your opinion about countries becoming involved in the politics of other nations? Explain.

____

____

4. **Rank** What do you think are the most important rights a government should provide its citizens? Rank the rights you identify in order of importance.

____

____

Name ____________________ Class ______________ Date ____________

MAIN IDEA

In reaction to economic and social conditions in Latin America after World War II, many Central American countries experienced revolutions that involved intervention by the United States.

Key Terms and People

import-substitution led industrialization a policy in which industries were developed to replace the need to import manufactured goods

Liberation Theology the belief that the church should be active in the struggle for economic and political equality

Fidel Castro leader who launched a revolution in Cuba and became its leader in 1959

Che Guevara revolutionary who wanted to set up a Marxist regime in Cuba

Sandinistas revolutionary group that took over Nicaragua in 1979

junta a group of leaders who rule jointly

Contras a U.S.-trained and funded rebel group in Nicaragua

Taking Notes

As you read the summary, use a graphic organizer like the one below to take notes on trends and conflicts in Latin America.

Trends	Conflicts

Section Summary

TRENDS IN LATIN AMERICA

After World War II, many Latin American countries struggled with issues of poverty and inequality that stem from their long history of colonialism. Many Latin American countries wanted to decrease their dependence on foreign countries. They adopted policies of **import-substitution led industrialization**. This means industries were developed so that the country did not need to import as many manufactured goods. Despite the growth of industry, many nations received foreign investments, loans, and military aid.

What is the goal of import-substitution led industrialization?

____

____

As countries industrialized, rural land use remained a major issue. Most land was owned by a few wealthy people, many of whom had ties to U.S. businesses. Meanwhile, peasants struggled to find land to farm. Some countries took land from large landholders and gave it to landless peasants, with mixed results. One group that tried to address the enormous gap between the rich and the poor in Latin America was the Catholic Church. Many priests supported the popular **Liberation Theology**, the belief that the church should be active in the struggle for economic and political equality. Peasants often moved to fast-growing cities to improve their lives, but found shortages of food, housing, and safe drinking water.

What are two ways that Latin American governments and others tried to close the gap between the rich and the poor after World War II.

____

____

THE CUBAN REVOLUTION

Although Cuba was one of Latin America's wealthiest, most developed nations, many of the people struggled with poverty. In addition to hotels and casinos, businesses based in the United States owned huge sugar and tobacco plantations in Cuba. These enterprises took up so much land that little was left for growing food. Business interests encouraged the United States to support several corrupt dictators in Cuba, including Fulgencio Batista, who seized power in 1952.

Many of Cuba's poor were unhappy under Batista's rule. A young lawyer named **Fidel Castro** started a guerrilla war that turned into a full-scale revolution. On January 1, 1959, Batista fled and Cuba was left in Castro's control.

How did Fidel Castro come to power in Cuba?

____

____

While some wanted democratic reforms, others, like **Che Guevara**, favored a Communist regime. Castro focused on ending U.S. dominance, redistributing wealth, and reforming society. He restructured Cuba's economy, society, government and foreign policy. He took full control of the government, and ended freedom of the press. As Castro led Cuba toward communism, the concerned United States tried again and again to oust the communist leader. In 1961, U.S. troops invaded Cuba's Bay of Pigs, but were easily defeated. In 1962, the CIA discovered that the Soviet Union was building nuclear missile sites in Cuba. President John F. Kennedy ordered a naval blockade to stop Soviet ships headed for Cuba. After a tense confrontation known as the Cuban Missile Crisis, the Soviet Union removed the missile sites.

Why was the CIA's discovery of Soviet missile sites in Cuba a cause for alarm in the United States?

____

____

The Cuban Revolution has had mixed results. The people have access to free health care and education, but they also have few civil liberties. The Cuban economy has struggled due to many people leaving the country, the loss of Soviet financial support, and the U.S. embargo on goods.

OTHER REVOLUTIONS

In 1954, the United States led a coup against Guatemalan president Jacobo Arbenz due to his communist leanings and pressure from a U.S. company hurt by his land reforms. This sparked a civil war that finally ended in 1996. In El Salvador in 1980, government assassins killed Archbishop Oscar Romero, a priest who supported Liberation Theology. This too led to a civil war between Communist-supported guerrilla groups and the U.S.-supported government that oppressed dissent.

Nicaragua also struggled with instability. In 1979, the ruling Somoza family was overthrown by a revolutionary group, the **Sandinistas**. The Sandinistas used a **junta** (HOON-tuh), a group of leaders who rule jointly. As the junta grew more radical, the United States ended its financial aid and backed a rebel group, the **Contras**, that fought the junta government. Economic troubles and violence continued throughout the 1980s.

Why did the United States switch its support to the Contras after having supported the Sandinistas?

____

____

MAIN IDEA

Spiraling economic and social problems and political turmoil in Latin America led military leaders to seize power and install repressive regimes.

Key Terms and People

Juan Perón Argentinean leader who rose to power in 1943 after a military coup

populist a supporter of the rights of the common people, not the privileged elite

hyperinflation an extremely high level of inflation that grows rapidly in a short period of time

Augusto Pinochet Chilean army commander who became president in 1974

Manuel Noriega dictator of Panama in the 1980s

Shining Path a guerrilla group that terrorized Peru in the 1990s

Taking Notes

As you read the summary, take notes on life under the dictatorship for each country listed in the graphic organizer below.

Argentina	
Brazil	
Chile	
Other countries	

Section Summary

ARGENTINA

In 1943, **Juan Perón** rose to power in Argentina following a military coup. Perón was a **populist**, a supporter of the rights of the common people as opposed to the privileged elite. With his wife Eva in charge of labor and social programs, Perón brought minimum wage, eight-hour work days, and paid vacations to Argentina. A booming postwar economy enabled him to build schools, hospitals, and homeless shelters. Lack of sufficient resources, however, kept industry from growing. Agricultural production fell after Perón put the cattle and wheat industries under government control. The economy suffered. Perón also turned Argentina into a one-party state and suppressed many freedoms. He had become a dictator.

How did Perón improve life for citizens of Argentina?

____

____

Perón's downfall in 1955 was followed by decades of economic and political turmoil. From 1976 to 1983, Argentina's military dictatorship killed tens of thousands of citizens in a secret "dirty war." A group of mothers organized protests to bring national and international attention to the situation.

BRAZIL

Brazil's story is similar to Argentina's. Juscelino Kubitschek won a democratic election in 1954. He promised Brazil rapid progress. Foreign investment flowed into the country, helping him reach his goal. Though the $2 billion capital city of Brasília quickly became a source of pride for the nation, the costs of modernization crippled Brazil's economy. Military leaders seized control in 1964. From 1968 to 1973, the country's economy grew faster than any other in the world, an achievement called the "Brazilian miracle."

How did Brazil's economy change after Kubitschek's election?

____

____

But progress came at a terrible price. Those who complained about the government freezing wages or the resulting decline in living standards were kidnapped, tortured, or killed. Opposition grew, and the economy crashed. Brazil fell deeply into debt when oil prices rose in the 1970s. This debt brought about **hyperinflation**, or an extremely high level of inflation that grows rapidly in a short period of time.

CHILE

Like Argentina and Brazil, economic problems led to drastic changes in government in Chile. In 1970, Chileans elected Salvador Allende president. Allende improved housing, education, and health care. He also redistributed land to peasants. At first, these measures succeeded. But as industrial and farm production slowed, prices rose, along with food shortages. Allende's socialist-style policies distanced him from business owners. His policies also worried the United States government, which began supporting opposition groups. In 1973, fighter planes bombed the presidential palace, killing Allende and 3,000 others.

The coup against Allende was carried out by **Augusto Pinochet**, (peen-oh-SHAY) commander in chief of the Chilean army. Pinochet became president in 1974. He quickly demolished his opposition, disbanded congress, and suspended the constitution. Thousands of citizens were tortured or killed; others fled into exile. Despite the turmoil, Chile's capitalism-supporting economy grew quickly.

Why were Chilean business owners and the United States government concerned about Allende's rule?

____

____

OTHER DICTATORSHIPS

In Haiti, the Duvalier family maintained a dictatorship for 28 years. Their rule made Haiti's struggling economy even worse. In 1986, riots broke out, ousting the Duvaliers. Turmoil followed as president Jean-Bertrand Aristide and the Haitian military vied for power.

During the 1980s, Panama came under the control of **Manuel Noriega**, a brutal dictator who used the country as a base for drug smuggling. Noriega was arrested by United States authorities in 1989 and imprisoned in Florida. Panama held democratic elections in 1994.

In 1990, Peru faced a poor economy and a terror campaign from a guerrilla group known as the **Shining Path**. Alberto Fujimori was elected president. When congress complained that he abused his power, Fujimori disbanded congress and suspended the constitution. He was reelected in 1995 due to a booming economy and decreased guerrilla activity. However, Fujimori resigned because of scandals and fraud after the 2000 election.

Circle the names of two Latin American countries whose dictators are discussed in this section.

Name ______________________ Class ______________ Date ______________

Latin America

Section 3

MAIN IDEA

In the 1980s, repressive regimes in Latin America fell, and more moderate elected leaders brought some measure of political and economic progress.

Key Terms and People

Violeta Chamorro moderate leader elected in Nicaragua

North American Free Trade Agreement (NAFTA) an agreement meant to eliminate tariffs on trade between Mexico, the United States, and Canada

Vicente Fox conservative PAN party candidate elected president of Mexico in 2000

Hugo Chávez elected president of Venezuela in 2000

Taking Notes

As you read the summary, take notes on the chain of events that brought democratic and economic reforms to Latin America. Use a graphic organizer like the one below to add key points. Add as many boxes as you need.

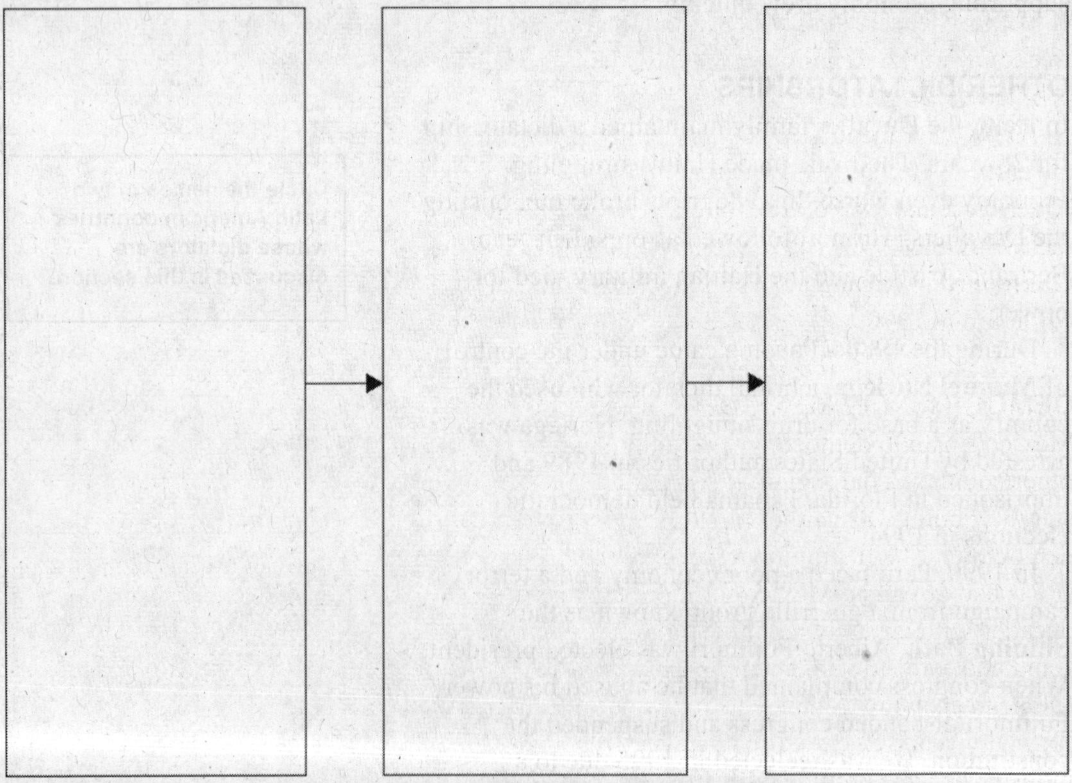

Section Summary

RETURN OF DEMOCRACY

After decades of political turmoil and civil wars, dictatorships across Latin America started falling in the 1980s and 1990s. Elected leaders put an end to military rule. Moderate civilian politicians began a series of political and economic reforms.

Latin America's military governments failed to bring about needed social and economic reforms. Poor landless peasants moved to cities, only to find themselves living in shantytowns with other job seekers. Economies did not get better, civil wars raged, and civil rights were repressed. People demanded change.

Underline the factors that led to the downfall of military governments in Latin America.

The return of democracy in Latin America turned out to be fairly peaceful. Pressure came from international lenders that demanded changes before they gave loans. Pro-democracy groups inside and outside the region wanted voting rights and the right to voice opposition to political leadership.

What groups put pressure on Latin American governments? How?

____

____

____

Military leaders slowly began to integrate some freedoms into their policies. When given the chance, people voted against the military in favor of new civilian governments. Democracy returned to Brazil in the early 1970s, and to Argentina in 1982. Central America countries elected moderate governments in the 1980s and 1990s, such as that of **Violeta Chamorro** in Nicaragua. The Pinochet regime in Chile fell in 1990.

DEMOCRACY IN MEXICO

Mexico's path to democracy was unlike that of any other country in the region. It had experienced relative stability, but it was neither a full dictatorship nor very democratic. The Institutional Revolutionary Party (PRI) had governed Mexico for more than seven decades with virtually no opposition. It often used fraud and force to win elections. However, the Mexican economy remained strong and industry grew for many years. Eventually, however, Mexican industry became dominated by foreign investors. Even as profits grew, most money left the country, leaving Mexico with foreign debt, poverty, and inequality.

How did the rule of the PRI in Mexico resemble a dictatorship?

____

____

Mexicans became increasingly dissatisfied with PRI rule. The country experienced several crises, including the murder of peaceful protesters in 1968 and a huge earthquake in 1985 that destroyed large parts of Mexico City. The high cost of rebuilding, along with high inflation and unemployment further increased the public's dissatisfaction.

In 1992, Mexico, the United States, and Canada signed the **North American Free Trade Agreement (NAFTA)**. This agreement was meant to eliminate tariffs on trade among the three countries to improve their economies. Many Mexicans, however, feared increased competition from imported goods.

Circle the names of the three countries involved in NAFTA.

Mexican voters ended 71 years of PRI rule in 2000, when they elected **Vicente Fox**, a member of the conservative PAN party, to be president. Fox worked to end corruption and improve relations with the United States. In 2006, Mexicans elected another PAN party member, Felipe Calderón.

MARKET REFORMS

The political shift to democracy that swept from Mexico to Argentina brought economic changes as well. Deeply indebted Latin American countries instituted difficult reform measures to stabilize their economies. Countries cut government spending and ended some government subsidies of businesses. Some government-run services and businesses were turned over to private ownership. Nations strengthened and established trade agreements.

The free-market reforms of the 1990s achieved mixed results. Brazil's inflation plunged, and Chile's poverty rate was cut in half. The economies of both countries improved. Other nations struggled. Argentina suffered a deep recession in 2001 and 2002. Many Latin American countries continued to face widespread poverty.

Which Latin American countries' economies benefited from free market reforms in the 1990s?

____

____

Latin Americans' dissatisfaction with economic problems led to more political and economic shifts in the region. Recent elections brought to power many populist, left-leaning leaders. These included **Hugo Chávez** in Venezuela, Evo Morales in Bolivia, and Luiz Inácio Lula da Silva in Brazil.

Chapter Summary

Globalization affects economies and lives around the world. It creates economic interdependence between developed and developing countries, bringing both opportunities and new problems in developing countries.

People and countries are working together to help solve problems such as poverty and disease, adjust to new patterns of immigration, and to protect human rights around the world.

Today's World

Terrorism, the use of weapons of mass destruction (biological, chemical and nuclear), and ethnic and religious tensions threaten security around the world.

Pollution and global warming are two serious environmental problems. People are working together to protect the environment, using science and technology to improve living conditions around the world.

COMPREHENSION AND CRITICAL THINKING

Use information from the graphic organizer to answer the following questions.

1. **Identify** What are some of the problems and threats faced by today's world?

____

____

2. **Analyze** What are some ways that science and technology affects modern life?

____

____

3. **Rank** Which challenge facing today's world do you think is the most serious, and why?

____

____

____

MAIN IDEA

Trade and culture link economies and lives around the world.

Key Terms and People

globalization the process in which countries are linked through trade and culture

interdependence the relationship between countries that depend on each other for resources, goods, or services

multinational corporations large companies that operate in multiple countries

outsourcing practice of having work done elsewhere to cut costs or increase production

free trade exchange of goods among nations without trade barriers such as tariffs

popular culture traits that are common within a group of people, such as food, sports, music, and movies

cultural diffusion the spread of culture traits from one region to another

Taking Notes

As you read the summary, use a graphic organizer like the one below to list the causes and effects of globalization.

Causes

↓

Globalization

↓

Effects

Section 1

Section Summary

ECONOMIC INTERDEPENDENCE

Despite issues that divide them, countries around the world are more tied together than ever before. Countries are linked through trade and culture in a process called **globalization**. Advances in transportation and communication make globalization much easier. Global trade increases economic **interdependence**, or countries' depending on one another for resources, goods, and services.

Nations are often described as developed or developing. Developed countries such as the U.S. and Japan have strong, industrialized economies. Their citizens have a high quality of life, with access to good health care, education, and technology. Developing countries have less productive economies and a lower standard of living. People lack opportunities for education and health care. Because of globalization, developed and developing countries are economically interdependent. They are linked through trade and international business.

Multinational corporations are large companies that operate in more than one country. Many use **outsourcing**, the practice of having work done in another country to cut costs or make more items. Opinion is divided over the corporations' practices. Some believe they benefit developing countries by creating jobs and wealth. Others believe outsourcing takes jobs away from the company's home country without improving life in the developing country.

Global interdependence means that the actions of one nation can affect many others. For example, in the early 2000s, the price of crude oil nearly tripled in two years. Developed countries had to pay much higher oil costs while developing countries often could not afford to pay the higher oil costs and faced fuel shortages.

Underline three things one country could depend on another country for.

How are developed and developing countries different?

____

____

____

____

____

Do you think outsourcing is good or bad? Explain.

____

____

____

GLOBAL TRADE

Another major element of globalization is **free trade,** the exchange of goods among nations without trade barriers such as tariffs. Several international trade organizations promote free trade. In 1948, the General

Agreement on Tariffs and Trade (GATT) was formed. It worked to limit trade barriers and settle disputes. GATT was replaced by the WTO, or World Trade Organization, in 1995. It has about 150 member nations. Other organizations have more limited membership. The Organization of Petroleum Exporting Countries (OPEC) attempts to control oil production and prices. The European Union (EU) and North American Free Trade Agreement (NAFTA) promote free trade and address regional economic issues.

There is much debate about global trade. Developing countries can benefit from the new technology and services provided, while the companies of developed countries benefit from having new markets in which to sell their products. But opponents say that free trade only benefits the developed nations; in developing nations, workers and the environment are exploited. Some opponents of free trade promote fair trade instead. This calls for companies to pay workers fairly and to protect the environment during production of products.

What is the difference between fair trade and free trade?

____

____

____

____

CULTURAL EXCHANGE

With globalization, countries are linked through culture as well as trade. **Popular culture**, or culture traits that are common within a group of people, includes food, music, movies, and sports. Though popular culture differs from one country to another, globalization is causing **cultural diffusion**, or the spreading of culture traits from one region to another. Trade and travel help people learn about other cultures and share their own.

Mass media such as television, music, movies, and the Internet are the most powerful methods of cultural diffusion. Satellite programming and the Internet are major sources of cultural exchange. Some people worry that mass media encourages the growth of consumerism, or a preoccupation with the buying of consumer goods like automobiles. Some people worry that traditional cultures are losing what makes them unique. Preserving traditional cultures while adding the best elements of other cultures is one of the biggest challenges presented by globalization.

Underline the definition of cultural diffusion. Then describe an example of cultural diffusion you have seen or experienced.

____

____

____

MAIN IDEA

People and countries are working together to help solve problems such as poverty and disease, and adjust to new patterns of migration.

Key Terms and People

NGOs non-governmental organizations; groups not affiliated with any government, formed to provide services or push for a certain public policy

famine extreme shortage of food

epidemic an outbreak of a contagious disease that spreads quickly and affects many people

refugees people who leave their own country to find safety in another nation

Taking Notes

As you read the summary, use a graphic organizer like the one below to take notes on the social challenges of human rights, poverty and disease, and migration patterns.

Social Challenges
1.
2.
3.

Section Summary

HUMAN RIGHTS

In 1948, the United Nations issued the Universal Declaration of Human Rights. It says that all people deserve basic rights. In 1975, countries that signed the Helsinki Accords agreed to respect human rights. But human rights continue to be abused around the world. Abuses include torture, slavery, and even killing. Some people are more at risk for abuse, such as people who disagree with their government or people who are members of a religious or ethnic minority. Women and children are also at greater risk.

Which groups of people are at greater risk for human rights abuses?

____

____

Many people and groups work to protect and improve human rights. The United Nations is a major force for monitoring, investigating, and improving conditions for all people. Non-governmental organizations, or **NGOs**, play key roles in assisting the UN. However, NGOs often work for the rights of specific groups such as women, children, or indigenous peoples.

How is the UN's work on human rights similar to the work of NGOs? How is it different?

____

____

____

____

Other changes in the world have also improved human rights. People's rights are often better protected in democratic countries. As more countries adopt democracy, conditions improve. Also, globalization helps by making the economic situation better, allowing more children to be educated and more women to find jobs. Slowly, protection of human rights around the world is increasing.

GLOBAL CHALLENGES

Globalization is improving some people's lives, but many still suffer due to poverty, disease, and natural disasters. More than 20 percent of people in the world live on less than $1 per day and do not have access to education or health care. Poverty can be caused by lack of resources, but also by war, poor government planning, and rapid population growth. One result of poverty can be a **famine**, or extreme shortage of food. Poverty is found even in wealthy countries, but it is most common in developing countries. Developed countries assist poor countries with millions of dollars in gifts or loans each year. If the money is used carefully, it can help reduce poverty.

Underline four causes of poverty.

Disease is another challenge for the world, especially as international air travel causes diseases to spread quickly around the world. An outbreak of contagious disease that spreads quickly and affects many people is called an **epidemic**. HIV/AIDS is an epidemic that has killed more than 25 million people since 1981 and has infected millions more. Organizations and governments have had some success controlling HIV/AIDS and other diseases by educating people about causes and prevention. Making medicines cheaper and more available has also helped.

Which problem do you think is most troubling to the world today—human rights abuse, poverty, disease, or natural disasters? Explain your reasoning.

____

____

____

____

____

Natural disasters such as hurricanes, earthquakes and floods also affect many areas, destroying buildings and killing people. Many individuals, governments, and organizations work to help regions suffering from natural disasters.

POPULATION MOVEMENT

Globalization has led to movement of many people around the world. Some choose to move to find better opportunities, but others are **refugees**, people who flee violence in their home country to protect their safety. Both "push" and "pull" factors influence people to move. Factors that push people away from their homelands include war, persecution, and poverty. Factors that pull people to new places include opportunities for better jobs, education, or quality of life. Most migrants go to wealthy, developed countries, such as those in North America and Europe. Many migrants do find better lives there, but some do not find jobs, or face discrimination. Some people want to limit the number of migrants that can enter their country, thinking that the migrants take away jobs and services from the native citizens, and may change the culture.

Sometimes migration happens within countries. In many places, people are moving from rural areas to cities. This is called urbanization. The world's fastest growing cities—and also the world's largest—are in developing countries such as India and Brazil. In developed countries, urbanization is much slower.

What is urbanization?

____

____

MAIN IDEA
Terrorism, the potential use of weapons of mass destruction, and ethnic and religious tensions threaten security around the world.

Key Terms and People

terrorism the use or threat of violence to cause fear and advance political goals

weapons of mass destruction weapons, including biological, chemical, and nuclear, that can cause an enormous amount of destruction

sanctions economic or political penalties imposed by one country on another to try to force a change in policy

Taking Notes

As you read the summary, use a graphic organizer like the one below to summarize the current threats to security around the world.

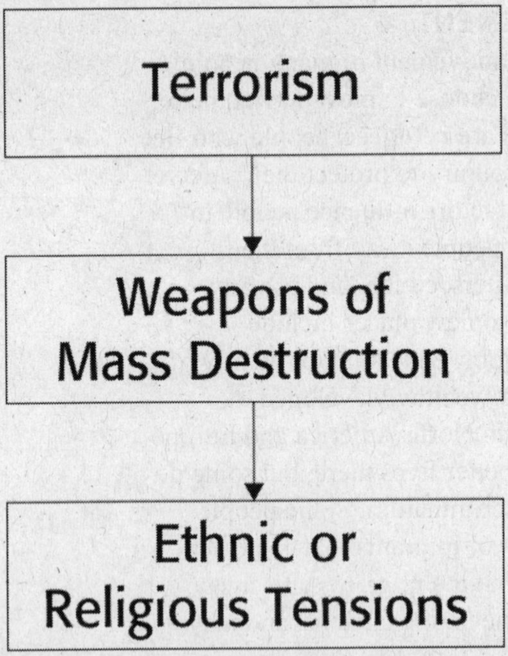

Section Summary

THE THREAT OF TERRORISM

Terrorism, the use or threat of violence to achieve political goals and spread fear, is a major threat to world security. Many of its victims are innocent citizens. Terrorism has been used for thousands of years to fight for independence, change society, or threaten foreigners. But acts of terrorism have become more common over the last 200 years. In the late 1800s and early 1900s, terrorist groups killed several political leaders. Recently, terrorist acts have taken place in Colombia, Peru, Great Britain and Sri Lanka.

Underline the names of modern countries where terrorist acts have taken place.

In recent years, the Middle East has become a center for terrorists. This is partly because of the ongoing Arab-Israeli conflict as well as the region's history of Western colonial domination, which have led to resentment of the West among some Arabs. In the 1980s, Islamist groups such as Hamas, Hezbollah, and al Qaeda increasingly used terrorist tactics against Israel and some Western nations. Some of these groups, such as Hamas, seek to destroy Israel and create an independent Palestinian state, while others want to rid the Middle East of Western influences. These groups are sometimes funded or aided by governments.

Name two reasons for the rise of terrorist groups in the Middle East.

____

____

____

The most notorious recent terrorist attack was on September 11, 2001, when terrorists hijacked four airplanes and crashed two of them into the World Trade Center and one into the Pentagon. The fourth plane crashed in Pennsylvania. Over 3,000 people died. The U.S. learned that al Qaeda, an Islamist terrorist organization led by Osama bin Laden, was responsible for these attacks. The government took several actions to try to prevent future attacks, such as strengthening intelligence services, increasing focus on border and transportation security, and disrupting terrorists' sources of funding.

List three ways the U.S has tried to prevent additional terrorist attacks.

____

____

____

____

In 2001, a U.S.-led military force invaded Afghanistan and forced out the Taliban government, which supported al Qaeda. In 2003, the U.S. invaded Iraq. Some government officials believed that its dictator, Saddam Hussein, had dangerous weapons and supported terrorist groups.

Other countries face similar issues. Spain and Great Britain both experienced bomb attacks on their train systems in the early 2000s.

OTHER THREATS TO SECURITY

Dangerous weapons and ethnic and religious conflicts also contribute to a lack of security around the globe. **Weapons of mass destruction** can cause enormous damage. They include biological, chemical, and nuclear weapons. Several countries have or may be developing biological weapons such as diseases and toxins. Anthrax sent through the mail killed five people in the U.S. in 2001. Chemical weapons were used during both world wars, and by Saddam Hussein. A religious cult used nerve gas in Tokyo in 1995.

Nuclear weapons may be the most dangerous threat. Nearly all nations have signed the Nuclear Non-proliferation Treaty, agreeing to stop the spread of nuclear weapons. However, at least eight countries are known to have nuclear weapons, and others are believed to be trying to develop them. One problem is that nuclear technology can also be used for peaceful purposes, such as for generating energy. So countries can claim they are building nuclear facilities for this purpose only. The International Atomic Energy Agency, or IAEA, monitors countries suspected of developing nuclear weapons. **Sanctions,** or economic and political penalties imposed by one country on another to try to force a change in policy, are sometimes placed those considered nuclear threats.

Underline the three different types of weapons of mass destruction. How do nations try to keep others from developing nuclear weapons?

____

____

____

In some places, violence from ethnic or religious tension is an even greater threat than weapons of mass destruction. In Rwanda in 1994, tension between Tutsi and Hutu ethnic groups led to the massacre of more than 1 million people. Another 2 million fled to refugee camps in nearby countries. A new Rwandan government reestablished order and in 1998, some of the people involved in the genocide were convicted and executed. In the early 2000s in Darfur, a region of Sudan, Arab militias supported by the government attacked African villagers, killing some 400,000 people by 2006 and forcing over 2 million others to flee.

MAIN IDEA
People are working together to protect the environment and using science and technology to improve living conditions around the world.

Key Terms and People

global warming the rise in the surface temperature of the earth over time

deforestation the clearing of trees

desertification the spread of desert-like conditions

sustainable development economic development that does not permanently damage resources

biotechnology the use of biological research in industry

genetic engineering changing the genetic makeup of a plant or animal to create a new type

green revolution an attempt to increase the world's food production by using fertilizers, pesticides, and new varieties of crops

cloning the process of creating identical organisms from a cell of an original organism

Taking Notes

As you read the summary, use a graphic organizer like the one below to take notes on the effects of recent advances in science and technology. Add more boxes as necessary.

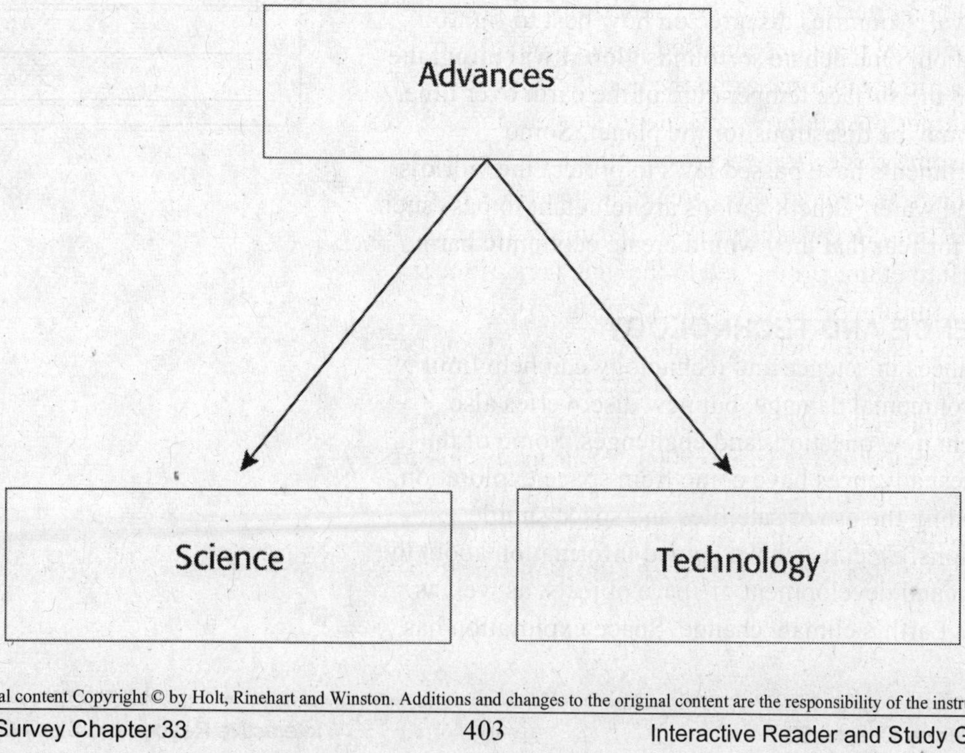

Section Summary

PROTECTING THE ENVIRONMENT

Industrialization and a quickly growing population harm the environment by creating or increasing pollution and problems related to the use of resources. **Deforestation**, the clearing of trees, is happening rapidly in areas of Africa, Asia, and Latin America, particularly in the Amazon region of Brazil. The forests are being cleared to make land for farming, ranching, or mining.

In the Sahel region of West Africa, the environmental issue is **desertification**, the spread of desert-like conditions. This is caused partly by drought and partly by people cutting down trees and allowing animals to overgraze the land. Without plants to anchor it, the soil blows away, making the land useless.

What is the difference between deforestation and desertification?

____

____

____

Despite these risks, industry is necessary, so the goal is to balance the need for development with environmental protection. **Sustainable development** does not permanently damage resources.

Pollution has been a problem since the Industrial Revolution. Industrial processes create waste products which harm the air, water, and land, and can kill or injure people. By the 1960s, some scientists were beginning to see pollution as a threat to human survival. Countries disagree on how best to fight pollution. One debate surrounds **global warming**, the rise in the surface temperature of the earth over time. This may be disastrous for the planet. Some governments have passed laws to protect the world's air and water. Others nations are reluctant to pass such laws for fear that they would create economic harm.

Do all countries agree on how to fight pollution? Why or why not?

____

____

____

SCIENCE AND TECHNOLOGY

Advances in science and technology can help limit environmental damage, but new discoveries also present new questions and challenges. Some of the greatest advances have come from space exploration, including the use of satellites and space shuttle missions. Scientists have gained information about the origin and development of space objects, as well as about Earth's climate change. Space exploration has also led to technologies and consumer products widely used today.

Other advances have changed how we transmit and receive information. Some call the age we live in the Information Age because information exchange is so important in modern life. Computers, cell phones, and Internet access are increasingly common, allowing instant communication. But in many places around the world, access to these technologies is rare. We call this the digital divide.

Why is it said that we live in the Information Age?

____

____

____

People are also benefiting from advances in biology. Developments in the study of genes and heredity have led to the rapid growth of the field of **biotechnology**, or the use of biological research in industry. Genetics is the study of genes and heredity, and **genetic engineering** is the changing of the genetic makeup of a plant or animal to create a new type. Scientists have used genetic engineering to make fruits and vegetables hardier and more productive. They can be planted in places where crops usually cannot grow well. This practice is part of the **green revolution**, the ongoing attempt by scientists to increase food production, using fertilizers, pesticides, and new varieties of crops. Increasing the amount of crops can support larger populations of people. But these practices bring some criticism. Some people wonder about the effects chemicals can have on food, the environment, and human health.

Do you think using genetic engineering on food products is good or bad? Explain your reasoning.

____

____

____

____

____

____

Cloning, the process of creating identical organisms from the cell of an original organism, is another use of genetic engineering that causes debate. While cloning creates possibilities for improving livestock and for medical research, it also raises serious moral, ethical, and legal questions. The study of genes has contributed to the development of new medicines. Other technological advances that have helped doctors include computer imagery and lasers. Science and technology will continue to be used for solving problems and improving lives.

Name ______________________ Class ______________ Date ______________

FOCUSING ON THE ISSUE
What challenges do old and new democracies face in promoting civic participation?

Key Term

devolution the redistribution of power from a central government to local governments

Issue Summary

CIVIC PARTICIPATION

In a 2005 survey, about two-thirds of people from 68 countries said they were generally satisfied with democracy. But only one-third said that their own countries were ruled by the will of the people.

When people feel that they have no voice in their own government, they often become discouraged. This may be why voter turnout has declined in many countries in recent years.

People can participate in democracy in many ways. Voting is just one way. People can also contact their representatives and stage protests. These activities let people influence government policies. Citizens are more likely to remain engaged in a democracy if a country has fair elections, honest government, free speech, and a lively opposition. Communities also depend on support from volunteer and charitable groups.

Underline ways in which a person can participate in democracy.

The United Kingdom has a long democratic tradition. In contrast, South Africa held its first democratic elections in 1994. Both countries are experiencing changes that will affect the future of their democracies.

The United Kingdom has several advantages as an old democracy. Its society is stable. The people respect the nation's laws and democratic tradition. People also participate in public life and volunteer in the community. However, in recent years voter turnout has declined.

South Africa had very high voter turnout in its first election. Since then, voter turnout has declined a great deal. Instead, South Africans often participate in the community through informal groups. The government is trying to create trustworthy institutions, but the country faces social and political unrest.

The United Kingdom has had a parliament for more than 700 years. However, political change has come slowly. It was not until the twentieth century that all adult citizens got the right to vote. In recent years fewer and fewer people have voted, especially among the poor and the young. Britain's Labor government has been trying to reverse this trend by reforming the country's democratic institutions.

One key reform has been **devolution**. Devolution is the process of giving power from the central government to local governments. In the late 1990s, Wales and Scotland were given more local power. Both countries remain part of the United Kingdom. Some supporters of devolution have been disappointed because the central government kept important powers.

Why do you think that the Labor government thought devolution would encourage people to vote?

____

____

____

In 2005 nearly two-thirds of South Africans said that their country was governed by the will of the people. In the first few years of independence, voter turnout in South Africa was very high. However, voter turnout has declined.

The ruling African National Congress (ANC) has benefited the most from voter participation. This group led the struggle against apartheid. The party has won greater majorities in each national election. Unfortunately, there is no strong opposition party to challenge and monitor the ANC. The party has had problems with corruption and inefficiency.

Why is an opposition party helpful in a democracy?

____

____

____

South Africans are committed to participating in civic life. Many join groups such as anti-crime organizations, women's groups, and trade unions. These informal networks strengthen society by offering flexible, creative ways to solve problems.

Issues in the Contemporary World

Case Study 2

FOCUSING ON THE ISSUE
How are developing countries such as Brazil and Mexico trying to meet the needs of their peoples?

Key Terms

megacity a city with a population of 10 million or more

maquiladora large industrial assembly plants located in Mexico, along the U.S. border

Issue Summary

DEVELOPING SOCIETIES

In order to thrive, developing countries have to become stable. Political stability helps businesses grow. Successful businesses attract foreign investment. Investment helps stabilize the economy. A stable economy creates jobs and helps build a middle class. A strong middle class helps create a society in which political order improves and democracy can take root.

How does political stability help create a stable economy?

____

____

____

Latin America has experienced broad instability over the last century. Large economic gaps between the rich and poor have led to political revolutions. Nations that depend on the sale of cash crops have seen prices for their goods change wildly. Large numbers of people have moved to cities to find work. Efforts by indigenous peoples to gain recognition and equal treatment have sometimes caused turmoil.

As countries such as Brazil grow in strength in the world market, they are competing with rising economic powers such as China and India. Latin American leaders are trying to find solutions that will create long-term stability. These leaders know that their nations' large populations are their greatest asset.

What countries is Brazil competing with as its economy gains strength?

____

____

Mexico and Brazil have experienced many political changes in recent years. Brazil was ruled by military dictatorships in the 1960s and 1970s. Since then it has become a modern democracy. Mexico was ruled by a single political party for seventy years. It held its first true two-party election in 2000. Even with these changes, both nations still face challenges.

Brazil is the largest country in Latin America. During the mid-1990s, Brazil expanded in global markets for agriculture, mining, and manufactured goods. Exporting more goods helped improve many aspects of Brazilian society. However, Brazil still has some of the world's worst poverty.

Circle the markets in which Brazil expanded in the 1990s.

Most of Brazil's urban poor live in dangerous shantytowns called *favelas*. These neighborhoods surround Rio de Janeiro and São Paulo, the country's **megacities**. Megacities are those with populations of 10 million or more. Many people avoid the streets of São Paulo because of gang violence and the high murder rate.

In the 1970s, Brazil opened its interior for resettlement and development. The government hoped this would ease the crowding in cities. However, this change led to destruction of the rain forests and criticism from other nations.

Mexico has the second-largest economy in Latin America. It has been able to expand trade under the North American Free Trade Agreement (NAFTA). Mexico generates income from its large petroleum reserves, tourism, and **maquiladoras**. Maquiladoras are large industrial assembly plants located in towns along the U.S. border.

Underline the ways in which Mexico generates income.

Mexico has the highest per-capita income in Latin America. Unfortunately, there is a huge gap between Mexico's rich and poor. Extreme poverty is still common. Only about 15 percent of Mexico's land can be used for farming. This makes it difficult for the government to ease rural poverty. The lack of land draws peasants to Mexico City, the only megacity in Mexico. Now the government focuses on urban poverty because it leads to violence, political instability, and damage to the environment.

The Mexican government encourages its people to migrate to the United States to find jobs. Meanwhile, Mexico is trying to create a better-educated work force. This is important in the world today.

Name ______________________ Class ______________ Date ______________

Issues in the Contemporary World

Case Study 3

FOCUSING ON THE ISSUE
How are the giant emerging economies of India and China affecting the world?

Key Terms

offshoring the practice of moving an entire factory or business to a different country

privatization ownership of companies by individuals or groups instead of the government

joint ventures a business partnership or co-ownership between two companies

Issue Summary

EMERGING ECONOMIC POWERHOUSES

Most observers believe that either India or China will someday replace the United States as the world's largest economy. India and China have the two largest populations in the world. Their economies are becoming vibrant market economies. China made limited reforms in the late 1970s, then began to allow private enterprise in the 1990s. The government hoped to make China the manufacturing capital of the world. India opened its economy in the 1990s when it first began to use the Internet to connect its workers to employers and customers around the globe.

Name two things that China and India have in common.

____

____

____

The rise of Asian economies began in the 1960s, when Japan, South Korea, and the other countries known as "Asian tigers" started to increase manufacturing and industry. Today, China emphasizes manufactured goods, while India focuses on service industries such as tax preparation and computer technical support.

What is China's main source of economic growth? What is India's?

____

____

____

Under communism, China's government controlled its economy. It tried to move from an agricultural to an industrial economy, but failed. The government did not allow private enterprise, so people did not have the incentive of making profits. Instead, productivity was low and inefficiency was high.

Since 1978, China has slowly reformed its economy. The government started to allow farmers to sell some of their crops on the free market. In some cases, regional officials make trade decisions instead of the central government. The government also began to encourage foreign investment in "special economic zones" such as the city of Shenzen.

These reforms led to impressive economic growth in the 1980s. More reforms were made in the 1990s. By 2005, China was the world's second-largest economy. In 2001, China joined the World Trade Organization (WTO), agreeing to its laws and standards. This made China even more attractive for **offshoring**, the practice of moving an entire factory or company to another country.

China has struggled to decide how fast to make changes and how much to change. Progress is slowed by corruption, slow government decision-making, pollution, and economic crimes. However, the economy continues to grow.

After India gained independence in 1948, it adopted a socialist economy. The government limited imports and foreign investment. India tried to create enough industry to meet the nation's needs without becoming dependent on foreign investments and imports. Unfortunately, heavy government regulation resulted in inefficiency and poor products.

In the 1990s, India's government allowed more **privatization**, the ownership of industries by individuals or groups rather than the government. It also allowed foreign companies to form **joint ventures**, partnerships and co-ownership with Indian companies. In the early 2000s, foreign countries started to invest directly in India's economy, especially in telecommunications. The economy has boomed, especially the service industry. It has benefited from government incentives and a large English-speaking population.

Economic growth has been steady since 1991. However, restrictions and tariffs remain. India continues to debate how much to open up its economy. Most Indians still work on farms or in small, traditional businesses. The creation of wealth has drawn attention to the differences between the "two Indias." One is largely rural and poor and the other is urban and prosperous.

What are some of the problems China is facing as a result of reforms?

____

____

____

Why did India chose to limit imports and foreign investments?

____

____

____

Case Study 4

FOCUSING ON THE ISSUE
How do historical and cultural trends affect the status of women?

Key Term

secular nonreligious

Issue Summary

WOMEN IN SOCIETY

Recent studies have revealed the low status of women around the world. One survey found that women did about 66 percent of the work, earned 10 percent of the income, and owned just 1 percent of the land. They are also underrepresented in parliaments around the world, holding about 16 percent of the seats.

Circle the percentage of the world's land that is owned by women.

Governments have pledged to improve the status of women. Globalization has led to a gradual shift in attitudes toward women. It emphasizes that to be economically competitive, developing countries need to recognize the value of women as a human resource. Countries that hold women back from participating in society consistently lag behind in development.

How have countries suffered when they have held women back from participating in society?

Efforts to improve women's lives often conflict with traditional culture and religious beliefs that keep women in a disadvantaged position. Even some women wonder whether too much is lost as changes come about. Two countries that have faced these challenges are Turkey and Ireland. Religious traditions have helped shape the role of women in both nations.

Most people in Ireland are Roman Catholic. Until the 1970s, most women stayed home and raised families. An Irish woman could be forced to quit her job when she got married.

In 1973, Ireland joined the European Economic Community, the forerunner to the European Union (EU). It then started the process of conforming to EU standards on the treatment of women. EU membership also opened Ireland to the world. With this came changing attitudes on a number of social issues.

Issues in the Contemporary World

Case Study 4

At the same time, the influence of the Catholic Church had begun to diminish. In 1972, a clause recognizing the "special position" of the Catholic Church in Irish society was removed from Ireland's constitution. Nevertheless, the church has continued to play a large role in politics. It has so far convinced Irish voters to uphold restrictions on abortion but it has failed to keep divorce illegal.

After a long struggle, the right of married women to work outside the home was guaranteed. The employment of women has increased, in part spurred by an economic boom in the 1990s. In 2004, women made up about 47 percent of the workforce, up from 36 percent in 1994. However, men in Ireland are still favored when it comes to job opportunities and access to living-wage pay and high-paying management jobs. Participation by women in politics remains low.

Underline how life has changed for married women in Ireland. How do you think life in Ireland may change as a result?

____

____

____

The modern nation of Turkey was founded in 1923. Although most people in Turkey are Muslim, leaders of the new nation sought to build a strong, modern country in which church and state would be separate. They created a **secular**, or nonreligious, government. Women's rights were written into law.

With the goal of joining the European Union, Turkey has tried to bring its laws further in line with EU requirements and to promote women's rights in general. However, women have trouble rising to managerial jobs, and women still earn far less than men do.

Turkey's founders wanted their country to be strong and modern. Underline words and phrases that show what they did to build that strength.

In 2002, the predominately Muslim Turkish people brought to power a party with Islamic ties. This was partly a reaction to corruption in the secular government of the 1990s.

Today, there is a generational divide among Turkish women. Older generations see being "modern" as being secular, seeing themselves as citizens of Turkey first and Muslims second. Some members of the new generation, however, seek to redefine women's right and feminism to better fit their religious beliefs.

Name ______________________ Class ______________ Date ______________

Issues in the Contemporary World

Case Study 5

> **FOCUSING ON THE ISSUE**
> What should the role of the United Nations be in international affairs?

Key Terms

charter a document that creates an organization and explains its goals

General Assembly the UN group that includes all member nations

Security Council the UN group whose role is to be the guardian of peace

Secretariat the part of the UN that carries out its administrative tasks

peacekeeping the process of sending military forces into countries to enforce ceasefires or truces among warring countries or warring groups within a single country

Issue Summary

THE ROLE OF THE UNITED NATIONS

The United Nations was created in 1945 as the result of efforts by the United States and its World War II allies. The document that created the organization, called a **charter**, states that the purpose of the United Nations is to settle disputes among nations and solve global problems. Today, its top concerns are security, human rights, economic development, healthcare, disaster relief, and refugee aid.

> **What are the UN's top concerns today?**
>
> ______________________
>
> ______________________

The UN's mission involves a balancing act. Although the charter states that nations are equal, the most powerful nations are given a greater responsibility for maintaining global security. The member nations shift in their goals and alliances. Even within the United States, the host country, there is debate about whether the UN should even exist.

Meanwhile, the number of nations belonging to the UN has grown from 51 to 192. Its mission has also grown. Globalization, terrorism, and nuclear proliferation have challenged the UN in ways the founders never could have imagined. As the UN has expanded, problems such as corruption have arisen. Also, the UN's credibility has been damaged because it has failed to prevent wars and genocides. Around 2005, the UN began to try to deal with these problems by making reforms, but critics remain skeptical that the UN can meet twenty-first century needs.

The UN consists of six main entities: the General Assembly, the Security Council, the Secretariat, the Economic and Social Council, the Trusteeship Council, and the International Court of Justice. The court is held in the Hague, in the Netherlands, while the rest of the operations are based in New York City.

The **General Assembly** includes all member nations. Each nation gets one vote. The votes are not binding, but they carry the weight of world opinion.

The **Security Council** guards the peace. It arranges ceasefires, brokers peace agreements, and sends armies to trouble spots. If countries violate agreements, the Council may impose sanctions. It can also order military action if necessary. There are 15 Security Council members. China, France, Russia, the United Kingdom, and the United States are permanent members. They all have veto power. Other member nations serve two-year terms. There have been recent discussions of adding other powerful nations to the Council, such as Germany and Japan.

What does the UN Security Council do?

____

____

The **Secretariat** carries out administrative tasks. The head of the UN is the secretary-general, who is elected for one or two five-year terms.

More than half of the UN's 30,000 nonmilitary employees serve in the field, providing humanitarian relief, monitoring human rights and elections, and fighting crime. The major field operation of the UN is **peacekeeping**, the process of sending multinational military forces into countries to enforce ceasefires and truces. In 2006, about 80,000 UN troops served around the globe, and about 70 percent of the UN's budget was dedicated to field operations.

What are some things UN workers in the field do?

____

____

____

Critics of the UN say it reacted too slowly to ethnic genocides in Rwanda and Bosnia in the 1990s. Critics also complain that the UN is ineffective in combating terrorism and preventing the spread of nuclear technology. Some think the UN should have taken stronger action against dictator Saddam Hussein before the United States invaded Iraq in 2003. In 2004, a major scandal broke. The UN had been allowing Iraq to sell its oil to buy food and medicine. Instead, Saddam Hussein skimmed billions of dollars from the program. Some UN officials were accused of profiting from the program.

What are recent criticisms of the UN?

____

____

____